THE SACRED EARTH

CCAR CHALLENGE AND CHANGE SERIES

The Sacred Table: Creating a Jewish Food Ethic

The Sacred Encounter: Jewish Perspectives on Sexuality

The Sacred Calling: Four Decades of Women in the Rabbinate

The Sacred Exchange: Creating a Jewish Money Ethic

The Sacred Earth: Jewish Perspectives on Our Planet

THE
SACRED
EARTH

Jewish Perspectives on Our Planet

Edited by Rabbi Andrue J. Kahn

Foreword by Karenna Gore

CENTRAL CONFERENCE OF AMERICAN RABBIS

5783 NEW YORK 2023

The ideas expressed in this volume are meant to foster robust and challenging conversation, and do not necessarily reflect the views of the Central Conference of American Rabbis or its official policies.

Published by Reform Judaism Publishing, a division of CCAR Press
Central Conference of American Rabbis
355 Lexington Avenue, New York, NY 10017
(212) 972-3636 | info@ccarpress.org | www.ccarpress.org

LIBRARY OF CONGRESS CATALOGING-IN-PUBLICATION DATA
Names: Kahn, Andrue J., editor.
Title: The sacred earth: Jewish perspectives on our planet / Rabbi Andrue
  J. Kahn, editor; foreword by Karenna Gore.
Description: First edition. | New York: Central Conference of American
  Rabbis, 5783 = 2023. | Summary: "The Sacred Earth: Jewish Perspectives
  on Our Planet is a contemporary Jewish response to the looming threat of
  climate change, the widespread desire for experiential spirituality
  rooted in nature, and the continually changing relationship between
  humanity, nature, technology, and the Divine. The leading thinkers in
  this collection examine conceptions of our place in cosmology, and
  grapple with environmental destruction. They creatively explore ways to
  redeem the sacred Earth"-- Provided by publisher.
Identifiers: LCCN 2022037959 (print) | LCCN 2022037960 (ebook) | ISBN
  9780881233858 (trade paperback) | ISBN 9780881233865 (ebook)
Subjects: LCSH: Climatic changes--Religious aspects--Judaism. | Global
  warming--Religious aspects--Judaism. | Human ecology--Religious
  aspects--Judaism. | Nature--Religious aspects--Judaism. |
  Environmentalism--Religious aspects.
Classification: LCC BM538.C58 S23 2023 (print) | LCC BM538.C58 (ebook) |
  DDC 296.3/75--dc23/eng/20221205
LC record available at https://lccn.loc.gov/2022037959
LC ebook record available at https://lccn.loc.gov/2022037960

Text designed and composed by Scott-Martin Kosofsky
  at The Philidor Company, Rhinebeck, NY
Printed in the United States of America

10 9 8 7 6 5 4 3 2 1 0

Contents

Foreword, Karenna Gore   xiii

Acknowledgments   xvii

Introduction, Rabbi Andrue J. Kahn   xix

PART ONE · *THEOLOGY*   1

1. Jewish Ecological Wisdom for the Anthropocene Age
   HAVA TIROSH-SAMUELSON, PhD   3

2. Healing *Adam* and *Adamah*: Ancient Torah, Action Today
   RABBI ARTHUR O. WASKOW, PhD   13

3. *B'midbar*: A Contemporary Midrash
   RABBI IAH PILLSBURY   23

4. Humanity and the Earth: Dominion versus Stewardship
   JEREMY BENSTEIN, PhD   31

5. A Natural Jewish Theology: God's Covenant with the Earth
   RABBI DAVID MEVORACH SEIDENBERG   39

6. God as the Connective Tissue of the Universe
   RABBI MORDECHAI LIEBLING   51

7. Earth, Water, Air, and Fire: The Four Elements
   as a Language for Sanctifying the Earth
   RABBI JILL HAMMER, PhD   59

8. What If the Earth Is Alive? A Post-halachic Theology
   SHAUL MAGID, PhD   67

9. *Yishuv HaOlam*: The Jewish Imperative of Sustainability
   RABBI NINA BETH CARDIN
   and RABBI AVRAM ISRAEL REISNER   75

PART TWO · *JEWISH TEXTS*   83

10. *Adam v'Teva*: A Renewed Relationship with Humanity
   and Earth
   RABBI NATE DEGROOT   85

11. Reclaiming *V'hayah Im Shamoa*:
   Our Actions Have Consequences
   RABBI DEVORAH DIANA LYNN   93

12. What Can Jeremiah Teach Us about Climate Change?
   RABBI ELIZABETH BAHAR   101

13. How to Change Minds: Lessons from Jonah
   MIRELE B. GOLDSMITH, PhD   111

14. The Songs of Songs: A Ritual Journey
   of Connection with Creation
   RABBI SHEFA GOLD   119

15. The Rivers Will Clap Their Hands: Shabbat Rituals
   for Connecting to the Earth
   RABBI LAURA RUMPF   129

   Yotzeir Or
   RABBI EVAN SCHULTZ   134

   Nature and Humility: A Reflection on Job
   ADRIANE LEVEEN, PhD   135

PART THREE · *ENCOUNTERING THE DIVINE*   139

16. Awesome Heights: Mountains in the Bible
   RABBI ERIC L. ABBOTT   141

17. The Sacred Whole of Creation: *Sefer Y'tzirah*
   and Jewish Eco-theology
   RABBI JILL HAMMER, PhD   149

18. *Hitbod'dut*: Finding the Divine through Solitude in Nature
   RABBI ELI HERB   159

19. Desert Torah: Listening for God in the Wilderness
    RABBI MIKE COMINS   167

20. Composting and Sacred Time: Lessons from a Pumpkin
    RABBI MICHAEL BIRNHOLZ   175

21. The Weight of the World: Spiritual Grounding
    through Making Art
    RABBI ADINA ALLEN   179

    Infinite Love
    RABBI EFRAT ROTEM   186

    The Story of the Pizza
    RABBI JOEL M. MOSBACHER, DMin   187

    The Sacred Power of the Shabbat Stroll
    RABBI DANIEL A. WEINER and RABBI AVI B. FINE   189

    Radical Confidence
    ROB WATSON   192

    Ferns/Passage
    CHAPLAIN DE FISCHLER HERMAN   195

PART FOUR · *SACRED TIME*   197

22. The Climate and the Calendar: A Talmudic Perspective
    RABBI DVORA E. WEISBERG, PhD   199

23. *Yizal Mayim*: Water Rituals and Meditations
    KOHENET SHAMIRAH BECHIRAH (SARAH CHANDLER)   207

24. Resetting the Planet through *Sh'mitah*
    NIGEL S. SAVAGE   217

25. Creating a Local *Lulav*
    RABBI SHOSHANA MEIRA FRIEDMAN   225

26. *Birkat HaMazon*: A Call to Environmental Awareness
    RABBI DENNIS C. SASSO, DMin   231

27. Yom Kippur: A Jewish Earth Day
    RABBAH GILA CAINE   239

    A Tu BiSh'vat Prayer for Creation
    RABBI WARREN G. STONE   247

    Voices of the Future: Stories from
    the Jewish Youth Climate Movement
    MICHAEL PINCUS, ANNA DUBEY, RAPHAELA GOLD,
    PENELOPE KOPP, and TALI DEANER   248

PART FIVE · *CONTEMPORARY RESPONSES*   259

28. Beyond *Bal Tashchit*: Developing an Environmental Halachah
    RABBI MARK WASHOFSKY, PhD   261

29. The Land's Still Small Voice Beckons Us All:
    Preserving a Collective, Zionist Environmental Ethic
    ALON TAL, PhD   267

30. "You Are but Tenants and Settlers":
    Ecology, Anti-colonialism, and the Theology of *Galut*
    DANIEL DELGADO   277

31. Healing the Environment through Global Interfaith Activism
    RABBI DR. SHMULY YANKLOWITZ   285

32. *Beit Atid*: Synagogues as Laboratories for the Future
    RABBI DEAN SHAPIRO   293

33. Achieving Zero Waste: A Synagogue Case Study
    RABBI JONATHAN E. BLAKE, RON SCHULHOF,
    and MICHELLE STERLING   303

34. Sustainable Eating and Eco-justice:
    Lessons from Jewish Tradition
    ROSA FINK, TANYA FINK, MS, RD,
    and RABBI DANIEL B. FINK   311

35. Indigenous Land Acknowledgments: A Jewish Perspective
    RABBI JESSICA ROSENBERG   319

36. Learning from Rocks: Sacred Stones in the Torah
RABBI SANDY EISENBERG SASSO, DMin   329

Dayenu! A Jewish Response to the Climate Crisis
RABBI JENNIE ROSENN   333

Contributors   337

Foreword

KARENNA GORE

IN SEPTEMBER 2014, an economist and a climate scientist joined forces to coauthor an essay in the journal *Science* that was essentially a cry for help: "Over and above the institutional reforms and policy changes that are required," they wrote, "there is a need to reorient our attitude towards nature and thereby ourselves." One of the authors, climatologist Veerabhadran Ramanathan, added that "eight decades of research between Dr. [Partha] Dasgupta and myself on the natural and social science aspects of environmental changes has led us to the doorsteps of moral leaders of religions to rescue humanity from climate change."[1]

The global ecological crisis is about more than data, science, and technology, as important as they are. It is about our moral obligations to one another across space, time, and even species. It is about the very identity of human beings in relationship to the rest of life (what we have come to define as "nature") and to the creative force behind the interconnected wholeness of it all. It is about whether we will listen to the voice of the earth, expressed through the undeniable signs revealed to each of us, whether in images in the news or in the course of our lives. Sooner or later, even the most secular minds turn to these points of inquiry with some measure of awareness that there are faith and wisdom traditions that have lived and wrestled with them for centuries.

There is particular urgency in the case of climate change. Ice shelves are breaking off in Antarctica and Greenland, permafrost is melting, people are dying of heat waves, floods, and wildfires, and others are fleeing coastal areas where sea levels are on the rise. As the latest Intergovernmental Panel on Climate Change report made ever more clear, we already have most of the technology we need to change this perilous trajectory, and we must do so in the next several years.[2] Yet emissions continue to rise. It is not the earth that needs fixing; it is us.

We must move away from the thought system that conceives of the earth as a set of resources to be dominated and exploited by humans, without regard to planetary boundaries. The modern megatrends of pollution (particularly methane and carbon pollution from the extraction and burning of fossil fuels, which trap heat in the atmosphere) and depletion (particularly of carbon sinks like forests) continue to accelerate. The industrial revolution that began those modern megatrends originated in Western Europe. Many have noted that it arose in tandem with a worldview that was shaped by a particular version of Christianity, one that took liberties of interpretation with the text it called "the Old Testament."

In 1967, a medieval historian named Lynn White wrote a paper called "The Historical Roots of Our Ecologic Crisis,"[3] in which he famously claimed, "The victory of Christianity over paganism was the biggest psychic revolution in the history of our culture." The agenda of the Roman Empire latched onto the concepts of dominion and *imago dei* (humans having been made in the image of God) in order to eradicate animistic beliefs that conceived of spirits within natural entities, like forests and rivers, and served as inhibitions to their destruction. White, himself a Christian, was not quarreling with the essence of the Scripture so much as with the way it had been interpreted and used. The belief system that set the ecological crisis in motion was borne of "the most anthropocentric religion the world has seen."

Although White does not explore it, it is important to note that this belief system flowed through persecution of female spiritual leaders as "witches" and through the papal bulls that came from the Vatican in the fifteenth century to launch the age of discovery. Those decrees put forth the mandate to "conquer, vanquish and subdue" the land and peoples of what we now know as Africa and the Americas, dehumanizing the human beings who lived there as "part of the flora and fauna."[4]

The Lynn White thesis has always been controversial, but recent efforts to identify and revive the ecological sensibility within the Christian tradition actually serve to reinforce its point. In 2015, Pope Francis published an extraordinary encyclical, *Laudato Si: On Care for Our Common Home*, which is full of Christian theology about the intrinsic worth of nature and the need to understand "dominion" in terms of responsible stewardship rather than domination.⁵ The endeavor to grapple with this theological knot is not only being undertaken in every Christian denomination doing eco-justice work; it is also necessary in secular discourse. We all hear echoes in political catchphrases such as "energy dominance" and in the almost cultlike refusal to hear the voice of the earth, getting louder with each new wave of climate impacts.

It is long since time to pay close heed to Jewish scholarship on climate. In one sense, Jewish thinkers are making the powerful shift that Susannah Heschel has described as "reversing the gaze."⁶ Just as a woman can bear witness to a domineering male gaze upon her in a way that reveals the flawed assumptions of the gazer, Jewish scholars bring special insight to an examination of the use of their sacred texts for the expansion of Christendom. Of course, there is much more to Jewish scholarship on climate than that critique, but it bears mentioning because of the historical roots of the crisis we are addressing.

The contemporary Jewish response to the global ecological crisis includes the prophetic, pastoral, practical, and personal. Even those without religious sensibilities can recognize the need for the epic sweep and probing depth of what this perspective has to offer. Engaging the most intense and complex aspects of Jewish tradition with the right guide can make this seem like the only modality weighty enough to process what we are facing with the climate crisis. Jewish scholars help us to take a God's eye view alongside the prophets, to see the idolatry disguised as social norms, to hear God's call to Jonah and God's answer to Job, to understand the message of the Burning Bush and the rocks crying out. And it is not only Scripture—it is the wisdom that comes from the Jewish experience. As I have learned from my friends Rabbis Burt Visotzky, Andrue J. Kahn, and Jennie Rosenn, among others, there are the matters of connection and disconnection to land, the power of ritual, the multidimensional realities of living in a political system that does not recognize the essence of who you are, the effect of trauma, the power of resilience, and the emotional and spiritual toll of living under the real threat of annihilation. This collection is a blessing and an invitation to correct course, in mutually respectful communion with one another, with ourselves, and with the sacred earth.

NOTES

1. Robert Monroe, "An Appeal from Science Leaders to Religious Leaders on Environmental Protection," Scripps Institution of Oceanography, September 18, 2014, https://scripps.ucsd.edu/news/appeal-science-leaders-religious-leaders-environmental-protection.

2. P. R. Shukla et al., eds., *Climate Change 2022: Mitigation of Climate Change; Contribution of Working Group III to the Sixth Assessment Report of the Intergovernmental Panel on Climate Change* (Cambridge: Cambridge University Press, 2022), https://www.ipcc.ch/report/sixth-assessment-report-working-group-3/.

3. Lynn White, "The Historical Roots of Our Ecologic Crisis," *Science* 155, no. 3767 (March 10, 1967): 1203–7.

4. "The Doctrine of Discovery, 1493," Gilder Lehrman Institute of American History, https://www.gilderlehrman.org/history-resources/spotlight-primary-source/doctrine-discovery-1493.

5. Pope Francis, *Laudato Si: On Care for Our Common Home*, 2015, https://www.vatican.va/content/francesco/en/encyclicals/documents/papa-francesco_20150524_enciclica-laudato-si.html.

6. Susannah Heschel, *Abraham Geiger and the Jewish Jesus* (Chicago: University of Chicago Press, 1998), 1.

Acknowledgments

FIRST AND FOREMOST, I must acknowledge and thank Rabbi Hara Person for her mentorship and guidance, both throughout my career and in particular towards the creation of this book. Without her vision for this series, her incredibly giving spirit both in time and care, and her friendship throughout the past eight years, this book would certainly not have come to fruition. I also thank Rabbi Sonja Pilz, for getting me started on the journey that became this book; Rafael Chaiken, for joining along the way and guiding us to our destination; and Chiara Ricisak for making sure we didn't drop any pieces along the way. During the creation of this volume, I was also greatly supported in process and editing by Rabbi Jan Katz, Rabbi Annie Villarreal-Belford, as well as by rabbinic intern Ariel Tovlev. I am grateful to the rest of the CCAR Press staff, Raquel Fairweather-Gallie and Debbie Smilow, as well as copy editor Debra Hirsch Corman, proofreader Michelle Kwitkin, designer Scott-Martin Kosofsky, and cover artist Barbara Leff.

My involvement and interest in the relationship between Judaism and the environment was begun and nurtured by many at the Institute for Jewish Spirituality, including Rabbi Myriam Klotz, Rabbi Jonathan Slater, and Cantor Richard Cohn. The catalyst for it becoming part of my rabbinate, though, was one particularly interested congregant at Congregation Emanu-El, Peg Watson. Peg's desire to get our community involved in environmental work led to her introducing me to the inimitable Karenna Gore, to whom I am deeply grateful for inspiring me to take on this project, and for contributing a beautiful foreword to the volume. Peg, Karenna, and I began meeting, Karenna graciously agreed to speak at the synagogue, and eventually at the CCAR Convention in March 2020. Without Peg's indomitable spirit, wonderful ability to connect people, and her instinct to inspire collaboration, I would never have considered putting together a book such as this one. Thank you, Peg, for your friendship, passion, and leadership.

I am particularly grateful for the amazing group of thinkers who became the editorial committee. Their contributions through reflection, guidance, and feedback led to the diverse viewpoints found throughout this book and helped inspire my vision for its format and organization. This group of visionary rabbis are truly some of the most inventive, passionate, and spiritual teachers of our time, and I feel honored to have been able to work with them on this project.

Thank you to my parents, Jo Ann Kahn and Mike Kahn, z"l, for raising me in the Pacific Northwest and showing me how beautiful, important, and indeed spiritual our sacred planet is, and my sister Sarah for being my friend and companion exploring it all as we grew up together. Thank you to my incredible mentors throughout my academic career, particularly Dr. Miriam Dean-Otting, who ignited my passion for Judaism and social justice; Dr. James Miller, who completely blew open my conception of the relationship between nature, religion, technology, and humanity; and Dr. Benjamin Sommer, who showed me that Jewish theology is much broader, deeper, and stranger than I could have ever imagined.

And finally, thank you to Mia Wilson, my partner in everything, for your love, support, occasional goading, and listening to me ramble about so many different aspects of this work as I tried to cohere it all together. Our foundation as a family provided me the stability, clarity, and space to pour my energies into making this dream of a book a reality.

—RABBI ANDRUE J. KAHN

Introduction

RABBI ANDRUE J. KAHN

NEARLY A DECADE AGO, Rabbi Zalman Schachter-Shalomi wrote, "To me, the sight of our Earth from outer space is not only a scientific triumph but today's most potent *religious* icon as well. More than I want to talk about *avodat ha-Shem*, serving God, I want to talk about serving the planet. . . . The question is: can Judaism respond?"[1]

This book is a collection of responses to Reb Zalman's question. *Avodah*—serving—holds the meanings of both physical labor and sacred service. Responses range from new innovations to ancient customs, all of which provide modes of *avodah*. Our tradition tells us, in fact, that our ancestors considered *avodah* within the Temple to be the balancing force for the whole world, allowing it to be blessed, and for rains to fall in their proper seasons (*Avot D'Rabbi Natan* 4:4). By approaching this moment of environmental crisis from the point of view of *avodat HaShem* (service of God) and *avodat haaretz* (service of the earth), this volume reinvestigates our Jewish approach to the earth as a whole, seeking to regain that balance.

An ancient midrash provides a Jewish context for understanding the relationship between the Divine, the earth, and humanity. In *Pirkei D'Rabbi Eliezer* 12:4 and 12:6, the midrashist tells us:

> And [Adam] was at his leisure in the Garden of Eden, like one of the ministering angels. The Holy One, blessed be God, said: I am singular in My world and this one is singular in his world. There is no propagation before Me and this one has no propagation in his life; hereafter all the creatures will say: Since there was no propagation in his life, it is he who has created us. It is not good for man to be alone, as it is said, "And God, the Eternal, said, 'It is not good for man to be alone; I will make a helpmeet for him'" (Genesis 2:8). . . .
>
> When the earth heard this expression thereupon she trembled

and quaked, crying before her Creator: Sovereign of all worlds, I have not the power to provide for the multitude of humankind. The Holy One, blessed be God, replied: I and you will (together) feed the multitude of humankind. They agreed to divide (the task) between themselves: the night was for the Holy One, blessed be God, and the day [was apportioned] to the earth. What did the Holy One, blessed be God, do? God created the sleep of life, so that a human lies down and sleeps while God sustains and heals that human and [gives] them life and repose, as it is said, "I should have slept: then had I been at rest" (Job 3:18). The Holy One, blessed be God, supports [a human being] with the earth, giving it water; and it yields its fruit and food for all creatures— but the first man's food "in toil shall you eat of it all the days of your life" (Genesis 3:17).[2]

This midrash posits a novel relationship among humanity, God, and the earth. The earth becomes concerned with the capacity to sustain humanity. The words used, *lazon tzono* (translated above as "to provide for the multitude"), are of particular interest here. This is the crux of the relationship. The first word, the verb, is clear: to provide. But the second is slightly less so. It could mean "his waste," "his flock," or through a slightly less clear conjugation, "his offspring." Regardless of the actual meaning, it is a moment addressing covenantal cooperation between God and the earth to provide for humanity.

God, in our midrash, provides sleep. Sleep is the realm of dreams, rich with divine communication.[3] Sleep is a respite from the reality in which we all exist in daily life—the earth and all it encompasses. That which we cannot see with our eyes visits us in the night, lingering in our mind during our waking hours and influencing our actions. The earth, then, is all that we experience while conscious: where our lives happen; what sustains us through air, water, and food; the atmospheric womb that holds us throughout our lives; and the stage upon which our greatest victories and most devastating losses play out. Humanity's role in this nexus is to create—whether it be waste, flock, or offspring—during the waking hours with the earth, while God provides for us rest and, perhaps, guidance for our actions on earth, during the night.

Humanity's role is the crux of the midrash, as humanity created this midrash. The fable of God and the earth forming a covenant to provide for humanity is deeply anthropocentric. But what else could it be? We human creatures can only create from our own limited senses and perspectives, and these perspectives are also sacred. Only through them can we experience and reflect upon God. Hence, our time of dreaming and revelation comes when God rules over the night. Moreover, the earth's role is also revelatory. The earth in this midrash is all that we experience during the day. It is where Mount Sinai still stands, echoing from the great Revelation. It is where the Burning Bush was not consumed. It is where Abraham, Isaac, and Jacob, Sarah, Rebekah, Rachel, and Leah all encountered God.

Revelation during waking hours is God speaking via the earth. Our Rabbinic ancestors knew this, pointing out in the Talmud that many lessons taught directly in Torah present themselves in one form or another through the natural world (Babylonian Talmud, *Eiruvin* 100b). Reform Jewish theology teaches us something similar, that we may find divine inspiration everywhere—be it in the pages of the Bible or in the scientific method—for our ultimate conclusion is the same: "How many are the things You have made, O God; You have made them all with wisdom" (Psalm 104:24).[4] The Torah's revealed divine wisdom may also be found through encountering our earth as a teacher, for we experience the earth in every waking minute. The earth colors the whole of our creative endeavors, even while divine inspiration from our non-waking hours may fuel these endeavors. The midrash reflects both the human point of view and hints at the nature of our relationship to God and the environment, bringing us back to the purpose of this volume.

Judith Plaskow, the pioneering Jewish feminist theologian, once wrote, "Highlighting aspects of Jewish experience that had previously been obscured and neglected, and valuing these as Torah, offers a richer and more diverse Judaism on which to reflect theologically."[5] In today's moment, we must continue the core revelation of this midrash by lifting up previously hidden aspects of Jewish experience, as well as new Torah from our own era. The midrash is a continued response to the event at Sinai in its elaborating the Torah's very opening moments of human-divine-environmental relations. Thus, it is upon us to inclusively and diversely participate in this ongoing revelation by seeking out sources and experiences previously obscured and neglected. In doing so, we will find new and diverse ways to relate to our environment Jewishly in our day and age, responding to the ultimate question of what it means to serve God and the earth today.

One central contemporary source, used by Rabbi Schachter-Shalomi and referred to by a great number of the authors of this volume, is the Gaia hypothesis, developed by Lynn Margulis, a groundbreaking Jewish evolutionary biologist, and her cocreator, environmentalist and futurist James Lovelock. Lovelock and Margulis defined the Gaia hypothesis, writing, "The total ensemble of living organisms which constitute the biosphere can act as a single entity to regulate chemical composition, surface pH and possibly also climate. The notion of the biosphere as an active adaptive control system able to maintain the earth in homeostasis we are calling the 'Gaia' hypothesis."[6]

Lovelock adds to this in his most recent work: "[Humanity's] mastery of information should be a source of pride, but we must use the gift wisely to help continue the evolution of all life on Earth so that it can cope with the ever-increasing hazards that inevitably threaten us and Gaia. We alone . . . are the ones who evolved with the ability to transmute the flood of photons into bits of information gathered in a way that empowers evolution. Our reward is the opportunity to understand something of the universe and ourselves."[7]

If we combine these thinkers' revolutionary views on the earth—that is, that all life on the planet works in concert to regulate its atmosphere, and that each piece of the whole has its own role to play—we find a new vocabulary for articulating the same message in the contemporary world as our original midrash. Just as the Rabbis saw that nature can teach us sacred lessons, Margulis and Lovelock remind us that we always have more to learn from nature. The chapters of this book each contribute a different perspective on the roles humanity, and Jews in particular, have to play in this ongoing covenant between the Divine, humanity, and the earth.

We, in our human way, have the capacity to gather and transmit information that allows us to participate in the ongoing regulation and balance of Gaia, whether passively or actively, and we need not overwhelm the earth with our creativity, especially now as we gain greater and greater understanding of ourselves and our role. As Jews, we have the capacity to continue the ever unfolding process of Torah with regard to our responsibilities in the Divine-human-earth nexus. Each piece in this anthology strives to provide us a way to understand these responsibilities—our *avodah*—by way of the infinite perspectives Torah can hold.

This book is divided into five sections on different Jewish approaches to the earth: theology, Jewish text, encountering the Divine, sacred time, and contemporary responses. Each section opens a door to a new form of understanding our relationship to the earth and the Divine, and each section interweaves with the others, supporting each other by filling out a wider context for our contemporary day.

Chapters in part 1, "Theology," reflect in multiple ways on how our relationship to God guides our relationship with the earth, laying a foundation for the rest of the volume. The frameworks of these chapters range from biblical to historical, mystical, and scientific. Part 2, "Jewish Texts," draws from our ancestors' wisdom as recorded in a wide variety of Jewish texts from throughout history, all in search of new perspectives on Jewish approaches to the earth. Part 3, "Encountering the Divine," explores personal experiences of the Divine as revealed through the earth. Part 4, "Sacred Time," reflects on our Jewish year and the place of the earth throughout the calendar. Specifically, this section looks at how the Jewish calendrical cycle intimately connects us to the earth's cycles and is itself a reflection of our relationship with the earth. Part 5, "Contemporary Responses," focuses on concrete ways Jews are serving the earth today. From greening synagogues to forming new institutions, these chapters contribute tangible action items for working toward a healthier relationship between us and the earth.

This anthology includes a wide spectrum of viewpoints, opinions, and modes. By including contributors from diverse backgrounds across the Jewish denominational spectrum, as well as many who may not identify with any denomination at all, this volume is enriched with a range of voices and often overlooked perspectives. From clergy to academics to activists, Jewish leaders from a wide variety of backgrounds have contributed their expertise in the following chapters. Contributors may at times disagree with each other, and some chapters may be challenging and even controversial. The ideas expressed do not necessarily reflect official views or policies of the CCAR. We hope that this range of perspectives will promote mutual learning and understanding. At the end of each section, shorter, more personal pieces and poems elucidate and provoke lived experiences of serving the earth and God. This anthology also includes reflections from the next generation of Jewish environmental consciousness. Leaders from Hazon's Jewish Youth Climate Movement share the experiences, ideas, and dreams that have been instrumental to their work on the leading edge of the future of our community's response to the climate. Their inspiring visions and work bring to the fore visions for a future led by powerful, active thinkers centering our responsibility in service to the world.

Each individual has a role to play in *avodat HaShem* (service of God) and *avodat haaretz* (service of the earth). The many authors in this volume have labored to share theirs with humanity through the following chapters. May you, dear reader, find guidance to your own *avodah* in these pages.

NOTES

1. Zalman Schachter-Shalomi and Joel Segel, *Jewish with Feeling: A Guide to Meaningful Jewish Practice (For People of All Faiths, All Backgrounds)* (Woodstock, VT: Jewish Lights, 2013), 150–51.
2. Based on trans. Gerald Friedlander (London, 1916), on Sefaria.org.
3. See Numbers 12:6, "When prophets of the Eternal rise among you, I will make Myself known to them in a vision . . . in a dream."
4. Kaufmann Kohler, *Jewish Theology: Systematically and Historically Reconsidered* (New York: Macmillan, 1918), 139.
5. Judith Plaskow, *The Coming of Lilith* (New York: Beacon Press, 2015), 153.
6. James E. Lovelock and Lynn Margulis, "Atmospheric Homeostasis by and for the Biosphere: The Gaia Hypothesis," *Tellus* 26 (1974): 1–2, http://www.jameslovelock.org/atmospheric-homeostasis-by-and-for-the-biosphere-the-gaia-hypothesis/.
7. James Lovelock, *Novacene: The Coming of Age of Hyperintelligence* (Cambridge, MA: MIT Press, 2019), 92.

PART ONE
Theology

To begin this volume, we investigate the assumptions and core values that Jewish thought and theologies generate, which guide our conceptions of how we ought to live in and with the natural world. These perspectives of theology both help us address the psycho-spiritual stress and sadness of living in a time of extreme environmental change and destruction and also push us toward *t'shuvah*, turning toward a more holistic, sacred form of living.

We begin with Hava Tirosh-Samuelson, PhD, confronting the concept of the Anthropocene using Jewish text and thought. Rabbi Arthur O. Waskow, PhD, re-renders the Torah's core narrative as one of ecological reflection. Rabbi Iah Pillsbury provides a contemporary midrash, using fiction to guide our thoughts toward a greater conception of rest and wholeness. Jeremy Benstein, PhD, investigates the way in which the Book of Genesis's prescription of humanity's relationship to the world can be reframed, and Rabbi David Mevorach Seidenberg urges us to find a new covenant in the Torah, not just between Israel and God, but between God and the earth. Rabbi Mordechai Liebling shares a new model for seeing God as the force binding the universe together, and Rabbi Jill Hammer, PhD, reflects on the way that the four elements have been both used and often ignored in Jewish thought. Shaul Magid, PhD, reframes our Jewish conception of the earth for the future, outside the bounds of traditional halachah, and Rabbi Nina Beth Cardin and Rabbi Avram Israel Reisner provide firm grounding in Jewish sources for sustainability as a mitzvah.

1

Jewish Ecological Wisdom for the Anthropocene Age

Hava Tirosh-Samuelson, PhD

The Anthropocene

A massive ecological crisis threatens the future of human life on planet earth. Global warming, climate change, extreme weather events, retreats of glaciers, rising sea levels, mega droughts and fires, creeping desertification, threats to available water, food, and shelter, mass extinction of species, loss of fisheries and forests, acidification of oceans, pollution of air, water, and soil, and shifts in the range and prevalence of diseases manifest wide-ranging ecological collapse. These are brought about by human activities, including industrialization, urbanization, overpopulation, excessive consumption, wastefulness, and pollution. People and nature interact reciprocally to form complex feedback loops, and all forms of life on the earth are impacted by human activities permanently and irreversibly. Scientists call the new geological era the Anthropocene (i.e., the Age of Humans), although there is no consensus about its causes, scope, and ramifications.[1]

How are we to respond to the specter of the Anthropocene? Are we to celebrate the dawning of the new geological era or lament it? Will the human species and all other forms of life be able to flourish or experience irreversible decline? Scientists and engineers debate these questions. The techno-optimists among them see the Anthropocene as an extraordinary opportunity to remake the world as Eden on earth by means of innovative technologies, such as climate engineering.[2] The Anthropocene is thus imagined as the "post-natural" age. By contrast, the techno-pessimists counsel caution and demand modification of human behavior and curtailment of the human hubris that has given us the environmental crisis in the first place. In between, there are the techno-pragmatists, who recognize that although technology is not an unproblematic solution to environmental problems such as climate change, geo-engineering might be the best available option for the future of the human species. Social scientists focus not so much on what could be done technologically, but on who is responsible for the environmental collapse, pointing fingers at global capitalism and voracious consumerism as major culprits.[3] Their solutions highlight the need to change human consumption habits and restructure social, economic, and political institutions.

For humanists, especially the religious among them, the dawning of the Anthropocene signifies a profound spiritual crisis brought about by modern secularism and its scientistic mindset. Modern technoscience and modern capitalism have yielded the eco-crisis because humanity has banished God from its self-understanding, replacing it with its own Promethean Self.[4] The natural world indeed will not disappear in the Anthropocene, but to ensure its fecundity and the flourishing of all forms of life, including human, we must reconfigure the relationship among God, humanity, and nature. All world religions have responded to the environmental crisis by reexamining and reinterpreting their canonical sources and generating faith-based religious activism.[5] Since the 1970s, across the entire spectrum of modern Judaism, Jews too have reexamined, reinterpreted, or reconstructed the sources of Judaism to address the eco-crisis.[6]

Jewish environmentalism offers a meaningful response to the specter of the Anthropocene, and Judaic sources harbor deep ecological wisdom. Judaism recognizes the grandeur of the world created by God, honors the innate dignity of all creatures and appreciates their interconnectedness and interdependence, hallows human physical embodiment as the foundation of the spiritual life, tasks human beings with the moral responsibility to care for the earth justly, and recognizes that human actions toward the natural world impact the quality of the human relationship with God and with other humans. Of course, the multivocal, layered Judaic tradition encompasses many voices that sometimes conflict with each other, but together their symphonic sonority offers a coherent vision that frames our orientation to life's challenges. A detailed exposition of Judaism's ecological wisdom goes beyond the scope of this short chapter,[7] but here are some insights relevant to the specter of the Anthropocene.[8]

Jewish ecological wisdom is rooted in the doctrine of Creation. That the world was created by God means that the earth and its fullness belong to God (Psalm 24:1) and that humans are but temporary tenants of the earth (Leviticus 25:23–24. Although humans were given the right to use and enjoy the goodness of the created world (Genesis 1:26), they were not given the mandate to destroy what does not belong to them.[9] Being created in the "image of God" (1:27) enables humans to imitate God's benevolence, and for that reason humans were tasked with the obligation to "till and protect" the earth (2:15). Acting as responsible caretakers or conscientious stewards is the heart of the Bible's ecological vision.[10] Biblical land ethics spell out how to treat soil, vegetation, animals, and other human beings to ensure the fecundity of the earth, its biodiversity, and the possibility of future generations.[11] When we mindfully care for the earth and its inhabitants, the created world thrives and humans flourish, but when we engage in destructive behavior, we bring about the "unmaking of Creation," according to Everett Gendler, a pioneering Jewish environmentalist.[12] Creation care requires that we curb our self-centered desires, put limits on our perpetual expansion, and be mindful of the harm we inflict on the well-being of others, both humans and nonhumans.

The Sabbath frames Jewish ecological consciousness. As a day of imposed rest and cessation of productive work, the Sabbath expresses the Judaic commitment to self-control, attentiveness to the needs of others, and awareness of our creatureliness. The late Rabbi Jonathan Sacks put it succinctly, stating that the Sabbath is "the most compelling tutorial in human dignity, environmental consciousness, and the principle that there are moral limits to economic exchange and commercial exploitation."[13] The Sabbath reminds us of God's ownership and control of Creation, and Sabbath observance "teaches us that we are not God, that we are not in control, and that the goal of creation is not to be found within us."[14] As Abraham Joshua Heschel beautifully put it, Sabbath rest is an invitation to participate in the delight and stillness of divine life that is the purpose of Creation.[15] The environmental merits of the Sabbath are self-evident: instead of perpetual consumption and busy pursuits, we take time to rest, and appreciate the beauty of Creation. On the Sabbath we recall that God declared Creation "very good" (Genesis 1:31), and we recognize that biodiversity is intrinsically good and that humans must protect it if they are to have a relationship with their Creator.

The Sabbath is not only the symbolic remembrance of Creation, but also a reminder that we were once slaves in Egypt and that God liberated us from that oppression (Deuteronomy 5:15). The memory of Exodus instills the ever-present danger of oppression and exploitation, instructing us to care for other people, especially the socially vulnerable, and to treat them justly. The moral message of the Sabbath was extended to the land in the laws of the Sabbatical year (Sh'mitah), whose goal was to let the land rest, releasing it from human use and control.[16] For humans, as Michael Lerner explains, the Sabbatical year "provides us with an opportunity to rethink what we are doing with our own individual lives and how much we are serving our own understanding of the common good."[17] The Sabbatical year enhanced the notion that the earth belongs to God, and its call for debt relief indicated the awareness of the dangers of slavery and destitution. The ancient institution of the Sabbatical year serves as a major inspiration to Jewish environmentalism today both in Israel and in the Diaspora.[18]

The Sabbath and the Sabbatical year establish the causal relationship between social justice and ecological well-being. From Torah we learn that when Israel pursues justice, the Land of Israel flourishes and the people of Israel enjoy peace and prosperity, but when violence, injustice, and exploitation dominate, the Land suffers, its fecundity is lost, and the people are punished by exile.

God, Humanity, and Nature: Two Paradigms

In the Middle Ages, when Jews were living in exile from the Land of Israel and no longer engaged in land cultivation, Judaism continued to evolve in two main meta-halachic reinterpretations: philosophy and Kabbalah. The philosophers highlighted the rationality of created nature whose laws are accessible to human reason. To interact with God, a Jew must study the natural world, understand the laws that govern it, and live by the divine wisdom that is implanted in nature. In contrast, the kabbalists held that the created world is a symbolic text whose building blocks are the twenty-two letters of the Hebrew alphabet and whose infinite permutations symbolically mirror the dynamic processes within the Godhead. Human performance of the commandments of the Torah with proper intention (*kavanah*) can not only repair the broken world but also bring about a mystical union with God and human participation in the rhythm of divine life. In their distinctive ways, both medieval philosophy and Kabbalah contributed to Judaic ecological consciousness.

Moses Maimonides (d. 1204), the paramount philosopher and jurist, insisted that "the Torah corresponds to nature."[19] Presenting Moses as the most perfect philosopher and most perfect prophet, Maimonides held that the Torah teaches philosophic-scientific truths conveyed through spoken human language. To grasp the truths of the Torah, one must study the philosophy of Aristotle, observe the natural world, and live by the laws of the Torah. Nature is a law-governed system that manifests the wisdom of God, recognized by the stability, orderliness, permanence, and purposefulness of nature.[20] By studying nature, human beings learn how God manages the world with wisdom, justice, and mercy, and they can imitate God's ways by observing the commandments. The perfection of the Torah is evident as well in the social sphere, since its laws (as Maimonides systematized in the *Mishneh Torah*) establish the perfect social order within which human beings flourish—namely, experience happiness.[21] Interpreting Judaism through the lens of Aristotle's virtue ethics, Maimonides asserted that the life of Torah ensures the "well-being of the body" (*tikkun haguf*) and the "well-being of the soul" (*tikkun hanefesh*). The former consists of physical health and moral virtues necessary for human flourishing in this life, and the latter consists of the intellectual virtues, culminating in intellectual perfection, by which humans attain immortality. Although Maimonides was not attuned to the environmental significance of virtues, today environmental ethicists promote the virtues of sustainability (e.g., humility, modesty, patience, gratitude, simplicity, and generosity), all of which are extolled by the Judaic tradition.[22] The Maimonidean interpretation of Judaism informs modern Orthodoxy as much as it inspires Reform Judaism.

If for Maimonides the scientific study of nature facilitates human flourishing and leads to immortality of the intellect, for the kabbalists the Torah discloses the mysteries of the created world, not because it coheres with Aristotle's natural philosophy, but because God created by the Hebrew language, literally speaking. The created world is thus a linguistic construct whose foundational "building blocks" are the twenty-two letters of the Hebrew alphabet, whose infinite permutations are governed by ten forces or vectors, the ten s'firot.[23] Together the letters and the s'firot constitute the "algorithm" of God's inner life, so to speak, which constitutes the "code" of the natural world, a vast information system that symbolizes the processes of divine life. Instead of accentuating the transcendence of God and Creation, Kabbalah highlights immanence and interconnectedness. All aspects of reality manifest the presence of God, since the ineffable YHVH is "stamped" or "sealed" into all existents. Not only humans were created in the "divine image," but all beings, terrestrial and celestial, human and nonhuman, were so created.[24] In the kabbalistic worldview, Creation is a vast information system that can be deciphered by those who possess the "code" of Creation, namely, by those who know the mysteries of the Hebrew letters, the ten s'firot, and the divine names. Like reading Torah, the decoding of symbolic nature is a hermeneutical process par excellence.

Medieval and early-modern Kabbalah and its further interpretations and elaboration in Chasidism accentuated the sacrality of all aspects of reality. The world of planet earth where humans dwell is suffused with the omnipresence of God, as each blade of grass, each drop of water, and each living cell is enlivened by divine "sparks" (nitzotzot) that are trapped in corporeal reality as the result of the catastrophic events (the "Breaking of the Vessels") of the creative process.[25] Whether one interprets the omnipresence of God pantheistically or panentheistically, literally or metaphorically,[26] Kabbalah and Chasidism resonate with the contemporary environmental philosophy of deep ecology, which cultivates a spiritual orientation of intimacy and reverence for the earth.[27] For those who live by Kabbalah and Chasidism, performing the rituals of Judaism with the proper intention is believed to facilitate the contact between the human soul and the divine sparks releasing energy that brings about tikkun olam, namely, the healing or repair of the broken world. The eco crisis manifests the brokenness of the world. Since Kabbalah and Chasidism accentuate human responsibility for the well-being of the world, it is not surprising that adherents of these strands of Judaism have promoted Jewish environmentalism under the banner of neo-Chasidism. Thus Schachter-Shalomi, Arthur Green, David Seidenberg, and Ariel Evan Mayse have advocated "Kabbalah for the environmental age," showing that commitment to traditional Judaism is utterly congruent with environmental sensibility. [28] Reform and Progressive Jews who are not familiar with Kabbalah and Chasidism or who may not be comfortable with Kabbalah's mythical worldview or its shamanic performance of halachic rituals readily adopt the concept of *tikkun olam* to justify climate activism, opposition to mineral extraction and hydraulic fracking, or engagement in eco-social justice.

Conclusion: An Inclusive Vision

Modern humans have profoundly destroyed the created world, intervening with and transforming many ecosystems, which they have not created. Therefore, the responsibility for mending the damage falls on human beings. We will be able to rise to the challenge if we listen to the voices of our religious traditions. Judaism articulates a framework that acknowledges human moral responsibility and spells out norms of conduct and ethical values that ensure the well-being of Creation in perpetuity. Judaism reminds us that humans did not bring the world into existence and that the world is not ours to recklessly destroy. To be Jewish means to participate in a conversation with the tradition, reinterpreting, reconstructing, and applying its deepest insights. Jews today should cultivate ecological consciousness and take a stand on a range of social, economic, and political issues posed by the Anthropocene. To become environmentally engaged, we will need to go beyond denominational divides; we will need to listen to the instructive insights of our tradition, even if we do not endorse every aspect of it; we will need to cooperate and collaborate with other religious traditions; and we will need to be scientifically informed about the extent of environmental degradation. The environmental spirituality advocated in this essay accommodates religious and secular perspectives, halachic and post-halachic practices, scientific and mythic outlooks, Jewish and non-Jewish perspectives. The future of life on earth indeed depends on us, so we need to act rightly and justly if we are to "till and protect" our planet earth, our only home, as the Torah enjoins us to do.

NOTES

1. On the Anthropocene, see Clive Hamilton, Christophe Bonneuil, and Francoise Gemenne, eds., *The Anthropocene and the Global Environmental Crisis: Rethinking Modernity in a New Epoch* (London and New York: Routledge, 2015); Christophe Bonneuil and Jean-Baptiste Fressos, *The Shock of the Anthropocene*, trans. David Fernbach (London: Verso, 2017); Erle C. Ellis, *The Anthropocene: A Very Short Introduction* (Oxford: Oxford University Press, 2018).

2. On religion and climate engineering, see Forrest Clingerman and Kevin J. O'Brien, *Theological and Ethical Perspectives on Climate Engineering: Calming the Storm* (Lanham, MD: Lexington Books, 2016).

3. See Jason W. Moore, ed., *Anthropocene or Capitalocene? Nature, History, and the Crisis of Capitalism* (Oakland, CA: PM Press, 2016); Ian Angus, *Facing the Anthropocene: Fossil Capitalism and the Crisis of Earth Systems* (New York: Monthly Review Press, 2016).

4. In Greek mythology, Prometheus, the Greek Titan, or demigod, was depicted as a clever trickster who stole the fire from the gods of Mount Olympus and gave it to humanity along with the skill of metalwork. For this rebellious act Prometheus was severely punished by Zeus. In modern culture, Prometheus became the symbol of technoscientific innovation that asserts human power over God and/or liberation of the individual from social ties. For example, Mary Shelley's influential work *Frankenstein* (1818) was originally titled *The Modern Prometheus*, and it told the story of Victor Frankenstein, a young scientist who created a sapient creature in an unorthodox scientific experiment. Victor Frankenstein's science gave humanity what once belonged only to the gods, namely, immortality. The Promethean Self is a trope used to signify the spirit of modern technoscience.

5. See overviews in John Grim and Mary Evelyn Tucker, *Religion and Ecology* (Washington, DC: Island Press, 2014).

6. See overview in Hava Tirosh-Samuelson, "Judaism and the Environment," in *Oxford Bibliographies Online-Jewish Studies*, ed. David Biale (Oxford: Oxford University Press, 2015), https://doi.org/10.1093/OBO/9780199840731-0118.

7. See Hava Tirosh-Samuelson, "Judaism," in *The Oxford Handbook of Religion and Ecology*, ed. Roger S. Gottlieb (Oxford: Oxford University Press, 2006), 27–64; "Judaism," in *Routledge Companion of Religion and Ecology*,

ed. Willis Jenkins, Mary Evelyn Tucker, and John Grim (New York and London: Routledge, 2017), 60–69.

8. See Hava Tirosh-Samuelson, "Human Flourishing and History: A Religious Imaginary for the Anthropocene," *Journal of the Philosophy of History* 14 (2020): 382–418.

9. The command to "be fruitful and multiply; fill the earth and tame it; hold sway over the fish of the sea and the birds of the sky, and over every animal that creeps on the earth" (Genesis 1:28) has been the main proof text that the Bible mandates human dominion. The massive literature on this topic by Jews and Christians offers a more nuanced reading.

10. See Max Oelschaleger, *Caring for Creation: An Ecumenical Approach to the Environmental Crisis* (New Haven, CT: Yale University Press, 1994); Steven Bouma-Prediger, *For the Beauty of the Earth: A Christian Vision of Creation Care* (Grand Rapids, MI: Bakers Academics, 2001).

11. See Hava Tirosh-Samuelson, "Jewish Environmental Ethics: The Imperative of Responsibility," in *The Wiley-Blackwell Companion of Religion and Ecology*, ed. John Hart (Malden, MA: Wiley Blackwell, 2017), 179–94.

12. See Everett Gendler, "A Sentient Universe," in *Ecology and the Jewish Spirit, Where Nature & the Sacred Meet*, ed. Ellen Bernstein (Woodstock, VT: Jewish Lights, 2000), 57–68.

13. Jonathan Sacks, *To Heal a Fractured World: The Ethics of Responsibility* (New York: Schocken Books, 2005), 169.

14. Norman Wirzba, *The Paradise of God: Renewing Religion in an Ecological Age* (Oxford: Oxford University Press, 2003), 37.

15. Abraham Joshua Heschel, *The Sabbath* (New York: Macmillan, 1995 [1951]). A good example of environmental interpretation of the Sabbath is offered by Rabbi Yonatan Neril, "Slowing Down on Shabbat: Rejuvenating Ourselves and Our Planet," "Jewish Eco Seminars," available at Jewcology.com. See also Yonatan Neril and Leo Dee, *Eco-Bible*, vol. 1, *An Ecological Commentary on Genesis and Exodus* (Interfaith Center for Sustainable Development, 2020).

16. For exposition of the laws of the Sabbatical year and its relevance today, consult Yigal Deutcher, Anna Hanau, and Nigel Savage, eds., *The Hazon Shmita Sourcebook* (New York: Hazon, 2013).

17. Michael Lerner, *Jewish Renewal: A Path to Healing and Transformation* (New York: Grosset/Putnam, 1994), 330–36, citation from 330, 331.

18. In addition to the sources mentioned in note 16 above, consult Adrienne Krone, "A Shmita Manifesto: A Radically Sabbatical Approach to Jewish Food Reform in the United States," *Religion and Food, Scripta Instituti Donnerian Aboensis* 26 (2015): 303–25; Einat Kramer, "The Shemita Year as a Laboratory for Jewish Sustainability," in *Sustainability and Jewish Peoplehood* (Center for Jewish Peoplehood Education). Kramer, the founder

of Teva Ivri, spearheaded the "Shmita Project" in 5775 (2014–2015), as well as the "Israeli Shmita" initiative for 5782 (2021–2021)."

19. Moses Maimonides, *Guide for the Perplexed* 2:40.

20. See Micah Goodman, *The Secrets of the Guide of the Perplexed* [in Hebrew] (Tel Aviv: Kinneret Zmorah-Bitan, 2010), 171–87; Eliezer Hadad, *The Torah and Nature in Maimonides's Writings* [in Hebrew] (Jerusalem: Magnes Press, 2011).

21. Hava Tirosh-Samuelson, *Happiness in Premodern Judaism: Virtue, Knowledge, and Well-Being* (Cincinnati, OH: Hebrew Union College Press, 2003), 192–245.

22. Jason Kawall, ed., *The Virtues of Sustainability* (Oxford: Oxford University Press, 2021); Hava Tirosh-Samuelson, "Jewish Environmentalism," in *Jewish Virtue Ethics*, ed. Alex Green, Geoffrey Clausen, and Alan Mittelman (Albany: State University of New York Press, 2023).

23. This idea is traced to the enigmatic book *Sefer Y'tzirah* (*The Book of Formation*), which became a foundational text of medieval Kabbalah. On *Sefer Y'tzirah*'s linguistic conception of nature, see Hava Tirosh-Samuelson, "Kabbalah and Science in the Middle Ages: Preliminary Remarks," in *Science in Medieval Jewish Culture*, ed. Gad Freudenthal (Cambridge: Cambridge University Press, 2011), 476–510.

24. See David Mevorach Seidenberg, *Kabbalah and Ecology: The Image of God in the More-Than-Human World* (Cambridge: Cambridge University Press, 2015).

25. Lurianic Kabbalah explicated the details of the dramatic process that brought the world into existence. The cosmic myth of Lurianic Kabbalah is summarized most usefully in Lawrence Fine, *Physician of the Soul, Healer of the Cosmos: Isaac Luria and His Kabbalistic Fellowship* (Stanford, CA: Stanford University Press, 2003).

26. Pantheism identifies God and the world, whereas panentheism insists that the world is in God but does not exhaust God.

27. See Eric Katz, "Faith, God, and Nature: Judaism and Deep Ecology," in *Deep Ecology and World Religions: New Essays on Sacred Ground*, ed. David Landis Barnhill and Roger S. Gottlieb (Albany: State University of New York Press, 2001), 153–62.

28. See Arthur Green, "Kabbalah for the Environmental Age," in *Judaism and Ecology: Created World and Revealed Word*, ed. Hava Tirosh-Samuelson (Cambridge, MA: Harvard University Press, 2002), 3–15; Arthur Green and Ariel Evan Mayse, eds., *A New-Hasidism*, 2 vols. (Philadelphia: Jewish Publication Society, 2019).

2

Healing *Adam* and *Adamah*
Ancient Torah, Action Today

RABBI ARTHUR O. WASKOW, PhD

THE *TANACH*, the Hebrew Bible, is a treasury of stories, outlooks, and practices that arose from a people of shepherds and farmers. They connected closely with the earth and saw that connection as the most sacred way to be in relationship with a God whom they named *YHWH*. "Pronounced" with no vowels—*YHWH*—the name invoked just breath, the Breath of Life that interbreathes all living beings on planet earth. The bringing of food from the earth to *YHWH*, *burning* it so that its smoke merged with the Breath of Life, became their crucial way of drawing near to *YHWH*.

Rabbinic Judaism emerged from the earthquake of being severed from the soil of *Eretz Yisrael* and indeed from close connection with any specific land. The people lost that emotional, political, intellectual, and spiritual impulse to construct their sacred life around an eco-harmonious relationship with the earth and turned to focus on themselves as the most important carriers of holiness, with their words of prayer and midrash now the most important medium for encountering God. "*YHWH*" turned into "*Adonai*, Lord," resulting in a hierarchical rather than ecological model for the sacred. Much was gained and much lost in that transformation. How much was lost did not become clear until the human race as a whole, through the Industrial Revolution, brought unexpected and worsening disaster on the planetary web of life—corrupting and poisoning the Interbreath of Life by pouring so much carbon dioxide into the atmosphere that all the earth's vegetation could not transmute it into oxygen. The surplus of carbon dioxide and other heat-trapping gases began to scorch the planet.

From the standpoint of science, these catastrophic environmental changes became the climate crisis. From the standpoint of religion and the Spirit, we face a crisis in *YHWH*. The earth itself is choking, and the Breath of Life, *YHWH*, is faltering. It is in this moment that the treasury of wisdom of an ancient earth-based people can have crucial relevance—not that their tales and practices could be enough. What had sufficed to make eco-harmony in a thin sliver of land on the eastern shore of the Mediterranean Sea will not adequately address a crisis afflicting the whole planet. Yet this treasury can point us toward doing what we need. Moreover, deemed sacred texts by a very large proportion of the human race, their teachings, midrashically transformed, could reawaken many communities of faith to heal the relationship between *adamah*, earth, and *adam*, human earthlings.

What then is the biblical teaching for our time? There are both a set of stories and a central practice that reveal how human action will damage and destroy the earth's abundance and also how human action can heal that broken relationship. Moreover, we can renew festivals that grew out of celebrating the dance of earth, moon, and sun, which can be renewed to give that dance new life.

There is a through-line in Torah that begins with lush abundance and then its loss in Eden, just as childhood becomes adolescence and then an adulthood of drudgery. This through-line continues in the plagues that Pharaoh brings upon the *Mitzrayim* (Egypt, or "narrow place") piece of earth, begins the journey back to abundance with manna and Shabbat, then looks toward the Song of Songs as a return to Eden for a maturely adult human race in loving harmony with the earth. Thus the stories, parables, and poems guide us toward a practice that can preserve the harmony through a pulsating economy, one that grows and quiets, grows and quiets.

Before Eden, the Torah makes the interrelationship of farmer, grain, and rain the context for the birth of *adam* from *adamah*. Then the Breath of Life voices a truth on behalf of a farmer's reality: there is extraordinary abundance, but it must be safeguarded by human self-restraint—do not gobble everything; leave one tree's fruits, the Tree of Knowledge of Good and Evil, uneaten. The humans are like children, naked (*arumim*) but not ashamed. The snake, most naked (*arum*) of all animals because it sheds its skin, approaches the girl-child: "You will soon be growing up, shedding your skin as I do. There will even be blood; it may be frightening. You may think you are dying. But you will not; you will be transformed instead. The Voice said you will die if you eat from this tree. It is not true; by eating you will be transformed."

And the girl-child like any adolescent takes a step of independence, refuses to restrain herself, and eats. She ingests the knowledge of opposites: good and evil, dark and light, God and human, this and that. She leaves behind the flow of life, taking only one aspect of the eco-truth: the uniqueness and separateness of each fact in the flow, but not how they fit together like the pieces in a jigsaw puzzle into the greater living One. Her male companion joins her. They separate themselves into an "it."

And so the abundance vanishes. The earth will now give forth only thorns and thistles, and humans will have to work every day of their lives to garner just enough to eat. Hierarchy enters this adulthood of drudgery. Men rule over women. The one human relationship most obviously meant for attunement, for eco-harmony, is corrupted by power of one over the other. These are consequences, not commands. No one ever took the first consequence as a command to not make tools, a rake or hoe, a plow, a harvester, to ease the toil of growing food. In the same way Torah urges us to grow up beyond the gender hierarchy.

In the Torah we witness hierarchy in the Joseph narrative as he concentrates enormous power in Pharaoh. Pharaoh not only responds by making us pariahs to his own people, as unwanted illegal immigrants with a foreign religion and a foreign language, but ultimately enslaves us, eventually verging on genocide. Pharaoh is challenged by those who know that *YHWH* is the Interbreath of Life, that tyranny over humans will inevitably generate destruction of the earth, that plagues are not just an accident. He turns his stubbornness and cruelty against the earth's abundance. His utter lack of self-restraint brings disaster upon his own people, even while those same plagues become an avenue of liberation for the enslaved.

After the people of Israel—we—birth ourselves anew not once but twice, through the doorway smeared with blood like the womb, through the broken waters of rebirth of the Reed Sea when we chose the Unknown rather than Pharaoh's army, we face the quandary of food once again. This is a wilderness—what can we eat? The earth gives forth abundance yet again in the form of manna—*mahn hu*, "what's that"? It comes with self-restraint: enough to eat, but if we gather more, it rots and stinks. On the one day, Shabbat, when it does not come, we must not even go out to gather it, because we are provided with enough on the sixth day. This self-restraint is quite different from the asceticism in the Garden of Eden. Self-restraint on Shabbat is delicious—it will preserve Shabbat for us just as the manna in the desert sustained our ancestors.

The parable above may stem from the teaching on *Shabbat Shabbaton*, the seventh year, the *Sh'mitah* year of release, or more likely, intended to encapsulate the wisdom of the *Sh'mitah*. For one year we would eat what grew freely from the soil and what we had stored, but we and the land would rest from the work of organized agriculture. Debts would be annulled; each family would reconnect with its ancestral land (at least in the year of seven times seven plus one). Leviticus 26:34–38 asks, "What will happen if you refuse to let the earth make its Shabbat?" And the answer comes, "The earth will make Shabbat anyway—on your heads! Pestilence and plague, fire and flood, exile and estrangement will engulf you."

Centuries later, even the *Sh'mitah* and the warnings of its rejection were not enough. The vision of Eden for a fully grown-up human race resurfaced. Rabbi Akiva and the Sanhedrin on "that day"—the revolutionary day when they had forced their arrogant chair to resign[1]— went beyond the *Sh'mitah* to include among the sacred books the Song of Songs (*Shir HaShirim*), the Song beyond all songs. In it, women and men are fully equal and beloved of each other. They are naked and not ashamed, with the erotic and the spiritual fully blended. They love the earth, and the earth delights in them. The Mama-Papa God is not commanding them, because they have internalized both the ethic of love and the need for joyful self-restraint. Yet there is a moment of violence, when the woman-hero goes out at night to seek her love and is assaulted by some men. This encounter hints at the world we are used to, in which violence and subjugation are endemic, and love is present but fleeting—as if to say that this world of love and abundance is achievable, not only as fantasy, not as sheer utopia. We are urged to grow into it. If we put our minds and bodies, our heart and soul, into the journey, we can arrive; it is not merely a dream to vanish in the morning.

How then do we put our minds and bodies, heart and soul, into the journey? I turn to the cycle of our holy days. Most of these days are the Jewish offspring of a long love affair between earth and humanity. Now that both earth and human earthlings—*adamah* and *adam*, in Hebrew— are wounded and in serious trouble, let us reawaken and reframe their offspring, our festivals and fast days, to rejuvenate their endangered parents. Following are only some examples.

Sukkot

Sukkot is the festival that moves us almost outdoors, into a hut with a leafy, leaky roof. We must construct it. A sukkah is not a cave; sitting in it is not the same as sitting beneath a tree. Each year we echo the earliest kind of shelter that human beings made—one step away from the Garden of Eden, but only one small step. We are taught to celebrate the harvest, not only for ourselves but for all the "seventy nations" of the world (Babylonian Talmud, *Sukkah* 55b). We wave four species of tree from four different sub-ecosystems of the Land of Israel in the seven directions of the world: left, right, up, down, front, back, and inward to our hearts. The first time I did this and showed my ten-year-old son how to do it, I asked him an untraditional question: "How did that feel?" He answered, "I felt like I was a tree, my own branches waving in the wind." We learn that the four species embody the four letters of the *YHWH* name of God. If we hold the four species as tradition teaches, the letters are reversed: *HWHY*. Only someone else facing us can see the name in correct order—as if to say, "This name is not just your breath but Interbreath." In America, where like Sukkot the national elections are keyed to the harvest in what was once an agricultural society, we could shape the holy day toward fruitful action with a slogan like "Share Sukkot: Green and Grow the Vote."

Chanukah

Chanukah comes at the darkest time of year in the Northern Hemisphere, close to the winter solstice at the twenty-fifth day of the lunar month, when the moon is disappearing, reappearing for the new moon, and still growing by its eighth day. The legend of the olive oil that was supposed to light the Great Menorah for one day but lasted eight is a teaching about the conservation of energy and the use of renewable resources for the light. As we realize that the golden Menorah is itself modeled on a tree, with branches and buds and blossoms, we are awe-struck by the vision of Zechariah, who imagines in a Temple rebuilt that not only are two olive trees growing beside the "Menorah Tree," but he also sees them pouring their oil directly into the Menorah, without human intervention (Zechariah 4:2–3, 11–12). This is the work *of adam* and *adamah* intertwined! The eight days could be used not only to raise consciousness about sacred earth, but also to take action for energy conservation and to encourage households to form congregation-based or neighborhood-based solar co-ops. These small but active communities of resilience would spring into action in case of natural or unnatural disaster. They would also work toward national and international funding for such solar co-ops everywhere.

Tu BiSh'vat

We celebrate the Re-birthday of the Trees and of the mystic Tree of Life as sap stirs and begins to rise in some midwinter climates. On a planet increasingly denuded of trees that could absorb and transmute carbon dioxide, this holiday could focus on reforesting the earth, not only to raise the money and demand support from governments, but also to go out in groups to physically plant seedlings. Could we introduce into our sacred texts *The Overstory*, a novel in which trees are characters and their suffering is as poignant as our own?

Pesach

Pesach began as two spring festivals, one of shepherds and one of farmers—a time not only of the birth of lambs and the rising of barley, but the rebirth of a people in their uprising against Pharaoh. The Rabbis insisted on a combined lunar-solar calendar because they knew Pesach must be in the spring. Just as cruel, stubborn Pharaoh got addicted to his own power over people and his local slice of the planet, just as his own hardening of the heart became addictive beyond the capacity to heal, so too, we have climate pharaohs today: in corporations and in governments who for the sake of hyper-profit are willing to bring flood, ice, and fire on the earth and humankind. At Pesach we might include supplements to the Haggadah to recognize the need for the continuing liberation of all peoples from the plagues brought on by climate pharaohs. Leaping off the written pages, people might wave the matzah of the "fierce urgency of Now," nonviolently challenging the reckless power of fossil-fuel companies, the banks that fund them, and the politicians who obey them.

Shavuot

Shavuot reunites the biblical festival and the anxiety-ridden counting of the days (*S'firat HaOmer*) until we knew whether the spring wheat harvest would be fruitful, along with the Rabbinic celebration of wisdom that is Torah, renewed in every generation, in every year. Counting the Omer is a miniature yearly version of the *Sh'mitah/Yoveil* cycle. This year, can our Torah rise to the occasion of this existential crisis and save the abundance, learn to share it, heal the earth and our own greed?

Tishah B'Av

Traditionally, Tishah B'Av is a time of grief as we remember the destruction of the Holy Temples in Jerusalem by invading imperial armies. I suggest that we intertwine a theme of grief for the endangered Temple Earth. Today earth is the sacred Temple of all the interbreathing life that makes up this planet, and it is in great danger of desolation by corporate carbon empires—the Babylonian and Roman Empires of our day.

There is an ancient notion that the kernel of Tishah B'Av contains deep sacred meaning going beyond the Jewish people. It is embodied deep into the experience of the Temple as a focus of universal holiness.

The Book of Lamentations, which bewails the destruction in a limping, painful melody, is called in Hebrew *Eichah*—"How?!" as to howl "Alas." The ancient Rabbis asked when was the first *eichah*? They answered that it was in the Garden of Eden when God called out, "*Ayekah*—Where Are You?" (Genesis 3:9) to the human race as we despoiled earth's abundance, foreshadowing the first and universal exile. For *eichah* and *ayekah* share the same Hebrew consonants, with only the signs of breathing vowels distinguishing the two (*Eichah Rabbah* 1:1). This good-humored and deeply serious wordplay by the ancient Rabbis hints strongly that ruining the earth is a noxious foretaste of the destruction of the Temple—and an aftertaste as well.

In Rabbinic and kabbalistic thought, the ancient Temples were microcosms of the created universe, where light (by burning olive oil in the Menorah), minerals (salt), vegetation (fruit, spices, pancakes, grain), animals (sheep, goats, bulls, doves), and the joyful sound of human song (by the Levites) were all brought near to *YHWH*, the Interbreath of Life. Thus there is warrant for intertwining the traditional concerns of Tishah B'Av with the planetary concern of our own generation.

One possible resource for synagogues, *chavurot*, and other sacred congregations is an entire Tishah B'Av service centered on the English "*Eichah* for the Earth" composed by Rabbi Tamara Cohen. It was first chanted in traditional trope at the US Capitol during the summer of 2010, at the time of the BP oil eruption in the Gulf of Mexico, and since then at such other venues as the National Havurah Institute.[2] One could add to the element of grief a simple act of healing in the spirit of the end of *Eichah*: "*Hashiveinu, Adonai, eilecha v'nashuvah; chadeish yameinu k'kedem*—You who breathe all life, turn us to You and we shall ourselves turn; make new our days as our days were new long ago" (Lamentations 5:21).

We could also do the important sacred act of writing a letter or paying a visit to our senators or congressperson to urge the inclusion in federal law of massive grants for solarizing homes, building electric railway systems and frequent service stations for electric autos, requiring retrofitting for all public buildings in renewable energy, organizing coastal wind-turbine arrays, and financing restorative agriculture and urban organic gardens/farms, and so on.

Rosh HaShanah and Yom Kippur

After seven Sabbaths of consolation with perhaps new haftarot from ancient texts or our own, we turn from mourning death to renewing life. Traditionally, Rosh HaShanah is the anniversary of the creation of the world or of humankind. In the Ten Days of Awe and Turning that conclude with Yom Kippur, we can face the awe that our astounding world inspires and learn again what we need to do.

In all this, we may live out the teaching of the manna. Our self-restraint should be joyful. We gather to sing and dance, to be serious but not downcast. We together take joy in the very fact that we are transforming Torah and taking action today.

Notes

1. See the story of the revolutionary deposition of Rabban Gamliel as leader of the Sanhedrin on "that day," and the many resulting changes that followed in the Babylonian Talmud, *B'rachot* 27b–28a.

2. You can see this prayer and other elements of an earth-oriented Tishah B'Av service at https://theshalomcenter.org/node/1733.

3

B'midbar
A Contemporary Midrash

RABBI IAH PILLSBURY

"Addy, can you give me a hand with this? No, not like that, like this."
"Has the manna been gathered? And the floor swept?"
"Would you help me with this?"

It was always something.
Always another thing. One after the other.

Wanting. Wanting. Wanting.
  Always asking.
  Always taking.
Always assuming she had more time and more energy to give.

But didn't she?
What would she be doing, otherwise, after all?

And so she said yes. Always yes.
  Always with a smile on her face and music in her voice.

Addy liked being liked and enjoyed being needed. And there was always so much to do, it was only right that she help, she told herself. It's what being part of a community meant after all—helping each other and doing it with joy. That's what freedom was all about! Becoming a people and being in it together, no matter how long the wandering took.

"Adeleh, would you mind watching the baby for a bit? And teaching the children their letters?"

"Could you give me a hand with the mending?"

If it wasn't help with a physical task, Addy's friends and family were asking for help solving their problems. Asking for advice and blaming her for the outcomes. There was never any time to rest, nor anywhere for Addy to put their pain or their problems. There was never any time to think about her wants or dreams. There was just yes, always yes, to everyone other than herself. Always, "I'd be happy to help." And no one seemed to see the tightness around Addy's mouth nor the shadows under her eyes. No one noticed how she began to move more and more slowly, and how her smile became less and less bright. They just heard "yes" and told themselves, "Adamah lives to serve. She's always so nice, I'm sure she loves it. One day she'll have a partner and children of her own, but until then we are helping her. She'd be all alone without us. It is a kindness that we let her help us so much."

And so, they kept asking and taking.

More and more.

And even more.

And Addy did not say anything, not even to herself. She just knew she was exhausted. And overwhelmed.

It was hard to think.

Harder to teach. Harder to enjoy herself.

She knew this wasn't what she dreamed freedom would look like or feel like. And if this wasn't what had been promised, she must be the one to blame, she decided. She called herself ungrateful and tried to ignore that it was getting harder and harder to breathe.

Instead of sleeping soundly at night, Addy would lie awake thinking about the last day and the ones to come. First, she would pick out all her mistakes from the day just lived, remembering every task and every interaction until she found her wrongdoings. She then repeatedly thought about them, poking them over and over like a sore wound. After the bruises abated, Addy would remind herself of task after task left to perform in the coming days. And with every mistake and every task she thought of, her chest constricted a little bit tighter, one small stone lying upon her chest and then another and another—until she felt each of them piled upon her like a funeral pyre, leaving her paralyzed and afraid. She never knew when exactly she managed to finally fall asleep each night, but she woke more and more exhausted with each passing day.

There was always the manna to
collect. And children to teach and to
feed.
And water to draw and endless things to
    wash. And never any sense of ever
    being done.
    There was always something else that needed doing and someone
else that needed helping.

And then the frustration and the anger came. First in small, short
bursts that were easier to hide. And then in larger, longer flares brought
on by everyone and everything. Suddenly, the world was fundamentally
infuriating in every way. Why did Ima have to ask her for help all the
time? And always when Addy had just sat down to her own task! And
why couldn't the children stop fighting for five minutes and just practice their letters in the sand? If God could provide manna, why should
Addy have to do the endless arduous work of collecting and preparing it
every day? Why was the sun so very hot and her tunic so incredibly itchy
and the camp so very smelly and so deliberately and annoyingly loud?
And why must they wait in this crowded wasteland forever?

There were too many people around. And they were always wanting
something from her. Always asking for help. Always needing her.

"Adeleh, do you have a moment? Can you help me with this?"

They never stopped. Addy thought of all the thankless labor lying in
front of her, all the wanting and the complaining and the endless guilt
and shame of never being good enough and never being finished. She
was sitting at the entrance of her family's tent, right in the middle of the
camp, surrounded by her family and friends, and she had never felt so
guilty and so alone.

She just wanted it all to
stop. To cease.
Not to be.

She just couldn't be bothered anymore. With any of it. With helping.
With teaching. With being nice. With this journey toward the Promised

Land that clearly didn't really exist at all.

It was all too much.

And so, one night, a little before dawn, Addy simply got up and started walking. She just needed to be Away and to Breathe. She walked past all the sleeping tents—past Ima and Aba, past Kohat, and Merari, and the children—all the way to the desert on the other side. It took a long time to walk through the whole camp to the edge, but it felt good to be moving and to be alone as they slept. And so, she kept walking and walking, past the tents and the banked fires, past the sentry posts and out into the wide unknown. The desert air was crisp and the stars were uncountably numerous. It was quiet out here. Addy appreciated the sound of wind on sand and rocks, the cry of a bird, and the rustle of the brush. Addy kept walking, watching the sky and the ground transform around her, feeling her body loosen and her breath come more and more easily. She began to walk faster and faster, and then she was running—grinning, heart pounding, breath fast. Slowly the darkness of the night gave way to the purple light before morning, and then colors began to appear. The sky turned from black to purple to pink to orange to white to blue. It was good to be alive in this beautiful world, good to Be. Addy slowed as the terrain grew steeper but kept walking, breath ragged, sweat dripping. She tied up her tunic and knotted her hair more firmly, hands scrabbling at rocks and shrubs, reveling in her own strength. She climbed and she climbed, breathing in the scent of sand and earth, of sage and acacia and hyssop. She stubbed her toe on a rock and tripped, laughing a real laugh for the first time in what felt like forever, no longer frustrated with the world for existing. She laughed and she laughed and she laughed, so hard she had to stop and gasp for air, so hard her sides hurt and tears streamed down her cheeks. When she was done laughing she kept climbing and climbing, higher and higher into the wide-open sky. All of a sudden Addy climbed past an unfamiliar bush and then there she was—way up in the middle of the rising sky, on the top of a mountain, with the sun in her eyes and the wind rushing by. Around her and below, there was desert. Wilderness. Possibility. She was in the very middle of everything and nothing. *B'midbar.* In the wilderness. In the middle of becoming.

Addy took a deep breath and grinned. She could use this time of wandering to become anyone she wanted to become. To do anything she wanted. To help her family or not. To do both. Or even neither. But whatever she did, she would do it on her own terms, in her own way, in her own time. It didn't matter how long the wandering lasted, she would make it her own, Addy promised herself. She could do it and she would.

> "*Hineini*!" Adamah thought as she breathed in deeply. "I am here. And I can be myself. Wholly myself. Holy myself. I have to be." Adamah looked out at the sky and the desert and the mountain around her, "This place is holy and so am I, even if I did not know it."

Addy watched the sun continue to rise over the vastness of the wilderness all around her, humbled and awed and filled with wonder. She dug her toes into the earth, feeling each grain of sand, each rock and seed, and each possibility for life or for death. She breathed in the early morning air and the sun, the possibility of all that ever was, is, and ever will be.

"*Ani m'kudeshet li*. I am holy to myself and for myself. And I get to say no. I have to say no or no sometimes. And that's okay. That's good even. For all holiness requires separation. I get to choose the terms of my own boundaries. I get to draw my own borders and it will be beautiful. My boundaries are holy and beautiful."

Addy breathed deep, arms outstretched, heart open to the terrifyingly beautiful wilderness everywhere she looked. And then from somewhere deep within, she felt herself begin to sing. She didn't know what she was singing, nor from where it came—just a wordless melody overflowing with everything she was feeling and could not name. *Lai lai lai*. So softly at first—*lai lai lai laiiii laiiiii*—and then louder and louder and louder, faster and faster, *lai lai laaaiii lanai laaaaiiii* and then she was spinning and dancing and singing with the sky and the wind and the wilderness.

Her own wordless
melody. A *nigun* all her
own.

She sang and she sang and she sang. *Lai lai laiii laiiiii laaiiiii laaaiiii laii*. The wind whirled in time with her *nigun*, and the branches of the desert shrubs added to the pattern as they waved. Birds called in perfect counter to the melody, and all around her small creatures scraped and slithered about their days in time to the beat. They sang and they danced all together—woman and creatures, wind and sun. And then from somewhere far away in the valley below, Addy heard familiar voices raised in a chorus of song that echoed her own. And the patter of dancing feet. And drums. And timbrels. And the call of the shofar. And so she sang louder and danced with more feeling and the Israelites dancing and singing in the camp far below added to the *nigun*. They passed it back and forth from mountain to valley, from heavens to earth, allowing the melody to transform and to be transformed, growing and changing with each passing note and musician. And so Addy and the Israelites and the sun and the wind danced and sang all day on the mountain and in the camp, giving voice to all their pent-up feelings, all their frustrations and secret desires, their guilt and their dreams. They danced and they sang until there was nothing left to say or to feel and their bellies were rumbling for manna.

When the sun began to make its descent in the sky, Addy too began to make her way down the mountain, legs shaking ever so slightly. She was more tired than she had been in a long while, but it was a different kind of tiredness, a deeply satisfying kind of tiredness that permeated all of herself. She had done something entirely on her own terms and been somewhere beautiful and made it more beautiful. It had been good. It had been great even, she corrected herself. From now on, she was going to start making more decisions for herself, to say yes to the kind of work that fed her soul, and no to the kind that didn't. She was going to spend more time really resting and less time criticizing herself. She thought of Miriam leading the women in song at the very beginning of the wandering and how wonderful it would be to learn from her to do that kind of sacred work. "Tomorrow I will ask Miriam if she is in need of an apprentice!" Adamah decided.

She was going to take her life into her own hands and really start living it. She would ask for help and also say no, she promised herself. And it was going to start right now, with asking for something to eat and help drawing water to wash her tired feet!

Nimshal—The Message of the Midrash

This is a story about holiness: what it is, what it means, and what it needs. This is a story about the sanctity we find when we engage with our sacred earth: when we commune with her, contribute to her, nurture her, protect her, and appreciate her. This is a story about the restorative power of nature and coming back to ourselves, about making time and space to go outside and feed our souls. And this is also a story about burnout and the importance of boundaries, about the difficulty and importance of saying real noes and real yeses. This is a story that reminds us that no one person's resources are infinite—not any one human nor any one planet. Our planet, our sacred earth, gives endlessly and generously to our bodies, minds, and souls, even as we return those gifts with more demands, more pollution, and more pillaging of resources. Adamah's story is a reminder to each of us of how intertwined we are with our world and with our planet. It is a reminder that taking care of our sacred earth is a sacred partnership. We take care of the mountains, and the mountains in turn take care of us.

4

Humanity and the Earth
Dominion versus Stewardship

Jeremy Benstein, PhD

If the Bible were meant to be exclusively the lawbook of a particular tradition or just the historical narrative of one people, it could have dispensed with the opening chapters of Genesis. These chapters tell a cosmic tale, beyond any legislation or particularistic story of one nation, which puts those laws and narratives of later sections into a universal context of all Creation. This tale paints a complex portrait of Creation and of humanity, a single family (eventually split into distinct branches) inhabiting that world. Moreover, it presents, both descriptively and prescriptively, the intricate, at times contradictory, relationships between the two.

Fundamentalist readers often read Genesis as science, that is, a source of incontrovertible, empirical data about the formation of the physical world. Yet, "creationism" does not hold wide currency in the progressive Jewish world, most probably because of the strong tradition of multilayered interpretation, including midrashic approaches, which free the text from the straitjacket of a narrow literalism. Moreover, to read the magisterial chapters of Creation, which deal with some of the fundamental mysteries of existence, as a textbook of paleontology is, in traditional Jewish terms, to miss the *ikar*, the main thing: it is to focus on trivial, temporal physical events (*shaah*) instead of the significant eternal spiritual truths (*netzach*). We are searching for values, not facts.

Another approach states that since the Bible is a religious book, it is mainly about God, and we should read it for theological reasons. In response to this, Rabbi Abraham Joshua Heschel has written that more than human theology, what people think about God, the Bible is "divine anthropology"—a God's eye view of people. In other words, we are not looking primarily for scientific, historical, or even theological insight;

we are looking for wisdom and understanding about human existence and for guidance about understanding our place in the world.

Our rights and responsibilities—our duties and privileges—with respect to the world, which is our common home, are elaborated and specified in other parts of the Bible and Rabbinic literature, but their fundamental conceptual basis is here in Genesis and the Creation stories. Yes, *stories*, for Genesis presents us with two distinct versions of the creation of the world and of people, each with its own internal complexities and layered meanings. Moreover, when read together, these stories (in chapters 1 and 2) use a sort of "literary parallax," to create a composite portrait that strives to do justice to the many sides of its subjects: the Creator, the creating, the creation, and the creatures, including ourselves. Biblical scholar and literary critic Robert Alter likens the artistry of the biblical author/editor to that of a post-Cubist artist, able to present different perspectives of a complex and even contradictory multidimensional subject together in the same text.[1]

Genesis 1: Master and Rule—The Demands of Dominion

The most "ecologically notorious" part of the Creation narrative is the charge of Genesis 1:28, which states, "God then blessed them, and God said to them, 'Be fruitful and multiply; fill the earth and tame it; hold sway over the fish of the sea and the birds of the sky, and over every animal that creeps on the earth.'"

There is no linguistic way to get around the central terms here. They cannot be reinterpreted to align with twenty-first-century environmental sensibilities. We humans are indeed enjoined to breed like rabbits (or more specifically like fish and birds, for they receive the same divine blessing of fecundity; cf. Genesis 1:22), but distinctive to the human *telos*, we are to "tame" (or "master," "conquer"—*v'chivshuha*) the land and "hold sway over" (or "rule," "dominate," "have dominion over"—*urdu*) the rest of the fauna. The root *kuf-vet-shin* means literally "to trample or crush" (which is done in pickling vegetables, *k'vushim*, or in paving a road, *k'vish*).[2] And "dominate," *resh-dalet-hei*, gives us the modern Hebrew word for dictator (*rodan*).

But the easy, superficial, and therefore mistaken reading would be one in which Genesis 1 is stereotyped as the environmentally "bad" chapter and Genesis 2 as the "good" one. Not only are the larger narrative texts in which these lone verses are embedded more nuanced and complex, but we must also remember the difference in historical context. Genesis 1:28, mandating conquest and dominion, is categorically a *blessing*, and an uplifting and empowering one at that. Some 3,000 years ago (and 2,000, and 1,000 as well) this vision promised hope and dignity for a society with a short average life span and great susceptibility to natural threats.

But let's go deeper: What is the nature of this mastery and dominion? What type of behavior does it sanction? Are we truly meant to govern the wild animals, or does this just mean to domesticate some? The medieval commentator Nachmanides on this verse emphasizes that God gave humans "strength and authority to do whatever they wish with animals and all crawling creatures, to build and to uproot, and to mine copper from the mountains." Yet a close reading of the verses themselves reveals the surprising fact that whatever else dominion of the animal kingdom may have meant, it did not include eating them! The very next verse, Genesis 1:29, states, "And God said, 'Look, I have given you all the seed-bearing plants on the face of the earth, and every tree that has in it seed-bearing fruit—these are yours to eat."

Though no ban on meat eating is explicitly stated (there are no prohibitions of any type in Genesis 1), the affirmation of permitted fare makes the limitation clear (Babylonian Talmud, *Sanhedrin* 59b). And as Genesis 1:30 attests, this was true of all living things; there was no carnivory in Creation as originally conceived.[3] This condition also implied a deeper affinity or fellowship between humans and other animals than what might be otherwise inferred from the verses on subjugation; here all humans and animals were on the same side of the knife and fork (and tooth and claw). This situation changed after the Flood (cf. Genesis 9:3), when overt permission to eat meat was granted, in the context of the Noachide Laws of general morality. According to one interpretation, this concession was made as an outlet for humans to sublimate their aggression, the lack of which had led their antediluvian predecessors to lawlessness and violence.

Another significant aspect of the narrative of Genesis 1 is the often overlooked fact that God famously deems "good" all the various creations throughout the process, crucially before the appearance of humans. There is no hint that light, earth, water, vegetation, stars, planets, and other animals are good for their eventual functional value to humans. They are proclaimed good on their own terms, for their own or general divine purposes. It is the whole of Creation, including the human, that is declared "very good" (Genesis 1:31). Each part of that whole clearly has its own intrinsic value. This is emphasized by Maimonides in his *Guide for the Perplexed*: "All beings should not be believed to exist for the sake of humanity's existence. Rather, all other beings too were intended to exist for their own sakes, not for the sake of something else" (3:13).

So even in the context of the Creation story of Genesis 1, dominion and conquest are not as rapacious as they have been made out to be. Likewise, throughout the ages this verse was rarely used as a mandate to engage in acts connected to "subduing nature"; much more attention was given to the first half of verse 28 and questions surrounding the demands of procreation.[4]

The common vegetarian diet, the joint blessing of fecundity (Genesis 1:22 and 1:28), even the creation of humans on the same day with all other mammals bespeak a fellowship with the rest of the created world that is a powerful counterpoint to the assumption of the uniqueness of the human implied in having been the only creature to be created in the image of God.

Genesis 2: Serve and Preserve—The Stipulations of Stewardship

And what of the second story? Here too there are nuances and complexities. On the one hand, the human, formed of the dust of the earth, is placed in the Garden of Eden with a much gentler charge—not to rule, but in effect, to serve—and the animals are seen as candidates for companionship. This implies deep affinity and connectedness. But on the other hand, the human is still set apart as having uniquely received the divine breath of life, and no less importantly, the animals are ruled out as soulmates of the human. Let us look at the central charge of "to work it and keep it," *l'ovdah ul'shomrah* (Genesis 2:15).

Avodah is "work" or "labor" (and in the context of land, cultivation), and *sh'mirah* is "guarding" or "protecting." *L'ovdah ul'shomrah* has been variously translated as "to work and to watch" or "to till and to tend." One of my favorites is "to serve and preserve." One can add to that "observe" (as in commandments, like *sh'mirat Shabbat*, "observance of the Sabbath"), for it is surely no accident that both these terms have such cultic associations. Cultivating the soil and worshiping God are the same word in Hebrew (*avodah*); indeed, the English word "worship" is from "work," just as "cult" is the root of "cultivate."

If we try to divine the meaning of these terms from their referents in other contexts, our relationship to the Garden, and by implication the world, is homologous to our relationship with God—we are enjoined to do to the Garden what we do for God (*avodah*, "service")—and also what God does for or to us, as in the Priestly Benediction of Numbers 6:24, "*Y'varech'cha Adonai v'yishm'recha*, The Eternal bless you and protect you."

But let's dig deeper into the dynamic of *l'ovdah ul'shomrah*. From what exactly are we meant to protect or guard the Garden? I would suggest that the main threat to the Garden, and by extension the world, is precisely the other pair of the dyad: to master and dominate—the cultivation; the human work.

The mission is to work, to produce, to develop—but at the same time to guard, to be vigilant that the work doesn't get out of hand. It must remain, in a word, *sustainable*. Indeed, perhaps the best translation of the biblical phrase *l'ovdah ul'shomrah* is "sustainable development." Working the land is crucial for human flourishing—but guarding the earth is the critical complement. We need to guard the world precisely from our *avodah*, the effects of our own work. In our struggle for the earth's fruits, we sow the seeds of our own, and the world's, destruction—unless we temper our toil with responsibility and concern for posterity.

This responsibility is at the root of the very important contemporary notion of stewardship. Classically, to be a steward is to be in the middle: above is the lord of the manor, who has entrusted his domain to the charge of the servant-steward; below is the realm of responsibility. The steward is responsible *to* the one who is really in charge and at the same time responsible *for* the things entrusted. There is no traditional Hebrew term for the idea of stewardship, but it seems clear that this is another good translation of the biblical ideal of *l'ovdah ul'shomrah*.

The image is developed in the mystical text *Zohar Chadash* (5a), where Creation is likened to a king who ruled a city, who built it and maintained it, and then decided to appoint one of the residents as ruler over it in his stead. Everything would be handed over to him, his job being *m'lechet olam*, "the work, or craft, of the world"—to provide for the needs of the world and its perpetuation. Here we see a synthesis of Genesis 1 and 2: preserving, sustaining, and developing the world as an expression of dominion.

Between Apes and Angels: On Being a Part of and Apart from

> What is the question now placed before society with a glib assurance the most astounding? The question is this: Is man an ape or an angel? My Lord, I am on the side of the angels!
>
> —*Benjamin Disraeli*

> The Torah inculcates in us a sense of our modesty and lowliness, that we should ever be cognizant of the fact that we are of the same stuff as the ass and mule, the cabbage and pomegranate and even the lifeless stone.
>
> —*Ibn Kaspi*, Adnei Kesef, *commentary on Deuteronomy 22:6*

The very existence of a human-caused environmental crisis argues for exceptional human capabilities, which bestow upon us an exclusive status with concomitant responsibilities. Is it not understandable, though, that we have an anthropocentric view of the world—that we see ourselves somehow at the center of our environment? Wouldn't a fish have a pisco-centric view of the world (in their case probably just the ocean), and the horse an equo-centric philosophy? Anyone who knows cats knows that they absolutely have a felino-centric ideology. Seeing the world as surrounding us at a special place at the center may be the most commonplace, *natural* point of view.

But therein lies a paradox, for a religious conviction that affirms the divine character of the human spirit should require us to transcend that natural species-centric perspective and assume a God's eye view of the world and its ongoing functioning—as environmental philosopher Aldo Leopold put it, to "think like a mountain,"[5] to assume the point of view of the whole system, which may demand different conclusions than those concerned solely with the benefit of a single species.

This returns us to that difficult verse from Genesis 1:26: "God now said, 'Let *us* make human beings in *our* image, after *our* likeness.'" Who was God addressing? The possibility of plural deities is of course theologically ruled out. The most sensible, yet also most radical, interpretation is presented in a midrash (*B'reishit Rabbah* 8:3), which says plainly that God consulted with all of God's creations. Similarly, the commentator Rabbi David Kimchi (the RaDaK) wrote that God proposed to all the elements (*y'sodot*), "Let us, you and I, make the human together in partnership [*b'shituf*]."

Precisely because humans are created with the capacity to transcend nature, we are commanded by God to protect nature. In the words of Michal Smart Fox, we must "acknowledge our separateness in order to take responsibility, and to recognize our creatureliness in order to apprehend our limits."[6] It would be a repudiation of our divine nature and our appointed task in the world to be merely anthropocentric; we must take a God's eye view of the whole (of which we are a dependent part) and the conditions for its flourishing.

So, if it is moral agency and responsibility that is the crux of *imago dei*, "the divine image" (and not, say, shrewdness or technological know-how), then we best fulfill our divine image/destiny through acknowledging our moral responsibility for the world, rather than playing out the material possibilities of civilization and its development.

Part of that responsibility, again mimicking behavior attributed to the Divine, may be best described by the kabbalistic concept of *tzimtzum*, "contraction." According to Lurianic Kabbalah, the world could only come into being if God, whose presence was the totality of all being, "made room" for Creation. We too have a strong presence, filling up places that were once not humanly affected or defined, no longer leaving much room for what was once a vast nonhuman creation. It may now be time to fulfill that other divine precedent and undertake a willful contraction of our impact, for the sake of the whole of which we are also a part.

Again, this is not to downplay the awe-inspiring achievements of human civilization through the ages or the manifold blessings we enjoy today. This eternal dance of human empowerment and restraint, grandeur and humility, is expressed well in the Chasidic maxim of Reb Simcha Bunim: We should all walk around with two notes in our pockets. On one is written "the world was made for me" and on the other "I am but dust and ashes." The better part of wisdom is simply knowing when to take out which note.

NOTES

1. See Robert Alter, *The Art of Biblical Narrative* (New York: Basic Books, 1981), 146.

2. It is also the word used in contemporary Israel to refer to "the occupation" (of the territories)—*hakibush*, with all the attendant connotations.

3. Whether this accords with evolutionary or physiological data is not entirely clear—or germane. The point of the story is not the prehistorical data (i.e., Were we gatherers? Hunters? Both? Was the Garden envisioned as a place of work? Of leisure?), but the ultimate vision of paradise, the end of days. As Isaiah (cf. chapter 11) prophesied, the ideal world of eternal peace implies no harm to any of God's creatures by any of them, and the idyllic messianic era implies a "re-creation" of this initial paradise (cf. also Hosea 2:20).

4. See Jeremy Cohen, *Be Fertile and Increase, Fill the Earth and Master It: The Ancient and Medieval Career of a Biblical Text* (Ithaca, NY: Cornell University Press, 1989), 5ff.

5. Aldo Leopold, *A Sand County Almanac* (London: Oxford University Press, 1949), 129ff.

6. Michal Smart Fox, "Genesis as a Foundation for a Jewish Environmental Ethic," in *Operation Noah: Defending God's Endangered Creatures: Texts and Commentaries* (New York: Coalition on the Environment and Jewish Life, 1997), 8–15.

5

A Natural Jewish Theology
God's Covenant with the Earth

Rabbi David Mevorach Seidenberg

Sending Your Spirit, Your breath, all creatures come to life, and
You renew the face of the earth.

—*Psalm 104:30*

The greatest challenge of this century, and perhaps the coming
centuries, will be to address global climate disruption. For humanity to meet this challenge, we need to de-center humanity and re-center
the principle of life in all beings, which we may collectively call the
biosphere or Gaia.[1] Technological innovation alone will not suffice to
address the challenge. In Jewish terms, we need to remake our actions
to be in service to the *chiyut*, or life force, in all things; to *shefa*, which
means making the flow of divine sustenance more abundant; and to
adamah, the ground, which includes not just the soil but the whole community of life that lives on (and in) the soil.

Renewing the earth is an important part of *tikkun olam* not just in
our own time; it is the one issue we must face if we are to accomplish
anything else. The global scope of this threat may be new, but the kind
of tragedy we face is not new. In fact, Israelite religion and civilization
arose in the long shadow of the ecological collapse of Mesopotamia.
Sumer, the ancient civilization that invented writing and the plow,
destroyed its agricultural land when the soil became impregnated with
salt, leading to the abandonment of what were once among the most
fertile lands known to humanity. In our Torah story, this is represented
by the idea that Abraham and Sarah left Mesopotamia behind to come
to Canaan.

Our ancestors understood that the destruction of what we call the
environment or nature was both possible and real. That is why the
Torah begs us to "choose life!" (Deuteronomy 30:19). This is an invitation, but also a warning to human beings to restrain our destructive

power. That call to restraint is trumpeted in myriad ways by the Torah. For example, Torah forbids taking a parent bird and its young together (Deuteronomy 22:6–7), because, as medieval commentator Nachma nides explained, to do that is to act like someone who would willingly cause the extinction of a species. The Torah forbids cutting down fruit trees (Deuteronomy 20:19), because destroying the trees that freely provide food to all is not only unsustainable, but it is also repaying the goodness of giving life with evil. The Rabbis understood the possibility of ecological collapse, for they imagined God showing the first human the trees of the Garden of Eden and saying, "Don't destroy my world, for if you do, no one will come after you to fix it" (*Kohelet Rabbah* 7:13).

Torah laid out a plan for a civilization that would be sustainable, that would align with the needs of the land, as the second paragraph of the *Sh'ma* exhorts, "so that your days and the days of your children on the land will increase" (Deuteronomy 11:21).[2] In this civilization, agriculture would be radically different than that of Mesopotamia. The centrality of agriculture as a motif in Torah is already signaled in the second story of Creation, which tells us—three times—that humanity's purpose is to serve the land, *laavod et haadamah* (Genesis 2:5, 2:15, 3:23). The *adam*, the first human, comes from the *adamah*, the soil, and the *adam*'s purpose is to serve the *adamah*.[3] Because we are so distant from the roots of the Torah, we mistranslate and misinterpret this clear directive, saying instead that God tells us to "work" the land (as in the Revised Plaut translation of Genesis 2:15), or in other words, that we should make the land serve us.[4]

The plan for this new approach to agriculture is rooted in the story of Creation and the Sabbath, which is Creation's climax. "Remembering Creation" (*zikaron l'maaseih v'reishit*, as we say in Shabbat evening *Kiddush*) and imitating God, as the Torah guides us (Exodus 20:8–11), we let all of nature rest from our manipulation one day in seven. Shabbat was a weekly opportunity to practice for living a full year of allowing nature to rest in the seventh, or *Sh'mitah*, year. *Sh'mitah* means "release," and in that year, the Torah tells us, our fields are not ours. Their fruits belong again to the wild animals (Exodus 23:11; Leviticus 25:7), and they are free for all people to take (Leviticus 25:6). From this principle, the Rabbis learned that we must take down our fences to let people and animals enter any field they wish, and that we can only eat in our homes what the wild animals can find in the fields (*Mishnah Sh'vi-it* 7:1, 9:2–6).[5]

During the *Sh'mitah* year, humanity would share all food, and hoarding and storing food to sell were strictly forbidden (*Mishnah Sh'vi-it* 8:3, 9:4). At the end of the *Sh'mitah* year, all debts were canceled (Deuteronomy 15:1–2). The *Sh'mitah* year itself was a kind of practice for the year after the seventh *Sh'mitah*, the *Yoveil* or Jubilee, the fiftieth year when the land is redistributed in a manner that gave every family an equal portion. In that year, radical land reform goes hand-in-hand with radical freedom for all human beings.[6] As the Torah commands us, "You shall proclaim release throughout the land for all its inhabitants" (Leviticus 25:10). The lesson to be learned is this: we are "strangers" in the land, which belongs not to us but to the Creator (Leviticus 25:23). Moreover, the refugee or foreigner, whom we might label a stranger, is no different from ourselves, for we are also strangers (Exodus 23:9; Leviticus 19:34). Our central story, that our existence as a people was forged in Egypt, where we arrived as strangers and were forced into slavery, reminds us of this.

As we can see, the Israelites believed in a different kind of agriculture that would treat the land as sacred, as a subject with innate rights, needs, and desires. And they believed in a covenant between God and the land, even to the extent that the land's desires come before our own needs. God's covenant with the Land of Israel is foreshadowed in the rainbow covenant with the entire planet after the Flood, a covenant that is made not specifically with humanity, but rather with the land and with all creatures (Genesis 9:9–17).

God's covenantal promise to the land is why the consequence of failing to observe *Sh'mitah* is exile. Even though exile sounds like a punishment, it was most importantly a solution for fulfilling the need of the land to rest (Leviticus 26:34–35, 43). Living in exile is also a refresher lesson for us about being strangers, after which we could return and fulfill our mission. The Torah's plan was to create a living society where the people served the land not just through ritual but through justice. *This* was the mission of the civilization that formed the Jewish people. It is a mission for which the land of Canaan was uniquely suited:

> For the land that you are coming to is not like the land of Egypt, from which you came out, where you sowed your seed and gave drink with your foot (by pumping water from the Nile), like a garden of greens. [For] the land to where you are passing over is a land of mountains and valleys—through the rain of the heavens will she drink water. (Deuteronomy 11:10–11)[7]

In the next verse (Deuteronomy 11:12), the Torah teaches that this land of promise is under God's special care, that "the eyes of YHVH your God are continually upon her" (JPS: "on which the Eternal your God always keeps an eye"). This mystical-sounding relationship describes a simple ecological reality: as a hilly, arid land that is only watered by rainfall, Canaan could quickly succumb to drought. Imagined from a divine perspective, this meant that God was continually assessing whether the people merited rain. Our ancestors craved that kind of intimacy with God, even though it may sound judgmental to our ears. The very fact that everyone's tenure was tenuous, that they could not control the land, is what made Canaan/Israel/Palestine a holy land.

Canaan's rain-fed agriculture was the opposite of the land of Egypt, which could be sustained by the Nile's flooding and the technology of the pedal pump, and also the opposite of the land of Mesopotamia, which could be watered even more easily by canals dug from the Tigris and Euphrates to the fields.[8] No matter the state of the weather or the state of justice, those lands could go on producing for centuries without rain, until finally Egypt got its proverbial seven years of famine and its ten all-consuming plagues, or until Mesopotamia's soil became so salinized that it had to be abandoned.

Modern-day Canaan is run differently, however. Our Jewish state controls land by uprooting olive groves and demolishing homes, waging a low-intensity war on the Palestinian people who may be strangers to us, but who are not strangers to the land. And as Israel controls the land, Israel also controls the water. One of the consequences of our human technology is that Israel can pump water from deep aquifers and thereby become more like Egypt.

For all its benefits, humanity's technological prowess has more than one downside. There are the obvious and massive problems of pollution and destruction. But more than that, technology enables us to defer the consequences of those problems for centuries. Now the consequences are becoming so vast as to encompass the entire globe. In California, we already see fires more massive than any ever witnessed; in Bangladesh, vast flooding. In Israel and Palestine, as the climate changes, people won't be able to pump enough water from the aquifers to make up for the expected loss of rain.[9]

We may think of climate change as the consequence of industrialization, but it is equally the consequence of agriculture, which brings along with it the loss of forests as vast as continents and the loss of habitat for multitudes of creatures. Everywhere people go, we act like invasive species, driving native plants and animals to extinction, ending whole ecosystems. This is the sixth mass extinction, the culmination of the Anthropocene—the geological era of no Shabbat—in which humanity became a force so great as to change the planet itself.[10]

Our ancestors imagined another world was possible, based on a different kind of agriculture with a different value system, rooted in a holy relationship to the earth. The Torah inducted the Jewish people into the mission to create that new world, a world that perhaps could have averted the catastrophe that is the Anthropocene. The strategy was to create a model society living in service to a model land. We failed in that mission more than once in ancient times, and it is a mission we are failing now. Meanwhile, most nations, including Israel, continue to skirt the big steps we must take in order to change course. Is another world still possible? That is an open question. To change course, it will not be enough to manage the earth more and more intensely in the struggle to limit the tragic consequences of climate change. To create a sustainable world, we will need to plumb deep to understand how Western civilization, carrying along with it so many cultures and other civilizations, arrived at this point, spiritually and psychologically. What assumptions were made about the earth, about human life, about other creatures, about God? What did we human beings ignore or minimize in order to aggrandize ourselves? And we Jews must also ask: What stopped the Israelites, and later the Jewish people, from fulfilling the mission to transform civilization?

The scope of these questions is huge, and there is hardly enough space here to do more than scratch the surface.[11] Here are a few thoughts about that failure. Imperialism (whether Babylonian, Greek, or Roman) makes it hard for those subjugated to think well about the land and one's relationship to it. Even on a practical level, the Rabbis decided that in a time of exile, when Jews lived under foreign dominion even in the Holy Land, the *Sh'mitah* commandment to release the land was itself optional or evadable. Hillel's innovation of the prosbul[12] also annulled the Sabbatical year cancellation of debts, which was the only rule that applied even in the Diaspora. Persecutions and expulsions also make it hard to imagine that freedom can come from letting go of controlling the land that "God gave us"—even though the message of the Torah is that exercising control over the land is morally and literally disastrous.[13] Furthermore, we internalized beliefs that we stand in the place of God as rulers over Creation, along with other ideas such as the ancient division of spirit from matter and bodies or the more modern idea that humans, but no other animals, have souls.

Part of the process for restoring our mission may be to free Judaism from these accretions. We may also need to reconfigure the Torah's original message. That message, at least on its surface, seems to say that only human beings are created in the image of God. As we will see, Kabbalah can help us rectify this apparent flaw. More shockingly however, the *Tanach* (especially the Book of Joshua) also tells us that the way the Israelites began their new society was to commit genocide against the seven Canaanite nations. It is critical to note that there is *no archaeological evidence* that such a genocide ever happened. But even just as a story, it poisons the mission. The experience of exile itself, which must deepen our empathy with the stranger, can help us repair this flaw.

It is also true that while in exile, we accomplished great things and created new resources to help us in our mission. For example, Kabbalah found God's image in the structure of Creation itself, seeing humanity as being in God's image because it was in the image of Creation.[14] Maimonides urged us to completely reject anthropocentrism; he also saw the whole universe as a single being that is alive.[15] Moshe Cordovero demanded that we take responsibility for the lives *and souls* of every being, plant or animal, that we use in order to live.[16]

Some teachers of Chasidism, including the Baal Shem Tov, also took the Lurianic idea that physical reality trapped divine sparks, and they turned it upside down, believing that divinity could flame forth from within the physical realm.[17] And Martin Buber, Abraham Joshua Heschel, and Abraham Isaac Kook all gave us powerful language for rejecting the commodification of the world and lifting up the holiness of pure relation, wonder, and love. There is also today a vibrant Jewish environmental/farming/wilderness scene in North America, along with corresponding elements in Israel, including many feminist voices from institutions like the Kohenet Institute, that are deeply revaluing Judaism.

Revaluing what we have learned and are learning from exile needs to go hand in hand with what lessons might come from returning to the ancestral land. While *Sh'mitah* may teach us the idea of being strangers in the land, our journeys through the Diaspora help us identify with refugees and immigrants, making us so much more sensitive to that powerful lesson. What we have learned can also help strip the tarnish from older ideas and words that were in themselves magnificent. For example, the Chasidic turn toward divinity in the physical realm can illuminate the meaning of Isaiah 6:3, which is most accurately translated as "Holy, holy, holy is *Adonai Tz'vaot*, the fullness of the earth is God's glory."[18] Notice that the glory of God is not found in the angelic hosts but in the hosts on earth, as the angels themselves declare. "Fullness" here doesn't just mean that God's glory is everywhere; it means that the diversity and abundance of life *is* God's glory.

We can integrate the wonderful flowering of new ideas in the secular and broader religious world, including theology about Gaia, the idea that our planet is alive, and ecopsychology, which explores how the more-than-human world teaches us to inhabit our humanity, along with the sciences of ecology and evolutionary biology, which teach us so deeply about the interconnections between all beings in the Tree of Life.[19] In this fragile moment, we are called to utilize every available resource, in a process many ecological writers call "the Great Turning," to undertake to shift society away from industrialization and toward sustainability.[20]

We are being called to reforge our relationship to the more-than-human realm that comprises nature, earth, life, other creatures, and God.[21] Even as we may have to "say *Kaddish*" for the many species we have driven to extinction (how does one even say *Kaddish* for a whole species?), it will take all our spiritual resources to overcome grief and numbness, to stay connected to both the task and the hope we need to carry it out. But the flip side is that by connecting with and caring for other species, we may also connect to that part of ourselves that still belongs to the Eden of our stories.

In order for humanity to turn back from defacing the earth, we must turn to behold the earth's face. When we do so, we are reaching toward much more than a solution to the climate crisis. We may restore our hearts to the natural world, retune our senses to the many creatures that surround us, and reclaim our companionship with them. We may re-root the diversity of our personalities and ideas in the diversity of life itself. We may reignite passion as full as the Song of Songs, where love between two people is sung in harmony with the hills and mountains and interwoven with love for the birds and foxes and flowers. And as we renew the face of the earth, we may also restore ourselves to God, who is, after all, imaged not just in human beings, but in all the innumerable beings and ways of being and evolving—all of us related, all of us composing this universe, which also holds our bodies, our spirits, and our dreams.

NOTES

1. The "Gaia hypothesis" is outlined in this book's introduction. For a wonderful and literary exposition of Gaia theory, see Evan Eisenberg, *The Ecology of Eden* (New York: Knopf, 1998), chap. 21, esp. 262–65, 274–77. For a useful introduction to Gaia from a Jewish perspective, see Lawrence Troster, "Created in the Image of God: Humanity and Divinity in an Age of Environmentalism," in *Judaism and Environmental Ethics*, ed. Martin Yaffe (Lanham, MD: Lexington Books, 2001), 172–82, 176–77.

2. Author's translation. The standard JPS translation has "so you and your children may endure," which is less about sustainability than the actual Hebrew idiom.

3. The word *adam* is not initially a name of a person but rather the name of a species.

4. The grammatical form of serving and protecting the land in Genesis 2:15, *l'ovdah ul'shomrah*, is exactly the same as the command to serve God in the traditional second paragraph of the *Sh'ma*, "to serve [God] with your whole heart," *l'ovdo b'chol l'vavchem*. That paragraph also promises

that if we don't live rightly on the land, the climate will be ruined. It is a great loss to earth-based Judaism that many prayer books in the liberal movements removed the second paragraph of the *Sh'ma* from the liturgy, ostensibly because it was seen as superstitious.

5. Rashi on Leviticus 25:7; Maimonides, *Mishneh Torah, Hilchot Sh'mitah* 4:24, 7:6.

6. An excellent resource on these issues is Ellen Davis's *Scripture, Culture, and Agriculture: An Agrarian Reading of the Bible* (New York: Cambridge University Press, 2009). On *Sh'mitah*, see pp. 92–94.

7. Author's translation. The JPS (Jewish Publication Society) *Tanach* actually reverses the meaning of the passage. JPS translates: "For the land you are about to enter and possess is not like the land of Egypt from which you have come. There the grain you sowed had to be watered by your own labors, like a vegetable garden; but the land you are about to cross into and possess, a land of hills and valleys, soaks up its water from the rains of heaven." The implication of the JPS version is that you had to work hard in Egypt to water your garden, but in Canaan you won't have to work so hard, because the rain will fall. As explained, the whole point of the passage is that in Canaan agriculture is more vulnerable, because one cannot control irrigation.

8. The banks of these rivers had naturally built up over millennia, meaning that the water level in the rivers was higher than the fields, so that irrigation did not even require a pedal pump.

9. See "Choosing Life by Rosh Hashanah 5790" (*Tikkun*, October 16, 2019), where I summarize the current science on how climate change will affect the land of Israel/Palestine: https://www.tikkun.org/choosing-life-by-rosh-hashanah-5790/.

10. See Elizabeth Kolbert, *The Sixth Extinction: An Unnatural History* (New York: Holt, 2014).

11. Resources to explore include Evan Eisenberg, *The Ecology of Eden*; Ellen Davis, *Scripture, Culture, and Agriculture: An Agrarian Reading of the Bible*; and my book, *Kabbalah and Ecology: God's Image in the More-Than-Human World* (New York: Cambridge University Press, 2015), especially the introduction, which you can read online at kabbalahandecology.com.

12. A prosbul was a Rabbinic writ established by Hillel in the Second Temple period that changed the status of an individual private loan into a loan held and administered by the court. This allowed money lent before the *Sh'mitah* year to be collected after the *Sh'mitah* year. Its purpose was to make it easier for needy people to obtain interest-free loans.

13. See my "The Third Promise: Can Judaism's Indigenous Core Help Us Rise above the Damaging Politics of Our Time?," *Tikkun*, June 25, 2020, https://www.tikkun.org/the-third-promise/.

14. See Seidenberg, *Kabbalah and Ecology*, 250–55. Of special note is Yosef ben Shalom Ashkenazi (thirteenth century), who explains that the problem with idolatry is not that an idol is divorced from God. It's that Creation as a whole is in God's image, the idol as well as everything else, but directing one's worship toward an idol separates out that idol from the rest of Creation, thereby *disconnecting* it from God's image (*Kabbalah and Ecology*, 181).

15. Moses Maimonides, *Guide for the Perplexed*, trans. Shlomo Pines (Chicago: University of Chicago Press, 1963), 1:72, 3:12, 3:13, pp. 183, 187, 442, 452. Maimonides's vision of the universe as alive in many ways parallels modern Gaia theory, the idea that the earth is a self-regulating system where life creates, magnifies, and elaborates the conditions that allow life to thrive (*Kabbalah and Ecology*, chap. 10). Another point to note about the *Guide* is that whenever Maimonides discusses animals in comparison with human beings, he always speaks about humans and "the other animals."

16. See *Tomer D'vorah* (Jerusalem: Or Yikar, 1969) or *The Palm Tree of Deborah*, trans. Louis Jacobs (New York: Sepher Hermon, 1974), end of chaps. 2–3.

17. This idea evolved over generations. See David Mevorach Seidenberg, "Building the Body of the *Shekhinah*: Reenchantment and Redemption of the Natural World in Hasidic Thought," in *A New Hasidism: Branches*, ed. Arthur Green and Ariel Evan Mayse (Philadelpia: Jewish Publication Society, 2019), especially the sections on Nachman of Bratslav and Menachem Mendel Schneersohn therein. In Seidenberg, *Kabbalah and Ecology*, see pp. 206, 294–95, 330–31, 338.

18. JPS's very animated and idiomatic translation reads: "Holy, holy, holy! The LORD of Hosts! His presence fills all the earth!" On the interpretation given here, see Jeremy Benstein, "Biodiversity Is God's Glory," My Jewish Learning, https://www.myjewishlearning.com/article/biodiversity-is-gods-glory/; and David Seidenberg, "Being Here Now: This Creation Is the Divine Image," *Tikkun*, Winter 2017, https://www.academia.edu/31387102/Being_Here_Now_This_Creation_is_the_Divine_Image.

19. Resources to explore: Rosemary Radford Ruether, *Gaia & God: An Ecofeminist Theology of Earth Healing* (New York: HarperCollins, 1992); David Abram, *Becoming Animal: An Earthly Cosmology* (New York: Vintage Books, 2011); and Robin Wall Kimmerer, *Braiding Sweetgrass* (Minneapolis: Milkweed, 2013).

20. On this phrase, see Joanna Macy, "The Great Turning," Center for Ecoliteracy, June 29, 2009, https://www.ecoliteracy.org/article/great-turning.

21. The term "more-than-human world" was coined by David Abram in *The Spell of the Sensuous* (New York: Vintage Books, 1996) as a substitute for "nature." "More-than-human" emphasizes that humans are part of the whole, but it can fittingly also include God.

6

God as the Connective Tissue of the Universe

Rabbi Mordechai Liebling

W E NEED a Jewish theology that inspires, strengthens, and guides us in building a society that has a sustainable relationship with our living earth (*adamah* in Hebrew, *Gaia* in Greek), one that equally values every human being so that each feels comfortable changing places with any other, knowing that neither would lose any opportunities. We need a theology that can provide us with the spiritual sustenance to persevere over the "long haul," to help us grieve all that is dying, and to find active hope amid moments of despair. In truth, despair only colludes with those forces drawing power and profit from the inequities of our current systems, immobilizing us, and threatening all forms of life. Instead, let us attune to the Source of Life to provide comfort in our mourning and to energize our actions.

We need a sacred story about the possibility of a socially just, environmentally sustainable, and spiritually fulfilling future that takes into account the inevitable losses and changes caused by massive ecological shifts, for the "stories" we tell and believe usually determine our deeds. The most important of cultural narratives is the "Big Story," the meta-narrative that defines for its society what the sacred is. There can be no more pressing cause than formulating and articulating that meta-narrative for today. As David Korten has written, "When we get sacred wrong, we easily become entangled in a web of self-destructive, even suicidal, deceptions."[1] Thus, let us begin telling a new story rooted in Jewish tradition and values that transmits a new Jewish theology of connection.

Biography shapes our understanding. As the son of immigrants, I felt that this land, America, was not mine. On a deeper level, Judaism, reshaped in two thousand years of exile, had become a religion more of time than of space.[2] In the absence of our own sovereign territory, Jews kept Judaism alive largely through set times for prayer and study and through the sanctification of our holy days. Rabbinic Judaism sought to downplay the connection to the land to avoid further uprisings like the Bar Kochba Revolt, which ended in a disastrous defeat and Jews being banned from Jerusalem for decades. In addition, repeated forced exiles over centuries eroded the connection to the earth-rooted Judaism of the Torah. While this connection was reclaimed in Israel by the *chalutzim* (early Zionist pioneers), it lies mainly dormant in the largely urbanized Jewish Diaspora. This needs to change and, thankfully, is beginning to happen.

From Plato through Descartes and beyond, Western culture has principally embraced a dualistic view of the world. In turn, classical Christianity has preached a pronounced dualism of body and spirit, good and evil, heaven and hell. Such thinking has led to a hegemony of binary thinking, used to sanction cutthroat competition, domination, racism, oppressive patriarchy, and an unbridled exploitation of the earth's resources.[3] Judaism in Western culture has absorbed some of these ideas, while in biblical Judaism there is no bifurcation of body and spirit.

In recent decades many Westerners have become more familiar with the non-dualistic views of existence embedded in Taoism, Hinduism, and Buddhism.[4] The contemporary Buddhist teacher Thich Nhat Hahn refers to the interconnection of all that is as "inter-being" and sees it as the foundation of any informed, contemporary theology.[5] From the latest discoveries in physics, biology, and environmental science to the millennia-old wisdom of Indigenous peoples, we learn that nothing exists in isolation, that everything is part of a system.[6] The system that we are a part of has its origins fourteen billion years ago in the big bang. Everything is energy, composed of atomic particles that originated in the stars; to echo an old Joni Mitchell song, we are stardust.[7] The Life Force (another way to think of God) manifest in and through evolution has brought us to this moment. Consciousness or awareness has gradually emerged through the evolution of life. Though human beings seem to be the furthest along in self-awareness, we should not assert that our species is the purpose or center of existence. The great lie of

Western civilization is that we are essentially separate beings. It is not possible for humans to live outside of community with others, be that other humans or the other creatures with whom we share this planet. Perhaps foremost among my experiences of the Divine, I see God to be the Connective Tissue of the Universe.[8] For me it follows that sin—a disruption of godliness—is any time we break or violate the connective tissue.

Rabbi Arthur Green, among others, has begun to articulate a non-dual Judaism grounded in the teachings of Jewish mysticism.[9] This panentheistic[10] understanding of reality asserts that Divinity envelops, infuses, and pervades all that is. The entire system of inter-being is a manifestation of the Divine, and thus each new evolutionary development is yet another expression of the Source of Life. Evolution moves toward greater complexity as well as greater awareness of this complexity; awareness is evident both in our bodies and social structures. Human beings participate in furthering evolution through imagination, creativity, and cultivating awareness. We are probably the first life-form that can take responsibility for consciously participating in evolution. As manifestations of the Source of Life, what is our responsibility to fourteen billion years of evolution that brought us here? Rav Kook addressed evolution in light of Jewish sources:

> The doctrine of evolution has a greater affinity with the secret teachings of the Kabbalah than all other philosophies. Evolution sheds light on all the ways of God. All existence evolves and ascends toward the height of the absolute good. The good and the complete all go together. Existence is destined to reach a point when the whole will assimilate the good. No particularity will remain outside, not a spark will be lost from the ensemble.[11]

The first story about humans in Genesis is that of Adam and Eve. After they eat the forbidden fruit, God asks, "*Ayekah*—where are you?" (Genesis 3:9). Classically God was considered all-seeing and all-knowing. Thus *ayekah* must be an existential rather than a geographic question, a call to responsibility. Judaism's foundational text first situates us in connection to all that is around us; we are formed from *adamah*. The text then calls on us to take responsibility for our actions. From a panentheistic perspective, this call to responsibility is bound into the very fabric of being, not dissimilar from existentialism. A bedrock principle of Judaism is that each human being is created in the image of God—*b'tzelem Elohim*—and thus deserving of equal dignity. Indeed, a case has been made, grounded in Jewish text, that all creatures are in God's image.[12] Respect for the inherent dignity of each person, each creature, and all that is remains a sound basis for working for justice.

Scholars have long pointed out that within the Torah there are two names for the Divine, each denoting a different set of attributes. We are first introduced to *Elohim*, the God of Creation, of the way things are, the God of being. Later in the text *YHVH*, the God of history, appears to Moses. This is the God who calls for us to bring about a world of justice, the world as it ought to be, of linear time, the God of becoming. Michael Lerner wrote that the genius of Judaism was incorporating both spirituality and ethics, Being and Becoming.[13] Despite classical Judaism's embrace of dualism, it never went so far as to advocate a strict dichotomy between body and spirit.

If Divinity both envelops the world and exists in this world, theology, of necessity, must be embodied, grounded in the lives of people, in our bodies, in our conduct and relationships, and in our history. In response to the exhortation "You shall be holy people to Me" (Exodus 22:30), the nineteenth-century Chasidic master Mendel of Kotzk reminded us that God has enough angels in heaven. The Holy One calls us to embodied sanctity here on earth.[14]

Our ongoing, actual life is dependent on Gaia—on our unique relationship to a star (our sun), soil, air, and water and on our relationships to others, to everyone we interact with to get the material and emotional necessities of life. In Genesis, the original human is called *adam* because we come from humus, *adamah*, the earth. Rabbi Ellen Bernstein has carefully looked at the Creation story in Genesis to illustrate how the original Jewish teachings understood our connection to all of life.[15] Our requirement to care for the earth is evident in many biblical laws. We violated the terms of our stewardship with the rise of an industrial society that sanctioned the exploitation and pollution of our natural environment. No other species consciously and systematically destroys its habitat. Theology must call us back to having a sustainable relationship with the world in which we exist, because the alternative is mass destruction. We are already living in what scientists call the sixth great mass extinction; the last one was sixty-six million years ago, when the dinosaurs vanished.

The contemporary Jewish environmental movement is reexamining the Torah and bringing to the fore its rootedness in agricultural traditions. I am a lifelong urban dweller, yet an important part of my spiritual life, of my experience of the Source of Life, is in the natural world. I firmly believe that only an embodied theology will lead us to cultivate spiritual practices that connect us more deeply with the earth. This can be a source of strength, guidance, and well-being.

Our connectedness to All That Is calls us to approach others and ourselves with humility, compassion, and curiosity. It takes us out of male-female, black-white, straight-queer, win-lose dichotomies that often justify injustice and oppression. The energy of domination, competition, patriarchy, racism, and unbridled exploitation has long been dominant in Western civilization. The Connective Tissue of the Universe calls us toward a rebalancing that would emphasize a "power with," cooperation, the enfranchisement and leadership of women and people of color, and the preservation—indeed the restoration—of earth. After all, healthy living systems move toward rebalance; the unhealthy ones wither and perish.

By embracing our interdependence, non-dualism is consistent with systems theory—the paradigm that undergirds current math and science. A Jewish theology for this time in history needs to incorporate non-dualism as we embrace both cyclical and linear time. The Source of Life contains all within it, competition and cooperation, which both propel evolution. Evolution shows that the species that thrive are those that cooperate with other life-forms. The redwoods, one of our oldest living relatives, stay alive through their connections to each other; they can only live in groves.

Our theology also needs to be a source of comfort and courage, as we experience the devasting losses of species extinction, desertification, forest fires, and the multiple ways climate change leads to increased deaths. My teacher Joanna Macy recently echoed Reb Nachman's teaching that we walk a narrow bridge across fear. She taught that we walk a narrow path on both sides of which there are ditches of fear—on one side is the fear that leads to denial, sticking our fingers in our ears, or downplaying what we hear; and on the other side is the ditch of hysteria, announcing human extinction and the apocalypse. The only way we stay on the path is by holding on to each other for strength and clarity, knowing that we all belong to each other and to the earth.[16] Judaism teaches that we are of the earth and bound to each other. Our courage and comfort are rooted in being a part of the life force of evolution, which includes an appreciation for all of our ancestors on whose lives we stand as a link in the chain.

One of the wisest aspects of Jewish ritual life is the way we respond to death. We make the time for grief in our personal lives through observing our mourning rituals and in our communal lives through remembrances such as Tishah B'Av and Yom HaShoah. It is time that we use this wisdom to respond to the devastating losses of climate chaos in our midst—the massive forest fires, flooding, climate change, desertification, the mass extinction of species. We must provide the communal framework to take in the enormity of what is happening, for it is too big to take in alone. And only when we are able to feel the scale of what is happening to our home—*adamah*—will we be able to respond with the amount of power needed to make the necessary changes. God the Life Force is calling us: *Ayekah*?

A Creation-inflected spirituality means that we celebrate the divine presence within all of God's creatures, however we spell out the details of that presence. A sense of spirituality is precisely that which brings us closer to an appreciation of nature and a sense of awe before its wonders. That sense of wonder and its renewal is at the core of our ability to act on behalf of life. Awe is a divine gift and a sacred opportunity. In it may lie humanity's greatest hope for liberation from the self-destructive forces destroying our means of existence. We all belong to each other and to the earth.

Our sense of connection can cause us to feel and express love and compassion—not to save or to fix, but to be open to sensing the pain of others and letting that transform how we live in the world. This openness does not need to lead to paralysis or depression, but rather to being fully present to life in every moment, however it manifests. This approach, the opposite of othering, arises from a loving mindset, in which we experience universal compassion toward all beings.

Ultimately, for a theology to have any import it must move our hearts. In many ways I still embrace the notion of my younger days, that God is Love; and when our actions are guided by love, we are most in harmony with Spirit. It takes ongoing spiritual practice to cultivate the compassion and gratitude necessary to strengthen our hearts, guide our actions, and calm our fears. If we accept that we are connected to all of life, then love is the most sensible response. If God is the Connective Tissue of the Universe, then action guided by love is prayer.

NOTES

1. David Korten, "Ecological Civilization and the New Enlightenment," *Tikkun* 32, no. 4 (2017): 17–24, https://doi.org/10.1215/08879982-4252947.

2. Abraham Joshua Heschel, *The Sabbath: Its Meaning for Modern Man* (New York: Farrar, Straus and Giroux, 2005).

3. This is not to say that non-Western civilization has been totally free of such evils, but here we are concerned with developing a theology for North American Jews, who share in both the blessings and the shortcomings of Western culture.

4. None of these Asian traditions have been totally immune to the curse of militant ethnic exclusivism, as witnessed by the Myanmar Buddhist persecution of the Muslim Rohingyans or the Hindu-Muslim violence in Kashmir.

5. Thich Nhat Hahn, *Essential Writings of Thich Nhat Hahn* (Maryknoll, NY: Orbis, 2001).

6. Joanna Macy, *Mutual Causality in Buddhism and General Systems Theory* (Albany: State University of New York Press, 1991).

7. Joni Mitchell, *Ladies of the Canyon* (Reprise, March 1970).

8. Brian T. Swimme and Mary Evelyn Tucker, *The Journey of the Universe* (New Haven, CT: Yale University Press, 2014).

9. Arthur Green, *Radical Judaism: Rethinking God and Tradition* (New Haven, CT: Yale University Press, 2010); and Jay Michaelson, *Everything Is God: The Radical Path of Nondual Judaism* (Boston: Trumpeter, 2009). Non-duality is a continuing feature of Islamic Sufi mysticism. Cynthia Bougeault, an Episcopal priest, is a leading contemporary theologian of Christian non-duality. See "Christian Nonduality: A Q&A with Cynthia Bougeault," Garrison Institute, February 13, 2017, www.garrisoninstitute.org/blog/cynthia-bourgeault-christian-nonduality/.

10. Panentheism is a theological framework that positions God within nature and also transcending beyond nature.

11. Abraham Isaac Kook, *Orot Hakodesh*, as cited in David Mevorach Seidenberg, *Kabbalah and Ecology: God's Image in the More-Than-Human World* (New York: Cambridge University Press, 2015), 29.

12. Seidenberg, *Kabbalah and Ecology*, 129.

13. Michael Lerner, *Jewish Renewal: A Path to Healing and Transformation* (New York: G. P. Putnam's Sons, 1994).

14. Alexander Zusia Friedman, *Wellsprings of Torah* (New York: Judaica Press, 1990), 157.

15. Ellen Bernstein, *The Splendor of Creation: A Biblical Ecology* (Cleveland: Pilgrim Press, 2005).

16. For more on Macy's teachings, see Joanna Macy, *Despair and Personal Power in the Nuclear Age* (Philadelphia: New Society Publishers, 1983).

A previous version of this chapter was published as "Imagining a Jewish Theology of Liberation: An Invitation," in *Seeking Redemption in an Unredeemed World*, edited by Howard Avruhm Addison (Mishsawaka, IN: GTF Books, 2019).

7

Earth, Water, Air, and Fire

The Four Elements as a Language
for Sanctifying the Earth

RABBI JILL HAMMER, PhD

IN ENCOUNTERING the diversity of the world, numerous cultures have developed the language of the four elements. Earth, water, air, and fire are considered the traditional material elements by many societies, from Greece to India. Some traditions include ether or spirit as a fifth element; the Chinese system includes fire, air, water, wood, and metal.[1] Jews too have used this language to express the ongoing cycles of the earth, the composition of physical matter, and even the layers of the soul.

The four elements offer a kind of "alphabet" for the multiple components of Creation, which are interwoven to create all things. They embody the sacred earth, not as a single entity but as a collaboration of multiple entities. A conscious Jewish return to the four elements as a ritual language for Creation may be one way to center the sacredness of ecology and foreground the complex interdependent relationships that characterize life on earth.

To offer one prominent example of an ancient Jewish text that uses the four elements to signify the structures of the natural world, in Ecclesiastes 1:4–7 we read:

> A generation goes, a generation comes,
> But the earth exists forever;
> The sun rises and the sun sets, and returns to rise again;
> Running southward, turning northward,
> The wind runs ever-turning,
> The wind returns on its rounds;
> The rivers run to the sea,
> But the sea is never full;

> To the place from where the rivers come,
> There they return again.

This passage references the four elements—earth, sun (fire), wind (air), and water—not only as substances, but as cycles or systems, patterns God has set within Creation. Ecclesiastes dates to somewhere between the third and fifth centuries BCE (the Second Temple period) and may show the influence of Greek thought and culture, including a belief in the four elements.

Yet we also may see something like the four elements in an earlier stratum, in the Torah itself. Consider the layout of the Tabernacle in Exodus. To the west, we have the washing basin (water); to the south, the menorah or candelabrum (fire); to the north, the twelve loaves of showbread (perhaps indicating earth); and to the east, the incense altar (perhaps indicating air, since the smoke rose to the sky). Jewish legend understood the Tabernacle/Temple to be a kind of model of the universe: the wash basin symbolizing the sea; the menorah the sun, moon, and stars; and so forth.[2] If so, the inclusion of the elements in the layout of sacred space was a way of depicting the cosmos as a whole. In a similar vein, Josephus suggested the curtain of the Holy of Holies represented the four elements: "It was a Babylonian curtain . . . a kind of image of the universe; for by the scarlet there seemed to be enigmatically signified fire, by the fine flax the earth, by the blue the air, and by the purple the sea."[3]

Maimonides clearly states his belief that the four elements (*arbaah y'sodot*) are the fundamental components of the physical world, making up "all bodies below the sky." Everything—stone, plant, animal, human—is composed of a combination of these elements. He is careful to emphasize that the four elements do not have souls and are not alive; furthermore, the soul is not composed of the elements.[4] Maimonides seems anxious lest anyone take the four elements to be entities worthy of reverence; he wants to understand them, not relate to them.

But the Jewish mystical tradition went in a different direction. For the ancient mystical work known as *Sefer Y'tzirah*, the elements—air, water, and fire—proceed directly from the divine breath and thus are in some way imbued with divine substance.[5] For the *Zohar*, the four elements are not merely the components of the soul, but components of the divine Being, corresponding with *s'firot*, or divine attributes. The *Zohar*, like Maimonides, states that the four elements are the foundation of all things, adding that they are associated with the four directions.[6] The text connects divine attributes with various elements (*Shechinah* or *Malchut* with earth, for example, or *Chesed* with water).

Lurianic Kabbalah has its own elemental system. The Lurianic school identifies the elements with both the manifest and the hidden worlds, from *asiyah* (earth, physical matter) through *atzilut* (fire, spiritual essence). Kabbalist Chayim Vital, Isaac Luria's student, suggests that the material world is created from the four physical elements (*y'sodot gufaniyim*), and so too the upper worlds are created from the four spiritual elements (*y'sodot ruchaniyim*).[7] Vital even speaks of the "souls of the four elements" (*n'fashot arbaah y'sodot*). These elements have a physical and a spiritual manifestation, just as humans do.

Ultimately, kabbalists understand that the language of the elements can be used to describe divine as well as material realms. Indeed, Rabbi Isaiah Horowitz (1555–1630) extrapolates from kabbalistic texts that God's image exists in the conjoining of the four elements.[8] Contemporary eco-theologians, in understanding the ecological whole as a complex interweaving of entities and a diversity worthy of reverence, have much in common with the mystics.

It is important to note that in kabbalistic sources, the elements are sometimes "ranked" in a hierarchy: fire closest to the Divine, air next, water next, and earth the most physical and farthest away from the Divine. This hierarchy conflicts with an egalitarian and less dualized view in which all of the elements matter equally as both matter and spirit. Indeed, we have the possibility of reimagining these Jewish views of the elements for our own age.

In his book *Kabbalah and Ecology*, eco-theologian David Seidenberg writes, "From the perspective of constructive theology, we would want to find teachings that recognize diversity to be something fundamentally desired by God." Seidenberg speaks of "a theology of diversity" as "an essential element of any theology of Nature."[9] The four elements are one image of sacred diversity. In this vein, Buddhist ecofeminist Dido Dunlop echoes Chayim Vital: "We are made of earth, water, fire, and air; all creatures are made of the same elements in different combinations."[10] Whether we speak of a mythic four or five elements or of the periodic table, the elements encode the message that we are all made of the same substance, no matter how unique each of us may be. We are diverse, yet all part of the larger world-body. Scholar Shaul Magid describes this attitude toward the sacred as "infinite divisibility"[11]—the divine Oneness fractures into multiplicity and then into creatures of endless variety.

Poet Elizabeth Cunningham writes, "When we breathe, drink or eat, sweat or shed a tear, in every moment of our lives, we connect through the elements to all the life that has gone before us and all the life that is to come."[12] As Ecclesiastes notes, narratives of the elements—and rituals invoking them—turn our attention to the cycles of rain and river, light and darkness, in-breath and out-breath, directing us not to an abstract idea or a hidden reality, but to the world as it is.

The Four Elements in Jewish Ritual Life

If the four elements have laid such a trail in Jewish theology, where are they manifest in our ritual lives? I confess that the first time I saw the four elements invoked in a Jewish context, I felt uneasy. I knew the four elements were at times invoked in Wiccan and other earth-based ceremonies, but I did not understand how they could be Jewish. Yet, drawn to the elemental powers of earth, water, air, and fire, I embarked on a journey to seek out the elements in Jewish sources and consider how I might weave them into my ritual life. As the scholar and theologian Julia Watts Belser has pointed out, religious experiences "become Jewish as individuals and communities learn to express them Jewishly."[13] Since that first uncertain encounter, I have been learning how to express the elements' message of sacred diversity in a Jewish language that draws on traditional rituals, biblical texts, kabbalistic concepts, and contemporary personal experience. This Jewish language could be adapted by many individuals and communities.

The Shabbat table ritual, for example, includes candlelighting (fire), handwashing (water), and challah (earth). We might imagine the accompanying prayers and songs as an offering of breath, or air. Or consider *Havdalah*, the brief, sensuous ceremony that ends Shabbat. We could easily imagine the wine as water, the spices as earth (or air, since we breathe in the fragrance), and the candle as fire.[14] The sensory powers of Shabbat and *Havdalah* come from the diversity of elements they bring together. This is surely a Jewish ritual moment we could imbue with an elemental consciousness.

We can also infuse daily prayer with an elemental awareness. In some Jewish Renewal communities, the parts of the morning service—the Morning Blessings, Psalms of Praise, blessings surrounding the *Sh'ma*, and the *Amidah*—parallel the four worlds of *asiyah* (body), *y'tzirah* (emotion), *b'riyah* (mind), and *atzilut* (soul). They also correspond with the elements of earth, water, air, and fire, in line with a Lurianic approach to prayer.[15] This practice could become sensory as well as symbolic, with the addition of moments to touch earth, wash in water, draw attention to the breath, and contemplate light. Such a practice might explicitly invite us to locate the Divine Presence in the material world.

We see the elements throughout the Jewish year as well. Consider how many holidays are focused on one or more of them: Chanukah celebrates fire; Tu BiSh'vat, the festival of the trees, is a holiday of the earth; Lag BaOmer is a holiday of bonfires; Sukkot celebrates earth (through the *lulav*) and water (through the prayers for rain). On Rosh HaShanah and Yom Kippur, the blowing of the shofar is, among other things, a ritual of breath and sound—gifts of air.

How would our perception of the Jewish year change if we thought about our sacred occasions as expressions of the diverse elements? How might our celebrations mark our relationships, not only through Jewish practice and our history, but also connecting to the substance of the world around us? Consider the four elements meditation by Noraa Neither Kaplan, which uses the frame of the Tu BiSh'vat seder to invite ritual participants to encounter the physical substances of earth/stone, water, air, and fire.[16] Consider Rabbi Tamara Cohen's "Eicha [Lament] for the Earth," which imagines planet earth as a destroyed Temple and uses elemental imagery to convey the diversity of planetary damage:

> Earth...
> like a beloved, deep in distress.
>
> Blue ocean, source of life—

Endangered and imprisoned.

. . . .

You Who Breathe all Life,
Breathe us into a new path.[17]

Yet another example is the contemporary Sukkot *Simchat Beit HaSho-eivah* (rejoicing in the water-pouring) ceremony crafted by Kohenet Sarah Shamirah Chandler, which includes a procession with torches and jars of water and a water libation around a firepit. This elemental celebration of the water cycle suggests that water is a sacred gift we must cherish.[18]

These calendrical offerings redirect our attention from only human concerns toward our embeddedness in the natural world and shift our understanding of which beings and entities count.

In the community I co-lead, the Kohenet Hebrew Priestess Institute, the elements are part of our spiritual discourse. We often sing a prayer referencing them near the beginning of our morning service. One of the songs is my loose translation of the passage of Ecclesiastes with which this article began:

Life is born and life moves on
and the earth has held and will hold it all.
The sun rises and the sun sets
and returns again to rise and fall.
The wind turns south and the wind turns north
turning, turning, returning still.
The rivers run from the clouds to the sea
and become the rain, and the sea is never filled.
So the beginning flows to the end
and the end flows on to begin again.
The One at the end is the One who begins
and the breath of breaths is within all things.[19]

The final line retranslates *haveil havalim* (vanity of vanities) as "breath of breaths"—the Divine as Great Breath—as air itself. This song offers a Jewish image of the four elements in prayer, the cycles of the natural world, and the larger unity within which our finite lives are contained. Its inclusion in our prayers is a statement of our values as an earth-centered Jewish community.

Out of necessity, humanity's attention must even more urgently turn to the world of which we are a part. A theology and ritual life solely focused on humans and on transcendent realms will not fully support this turning. As we create and re-create rituals that sanctify our relationship with the more-than-human world in all its fragility and diversity, the elements of earth, water, fire, and air can be a resource for wonder and gratitude, as they were for our ancestors.

Notes

1. For further discussion of elemental systems in various cultures, see Cait Johnson, *Earth, Water, Fire, and Air: Essential Ways of Connecting to Spirit* (Nashville, TN: SkyLight Paths, 2002).

2. See *Midrash Tadshei* 2.

3. Josephus, *Wars of the Jews* 5:5, trans. William Whiston, https://www.sefaria.org/The_War_of_the_Jews.5.5?lang=bi.

4. Maimonides, *Mishneh Torah*, *Hilchot Y'sodei HaTorah* 3:14–15, 4:1, 8.

5. *Sefer Y'tzirah* 1:9–12. See Jill Hammer, *Return to the Place: The Magic, Mysticism, and Meditation of Sefer Yetzirah* (Teaneck, NJ: Ben Yehuda Press, 2020), 34–71.

6. *Zohar* 2:24a.

7. Chayim Vital, *Shaarei K'dushah* 1:1–2.

8. Cited in David Seidenberg, *Kabbalah and Ecology: God's Image in the More-than-Human World* (New York: Cambridge University Press, 2015), 347.

9. Seidenberg, *Kabbalah and Ecology*, 19, 21.

10. Dido Dunlop, "What Is Ecofeminism? In a Nutshell—How to Save the World," *Permaculture Women Magazine*, https://www.permaculture-women.com/what-is-ecofeminism.

11. Shaul Magid, "Idolatry on the Other Side of Modernity," in *Idolatry: A Contemporary Conversation*, ed. Alon Goshen-Gotttstein (Boston: Academic Studies Press, 2022).

12. Elizabeth Cunningham, "The Elements Are Us," *Feminism and Religion*, April 19, 2015, https://feminismandreligion.com/2015/04/19/the-elements-are-us-by-elizabeth-cunningham.

13. Julia Watts Belser, "Making Room for the Divine She," *Zeek*, August 2007, http://www.zeek.net/708she.

14. Rabbi Shefa Gold was the first person I saw frame *Havdalah* in an elemental way.

15. See, for example, Marcia Praeger, *The P'nai Or Shabbat Morning Siddur* (Philadelphia: Pnai Or, 2009), 2.

16. Noraa Neither Kaplan, "The Four Elements: Mindfulness Ritual for

Tu Bishvat," Ritualwell, https://ritualwell.org/ritual/four-elements-mindfulness-ritual-tu-bishvat.

17. Tamara Cohen and Arthur Waskow, "Eicha for the Earth," Ritualwell, https://ritualwell.org/ritual/eicha-earth.

18. This ceremony has been performed multiple times at the Isabella Freedman Jewish Retreat Center in Falls Village, Connecticut, and is based on the Talmud's description of the Temple-era festival (Babylonian Talmud, *Sukkah* 51a–b).

19. Jill Hammer, *Siddur HaKohanot: A Hebrew Priestess Prayerbook*, ed. Jill Hammer and Taya Shere (Kohenet Hebrew Priestess Institute, 2015), 101.

8

What If the Earth Is Alive?
A Post-halachic Theology

Shaul Magid, PhD

The first chapter of Genesis tells a detailed story about the creation of all manner of life on earth. The beauty of the planet—its flora and fauna—rise in majestic detail through the poetry of these initial scriptural verses. But what about the planet itself? It is created, but is it alive? What does the term *eit haaretz* (earth, land) refer to in Genesis 1:1? Juxtaposed to the heavens, does it simply mean planet earth? And if so, what is the relationship between planet earth and all the living things that grow from and on it? Looking at that striking iconic first photo of the earth taken from the moon in June 1969, biologist Lewis Thomas wrote, "The astonishing thing about the earth, catching the breath, is that it is alive. The photographs show the dry, pounded surface of the moon in the foreground, dead as an old bone. Aloft, floating free beneath the moist, gleaming membrane of the blue sky, is the rising earth, the only exuberant thing in this part of the cosmos."[1] In some way, the moon landing enabled us to see what the ancients already knew. The notion of Gaia, a Greek mythological term referring to personification of the earth as a primordial deity, gestures toward this idea of the earth as alive.

James Lovelock, a British scientist, came up with what he called "the Gaia hypothesis" with microbiologist Lynn Margulis. A detailed scientific theory tracing the interactions of organic and inorganic matter, for the purposes of theological reflection, the Gaia hypothesis claims that the earth itself, and not just what grows from it, is a complex system, to quote Thomas again, that the earth "is alive."[2]

The implications of a living planet are tremendous in light of Scripture's early mandate, "So God Eternal took the man, placing him in the Garden of Eden to work it [*l'ovdah*] and keep it [*l'shomrah*]" (Genesis

2:15) and "to fill the earth and tame it" (1:28). It is one thing to work and keep, till and tend that which grows from the earth and another to tend to the earth itself—the earth that pulsates with life independent of the life it supports. It is one thing to "tame" the earth and another thing to destroy it.

It should be noted that Judaism's relationship to nature and the natural world is not monolithic and is arguably somewhat negative. Jewish philosopher Steven Schwarzschild even coined the term "the unnatural Jew" to illustrate that for the Jew, the focus was that which was "revealed" outside of nature and not nature itself.[3] Hava Tirosh-Samuelson notes, "The creative weaving of Judaism and ecology took place in North America and began in the early 1970s as an apologetic response to the charges that the Judeo-Christian tradition was the cause of the environmental crisis."[4] The turn toward caring for the planet, she implies (as opposed to caring for the Land of Israel), was not a natural inclination in the tradition but imported to respond to a growing environmental crisis that required religions of the world to respond from the sources of their tradition.[5] She further notes that "to date . . . the movement has not articulated a Jewish theology of nature."[6] Below I suggest that there has indeed been a move toward such a theological shift whereby the natural world, and the planet earth in particular, have become a central focus of a new theological paradigm.[7] Jewish theology often contains a practical, ritual component, and this is true in the recent Jewish awakening to environmentalism as well. A revisualization of dietary laws (kashrut) in light of the Gaia hypothesis in a post-halachic register exhibits such a move.

What Is Post-halachah?

The "halachic tradition" is a label for an ostensibly normative set of principles and practices that defines authentic Jewish living. Codified in Joseph Caro's *Shulchan Aruch* in the sixteenth century but gestating in various works long before, and then extending in subsequent works building from Caro's organized system, "halachic Judaism" has come to loosely define Orthodoxy. Classical Reform Judaism presented another model of Jewish life based not on the normative halachic tradition but on the ethical teachings that it believed better expressed the prophetic tradition. Conservative Judaism accepted the basic premise of halachah's binding nature but understood it as part of the warp and woof of changing historical circumstances, including scientific discoveries and ethical progress, which enabled halachah to become more fluid in practice and form. Some forms of Orthodoxy are also aware of changing circumstances that require halachic change, and thus its debate with Conservatism—setting aside theological differences, the origin of the Torah, etc.—is largely on the methodology and malleability of halachic norms to meet those circumstances.[8]

Mordecai Kaplan's magisterial *Judaism as a Civilization*, published in 1934, offered an entirely new sociocultural rendering of Jewish life and law by suggesting a civilizational model of Jewish post-halachic practice that rejected Reform's abandonment of halachah as well as Orthodoxy's and Conservative Judaism's fidelity to precedent in determining Jewish practice. It is here, perhaps, where post-halachah is truly born, with Kaplan's understanding halachah as "folkways"—an expression of collective consciousness.[9] Zalman Schachter-Shalomi even more forcefully expands legal innovation beyond the changing vicissitudes of historical circumstances to a notion of what he calls "reality maps."[10] Reality maps are more systemic ways in which we envision our lives and claim that the norms of our religious expression should respond to those changing shifts. Reality maps are not particularized but often have universal reach. A Jew in Israel and a Pashtun in Pakistan may see the vision of the earth from the moon within their particular traditions, but each view something extraordinary that challenges the very contours of their understanding of themselves. That photograph is not only a photograph of the earth. It is also us, all of us, viewing ourselves from space.

Schachter-Shalomi's post-halachic vision is Kaplanian in spirit but is also influenced by the kabbalistic notion that we live in different cosmic epochs. Each of these epochs contains its own "torah" as it were—its own specific way of living in concert with the divine call. Thus as the norms of the past required certain responses and normative halachah answered that call, new paradigms demand systemic and not simply incremental change to an old system. Schachter-Shalomi's experimental book *Integral Halachah* is a first attempt to rewrite the *Shulchan Aruch* from a new post-halachic perspective, one iteration being a new realization that the planet "is alive."

For Schachter-Shalomi, there were two paradigmatic shifts in his lifetime. The first encompassed the Holocaust, Hiroshima, and Nagasaki. He writes, "Terrible as the Holocaust was, the nuclear arms race threatened a Holocaust a thousand times bigger. For the first time in history we were faced with the possibility that all peoples, not just ours, might be annihilated—and by our own hand."[11] This was perhaps the greatest challenge to Genesis 2:15, "to work [the land] and keep it." Now, humanity has developed the ability to destroy it, to make the planet uninhabitable, to obliterate that which we have not made. The second shift—what he calls a seismic "aha moment!"—was the vision of the earth viewed from the moon. "To me, the sight of our earth from outer space is not only a scientific triumph but today's most potent religious icon as well. More than I want to talk about *avodat ha-Shem*, serving God, I want to talk about serving the planet."[12] This is a kind of reflection on Genesis 2:15. Part of our mandate as human beings, and as Jews, is to protect the planet, not a lifeless object upon which life exists, but a living thing itself. Ecology is not a nice practice but a theological mandate that serves as the foundation of the Jews, and humanity's, covenant with the Creator.

The Gaia hypothesis gives new meaning to older phrases. For example, "What happens if we re-imagine *Melekh ha-olam* ("King of the world") as the governing organismic wisdom of *ha-olam*—that is, of the planet earth? All of a sudden we see phrases like 'God is kind' or 'God is merciful' in a new light. . . . In our new understanding, such phrases become metaphors for the essential qualities of the planetary miracle we call life."[13]

A post-halachic approach absorbs this new insight, this new Gaia hypothesis that the earth is alive. Its dictates must thus conform to that new paradigm, something our predecessors may have intuited but did not know with such depth and visual certainty. Serving God is now becoming a companion to protecting the planet. The former without the latter is not only civilizational suicide but a desecration of the Creator. The notion of land—in Judaism, the land of Israel—has now been expanded to include the entire planet. As Jews, we believe the land is holy, as human beings, we see that the planet is alive, and thus we enact holiness by protecting its life.

Eco-kashrut: A Post-halachic Approach

Traditional laws and practices of kashrut have also been reimagined. If we assume that kashrut is not limited to what we eat and how we prepare food, but includes the broader notion of consumption more generally, then, as Schachter-Shalomi puts it, "kashrut pays attention not only to the end results, but the methods used to obtain them."[14] Through this outlook, kashrut's borders are broadened to include labor, production, genetic engineering, use of chemicals that may be damaging to human bodies and also to the planet, and even utensils, storing food, and replenishing the soil. In this instance, post-halachah is far stricter than classical halachah, for which these concerns are not paramount, although not absent either, such as prohibitions against waste (bal tashchit), observance of the Sabbatical year (Sh'mitah), and not eating fruits of a young fruit tree for three years (orlah). Post-halachic kashrut takes these prompts from traditional halachah and expands them under the new aegis of protecting the earth as a living being. Schachter-Shalomi remarks, "Our challenge is to maximize the kashrut of a given product of action—matter of degree, rather than a question with a yes-or-no answer."[15]

Sometimes that which made traditional halachah easier now becomes prohibited. For example, disposable dishes and utensils and Styrofoam make traditional kashrut more convenient because one can more readily prevent mixing meat and milk dishes. But in an eco-kashrut, post-halachah register, they become damaging to the planet and thus prohibited as part of conscious acts of consumption that include environment waste.

Transgression as a halachic norm now encompasses far more than the dictates of the *Shulchan Aruch*. For example, as long as a piece of meat was ritually slaughtered correctly, it is halachically permissible to eat. Most people do not inquire further. But in a post-halachic register we must now include issues of labor: How was it processed? How were the laborers treated? Was this fruit harvested by people deprived of a living wage? Non-union and/or exploited undocumented workers?

Yes, this is cumbersome and some of these things are simply impossible to determine, but if the consciousness is there, that is a start. Organizations such as Magen Zedek, Shomrei Adamah, the Coalition on the Environment for Jewish Life (COEJL), Camp Eden Village, and Grow and Behold have begun to implement these values within their kosher products. Indeed, there was a precedent set in the nineteenth century by Rabbi Israel Salanter, who refused to give kosher certification to a matzah factory because its workers were being unfairly treated.[16]

Arthur Waskow has been at the forefront of the eco-kashrut movement, for example, in his *Down-to-Earth Judaism: Food, Money, Sex, and the Rest of Life* (1995), as has Arthur Green in his *EHYEH: A Kabbalah for Tomorrow* (2004). But the larger theological premises were developed by Schachter-Shalomi and were founded on the Gaia hypothesis. Green develops a theological naturalism founded on the panentheistic notion popular in some forms of Kabbalah and Chasidism. Translating the divinity of the material into a contemporary key, Green writes:

> The One, I believe, is the only being that ever was, is, or will be. It is the One that undergoes the only sacred drama that really matters: the bio-history of the universe. . . . *I believe that it does so as a conscious and willful Self.* . . . I thus seek to re-vision the evolutionary process, not as a struggle of creature against creature and species against species, but as the emergence of a single life-energy.[17]

This theological revolution must also make serious inroads into a post-halachic practice. But how far can one take this? For example, if we dump toxic waste into a river, we not only kill the life *in* the river and pollute the river, we are essentially committing an act of murder *of* the planet. This is not merely an ecological disaster; it is an act against our divine mandate to "keep" or guard the earth. It is both an ecological catastrophe and a theological heresy.

Thus ecology, environmentalism, workers' justice, living wage, and other ethical concerns are not subsidiary categories adjacent to halachah; in this new post-halachic paradigm, they are the very rubrics of halachah. In a sense, post-halachah is an attempt to instantiate Reform's social consciousness inside Jewish ritual practice, interpreting Kaplan's "folkways" with a new cosmology, making sociology a productive form of theology. Liberated from the confines of the methodology of legal precedent and founded on the mystical assumption of each historical epoch having its own "torah," post-halachah confronts the earth not as a place where we happen to live but as a home we are commanded to keep (thus the term "ecology" comes from the Greek *oikos*, or "home.").

In this light, halachah functions as an answer to a somewhat different call than our ancestors heard and saw. Our contemporary abilities to end life on the planet through nuclear war or to view the image of the earth floating in space as testimony to our planet as a bright but fragile living organism in a universe of darkness become a call for radical recalibration of our world and its Creator. Whereas our ancestors viewed themselves as a particular community situated among (often antagonistic) strangers, we now must view the other (even given political realities) not as a stranger as much as a companion in the collective project of protecting the planet. The global COVID pandemic should teach us that. Borders, like halachah, are human creations of separation, and while they may serve a function of protecting human collectives from one another, they are destructive when threatened by that which knows no borders, in the heavens or in microorganisms.

Judaism has a repository of wisdom embodied in halachah that can serve as a gift to aid in this global project, but it can only do so if it is freed from the confines of its own paranoid particularity. For too long halachah has been a tool of separation, creating fences to minimize social interaction with the outside world. But now the world itself may be in peril, and creating an enclave will not save those within it. Solidarity means nothing on a dead planet. We need a new vision of the law—in some way, an inversion of the law. Regulating our consumption to include traditional models, even if some need to be discarded, combined with a new consciousness of a global emergency and a sense of human justice, requires us to reposition ourselves not merely as responsible for Jewish continuity, but as responsible for human and planetary survival.

NOTES

1. Lewis Thomas, *Lives of a Cell: Notes of a Biology Watcher*, cited in Connie Barlow, *From Gaia to Selfish Genes: Selected Writings in the Life Sciences* (Cambridge, MA: MIT Press, 1991), 35.

2. See "the Gaia hypothesis" in James Lovelock, *Gaia: A New Look at Life on Earth* (New York: Oxford University Press, 2016), 1–12.

3. Steven Schwarzschild, "The Unnatural Jew," *Environmental Ethics* 6 (1984): 347–62.

4. Hava Tirosh-Samuelson, introduction to *Judaism and Ecology*, ed. Hava Tirosh-Samuelson (Cambridge, MA: Harvard University Press, 2002), xxxvii.

5. See Arthur Waskow, "Is the Earth a Jewish Issue?," *Tikkun* 7, no. 5 (1992): 35–37.

6. Tirosh-Samuelson, *Judaism and Ecology*, xxxviii. More generally, see Hans Jonas, *The Phenomenon of Life: Toward a Philosophical Biology* (Evanston, IL: Northwestern University Press, 2001).

7. See Michael Fishbane, "Toward a Jewish Theology of Nature," in Tirosh-Samuelson, *Judaism and Ecology*, 17–26.

8. See Avi Weiss, *Journey to Open Orthodoxy* (Jerusalem, Urim Press, 2019), and David Rosenthal and Aharon Feldman, *Why Open Orthodoxy Is Not Orthodox* (New York: Yad Yosef Press, 2016).

9. This vision reached its full dimensionality in Jack Cohen's *Judaism in a Post-halakhic Age* (Boston: Academic Studies Press, 2010).

10. Zalman Schachter-Shalomi and Daniel Siegel, *Integral Halachah: Transcending and Including Jewish Practice through the Lens of Personal Transformation and Global Consciousness* (Victoria, BC: Trafford, 2007), x.

11. Zalman Schachter-Shalomi, *Jewish with Feeling* (Woodstock, VT: Jewish Lights, 2013), 151.

12. Schachter-Shalomi, *Jewish with Feeling*, 152.

13. Schachter-Shalomi, *Jewish with Feeling*, 169.

14. Schachter-Shalomi, *Jewish with Feeling*, 158.

15. Schachter-Shalomi, *Jewish with Feeling*, 159.

16. The story is cited often, but the exact source is not given. For example, see Nathan Ausubel, ed., *A Treasury of Jewish Folklore* (New York: Crown, 1948), 105.

17. Arthur Green, "A Kabbalah for the Environmental Age," in Tirosh-Samuelson, *Judaism and Ecology*, 9.

9

Yishuv HaOlam

The Jewish Imperative of Sustainability

RABBI NINA BETH CARDIN
AND RABBI AVRAM ISRAEL REISNER

OVER THE PAST FIFTY YEARS, despite an increased interest in a Jewish approach to environmental ethics, no language of mitzvah (commandment) has emerged that captures the full, all-encompassing, and urgent nature of the challenge of sustainability that the world currently faces. Though it is clearly true that Judaism speaks of the earth as God's creation and possession,[1] this general perception appears not to be presented as a command. In a religion that is so exquisitely designed to translate values into commandments, this absence is curious.

Upon further exploration, though, we believe that the mitzvah we have been seeking has been there all the while, hiding in plain sight—the commandment of *yishuv haolam* (from the Hebrew root *yod-shin-vet*),[2] the Jewish imperative of maintaining a livable, thriving, and flourishing world. *Sefer HaChinuch*, written by the itinerant Spanish preacher Pinchas ben Joseph HaLevi of Barcelona, expands on the first mitzvah in the Torah, "Be fruitful and multiply" (Genesis 1:28), as follows:

> The roots of this mitzvah [come to teach us] that the world is designed to be inhabited [*yod-shin-vet*],[3] for the Holy One wishes it to be inhabited [*yod-shin-vet*],[4] as it says (Isaiah 45:18): "God did not create the world [intending that it be] chaos [*tohu*]; God created it for habitation [*yod-shin-vet*]."[5] It is a premier mitzvah by virtue of which all mitzvot in the world stand.[6]

This passage declares that the very first mitzvah, "Be fruitful and multiply," encompasses a grander overarching imperative: the very purpose of Creation was to establish—and, therefore, not to extinguish—a thriving world. That was God's own desire and purpose.

In his call, Isaiah offers a midrash on Genesis: At the moment of

Creation, we are told that the world was *tohu vavohu* ("chaos, unformed"; Genesis 1:2), but *tohu vavohu*, says Isaiah, was not a state of being that God wanted to perpetuate. Creation itself was an expression of God's rejection of chaos and an embrace of a habitable world. According to *Sefer HaChinuch*, the fact that God created the world for habitation grounds the whole enterprise of Torah. God was seeking a thriving world for human habitation, which must necessarily include concern for the physical well-being of this world.

This was not an original insight by the author of *Sefer HaChinuch*, but rather a reflection on a very old Rabbinic reading of Isaiah. It first appears as a midrash on Isaiah in *Mishnah Eduyot* 1:13 in a discussion between the schools of Beit Shammai and Beit Hillel in the first half of the first century, when the Temple was still standing.[7] In *B'reishit Rabbah* 13:1, Rabbi Chanina calls God's creation of vegetation a step God takes to make the world habitable (*yod-shin-vet*).[8] In the Talmud, rainfall is likewise described as a part of God's Creation that was created for the right order and habitability (*yod-shin-vet*)[9] of the world (Jerusalem Talmud, *B'rachot* 9:2).

In fifteenth-century Spain, the biblical commentator Don Isaac Abarbanel recognized that this idea of *yishuv haolam* led to a fuller understanding of two somewhat unusually specific mitzvot. In his commentary to Deuteronomy 22:6, Abarbanel compares the mitzvah of this verse—send away a mother bird and refrain from taking her eggs in her presence (Deuteronomy 22:6–7)—to that of not destroying fruit-bearing trees during a siege (20:19–20). The first mitzvah is standardly interpreted as evidencing a concern for the mother's maternal feelings. Abarbanel acknowledges this interpretation, but further expands its teaching by comparing it to the second mitzvah:

> The Torah intended by this . . . that existence should continue to exist . . . as (in the case of) the fruit-bearing tree. The Holy One commanded us not to destroy that which gives birth or produces fruit. Rather, just as it is permitted to pick fruit but forbidden to cut down the tree . . . so God commanded that we take the children, who are the fruit, . . . but send away the mother . . . so the mother should produce other fruit and existence will be sustained and improved. . . . That is why the end of the verse is "so

that it may be good for you and so that you may live long [upon
the earth]." . . . It is good for humankind for existence to be
sustained.[10]

The Spanish kabbalist Joseph ben Abraham ibn Gikatilla, contem-
poraneous with *Sefer HaChinuch*, also wrote about *yishuv haolam*. He
pens this passage about our obligation to care for the world:

> One who enjoys the world but does not engage in its mainte-
> nance (*yod-shin-vet*)[11] is likened to what? To one to whom the king
> gave a beautiful garden and who was instructed to maintain it and
> enjoy its fruits. . . . For God gave God's world to humankind just
> like the king who placed the garden in the hands of a caretaker. . .
> . Every person who eats and drinks and benefits from the world,
> but only attends to their own benefit and enjoyment, such a per-
> son destroys the world and is liable to the sovereign.[12]

We may only enjoy the benefits of this world when we actively sustain its
existence; otherwise we are complicit in and liable for its destruction.

In the words of Eliezer Waldenberg of Jerusalem, "This mitzvah of
settlement of the world is a general mitzvah. [It] is obligatory on everyone to make efforts to assure that the world be made habitable [*yod-
shin-vet*]."[13] The fact that we have not fully stepped up to this mitzvah of
sustaining the habitability of the world is the failure we must now strive
to rectify. In reading "Be fruitful and multiply; fill the earth and tame
it" (Genesis 1:28), we have too often taken our commandment to conquer the world as an unlimited right, not taking into consideration the
obligations implicit in Genesis 2 that humankind's mission is to "work
it and protect it" (2:15).[14] It is ultimately this latter requirement that is
most consistent with the current demands of the mitzvah of *yishuv haolam*.

Generations of readers have noted that Genesis 1 and Genesis 2 offer
differing accounts of Creation. Perhaps no difference is more consequential to the issue we are exploring than the tasks that God assigned
to *adam*—humanity. In Genesis 1, all life is designed to be self-renew-
ing. Each life is born with seeds within it that hold the promise of the
next generation.[15] In the words of Nachmanides, "God created species
in the world . . . giving them the power to give birth so that those spe-

cies should continue forever, as long as God wished the world to continue."[16] This movement from chaos to continuity is the message of sustainability in Genesis 1. Into this world of sustained life, God created the humans and blessed them, saying, "Be fruitful and multiply; fill the earth and tame it; hold sway over the fish of the sea and the birds of the sky, and over every animal that creeps on the earth" (Genesis 1:27–28).

We need not balk, wonder at, or apologize for this blessing of mastery and dominance. Humanity, here, was in its infancy: weak, few, and naïve. Our footprint was small and our vulnerability great. The ingenuity and technology that would be the hallmarks of our species and the birthing ground of civilization had yet to fully emerge. In Genesis 1, humankind was blessed with the innate capacity, even the mandate, to explore, push boundaries, be curious, experiment, and use all the gifts of inspiration with which we were endowed to survive and thrive in this God-given world. It was unimaginable that earth's riches could be consumed into extinction. The earth was seen as an unending panoply of resources for our benefit and use. Our job was to flourish in a divinely constructed, eternally self-regenerating world. We believed there was nothing we could do to upset the earth's eternal systems. Flourishing and thriving were our primary task. So for thousands of years, we focused on just that. We tamed the rivers and felled the trees; we distilled potions from the plants to reduce our fevers and ease our pains; we built cities, roads, and museums; we planted and harvested and gathered in, changing the land, flora, and watercourses as we went. We were fruitful and multiplied, bursting the bounds of God's blessing. For generations we have lived into those blessings.

Such a vision of Creation and our human role in it only made sense before all our impacts on the earth reached catastrophic heights. Although we are still at the mercy of nature's power (storms, illness, earthquakes, viruses, and infections), collectively we are not few, not insignificant, and not innocent. Our footprint is larger than it ever was.[17] Over the last 150 years we have profoundly altered the contours of earth and the components of the world's operating systems in ways that are irreparable in any meaningful human time frame. As such, humanity's purpose must now be to place our capacities in service to the whole. Such is the task for which we are created in Genesis 2.

Genesis 2 expands the narrow, short-term, and human-centered cost-benefit analysis of human goals and efforts found in Genesis 1 to include the nonhuman sphere in the larger ecosystem, as well as the longer term encompassing future generations. While Genesis 1 is anthropocentric and inward facing, Genesis 2 is eco-centric and outward facing, embedding human behavior within and responsive to earth's complex operating system. Our job in Genesis 2 is not to consume and subdue the world's goodness, but to bring the earth into its own full fecundity and manage its richness and resources wisely.[18]

The goal of both Creation stories is the thriving of humankind. But in the first we thrive to the ultimate detriment of the superabundant earth, and in the second we thrive only in partnership with it. In contrast to the message in Genesis 1 of the earth being created for us, Genesis 2 teaches that we were created for the sake of the earth. Humanity and earth are a dyad, mutually reinforcing the well-being of each other and all the creatures who depend upon Creation. Such an interpretation yields not just a different literary reading, but a different theological charge.

Whereas in Genesis 1 the bounty of the earth predates the arrival of humans, laid out as a smorgasbord, a *shulchan aruch* (set table) for our use and hegemony, in Genesis 2 the bounty of the earth awaits the contributions of humanity, whose presence is necessary for the fulfillment of earthly goodness.

We know today, given the sheer numbers of humanity, that we are no longer the unconditional beneficiaries of the earth's preexisting bounty but must be its nurturers and cocreators. We are not the sovereigns we seem to be in Genesis 1, but God's—and the earth's—partners in bringing out the best Creation can offer.

For most of human existence, our small violations were tolerated. Humanity and the earth functioned well under a Genesis 1 worldview. While we did occasionally mistreat the earth, the breadth of our impact was limited. If we harmed the earth, we moved on; and in time, the earth recovered from our indiscretions.

Relatively recently, we have learned that humanity can no longer afford to live with a Genesis 1 mentality. We are too big, too powerful, too consequential for that. Our impact is global; there is no other place for us to go. This earth is all we have. In response to the earth's struggles to endure and absorb all our indiscretions, we must embrace the ideology of Genesis 2. We must come to terms with the geophysical powers we wield and develop an ethic that can honor, restrain, and guide those powers so we and future generations of all species can live in a healthy, regenerative world.[19] This calls us to the mitzvah of *yishuv haolam*, acting to ensure the habitability of the world, as Genesis 2 would encourage us to define it.

A Genesis 2 model argues for an eco-centric systems approach. We cannot ignore other forms of life or the interplay of environmental components. Nor can we ignore "externalities," the unintended consequences of human behavior that harm Creation (and ultimately us as well). Genesis 2 teaches us that we are responsible for what we do, and in order to pursue our own survival, we must also pursue the betterment of all. For it is only through the betterment of all that we, too, flourish.

This is not to say there is no "destruction" in the Genesis 2 model. All life leaves a trace. We must cut trees to build shelters, work the soil to grow food, mine the earth for stone and ore. Predators eat prey; ruminants eat plants. Consumption implies some measure of destruction, but when the traces we leave today are minimal enough to allow the earth to meet the needs of tomorrow, then it is regenerative destruction.

We all use earth's gifts. Our challenge is to use them in a fashion that allows their renewal, preservation, and reuse in an endlessly cyclical fashion. For as the earth knows no waste, neither should we. The human must be what we were called to be in Eden, the global "g[u]ardener"—the one who creates an enduring world out of our engagement with all its riches, all the while replenishing it for those yet to come.

NOTES

1. See Genesis 1:1, "When God was about to create heaven and earth"; Deuteronomy 10:14, "Mark, the heavens to their uttermost reaches belong to the Eternal your God, the earth and all that is on it!"; Isaiah 44:24, "It is I, the Eternal, who made everything, who alone stretched out the heavens and unaided stretched out the earth"; Jeremiah 10:12, "God made the earth by God's might, established the world by God's wisdom, and by God's understanding stretched out the skies"; Psalm 24:1, "The earth

is the Eternal's and all that fills it, the world and all its inhabitants"; and Psalm 146:6, "Maker of heaven and earth, the sea and all that is in them."

2. Also *yishuvo shel olam*, or simply *lashevet*. All these Hebrew terms share the Hebrew root *yod-shin-vet*, which suggests habitability. For references to habitability as a purpose for Creation, see Isaiah 45:18; *Sefer HaChinuch* 1:2; Babylonian Talmud, *Gittin* 41b; Jerusalem Talmud, *B'rachot* 9:2; and elsewhere. About this semantic range, see Jeremy Benstein, *Hebrew Roots, Jewish Routes* (Millburn, NJ: Berhman House, 2019), 60, Wordshop 11.

3. Hebrew: *sheyihyeh haolam m'yushav*.

4. Hebrew: *chafetz b'yishuvo*.

5. Hebrew: *lashevet y'tzarah*.

6. *Sefer HaChinuch*, mitzvah 1.

7. Interestingly, *Tosafot*, the school of Rashi's grandchildren, wonder why the Mishnah resorted to citing Isaiah to support the need to procreate, when it was, after all, the first mitzvah in the Torah, and a biblical mitzvah is surely preferable to a prophetic exhortation. Their answer (*Tosafot* on *Chagigah* 2b) is that the mitzvah of *lashevet*, though found only in Isaiah, is more fundamental than the mitzvah of procreation.

8. Hebrew: *l'yishuvo shel olam*.

9. Hebrew: *l'tikuno ul'yishuvo shel olam*.

10. Abarbanel does not name the concept of *yishuv haolam*. He speaks instead of continuing existence. But in his commentary in this place, in the next century, the Maharal of Prague, Judah Loew ben Bezalel, translated Abarbanel's concept into the more common idiom: "One who sends away the mother is maintaining the inhabiting of the world [*yishuv haolam*]" (Gur Aryeh, commentary to Rashi on Deuteronomy 22:8).

11. Hebrew: *eino mitasek b'yishuvo shel olam*.

12. *Sefer HaMeshalim*, 128. Baruch ben Yechiel Michel Epstein makes the same point in his commentary to Genesis 2:15, note 37: God placed humans in the Garden of Eden to "work it and to keep it," he writes, an allusion for those in the world that it is not fitting to enjoy benefit from the world without providing value and benefit in the establishment of the world and its continuity (*l'yishuv haolam v'kiyumo*).

13. Hebrew: *lihyot haolam m'yushav*; *Tzitz Eliezer* 4:16:12.

14. Genesis 2:15 has been translated by the authors.

15. Genesis 1:11: "God said, 'Let the earth grow vegetation, seed-bearing plants, fruit trees on the earth that bear fruit, each true to its type, with its seed in it!'—and so it was." Genesis 1:22: "God then blessed them [the animals of the sea and air], saying, "Be fruitful and multiply, fill the waters of the seas, and let the birds multiply in the earth!"

16. Nachmanides's commentary to Leviticus 19:19.

17. Half of all habitable land is used for agriculture (Hannah Ritchie, Our World in Data, November 11, 2019, https://ourworldindata.org/global-land-for-agriculture). There are no boundaries to some of our polluting behavior. "New data shows that rainwater in some parts of the US contains high enough levels of potentially toxic per- and polyfluoroalkyl substances (PFAS) to possibly affect human health " (Daniel Ross, "Rainwater in Parts of US Contains High Levels of PFAS Chemicals, Says Study," December 17, 2019, *The Guardian*, https://www.theguardian.com/environment/2019/dec/17/rainwater-pfas-us-potentially-toxic-levels-study).

18. See Genesis 2:4, 15, 20. Plants did not grow except through human tending. Animals found their proper function through the agency of Adam's naming.

19. This analysis of Genesis 1 versus Genesis 2 is strongly similar to the thesis of Kenneth E. Boulding's 1966 lecture "The Economics of the Coming Spaceship Earth," published in Henry Jarrett, *Environmental Quality in a Growing Economy* (Baltimore: Johns Hopkins Press, 1971), available online at http://arachnid.biosci.utexas.edu/courses/THOC/Readings/Boulding_SpaceshipEarth.pdf.

PART TWO

Jewish Texts

OUR TEXTUAL TRADITION informs every aspect of Jewish life, and our interpretation of these texts continues to evolve, change, and grow with time and engagement. The following chapters offer new frames for understanding our ancient textual heritage and craft the outlines of an eco-interpretive mode of Jewish commentary.

Rabbi Nate DeGroot provides a deep analysis of the Hebrew word *teva*, usually translated as "nature." In her chapter, Rabbi Devorah Diana Lynn revisits the second paragraph of the *Sh'ma*, long excluded from Reform practice, as a way of engaging with our relationship to the environment. Next, Rabbi Elizabeth Bahar uses the devastation experienced by the prophet Jeremiah to investigate our own experience of climate disaster. To elucidate principles of community organizing, Mirele B. Goldsmith, PhD, uses Jonah the prophet's reluctance as a test case for how to change our own community's reluctance. Providing us with a practical spiritual connection, Rabbi Shefa Gold repurposes the Song of Songs as a source for nature ritual. Reflecting on her own experiences, Rabbi Laura Rumpf shares an innovative approach to the liturgical use of psalms in nature as a deepening way into Shabbat. Rabbi Evan Schultz translates the prayer *Yotzeir Or* for contemporary audiences. To conclude the section, Adriane Leveen, PhD, reflects on the nature imagery in the Book of Job as a path to awe.

10

Adam v'Teva

A Renewed Relationship
with Humanity and Earth

RABBI NATE DEGROOT

WE BEGIN WITH A QUIZ: What is the Hebrew word for "nature"? *Teva!* Now, when would you guess that *teva*, meaning "nature," first shows up in Jewish sources? Maybe the Creation story, when God creates light and dark and land and sea? Nope. Maybe when the first humans are created in the Garden of Eden, surrounded by lush vegetation and fruiting trees? Nope. Maybe during the Flood, with rainbows and doves and a whole lot of water? Not there either. Surely, then, in Psalms, filled as they are with verdant allusions to natural elements and objects? Still no.

Surprisingly, the first time *teva* seems to appear in Jewish writing to mean "nature" is only in the twelfth century CE. How could it be that for some two thousand years, Judaism had no word for "nature" when Judaism is a wisdom tradition that is unequivocally and inseparably rooted in the natural world? We know that most Jewish holidays are based on agricultural cycles, such as Passover, Shavuot, and Sukkot. We know that Jewish time is tracked by observing the celestial lights, that Jewish months are calculated in concert with the phases of the moon, that Jewish hours were once relative to the amount of sunlight in a day, and that the Jewish Sabbath doesn't end until there are three stars in the sky. How about the fact that we receive Torah in the wilderness? Or that divine revelation happens on a mountaintop? Or that we are promised a land of abundance, defined by its overflowing milk and honey?

Judaism, as a religion, was established by people who were in profoundly intimate relationship with the lands on which they dwelled. In our daily prayer, the *Amidah*, when the rainy season is set to begin in the arid deserts of the Middle East, the land in which these prayers originated, still today all across the world Jews insert a special line asking for the rains to come speedily and with life-giving fullness. Around that time, our people shake palm fronds, march around in circles, and beat willow branches against the ground for rain. And if that rain doesn't come, we fast until it does. At its core, Judaism is an earth-based religion. With all of this in mind, we must ask again: How is it possible that Judaism could have no word for "nature" for the first two thousand-plus years of its existence?

For Jews, everything—including, and perhaps especially, nature—is part of the Divine. *Ein od milvado* (Deuteronomy 4:35), our Chasidim teach us: there is nothing other than God Godself.[1] Given that, there was no need for our ancestors to distinguish between God and the natural world, between divinity and physicality, and between that which will be and that which is. The natural world is very simply and profoundly a manifestation of the Source of All Life, an aspect of Divine Mystery made corporeal through the unbounded diversity and beauty of God's Creation. Nature is but a form of God, that is, a *l'vush* (garb) in which God dresses,[2] and thus nature cannot be separated or distinguished from God. Because there is no nature without God and no clear division between the two, there is no need or even possibility for a specific word that would need to contain the bountiful and majestic proliferation of the Eternal. Rather, all is just One. *Sh'ma Yisrael Adonai Eloheinu Adonai Echad.* "Listen." Jews' central credo demands, "Really listen, all who wrestle with God: the Infinite One, our God, the Breath of Life, is Infinite Oneness."[3]

To extend this idea, we can then say that how we treat nature is a direct reflection of how we treat God. And perhaps, the converse: If God and nature cannot be separated, then every toxic fume that gets puffed into the air is filling God's lungs with smoke. Every waste plant pumping harmful refuse into flowing streams is pouring straight into God's overflowing cup. Every leaky oil line, buried deep within our planet's water and soil, is poisoning the veins that course through the body of the Infinite One.

Jews haven't always practiced this truth, but we have always known it. If we obey the commandments that God gives, to love and serve Divinity with everything we've got, Deuteronomy 11:13–17 tells us, the rains will fall in their season, our harvests will be abundant, our cattle will have ample food to eat, and we shall be sated. But if we stray and worship idols, and profane and forget what is most sacred in this world, God's anger will flare up against us until the skies above our heads turn to copper and the earth below our feet becomes iron. The rain of our land will be dust, and sand shall drop on us from the sky until we are wiped out.

In the context of our current climate crisis, we now understand, perhaps more than ever, how this text is not prescriptive, but descriptive. God is not punishing us for straying, but rather is describing to us the natural result of our own careless and callous actions. In this way, Deuteronomy reads eerily similar to recent warnings from UN Climate Reports. The Torah text, alongside our scientists, is teaching us that when we neglect the sacred, the sacred will just as quickly neglect us. When we live outside of right relationship with the natural world, we curse ourselves. Is this not what it means to take God's name in vain in a twenty-first-century context?

When we hurt nature, we are not only hurting God; we are also hurting ourselves. In the Garden of Eden (Genesis 2:7), the first human (*adam*) is created from the earth (*adamah*) itself. The earth and we humans—both creations of the Divine—share a common root mythically, scientifically, linguistically, and spiritually. Knowing this connection, how are we going to treat the earth? How are we going to treat ourselves? Our kin? Our ancestors? The Divine? And those not yet born?

The earth, in this deeply embodied way, serves as a kind of mirror for us on a global scale—what we do to it, we do to ourselves. Our values, our norms, and our health as a human society are reflected back to us in the wellness—or unwellness—of the natural world. Sadly, as we look around at the convulsing state of our current climate, it's hard to conclude that we are anything but profoundly sick: idol-worshiping sick, copper sky and iron earth sick, and in need of desperate and liberatory healing.

From what earth, specifically, was *adam* formed? Our tradition offers many answers,[4] but the one that perhaps we need most today comes from *Midrash Tanchuma*, *P'kudei* 3: "Whereupon God began to collect the dust for the body of the first human from the four corners of the earth, so that no one part of the earth might say: 'The dust of the body of humanity is mine.'" By recognizing that we are composed of soil from all corners of this world, we know that wherever we go, we are home and the earth will welcome us. Conversely, since we are made up of all the soil, we must acknowledge that we are responsible for all the soil, for all the earth. And even when we don't see the direct impact of our actions where we are, we know that since all the earth is mingled within each of us, all the earth is affected.

However, the earth is not all affected equally. As Tamara Toles O'Loughlin, a Black woman and a leader with the environmental group 350.org writes in an article titled "If You Care about the Planet, You Must Dismantle White Supremacy":

> Black communities face the long-term effects of environmental racism, intentionally zoned into neighborhoods surrounded by factories, highways, pipelines, and compressor stations. Systemic exposure to toxic fumes has caused higher rates of asthma and disease in Black communities, making us more vulnerable to the coronavirus. This adds a grim familiarity to the death-throw pleas of "I can't breathe," made by both George Floyd and Eric Garner while they were choked to death by police in Minneapolis and Staten Island, respectively. Those pleas are the latest in a long line of unmet calls for a shared sense of humanity in the face of white-supremacist violence that has been built into the system itself....
>
> Racism is deeply embedded in the business model of the fossil fuel industry. In order to extract resources, there are always "sacrifice zones," usually Black, Indigenous, or other communities of color that are put in harm's way and plunged into a violent and multigenerational cycle of economic disinvestment. The history of devastation and the disproportionate impacts of the climate crisis on people of color are well known....
>
> The future of our planet demands that we recognize inequity and defend our communities against compound injustice.[5]

Of course it can feel overwhelming to see clearly the role that we each play in harming each other and the planet. It can be scary to honestly contend with such a level of interconnectedness and accountability. But, if we hope to avert the worst of climate catastrophe and environmental racism, we must celebrate that interconnectedness as essential. For surely it is our false precept of separation, of strict independence, and of perceiving the earth or the other as object, separate and distinct from us, to use as we see fit, that got us into our current climate reality.

In the Torah, shortly after that first human is formed, a new generation decides that they want to challenge the power of the Divine. Feeling spunky and arrogant, the generation of Babel builds a tower that stretches from the ground below to the heavens above, up into God's domain (Genesis 11:4). How tall was this tower? According to one commentary,[6] the tower was of such great height that it took a person a full year to climb from the base to the top. Eventually the tower grew so tall, a different midrash continues, that its builders began to see the bricks as more precious than the people. "If a person fell and died," the midrash says, "the people paid no attention. Their hearts did not even notice. But if a single brick fell, the people sat and they wept, saying, *'Oy lanu!* Woe upon us! Where will we get another brick to replace it?'" (*Pirkei D'Rabbi Eliezer* 24:7).

Sadly, this midrash is still our reality. Our sin is the sin of Babel. Our reality, socially and environmentally, is the inevitable outcome of a society that was founded on the premise of valuing the brick more than the person—from the genocide and forced displacement of Indigenous peoples to the enslavement of Black people—and now the wanton degradation of the earth itself.

Whether or not their original intent was pure, at some point the builders of Babel lost touch with the fundamental truth that all of life is created in the infinite and precious image of the Divine. Their sin, and ours, is building for the sake of anything other than the holiness of life and the celebration of the sacred. If we truly want to take our climate crisis seriously, and our commitment to living a Jewish life seriously, we must assert unequivocally the value of the earth, the other, and the Divine over and above all else.

About nine years ago, I was present when a rabbi told a full room that in the years ahead, we would be called to be both hospice caretakers of the old world and its old structures and midwives of the new one. That idea has stuck with me ever since, as I've attuned my awareness to what I imagine as a cross-fade—the volume of an old way is being turned down as the volume of a new song is rising. We are living through that urgent and transformative and irresistibly holistic consciousness shift today, situated in the overlapping midst of a grand societal cross-fade, hearing for the last time—please God, may it be so—the final gasps of that dissonant and wretched old song and those old structures, while the new tune picks up with bold and beautiful fury, rising into our hearts and into our minds.

We know that the climate crisis is just one face of a multipronged crisis of dignity and sustainability. Therefore, our response must be swift, and we must unequivocally prioritize the physical and material needs of those most vulnerable. But our response cannot end there; what is required now is also a mentality shift—a spiritually oriented and fundamental uprooting and replanting, inspiring us into new ways of prioritizing people and planet. What we need now, in the words of Dr. Martin Luther King Jr., is "a revolution of values."[7] We need a society-wide commitment to living lighter on this planet, to living in more right relationship with each other and the earth, and to transforming the systems that seek to make that impossible. What we need now is a jubilee: *tikkun adam*—a healing of spirit; *tikkun adamah*—a healing of soil; *tikkun HaShem*—a healing of the Divine. We need a new song.

Before leaving the Garden of Eden (Genesis 3:17–19), our relationship with the earth was cursed, in that we would suffer from toil and sweat, and thorns and thistles would grow from the ground all the days of our lives until we return to the earth. Typically, this is read as "the curse will be in effect until we die" and literally return to the soil. But instead, what if we understand it as "we will be cursed by the earth for as long as we see the earth as 'other' and remain separate from it"? Read this way, our "return (*shuvchah*) to the earth," is a kind of *t'shuvah*—a reconnection with the earth—as we repent and renew our sacred connection with the very substance from which we are formed. Only then will the curse be lifted, not because God said so, nor because our punishment will somehow be rescinded, but because we will be treating the earth better and, in so doing, helping to ensure a healthier and more sustainable earth for all. By returning to the earth, we will be lifting the curse we have placed upon ourselves.

Yes, for us to come out the other side of this larger, existential cross-fade, it will require that we lift our own curse. It will require that we soften our hearts enough to embrace a new way of being in relationship with each other and with the more-than-human world. It will require that we return to the earth.

And as that old song fades, we will continue to amplify and turn up and sing along to the fierce and powerful and sweetly sung songs of liberation—the prophetic lyrics of collective sustainability, humility, compassion, empathic caring, and mutual support, rising from all corners.

We will prioritize, once and for all, populace over productivity, person over brick. We will learn what it means to really take care of one another, what we are truly capable of, and what exactly is demanded of us by being alive in just this moment. And then, together, with that song on our tongues, following the leaders of this movement and this moment, we will return to earth—to ourselves, each other, and the Divine—and help midwife the future that we know is already on its way.

NOTES
1. E.g., *Tanya* 37.
2. E.g., *M'or Einayim* on Numbers 30:2–3.
3. Author's translation.
4. E.g., Babylonian Talmud, *Sanhedrin* 38a–b; *B'reishit Rabbah* 14:8; *Targum Y'rushalmi* to Genesis 2:7; *Pirkei D'Rabbi Eliezer* 11:6.
5. Tamara Toles O'Loughlin, "If You Care about the Planet, You Must Dismantle White Supremacy," *Fix* (blog), Grist, June 15, 2020, https://grist.org/fix/opinion-if-you-care-about-the-planet-you-must-dismantle-white-supremacy/.
6. *Sefer HaYashar* on *Noach*.
7. Martin Luther King Jr., "Beyond Vietnam: A Time to Break the Silence" (speech, New York, NY, April, 4, 1967).

11

Reclaiming *V'hayah Im Shamoa*

Our Actions Have Consequences

RABBI DEVORAH DIANA LYNN

> If, then, you obey the commandments that I enjoin upon you this day, loving the Eternal your God and serving [God] with all your heart and soul, I will grant the rain for your land in season, the early rain and the late. You shall gather in your new grain and wine and oil—I will also provide grass in the fields for your cattle—and thus you shall eat your fill. Take care not to be lured away to serve other gods and bow to them. For the Eternal's anger will flare up against you, shutting up the skies so that there will be no rain and the ground will not yield its produce; and you will soon perish from the good land that the Eternal is assigning to you.
>
> Therefore impress these My words upon your very heart: bind them as a sign on your hand and let them serve as a symbol on your forehead, and teach them to your children—reciting them when you stay at home and when you are away, when you lie down and when you get up; and inscribe them on the doorposts of your house and on your gates—to the end that you and your children may endure, in the land that the Eternal swore to your fathers to assign to them, as long as there is a heaven over the earth.
>
> —*Deuteronomy 11:13–21*

TRADITIONALLY THERE ARE THREE paragraphs after the opening line of the *Sh'ma*, the key principle of Judaism's monotheism. The first paragraph that follows *Sh'ma Yisrael* (Deuteronomy 6:5–9), beginning with *v'ahavta* ("You shall love the Eternal your God . . ."), is a recipe for reviewing and passing on the mitzvot to subsequent generations. The third paragraph (Numbers 15:37–41) is a plea to follow and elevate the mitzvot. By staring at and even kissing the fringes of the tallit—the tzitzit with their knots that represent all 613 mitzvot—we are prompted to not be seduced by our most dishonorable instincts.

The second paragraph following the *Sh'ma* (Deuteronomy 11:13–21, quoted above), often referred to as *kabbalat ol mitzvot*—the acceptance of the yoke of the commandments—has all but gone missing in the Reform Movement. Since Rabbi David Einhorn created the progenitor of the *Union Prayer Book* in the 1890s, it has been left out of the Reform siddur and other progressive siddurim, out of a desire to shorten the worship service. Thus, the second paragraph, containing much of the same language as the first, was deemed redundant. Deuteronomy 11:18–20 is certainly repetitious; however, verses 13–17 and 21 are a clear warning. The strong admonition in these six verses presented a theological problem to progressive movements. It affirms that God rewards the observance of the mitzvot through rainfall in its proper season and punishes violations through drought. According to Rabbi Richard Sarason, "To the modern scientific mind, this seemed rather primitive and gross, both as an account of the weather and as an understanding of divine providence."[1]

Ironically, the biblical mind required an acute level of observation of nature by herders, shepherds, and gardeners to simply survive. Yet, the paragraph remained sufficiently problematic into the twenty-first century to earn a recommendation from the Reform Siddur Editorial Committee and a vote by the CCAR Executive Committee to continue to eliminate it from the new siddur, *Mishkan T'filah*, as it had been for over a hundred years.

When *Mishkan T'filah* was published in 2007, climate was still a back-page news item. Al Gore's movie *An Inconvenient Truth* was just coming out in 2006, and climate change was way down the list of social issues that needed to be addressed. Drastic change in the global weather was incomprehensible—too vast, too far away in space and time—not to mention that economically sensible solutions to the problem were not widely developed. In addition, we now know for certain that large international companies that are dependent on fossil fuel revenue were waging a media war remarkably similar to the one used by the tobacco industry in the 1960s to deny the veracity of the direct link between cigarette smoking and cancer.

Today the climate crisis appears on the front page of major news outlets almost every day. Connections between issues once viewed as unrelated are now attributable to climate change, including mass migrations of insects, plants, land and sea animals, and humans. Territorial conflicts, famines, storms, floods, and droughts are exacerbated by rising temperatures and seas. The extensive research of the National Climate Assessment under the U.S. Global Change Research Program has been providing the United States with a progress report every four years since 1990 under Congressional mandate. The latest report from 2018 is comprehensive, frank, and urgent, providing four succinct statements: climate change is happening now and everywhere; it is caused by human activity; many communities are responding; however, no one is responding enough.[2]

The ominous language of closed skies and unproductive soil in the second paragraph of the *Sh'ma* echoes the headlines of drought in the American Midwest; flaring and out of control wildfires in Australia and in the American West; melting permafrost and ice in Alaska, Greenland, Antarctica, and the Arctic; and rising seas, forcing island and coastal people from their homes and off the lands that once sustained them. The year 2020, with the COVID-19 pandemic and shutdown, demonstrated how quickly the entire globe could be knocked off-kilter. Paradoxically, our retreat from business as usual saw skies and waters clear and wildlife thrive. It was a grim demonstration of both our power as a species and our impotence.

Since our exile from the Land of Israel, Jews have trudged through a multi-millennial history of loss of land, forced migration, pressure to move into urban environments, and a physical and spiritual separation from our source of agricultural livelihood and its produce. Kashrut may focus our mind on eating choices, but our food mostly comes in plastic wrap and from faraway places, created out of sight of the challenges faced by farmers and their eroding topsoil. Disruption of supply streams during the global shutdown suddenly brought home how we could become helpless to even feed ourselves.

Almost every one of our Jewish holidays has an agricultural origin, but we generally include that element only as décor, since we are connected only to the grocery store rather than to the land. The seven species suitable and used for Temple offerings in ancient times and highlighted during the Omer counting between Passover and Shavuot—wheat, grapes, olives, barley, pomegranate, figs, and dates—are colorful and delectable. However, the Temple is gone, and by purchasing them at a grocer, we dissociate them from the experience of growing and harvesting them from the land and the complicated balance of heat, winds, and rain they require. We have a fondness for the four species of etrog, myrtle, willow, and palm at Sukkot, and we might even order them from Israel to maintain some small connection with holy produce. Yet, as we gather and shake them together in the sukkah, it strikes some as "rather primitive and gross."[3]

Let's take a closer look at the three items mentioned in the second paragraph of the *Sh'ma*: grain, wine, and oil. In *The Natural Bible* by Baruch Sienna, a brilliant anthology on nature and the Torah, Beth Uval points out that these three species imbue our Sabbath tables with the sacred relationship between the Jewish people and the Divine every single week. Wheat, wine, and olive oil are the necessary ingredients for *Kiddush* every Friday night. We have replaced olive oil lamps with wax candles, but kindling the lights is still an essential member of this trio for blessing the entrance of Shabbat. Wheat, grapes, and olives were necessary ingredients for the showbread, libation, and *m'norot* (lamps) of the Temple and still grace the Sabbath today, establishing our dinner table as a *Mikdash m'at*, a "little Temple." Without these three, the Temple offerings would have been incomplete. Without them, our own Sabbath experience is impoverished. These three species—grain (*dagan*), wine (*tirosh*), and oil (*yitzhar*) represent three ecological niches—field, vineyard, and orchard. They were also staples of the Israelite diet.

Wheat, according to Nogah Hareuveni, founder of the Biblical Plant Reserve, Neot Kedumim, was as much as 50 percent of the local caloric intake.[4] *Lechem* (bread) is surrounded by religious rituals of blessing and washing beforehand and saying grace after eating. Wheat is very rain dependent; it is sown after the dry season around Sukkot to take advantage of the early rains, and then harvested in April/May to avoid the summer's heat.

Wine from the vineyards provided hydration for the Israelites, safer to drink than the water supply. The alcohol sterilized local beverages, just as hard apple cider was a staple in the new colonies of the United

States, thanks to Johnny Appleseed. Wine could be as much as 25 percent of the population's calories. Hot and dry weather is a blessing for the grapes and essential for pollination. Grapes are harvested in June/July.

The olive provided oil for cooking and needed fat calories from food, fuel for burning in lamps, healing for wounds, light for the Temple Menorah, and anointment for the priests. Olive trees are the redwoods of the Middle East and, though not as tall, can last for thousands of years. The blossoms come out in the spring, the trees need and are sustained by hot weather over the summer, and the fruit is harvested in the fall.

Wheat, wine, and oil are three ingredients that "bake" the relationship between the land, the people, and their God. So important are they to this relationship that these three survived as a regular ritual at the Shabbat table as well as in the biblical passage found in our mezuzot and t'fillin.

What is remarkable is that these three chosen products require weather needs that are in direct conflict with each other. Heat and rain are a blessing to all three in moderate amounts but can be fatal to each if too much or too little, too early or too late. In other words, it takes a miracle of timing, rain, temperature, and pollination to harvest a good yield for grain, wine, and olives in a part of the world prone to drought and *chamsin*, winds that can blow strong dust and bring oppressive dry heat. Thus, as much as farmers might want to pat themselves on the back for a job well done in the event of a great harvest, much depends on luck or God. When it all works out, we are inclined to say, "My own power and the might of my own hand have won this wealth for me" (Deuteronomy 8:17). When things go wrong, we are prone to blame God if there is no one else around.

We progressive Jews don't like thinking of a punishing God any more than we submit easily to an angered finger-wagging parent. However, from the experience of a global pandemic, we now know better that we are yoked to one another's behavior and the dire consequences of overlooking our connections to the land. We are consumptive, extortive, and destructive of the earth, including the land, air, and water. We have been idly standing by while environmental injustice plagues our neighbors, species are disappearing in a mass extinction, and rising sea levels force climate refugees to search for new homes.

The second paragraph of the *Sh'ma* demands that we change our behavior, enhancing our positive powers as earthlings made in God's image. To this end, we added prayers into our liturgy. We pasted Debbie Friedman's *Mi Shebeirach* (prayer for healing) onto the back cover of *Gates of Prayer* until it could be added to *Mishkan T'filah*. We added *m'chayeih hameitim* ("[God] revives the dead") back into the *Amidah*. The former offered comfort; the latter gave us choices. Adding the second paragraph of the *Sh'ma* would offer neither. It is not comforting; it is confrontational *and* it reminds us we have no choice. The second paragraph of the *Sh'ma* in the daily prayer alarms and alerts us that we are interwoven with each other; as long as we eat and drink and breathe, we are yoked to the earth and rain in the proper times and proper amounts, even if we live in the city. The reality of our global condition, that destructive climate change is here in our generation, is difficult and overwhelming to confront—but confront we must. We are fighting for our very survival, no longer as the people Israel, but as a species.

Rabbi Arthur Waskow has proposed that each day at *Shacharit* (morning prayer) we read the biblical verses on the appropriate day of Creation to remind us of its perfection: day one for Sunday, day two for Monday, etc. I suggest we add the second paragraph of the *Sh'ma* back into our lives in honor of what we have learned through climate science, in acknowledgment of a *Sh'mitah* (Sabbatical) year, and in recognition of what can go terribly wrong when we are seduced by greed or indifference. We can paste the second paragraph into the back cover or add it to our visual *t'filah* or online services. We can also take note of the excerpt from Rabbi Richard Levy's interpretation of the second paragraph, written in 1985. It was added to *Mishkan T'filah* on the interpretive side of the two-page spread, opposite the first paragraph of the *Sh'ma*. Yet here, too, are a few missing lines (in italics below) from the original. They don't mince words about our behavior and make the strong connection between environmental disaster and injustice:

> Making gods of our comfort or our power
> Then the holiness of life will contract for us.
> Our world will grow inhospitable

To rains from heaven
Or worse
It will be ours unjustly,
And our acts shall isolate us
From the flowing waves of green and gold.[5]

Rabbi Abraham Joshua Heschel teaches that prayer must be revolutionary.[6] Adding this controversial paragraph of the *Sh'ma*, direct from our sacred Torah, reminds us that everything is connected and that there is no Planet B. If the addition of these words ignites us to action as individuals and with others in communal and systemic change that rewards the globe with clean air and water, healthy soil and food, temperature mitigation, and a deep caring for one another, then the second paragraph should have a place of honor in all progressive siddurim.

NOTES

1. Richard Sarason, "The Three Paragraphs of the *Sh'ma*," *Ten Minutes of Torah*, February 2006, https://www.ccarpress.org/content.asp?tid=454.
2. Fourth National Climate Assessment, https://nca2018.globalchange.gov; U.S. Global Change Research Program, https://globalchange.gov/.
3. Beth Uval, "From the Soil of Ancient Israel to the Sabbath Table," in Baruch Sienna, *The Natural Bible* (New York: Behrman House, 2013), 91–93.
4. Uval, 91-93.
5. *On Wings of Awe: A Fully Transliterated Machzor for Rosh Hashanah and Yom Kippur*, ed. and trans. Richard Levy (Jersey City, NJ: KTAV in association with Hillel: The Foundation for Jewish Campus Life, 2011), 22–23.
6. Abraham Joshua Heschel, "On Prayer" (speech, U.S. Liturgical Conference, Milwaukee, WI, August 28, 1969).

12

What Can Jeremiah Teach Us about Climate Change?

Rabbi Elizabeth Bahar

TODAY, WE FACE EXISTENTIAL THREATS so significant that they have altered the planet to the point that we have entered a new geological era—the Anthropocene Epoch. These threats are so overwhelming that we don't know how to respond when confronted with headlines such as "Catastrophic Climate Change Is Already Taking a Toll on Texas: Will The Energy Grid Adapt?" So frightening is the experience of the changing landscape, of humanity's safety with increasingly intense storms, of changing animal migratory patterns, and of increasing health risks not just as a result of pollution, but also from drought, that we are too stupefied to know how to respond. We are forced to ask painful questions including: Where is God? How can we process this inordinate change confronting humanity, and can we even stop or slow the change?

The Book of Jeremiah, a book devoted to engaging with suffering, offers us lessons that we can apply to our endangered lives today. When we, as human beings, face life-shattering catastrophes, either we tend to want to deny their existence and therefore support the current situation and maintain the dominant culture *or* we believe that we can engage and change the circumstances or the crisis. Following a loss, we as humans struggle to understand why, create meaning,[1] and pray that the circumstances never happen again. Similarly, the study of trauma has demonstrated that humans confront trauma by recalling the trauma, examining the trauma by means of developing an internal narrative story, and creating meaning. These processes are evident in the Book of Jeremiah.[2]

To address the trauma and loss of the First Temple, the authors attempted to organize their thoughts, address their grief, and begin to create meaning. They did so by creating the work of art we now have—

the Book of Jeremiah. They organized the book in such a way that it appears disjointed, out of chronological order, and full of poetic language. This arrangement followed the disjointed thoughts humans naturally have post-trauma, according to Kathleen O'Connor in her book *Jeremiah: Pain and Promise*.[3] It also created a process of preservation to record prophetic warnings Jeremiah received while he was alive, to then warn Judah of the impending destruction, thereby demonstrating his later validity as a true prophet. The readers and editors who inherited this book also perpetuated the scattering of the warnings, to subsequently prevent later readers from being overwhelmed by the painful traumatizing memories of the destruction of the Temple so that they could heed the messages found in the book.[4] Parts of the Book of Jeremiah also provided pastoral companionship to the trauma survivors, specifically to those individuals who experienced extreme loss by the decapitation of government through the several waves of expulsion, the destruction of Jerusalem following a two-year siege, the loss of land, and finally, the loss of the ritualistic hegemony of the Temple. In the words of Kathleen O'Connor, "[Jeremiah is] survival literature. In the face of cascading needs of the destroyed nation, Jeremiah is a moral act, a healing therapy, a redeeming lifeline to survival. . . . It helps survivors to read out beyond 'embeddedness' in their overwhelmed state and to create meaning from the ashes."[5]

The Book of Jeremiah was written in response to a specific event—the destruction of the Temple and the loss of the Southern Kingdom. Today we are in the midst of our own global crisis. The Book of Jeremiah offers a model to inspire in us the courage to listen to climate scientists and encourage change. We have an opportunity for the "weeping prophet" to help us mourn the loss of the world that was and transition to a new reality of what is.

To understand just how Jeremiah guides that transition, we need to unpack both the structure and the overall message of the book. By having the opening and closing verses pertain to *galut* (exile), it is structured to create, as Walter Brueggemann states, "an envelope at the beginning and the end of the book, in order to assert that this entire literary tradition is preoccupied with exile."[6] The exile came from God and is embodied in the people of Israel. Brueggemann goes onto argue:

> The book of Jeremiah, in its main thrust, concerns the *ending of beloved Jerusalem*, an ending wrought by the purposes of Yahweh in the face of every kind of human resistance, and the *formation of a new beloved Jerusalem* wrought by the creative power of Yahweh against all the data and in the face of massive despair.[7]

One of the powerful ways in which Jeremiah communicates both in ancient times and today is using metaphor as a tool of persuasion. Direct communication often fails to transmit emotion and urgency or push us forward. Simple examples of direct communication are a sermon or a lecture, and while often well crafted, they can be meaningless for the listener. Metaphor, on the other hand, can reorganize thoughts, introduce associations, and challenge assumptions beyond current understandings.[8] Metaphor is a cognitive device that transforms perception and reorients perspective. Metaphor for Jeremiah is not a simple substitution; it is used to introduce new outlooks and perspectives.

There are more than two sign acts (a physical nonverbal act intended to communicate a message through them to the audience)[9] used metaphorically by Jeremiah. The two discussed below highlight the use of two metaphors delivered at two different chronological points with two separate goals. This rhetorical style used in Jeremiah parallels speakers today who employ metaphor to awaken us to the growing climate crisis. In both cases, Jeremiah's time and ours, humanity is loath to admit that the crisis is a crisis.

Jeremiah uses the metaphor of domestic drama in two acts and in two ways.[10] The initial description of the drama is of a wife (Judah) who strayed, as told from the point of view of the husband (God). O'Connor points out that regardless of the understood and recognizable themes for the ancient audience, "betrayed spouse, adulterous spouse, and soon, bereft of children—the text is about a nation's turbulent present, as perilous as that of a disposable wife."[11] God then unburdens Godself to Jeremiah in the second part of the drama. God shares with Jeremiah that this situation had occurred with a previous wife (the Northern Kingdom) 150 years earlier; Israel, also known as the Northern Kingdom, strayed and was destroyed by Assyria. God argues that Judah (the Southern Kingdom) should have returned to God if she had learned her lesson from the past (Jeremiah 3:6–25).

The message that Jeremiah teaches is that if we fail to learn from the past, we will repeat it. In understanding ecological studies, researchers are beginning to connect the two fields—history and ecology—to learn longitudinal lessons.[12] Even Charles Darwin understood the impact of humans on something as basic as moth population, which was impacted by the industrial revolution.[13] We, as a society, additionally have been struggling with oil and its impact for decades.[14] Climate scientists, anthropologists, sociologists, and others are striving to make the same argument Jeremiah makes—we must learn from our past.

Another metaphor or dramatization occurs when Jeremiah wears a yoke appropriate for an ox to signify that all the nations must submit to the yoke of Nebuchadnezzar.[15] This prophetic sign act occurs between December 595 BCE and January 594 BCE,[16] after the Babylonians exile King Jehoiachin and several thousand nobility to Babylon. This exile destroys the assumption of the dominant society—that Jerusalem would never be breached. At this time Jeremiah is portrayed as a minority voice during extreme turmoil. Jeremiah speaks to the population, but more specifically to King Zedekiah, as he articulates that exile will be longer than the ruling prophets and other kings who gathered near King Zedekiah have predicted (Jeremiah 27). Jeremiah encourages the Israelites to serve the Babylonian king (27:16–17). The oracles convey in a dramatic fashion the same message to both Zedekiah and the other kings supporting him.

These oracles are delivered at the height of a crisis. They are like protestors today telling us of the inflection point we are in because of climate change.[17] We have religious faiths articulating theological statements encouraging adoption of climate change policies to benefit humanity and save the planet.[18] All of these statements and activities are similar to the prophets in the second oracle of chapter 27 of Jeremiah who fail to see the change underway and believe maintaining the course is the correct response (Jeremiah 27:14–15).

Jeremiah understands that the present course means war, and war means destruction. He knows that the totality of destruction about to happen will be not just of the nation but also of an understanding of what life itself means. He uses metaphor to express fear. This metaphor could be shared, one can imagine, with those traveling past battlefields laid waste by the Babylonians—individuals witnessing the absolute devastation of their world. His words reflect a reversal of the Creation narrative in Genesis and express perhaps what the Israelites experienced as their world became undone.

Chaos Revisited (Jeremiah 4:23–28)
I saw the earth, and look! It was waste and void
And the heavens, their light was not there
I saw the mountains, and look! They were quaking
And all the hills were tossing about
I saw, and look! The human was not there
And all the birds of the skies had fled
I saw, and look! The garden land was a desert
And all its cities were ruined
Before God
Before [God's] burning anger
For thus said God:
All the earth will be desolate
Yet I will not make a full end
On account of this the earth will mourn
And the heavens above be dark
For I have spoken, I have laid plans
I have not repented and I will not turn away from it.[19]

This poem is presented in the text as a vision. This vision could just as easily have been experienced by all who saw the devastation wrought today as a result of climate change. Even as Jeremiah unravels Creation, "it manufactures a strange continuity with it by translating violent memories into the familiar terms of Judah's sacred story. It reverses Genesis' steady march toward lush abundance and harmonious goodness and turns it into a nightmare of terror."[20] Jeremiah struggled then, as we struggle today, to make meaning. Just as in the time of Jeremiah, our failure will end in our own destruction, and Creation will be reversed. Climate change is a reverse of God's Creation.

How do we respond to ongoing change beyond our control—change that will impact not simply us, but life and the planet itself? The beginning of human response is grief. Jeremiah is called the weeping prophet because throughout the Book of Jeremiah we read that he wept. The weeping was not done by Jeremiah alone, for even God wept for the disasters that were wrought.[21] Grieving is a moral act, as it involves living here in the present while acknowledging what was lost. "Tearless grief bleeds inwardly" is a quote from American writer Christian Nestell Bovee, who opens an article on loss, grief, and tears as part of a larger series on mourning.[22]

We struggle. We grapple. Eventually, we come to terms and begin to make meaning. The disorder of the Book of Jeremiah is a reflection of the disorder in the mind of the book's editors struggling to make order of the chaos.[23] The fall of Jerusalem was a watershed moment in the history of Israelite religion. "The life of the people of Israel came to an end; the history of Judaism began."[24]

Jeremiah leads the people on with hope. For the survivors, he offers a vision that the God who scattered them will now gather them; that there will be economic well-being, as once again songs can be heard from the heights of Zion, and grain harvest and wine produced.[25] We will change as a society because of climate change, and what Jeremiah assures us is that by doing so we will find a new era of growth and possibility.

On April 3, 1968, Martin Luther King Jr. gave a historic speech in Memphis, Tennessee:

> We've got some difficult days ahead. But it really doesn't matter with me now. Because I've been to the mountaintop. I won't mind. Like anybody, I would like to live a long life. Longevity has its place. But I'm not concerned about that now. I just want to do God's will. And he's allowed me to go up to the mountain. And I've looked over, and I've seen the Promised Land. I may not get there with you, but I want you to know tonight that we as a people will get to the Promised Land. So, I'm happy tonight. I'm not worried about anything. I'm not fearing any man. "Mine eyes have seen the coming of the glory of the Lord."

Dr. King spoke these words as he was leading his people (all people) from the wilderness, through change to freedom. May the words of Jeremiah continue to carry us through challenging times toward freedom.

NOTES

1. Think about our individual responses to the trauma of a car accident. We do not normally remember the sequential activities that led to the accident. We might even remember it in flashes. We then may attempt to make meaning of it (e.g., perhaps we missed the stop sign). This way of making meaning involves taking some responsibility and allows us agency going forward.

2. This assumes that much of the book was written after the destruction. Many of the prophecies were most likely preserved by Baruch, Jeremiah's scribe, and also redacted after the destruction.

3. For a description and impact of these "disjointed thoughts," see the introduction to Kathleen O'Connor, *Jeremiah: Pain and Promise* (Minneapolis: Fortress Press, 2012).

4. This assumes the scroll was read as a whole by scribal schools.

5. O'Connor, *Jeremiah*, 136.

6. Walter Brueggemann, *A Commentary on Jeremiah: Exile and Homecoming* (Grand Rapids, MI: Eerdmans, 1998), 22. By repeating the phrase *d'var Adonai eilav* ("the word of the Eternal" [Jeremiah 1:2, 4]) twice in the opening four verses, Jeremiah further stresses that God is the active agent in causing the people to enter exile.

7. Brueggemann, *Commentary on Jeremiah*, 26.

8. This is the primary thesis in Sharon Moughtin-Mumby, *Sexual and Martial Metaphors in Hosea, Jeremiah, Isaiah and Ezekiel* (London: Oxford University Press, 2008).

9. An example would be Jeremiah buying, wearing, and burying a new waist sash. When he discovers it, it is ruined and not good for anything (Jeremiah 13:1–7).

10. O'Connor, *Jeremiah*, 36. The first act is "Betrayal and Divorce" (Jeremiah 2:1–3:5), and the second act is "Aftermath of Divorce" (3:6–4:2).

11. O'Connor, *Jeremiah*, 39.

12. David R. Foster, "Conservation Lessons and Challenges from Ecological History," *Forest History Today*, Fall 2000, 2–11, https://foresthistory. org/wp-content/uploads/2016/12/foster_Conservation-lessons-and-challenges.pdf.

13. Darwin's study was later repeated with the following conclusion: "Our findings confirm the conventional story put forward by early evolutionary biologists—that changes in the frequency of dark and pale peppered moths were driven by changes in pollution and camouflage" (University of Exeter, "Study Confirms Truth behind 'Darwin's Moth,'" ScienceDaily, August 17, 2018, https://www.sciencedaily.com/releases/2018/08/180817093802.htm).

14. Margaret E. Atwood, "It's Not Climate Change—It's Everything Change," Matter, July 27, 2015, https://medium.com/matter/it-s-not-climate-change-it-s-everything-change-8fd9aa671804.

15. William Holladay, *Jeremiah 2, Chapters 26–52: A Commentary on the Book of the Prophet Jeremiah* (Minneapolis: Fortress Press, 1989), 123. Again, according to Holladay, Jeremiah acted similarly to the earlier prophet Isaiah, who went naked and barefoot for three years as a sign that the Ethiopian dynasty of Egypt would submit to Assyria and that the Egyptians would be led away naked into captivity (Isaiah 20:1–6).

16. Holladay, *Jeremiah 2*, 118.

17. See protestors like Greta Thunberg, for example. For other examples, see "Young Climate Activists Demand Action and Inspire Hope," UNICEF, https://www.unicef.org/stories/young-climate-activists-demand-action-inspire-hope.

18. See statement from various rabbis based on the Catholic Church's statement: "A Rabbinic Letter on the Climate Crisis," Shalom Center, https://theshalomcenter.org/civicrm/petition/sign?sid=17; for the Catholic Church's statement on climate change, see "Climate Change Teachings," Catholic Climate Covenant, https://catholicclimatecovenant.org/teachings. The following offers a wide collection from other faith traditions: "Religious Statements on Climate Change," Faith Climate Action Week, https://www.faithclimateactionweek.org/resources/religious-statements-on-climate-change/.

19. Translation from Jack R. Lundbom, *Jeremiah 1–20*, Anchor Yale Bible Commentaries (New Haven, CT: Yale University Press, 1999), 356.

20. O'Connor, *Jeremiah*, 52.

21. "For the mountains, I take up weeping and lamenting, for the pastures of the wilderness, a dirge because they are desolate and no one passes through and the sound of cattle is not heard. The birds and the heavens and the beasts have fled and gone. And I will make Jerusalem a rubble, a den of jackals, and I will make the cities of Judah a waste without inhabitant" (Jeremiah 9:10–11, translation from O'Connor, *Jeremiah*, 65).

22. As quoted in Mark Roth, "What Function Do Tears, Crying Have in the Grieving Process?," *Pittsburgh Post-Gazette*, March 14, 2006, https://www.post-gazette.com/news/health/2016/03/14/Tears-the-silent-language-of-grief/stories/201510050002. See also the value of crying in Leo Newhouse, "Is Crying Good for You?," *Harvard Health Blog*, March 1, 2021, https://www.health.harvard.edu/blog/is-crying-good-for-you-2021030122020.

23. O'Connor, *Jeremiah*, 126–27.

24. Yehezkel Kaufmann, *The Religion of Israel*, trans. and abridged by M. Greenberg (New York: Schocken Books, 1972), 447.
25. Jeremiah 31:10–14; Lundbom argues this vision is early and speaks to a time from the reign of Josiah, but its placement among another oracle following the destruction indicates it was reinterpreted to offer hope (Lundbom, *Jeremiah 1–20*, 426).

13

How to Change Minds
Lessons from Jonah

MIRELE B. GOLDSMITH, PhD

THE CITY OF NINEVEH, filled with corruption, was in denial that the path ahead was unsustainable. When God sends Jonah to save the city, he does his best to avoid this seemingly hopeless mission. Yet when Jonah finally arrives in Nineveh and delivers God's message, the people of Nineveh immediately repent, and the city is saved.

Jonah's message to the people of Nineveh is *Od arbaim yom v'Nin'veih nehpachet*, "Forty days more, and Nineveh shall be overturned!" (Jonah 3:4).¹ Jonah and the people of Nineveh understand the prophecy as a threat that the city will be destroyed. But Rashi, the medieval commentator, explains that Jonah does not actually say that Nineveh will be "destroyed," only that one way or another, Nineveh will be "overturned." If the people of Nineveh fail to repent, the city will indeed be destroyed; if they repent, they themselves will be "overturned" and transformed from bad to good. Immediately following Jonah's message, we read that "the people of Nineveh believed God; and they proclaimed a fast, and put on sackcloth, from the greatest of them even to the least of them" (3:5). Thus, Nineveh and its inhabitants are saved.

The story of an entire society turning itself around in a moment reads like a fairy tale. Is such a radical and immediate change in behavior possible? This is an existential question that applies as well to the accelerating pace of climate disruption. Scientists have made it clear that we need to move fast to reduce future climate change and to be resilient in addressing what is already happening. Moving fast means reaching net zero greenhouse gas emissions by 2050. Like the people of Nineveh, we are forewarned, but can we save ourselves?

The short answer is yes. We now have solutions to reduce emissions and repair the earth's atmosphere. Clean renewable energy is cheaper than energy from fossil fuels. The cost of electric cars will reach parity with gas-powered cars in the next two to three years. Better yet, education for girls[2] so that they can control how many children they have, regenerative agriculture that restores the ability of the soil to store carbon, and planting trees are solutions too. These solutions also further equity, as all too often people who are already at risk suffer the health impacts of spreading disease and are forced to migrate as drought increases hunger, and resources to adapt to rising seas are directed toward wealthier communities.

All we lack is political will. Although attaining that political will may seem unimaginable, we know that societies do change in seemingly unpredictable ways. Changing hearts to inspire individuals, activating communities, and building a broad social movement for change produce unstoppable momentum. Suddenly a tipping point is reached, and as in Nineveh, change happens overnight.

Changing Individual Hearts

The first step toward reaching a tipping point is motivating individuals. Before I address the practical applications, let us review some basic insights about how people change.

Decades of research have confirmed that people do not change their ways as a result of information or persuasion. Most behavior is driven by gut feelings. Jonathan Haidt, in *The Happiness Hypothesis*,[3] uses a metaphor to explain this. Haidt says that our brains are made up of an elephant and a driver. The elephant is our gut feelings and emotions, and the driver is our cognitive processing. If the driver wants to go one way and the elephant wants to go the other way, which way will we go? For most of us, most of the time, we go where our gut feelings and emotions take us.

In order to motivate individuals to take action, we need to appeal to their emotions. But, which ones? One aspect of the Jonah story that should not be a model for us is Jonah's message of doom. Research has found that fear does not work as a motivator toward action to avert climate change, because confronted by a threat, we go into fight-or-flight mode. Climate change has been described as a problem that our brains are wired to ignore. As climate communications expert George

Marshall explains in his book *Don't Even Think About It*,[4] our brains are wired to respond to immediate threats. In contrast, climate change is complex, unfamiliar, slow moving, and intergenerational. Furthermore, we are all contributors to the problem, so it brings up feelings of shame, guilt, and powerlessness.

For these reasons, we need to inspire people with a vision of a better future that we can bring about by tackling climate change. Knowing about solutions—or better yet, seeing them with our own eyes—gives us hope. For example, Jews are proud to learn that the first commercial solar field in East Africa was built on the grounds of the Agahozo Shalom Youth Village.[5] The field provides electricity to fifteen thousand homes, and the profits pay for health care for the students, who are survivors of the genocide in Rwanda. These kinds of solutions demonstrate that it is reasonable to think that our work can bring about a safer, healthier, and fairer world that will not reflect the most pessimistic projections about climate change.

In addition to offering hope, we can motivate people to action by inspiring a sense of moral obligation by way of profound Jewish values and, as philosopher Roger S. Gottlieb teaches, feelings of responsibility, compassion, and caring for people and the rest of nature.[6] Research has shown that these intrinsic motivations are more sustainable than extrinsic ones such as money and status.[7] Deep in our Jewish psyche is the belief that we can overcome any trial. Our foundational story is that of the Exodus from Egypt, in which a small group of slaves achieve freedom from a mighty empire. We can draw on this powerful story and the faith in the future that it gives us. Our tradition is rich in resources, including rituals, song, and prayer, that can activate positive and empowering emotions in each of us.

Turning Feelings into Action

In the Jonah story, the people of Nineveh repent to save their city and themselves, symbolized by the ritual of dressing in sackcloth and sitting in ashes. Rabbis and scholars point out that feeling regret is not adequate for repentance. Repentance is not a change of feeling or mind; it requires changes in outward behavior. According to Maimonides, we need to ask forgiveness, express remorse, and right the wrong we did.

The real test of repentance is to act differently if the same situation happens again.[8] Similarly, to achieve change on a systemic scale, a vision of the future and positive motivations are not enough. People need to move from feelings to action.

Fortunately, we know quite a bit about what works to get people to take action. People are social animals, and how we behave is based on what we see others doing. For example, we know that the strongest predictor of smoking is the proportion of an individual's closest friends who smoke. We also have compelling evidence that people are much more likely to install rooftop solar panels if their neighbors do so. As a way to change behavior, peer influence is incredibly powerful. We are influenced not only by those we know directly but by people at two and three degrees removed from us. Individual actions like talking to friends about climate change, cutting back on eating meat, and installing energy-efficient light bulbs are sometimes criticized as inadequate to the scale of the threat from climate change. This is a fair criticism but also discourages people from getting involved. They feel blamed rather than encouraged to participate in the inspiring global movement for a better world.

As Robert Frank discusses in his illuminating book *Under the Influence: Putting Peer Pressure to Work*,[9] small steps are the building blocks of systemic change. Small steps in the right direction change us. They change our self-image. We begin to see ourselves as humans who care about climate change. And, as we endeavor to sustain that caring image, each step we take motivates us to take another step. This path eventually leads us to engage in advocacy for systemic change.

The Essential Role of Communities

In Nineveh, change seems to happen overnight because the author of the Book of Jonah focuses on the dramatic moment when Nineveh finally reaches a tipping point. But that cannot be the whole story. Undoubtedly, there is a less dramatic story of incremental progress prior to the city's moment of repentance. If we could go back in time, we would probably find that years before Jonah arrived, a few Ninevites had grown concerned about their city and the corruptive behaviors of its inhabitants. They started speaking to their neighbors about their concerns. Those neighbors began to repent and change their ways, and their transformations started to catch on.

At some point, individual Ninevites began joining together in groups. New behaviors are passed from person to person individually, but it can be a slow process, accelerated only when individuals take support and direction from a group. In fact, experts have learned that forming groups is an essential step toward change. An example is the neighborhood-based Eco-Teams, developed by David Gershon, to scale up a program for people to adopt sustainable lifestyle changes. Members of the teams support each other and provide accountability. Gershon describes how before groups were actually formed, people would ask him, "Why bother? My actions are just a drop in the bucket." Gershon overcame this barrier by forming groups and emphasizing that "if enough of us do this, our drops will fill the bucket."[10]

Fortunately, we as Jews are poised for action because we already have powerful communities that are bound together by sacred values and personal relationships, along with structures for working together and an empowering history of monumental achievements. In my community, Adat Shalom Reconstructionist Congregation, our climate action team employed the step-by-step approach of Doug McKenzie-Mohr, to engage our congregation in two campaigns.[11] The goal of the first campaign was for members to subscribe to the purchase of electricity from the first community solar field to be built in our state. We employed research-based tools of behavior change to inspire congregants to overcome barriers to action.[12] The most important technique was to activate the power of peer influence by publicizing the participation of members who subscribed. One of the highlights of the campaign was calling up the seventy-plus subscribers for an *aliyah* to the Torah during Shabbat services. We used similar techniques to encourage congregants to switch to socially responsible credit cards issued by banks that do not finance fossil fuel projects.[13]

Building a Social Movement

The People's Climate March, which took place on September 21, 2014, aimed to put pressure on world leaders assembled at the United Nations to commit to concrete actions to avert the climate crisis. An unprecedented 150 Jewish organizations endorsed the march. Thousands of Jews joined the multi-faith contingent, many with *shofarot* in hand, waiting hours to join the four hundred thousand people assembled along Central Park West. When Rabbi Arthur Waskow called out, "*T'kiah g'dolah*," a tremendous blast rang out calling for change.

Why were so many Jews present at the march? In *How Change Happens: Why Some Social Movements Succeed While Others Don't*, Leslie R. Crutchfield documents patterns that distinguish successful social movements.[14] In addition to "changing hearts," Crutchfield puts "turning grassroots gold" high on her list. Successful movements build momentum from the bottom up. She emphasizes that community must be an end in itself, not just a means to an end, in order to be effective. With a strong base and support in place, communities can coordinate their actions to achieve common goals. Between 2009 and 2014, Hazon's Jewish Greening Fellowship demonstrated the potential for turning Jewish "grassroots gold." Fellows, appointed to champion sustainability in their organizations, were inspired through participation in monthly trainings that included Jewish learning and site visits. In turn, the fellows convened "green teams" to engage and motivate others in their organizations. With support from the Jewish Greening Fellowship, the fellows led their green teams to concrete accomplishments such as lighting retrofits to reduce energy use, the establishment of community composting programs to cut methane emissions and rebuild soils, installing gardens and solar energy systems, and more. Together, they engaged over 600 people in green teams, over 33,000 in education programs, and 175,000 through communication efforts. They attracted $3.6 million in donations and government funding for their projects. Viewed from a systems perspective, the fellows, green teams, organizations, and UJA-Federation of New York, which invested $2 million, created an interlocking network that added up to more than the sum of its parts.

Jewish organizations are often reluctant to take positions on political issues and get involved in advocacy. When it came time to take a stand by endorsing the People's Climate March, what was different was that a network of committed organizations was already in place. The fifty-five organizations that participated in the Jewish Greening Fellowship were the first to endorse the People's Climate March, and they set in motion a process of peer influence, so that many others followed their example.

Reaching a Tipping Point

In the Jonah story, the social movement that coalesces when Jonah reaches Nineveh has a successful political conclusion. Despite Jonah's lack of enthusiasm for his mission and the brevity of his prophecy, his message hits the target. When "the tidings reached the King of Nineveh ... he arose from his throne, and laid his robe from him, and covered him with sackcloth, and sat in ashes" (Jonah 3:6). The leader of Nineveh follows the lead of the people and he repents! He even goes on to proclaim a fast of repentance for all the people and animals of Nineveh.

As in the Jonah story, tipping points are reached all the time. Behaviors can spread exponentially like an epidemic. This phenomenon is called social or behavioral contagion. Researchers who study social networks have found that the average American has a network of six hundred people.[15] We influence those closest to us and second- or third-degree contacts as well. Since we are unaware of the extent of our influence on others, we—like the people of Nineveh and the readers of the Jonah story—may think not much is changing until the tipping point is reached. Erica Chenoweth, a public policy expert who is widely admired for her empirical research, has demonstrated that nonviolent civil resistance campaigns are successful if they are able to mobilize 3.5 percent of the population.[16] Perhaps we are not that far from bringing our society to a tipping point to finally act in response to the challenge of climate change.

As Jews, we have the tools we need to change hearts, inspire individual action, activate communities, and help to build a broad social movement for change. The movement we build, together with many others, will achieve the political will to put us on a sustainable path. Like Nineveh, our world will be overturned for good.

NOTES

1. Biblical translations in this essay are taken from *The Twelve Prophets*, ed. Abraham Cohen (London: Soncino Press, 1948).

2. For further information, see "Health and Education," Project Drawdown, https://drawdown.org/solutions/health-and-education.

3. Jonathan Haidt, *The Happiness Hypothesis* (New York: Basic Books, 2006), 4.

4. George Marshall, *Don't Even Think About It: Why Our Brains Are Wired to Ignore Climate Change* (New York: Bloomsbury, 2014), 46–51.

5. See "Rwanda," Gigawatt Global, https://gigawattglobal.com/projects3/rwanda/.

6. Roger S. Gottlieb, "The Environmental Crisis: What Do We Have to Teach? What Do We Have to Learn?" (keynote address, Judaism and Climate Change, Judaism, Science and Medicine Group Conference, February 28, 2021), https://jewishstudies.asu.edu/recordings.

7. Alfie Kohn, "Why Incentive Plans Cannot Work," *Harvard Business Review* September–October 1993, https://hbr.org/1993/09/why-incentive-plans-cannot-work.

8. Maimonides, *Mishneh Torah, Hilchot T'shuvah* 2:1.

9. Robert H. Frank, *Under the Influence: Putting Peer Pressure to Work* (Princeton, NJ: Princeton University Press, 2020), 262.

10. David Gershon, *Social Change 2.0: A Blueprint for Reinventing Our World* (West Hurley, NY: High Point, 2009), 48.

11. This process is described in Doug McKenzie-Mohr, *Fostering Sustainable Behavior: An Introduction to Community-Based Social Marketing* (Gabriola Island, BC: New Society Publishers, 2011).

12. For an additional resource, see Mirele Goldsmith, "Greening Synagogues: Lessons from the Jewish Greening Fellowship," *Synergy* 12 (2016), https://www.ujafedny.org/api/assets/787027/.

13. For further information on socially responsible credit cards, see Sarah Tarver-Wahlquist, "Why Switch to a Responsible Credit Card," Green America, https://www.greenamerica.org/responsible-credit-cards.

14. Leslie R. Crutchfield, *How Change Happens: Why Some Social Movements Succeed While Others Don't* (Hoboken, NJ: Wiley, 2018), 21–51.

15. See Andrew Gelman, "The Average American Knows How Many People?," *New York Times*, February 18, 2013, https://www.nytimes.com/2013/02/19/science/the-average-american-knows-how-many-people.html.

16. David Robinson, "The '3.5% Rule': How a Small Minority Can Change the World," *BBC Future*, May 13, 2019, https://www.bbc.com/future/article/20190513-it-only-takes-35-of-people-to-change-the-world.

14

The Song of Songs
A Ritual Journey of Connection with Creation

Rabbi Shefa Gold

WHEN IT CAME TIME TO DECIDE which of the holy books would become part of Torah, the Song of Songs almost did not make it. It was so earthy and sensual, it did not once mention God, and besides, they were singing it in all the taverns. It was only because of Rabbi Akiva's adamant defense that this text was preserved for us today. He stood up to the assembled rabbis and said, "All the writings of Torah are holy, but the Song of Songs is the holy of holies!" (*Mishnah Yadayim* 3:5). He also said, "Had the Torah not been given, we could live our lives by the Song of Songs."[1]

By saying the Song of Songs is "the holy of holies," Rabbi Akiva meant that it belonged at the center. When I put the Song of Songs at the center of my Jewish practice, everything changed. I now practice a Judaism that has *love* at the center, along with pleasure, beauty, and a deep connection to the rhythms and mysteries of nature.

When I took seriously Rabbi Akiva's suggestion that I could *live* my life guided by this holy erotic, earthy, embodied text, it set me on a Jewish earth-based, love-centered path that has transformed my life.

What follows are some excerpts from this text, including a chant practice, commentary, and a question that will guide us as "we live our lives by the Song of Songs."

By using melody, harmony, rhythm, and a focused intention, we can embody this sacred text, rather than just think about it.[2]

A Path of Love
The Judaism that I celebrate and teach is a path of love that connects me to my roots in earthiness and opens my heart to the wide expanse. The text at the center of this path is the Song of Songs. The Song of Songs is a journey (through love) toward peace and wholeness.

Oh, give me the kisses of your mouth,
For your sweet loving is better than wine,
Your juices are fragrant,
Your essence pours out like oil,
This is why all the young women want you.

—*Song of Songs 1:1–3*

I am called to intimacy, and my longing calls me to Life.
I request Your mouth; I invite the Supreme Risk.
Your kiss is Death as well as Revelation.
Yet I know that all the wine I have drunk is just a taste;
Each and every moment of ecstasy only stirs the coals.
A spark, my true spark, awakens, leaps, and then grows dark again.
Each time I feel Your breath on my face, my spark awakens and twinkles
with laughter or trembles with Terror.
And then, I am all lips, all expectancy, all hunger.
Your fragrance, the scent of Reality, lures me
Beneath the dry surface of this seeming world . . .
Behind the shadows that confound me . . .
Between the sureties of conception and form
The tantalizing fragrance of Your Presence calls to me.

PRACTICE: *Chant:* Kiss Me (*Yishakeini*), https://www.rabbishefagold.com/kiss-me-yishakayni/

COMMENTARY: The words at the beginning of the Song of Songs set the tone for passion, intimacy, yearning, and fulfillment as we journey forth into the adventure of Love that is *Shir HaShirim*. These words teach us that the stance we must take toward life is "being puckered up": being ready, willing, expectant, and committed to the journey of Love.

This verse is a request to invite God—Reality, the World-as-It-Is, Existence Itself—to an intimate and direct encounter. That divine kiss in turn invites us into our passion. Our practice is to release all passivity, pucker up, and engage with Life. To receive the divine kiss is to die in this moment and be reborn in love.

QUESTION FOR CONTEMPLATION: Can I receive the divine kiss in the color of the sky? In this breath? With this step? Can I open to the gift that God is giving me in "this"?

I Am the Rose of Sharon

The Song of Songs sends me on a journey of identification with nature's gifts—I am that flower!

I am the rose of Sharon
A lily of the valleys.
Like a lily among the thorns,
So is my beloved among the young women.
—*Song of Songs 2:1–2*

I flower: bursting with color, vibrancy, and proud seed,
I announce my life to the world.
So very bold!
And yet vulnerable to each passing breeze, each mood,
  each day's surprise.
Attentive to this patch of ground, I put forth my tendrils,
  encountering rich soil, immovable rock.
I root myself in the earth of this life, this family, these circumstances—
while knowing how fragile is my certainty, how delicate my identity.
The garden of my heart is surrounded by wilderness,
A treasure hidden by thick brambles and scrub-oaks
Whose roots spread with vicious intensity,
Blocking the paths, and yet . . .
I can smell that lily, that apple-blossom shimmering
At the center of my heart, its fragrance calling me.

PRACTICE: *Chant*: I Am the Rose of Sharon (*Ani Chavatzelet*), https://www.rabbishefagold.com/rose-of-sharon-ani-chavatzelet/

COMMENTARY: This is a practice of blossoming forth and rooting down. Although we cannot be sure exactly what flowers these are (various translations include rose, lily, tulip, hyacinth, narcissus, lotus, crocus, and wildflower), we do know that these flowers resonate in the prophetic traditions of Isaiah 35:1–2 ("The desert shall be glad, the wilderness shall rejoice and shall blossom like a rose") and Hosea 14:6–8 ("I will be as the dew to Israel, who will blossom as the lily").

As I chant these words, I am rising toward the sunlight of glory and redemption, and at the same time, I am connecting myself to the deepest places in the world and in myself. The word for "valleys" (*amakim*) also means "the depths." When we blossom from those depths, our beauty, however transient, is grounded in the fullness and power of our earthly existence.

QUESTION FOR CONTEMPLATION: Can I stay rooted in my depths, my lineage, my body, and my earthiness while reaching toward the heavens and the great expanse?

Calling Others, Calling Ourselves

The Song of Songs connects me to the mysteries of the earth by asking me to listen to her rhythms and attune myself with her cycles.

My beloved calls to me:
Arise, my friend, oh beautiful one,
Go to yourself!
For now the winter is past,
The rains are over and gone,
Blossoms appear in the fields,
The time for singing has come.
The sound of the turtledove
Echoes throughout the land.

—*Song of Songs 2:10–12*

For now, my struggle is over. I struggled with the belief that I shouldn't be exactly who I am and sing myself aloud from the nearest tree. I struggled with the belief that I should have a different fragrance—something sweet, or perhaps something smarter, a fragrance that might be acceptable, that might perhaps blend in. I lost the battle against who I am, yet in my losing I am victorious. In my losing, I have found myself. My song echoes throughout the land. I exult in the fragrance that is mine alone.

PRACTICE: *Chant*: Arise, My Friend (*Kumi Lach*), https://www.rabbishefagold.com/arise-my-friend-kumi-lach/

COMMENTARY: What if every relationship becomes an opportunity for us to call each other into the realization of our full potential?

What would it mean to let our gaze penetrate the façade of another to reveal a glimmer of that core, authentic divine essence, thereby sending that other to her truth? And, what would it mean to receive the gaze of the world as a force of sending, to respond to each and every being by rising up to our full stature and beauty as we take the journey to the center of our being, the place where self and other meet?

QUESTION FOR CONTEMPLATION: How can I treat every relationship as an opportunity for us to call each other into the realization of my full potential? (This includes my relationships with the nonhuman world of rocks, trees, blossoms, birds, clouds, etc.)

God's True Face

The Song of Songs sends me to a direct encounter of God in the beauty of this world.

The fig tree is ripening
Its new green fruit,
And the budded vines give of their fragrance.
Arise, my friend, oh beautiful one,
Go to yourself!
My dove in the clefts of the rocks,
Hidden by the cliff,
Let me see who you are,
Let me hear your voice,
Your sweet voice,
Your radiant face.

—Song of Songs 2:13–14

Yes, I have been hidden from my own eyes, and so hidden from You,
My only love. Hidden by shame in a crevice of the heart, I bend to fit this
dark cave.
My voice has been muffled, my light dimmed.
My treasure—
hidden away.

PRACTICE: *Chant*: True Face (*Harini*), https://www.rabbishefagold.com/true-face-harini/

COMMENTARY: The normal way of being is to live inside our thoughts about the world. We see what we expect to see. We are busy trying to figure out how to use the world or protect ourselves from it. We are identifying threats or allies. We are comparing and categorizing. We are planning our next step. When those thoughts quiet down or cease being the focus of our attention, suddenly the world appears.

Surprisingly, the world is more bright, beautiful, and radiant than anything we could have imagined. Colors delight. Our curiosity is kindled. We can engage with what is before us and receive its gift, enjoying both the blessing and the challenge of this world. When we are paying attention and become receptive, God's true face appears as this world. In a moment of inner stillness, we can relax, enjoy, and open up as the sounds of this world become music.

QUESTIONS FOR CONTEMPLATION: Can I quiet my mind's interpretation of the world before me so that I may encounter my world directly, without commentary, comparison, analysis, definition, or judgment? Can I become receptive to the beauty before me as the face of God?

Hearing Your Voice

The Song of Songs urges me to listen, pay attention to the transforming power of beauty, and savor the pleasures of embodied earthiness.

Your lips like a scarlet ribbon
And your voice so sweet.
The curve of your cheek
Like a pomegranate
Hidden behind the thicket of your hair.
Your neck is a tower of David
Built to perfection,
A thousand shields hang upon it,
All the armor of heroes.

—*Song of Songs 4:3–4*

And You, my Beloved . . . this world You wear as a garment is torn and stained; ripped apart:
by war;
by greed;
by despair;
by rage.
Your magnificent garment decays in disease and injustice. Its cloth is rotting in poverty and degradation.
And yet I know You truly in Your incomparable beauty and perfection. Beneath that beggar's disguise, You are my Shining King, without blemish.

PRACTICE: *Chant*: Your Voice in the Wilderness, https://www.
rabbishefagold.com/your-voice-in-the-wilderness/

COMMENTARY: These words direct our attention to the lips and the
voice that emerges through that lovely outlet. That voice brings wisdom
and inspiration to us. In creating this practice, I couldn't help but be
reminded that the word *midbareich*, which is translated as "your voice,"
or "your speech," or "your mouth," is a homonym for "your wilderness." I added the English words of this chant so that the images of the
Song of Songs might lead us to inquire, "Can we allow the divine voice
to emerge from the deep silence of the wilderness? Can we listen and
receive the beauty, majesty, and wide perspective that the wilderness
offers?"

When I step into the wilderness, the noise of the "civilized" world
recedes, and I can begin to hear another voice—more subtle, more profound, wider in its scope. It is that voice that asks for a response that is
sourced in my depths.

QUESTIONS FOR CONTEMPLATION: Can I allow the divine voice to
emerge from the deep silence of the wilderness? Can I listen and receive
the beauty, majesty, and wide perspective that the wilderness offers?

The Flow of Change

The Song of Songs illuminates my own beauty and hidden powers
through the mirrors of nature and invites me to luxuriate in the delights
of my own garden.

You are a garden spring,
A well of living waters
That flow from Lebanon.
Awake, north wind! Oh South wind, come!
Blow upon my garden
and let its spices stream out.
Let my lover come into his garden
And taste its luscious fruit.
                    —*Song of Songs 4:15–16*
Only You, my Beloved Mysterious Infinite Void, can call
Forth and receive this infinite flow . . . through the vessel

That I am becoming. With this stream of love,
You make me known to myself.
I invite the winds of change to blow into my life. Who can fortify against
them?
I do not resist,
I welcome them, honor them;
They whip through me—
I vow to ride the winds, to consciously use their force to
Free myself,
To liberate my true fragrance—
So that I might bless the world with my unique essence.
I vow to receive Life in both its awesomeness and its awfulness, all of it.
My garden is dynamic, ever-changing,
Ever-seeding, ever-sprouting, ever-greening,
Ever-blossoming, ever-fruiting, ever-rotting,
Ever-going-back-to-seed. I offer these seeds to the winds.
Catch them, carry them, take them! "You never know!"
You never know what seeds will take root, somewhere in someone. You
never know what will grow, how or when.
Within my garden that is buzzing with life and change, disaster and
renewal, storm and bright sun, fragility and resilience . . . there is a
center of calm, my still and spacious, waiting, open heart.
Into that center I invite the Beloved.

PRACTICE: *Chant*: Awake, North Wind! (*Uri Tzafon!*), https://www.
rabbishefagold.com/awake-north-wind-uri-tzafon/.

COMMENTARY: There is a natural tendency to resist change in order
to maintain the illusion of control and the fantasy of security. Yet life
moves on, bringing with it upheavals, losses, transformations, and
shifts in perception. What if instead of resisting the winds of change, we
surrendered to those powerful forces, as the messengers of expanded
consciousness?

In the spirit of welcome, those changes may become opportunities
for adventure, growth, surprise, and awakening. The spices of our garden represent the hidden inner strength and beauty unlocked through
times of tumult and change.

QUESTIONS FOR CONTEMPLATION: Can I acknowledge my own hidden depths? Can I let my secret powers flow out as unique expressions of the divine flow?

Rising Like the Morning Star

The Song of Songs opens my eyes to the cosmos and my place in it.

Who is that rising like the morning star?
Clear as the moon, bright as the sun,
Daunting as the stars in the sky.
—*Song of Songs 6:10*

100 billion galaxies.
I try to understand. I try to fathom
The wisdom of cosmologists.
We live in a tiny corner of one galaxy,
In a small cul-de-sac called the Milky Way. This is my daily practice:
I say to myself, "There are 100 billion galaxies!"
I try to fathom; I am daunted.
My mind, just a tiny corner of a galaxy,
Is not big enough to hold this, but I try . . .
And then my mind just shuts down.
I take a breath,
I close my eyes,
I fall into my heart . . .
Which is LARGER than 100 billion galaxies.
There, I rest, expanding toward the edges of the universe, leaning into
Love's embrace.

PRACTICE: *Chant*: Who Is That Rising? (*Mi Zot Hanishkafah?*), https://www.rabbishefagold.com/who-is-that-rising/

COMMENTARY: As we open to the power of Love, we are joining the Dance of the Cosmos.

QUESTIONS FOR CONTEMPLATION: Who is it? What is it that is rising within me as I turn toward those 100 billion galaxies?

Descending into the Garden

The Song of Songs sends me into the secret places of earthly bounty, to explore and celebrate the beauty that is always emerging.

I went down to the nut grove,
To see the new green by the brook,
To see if the vines had blossomed
And the pomegranates had bloomed.
                    —*Song of Songs* 6:11

My garden is ever-greening,
Ever-blossoming, ever-fruiting.
I am hidden, even to myself.
The secret is revealed in the unselfconscious flow of my love.
As it blossoms You make me known to myself.

PRACTICE: *Chant:* Going Down to See (*El Ginat*), https://www.rabbishefagold.com/going-down-to-see/

COMMENTARY: We usually go up to a higher place to see . . . but sometimes we need to go down. We need to descend into our own depths and use a different kind of vision to penetrate the complexities within. We enter the nut grove with an eye toward cracking that nut whose hard exterior hides a delicious treasure.

Our inner journey takes us to the *nachal*, which is a kind of "stream" that flows intermittently (the Arabic word would be a *wadi*; the Spanish word, *arroyo*). The "new green" that sprouts up in that *nachal* is mysterious and miraculous—found only by those who have the insight and courage to "go down" and explore the hidden places.

QUESTION FOR CONTEMPLATION: Can I "go down" into my own hidden places and find what is just beginning to blossom?

NOTES
1. *Aggadat Shir HaShirim Zuta* 1:6, as quoted in Abraham Joshua Heschel's *Heavenly Torah* (New York: Continuum, 2006), 196.
2. The practice for each section can be found at www.RabbiShefaGold.com.

15

The Rivers Will Clap Their Hands

Shabbat Rituals for Connecting to the Earth

RABBI LAURA RUMPF

T HE OLD *KOREN SIDDUR* I received during my first year of rabbinical studies in Jerusalem tells stories. It wears wine stains from raucous Shabbat tables, earmarked pages referenced repeatedly in silent prayer, and most notably, joyful dusty fingerprints from the summer I spent serving a vibrant Shabbat community at Camp Tawonga, a pluralistic Jewish summer camp nestled in the Yosemite Valley. Each Friday night after the sun went down and the campers tucked in, I circled up with a spiritually eclectic group of staff on some smooth sitting rocks by the Tuolumne River, which ran through camp. With flashlights, we huddled around one small siddur, to sing and sway to the lively verses of the *Kabbalat Shabbat* psalms, which seemed designed for the setting we found ourselves in.[1] We drew inspiration from verses that implied that nature herself joined us in rejoicing over Shabbat:

- Psalm 96 called us to sing a "new song" to a just God, who made the earth feel steadfast and glad: "Let the sea roar, and all that is in it; let the fields be jubilant and all they contain. [Then] the forests will sing for joy before God" (verses 11–12).
- Psalm 98 declared, "Let the rivers clap their hands, and the mountains sing together for joy" (verse 8), to witness God's justice, uniting humanity and the natural world.[2]
- Psalm 92 offered us a vision of human resilience rooted in nature: "The righteous will flourish like a palm tree and grow tall like a cedar in Lebanon. Planted in God's home . . . they will still bear fruit in old age, and stay vigorous and fresh" (verses 13–15).

Under the stars, those verses that offered a vision of God's justice that centered harmony in nature did not feel messianic or far off; they felt like an embodied, essential call to mindful connection with the environment as an integral part of Shabbat practice. Rather than drowning out the call of our earth with a cacophony of human-made distractions, we used our voices, our bodies, and our silences to attune to our place in the symphony of a Creation that makes room for the earth's flourishing.

The irony has not been lost on me that I now hum the *Kabbalat Shabbat* prayers in traffic on the way to the services I lead across the bridge and several freeways from my home. While I do my best as a rabbi to dwell in the sanctuary in time that is Shabbat, it is a rare Friday evening that I find myself communing with the natural world as viscerally as I did that summer. I recall now that anytime I can access my voice and my silence with those verses, and anywhere that I can light candles and engage in the simple blessings of the Shabbat table, I can taste that vision of earth-based justice that I felt so deeply that summer. Each Shabbat that I can connect in some embodied way to the justice of nature flourishing and renewing alongside us, I heal a bit of the separateness and estrangement I feel from Shabbat's essential call to environmental awareness.

It is with the yearning to feel more regularly enveloped in a sensory spirit of connection to our earth that I offer the following Shabbat rituals. Not all of us can reach a river or find a wild space to sing every Shabbat, but we are blessed with bodies that can connect us imaginatively to the natural world through our senses. My hope is that in doing so, we can reinvigorate a commitment to a mindful relationship with the land, and particularly with the natural resources that sustain our lives. The ritual series below is inspired by the psalms of *Kabbalat Shabbat* that call us to rejoice in the exuberance of the natural world. They may be done around a Shabbat table or anywhere you can gather, sing, light candles, and fill cups with water and wine.

Joining Nature's Chorus: A Pre-candlelighting Ritual for Reorienting toward the Rhythm of the Natural World

This ritual is best done in a circle where all can face each other and hear each other's voices. One ritual leader initiates the cues or designates another person in the circle to lead.

1. Offer these words of Rav Nachman of Bratzlav as inspiration
   for grounding the ritual:
   Each and every shepherd has their own special melody,
     according to the grasses and specific location where
     they are grazing. . . .
   Their melody is dictated by the grasses and place they pasture.
   Each and every grass blade has a song which it sings.
   And from the grass's song,
     the shepherd's melody is created.
                    —*Likutei Moharan 2:63:1:2, translation by Moshe Mykoff*
2. Invite each person gathered to choose one sound and movement inspired by the natural world, to elevate and bring an
   earth consciousness into Shabbat.
3. Designate one person to start the chorus with their nature-
   inspired sound and movement, repeating it rhythmically for
   a few beats, before the person to their left comes in with their
   sound and movement. Invite each person in the circle to enter
   the chorus organically, each contributing a sound and a movement inspired by the natural world.
4. Allow the chorus to reach a joyfully loud volume, and then
   subside to a hush, and finally into a silence, which may be held
   for several minutes. In the held silence, encourage an attention to faraway sounds, particularly natural sounds we don't
   hear when we are not listening with intention.
5. After one to two minutes of silence, designate one person to
   light Shabbat candles, lead the blessing for lighting candles,
   and then open the space for sharing on the reflection questions below.

BLESSING FOR CANDLELIGHTING:
*Baruch atah, Adonai, Eloheinu Melech haolam, asher kid'shanu
b'mitzvotav v'tzivanu l'hadlik ner shel Shabbat.*
Blessed are You, God, Source of life, who has blessed us with the
positive commandment to light the candles of Shabbat.

QUESTIONS FOR REFLECTION
- What wisdom has connection to the earth illuminated for me this week? How has nature inspired me?
- What excess use of resources can I release this Shabbat so that God and nature may experience greater rest and renewal?
- How can I make space to let the light of Shabbat reorient me to right relationship with the natural world?

Round of Earthly Applause before Blessing the Fruit of the Vine

1. Guide participants in a creative "round of applause" for the natural world. Pour cups of wine or *Kiddush* grape juice for all who are gathered. Before reciting the Hebrew blessing, invite each person present to share one experience of wonder or gratitude connected with their experience of the earth and her resources.
2. After each share, guide a collective clap for each experience.
3. After everyone has had a chance to share, prompt all to raise their glasses in a joyous *Kiddush* blessing, acknowledging the appreciation for the natural world that has been shared by the group.[3]

Attunement to Water before Ritual Handwashing

1. Prior to Shabbat, collect water from a special source (e.g., a local river, stream, clean drinking faucet), and have it ready to use in a small jug or basin.
2. Offer a special blessing for the source of the water (*m'kor mayim chayim*, "source of living water") at your table, along with the traditional blessing for handwashing prior to saying *Motzi* (see below). Invite participants to share any additional notes of gratitude for clean, potable sources of water in their lives and the ways water sources revive our bodies and spirits.

BLESSING FOR RITUAL HANDWASHING:
Baruch atah, Adonai, Eloheinu Melech haolam, asher kid'shanu b'mitzvotav v'tzivanu al n'tilat yadayim.
Blessed are You, Source of blessing, our God, who makes us holy through God's commandments and commands us concerning washing the hands.

Enhancing Challah Blessings with Food for Thought

1. Introduce the concept of the gift of a double portion that is part of God's vision of justice as inspiration for a brief reflection on food justice. As one participant holds up two challah loaves and invites others to join hands, offer the extended prayer that the earth and all of her inhabitants are able to access this feeling of abundance that a double portion promises.[4]

2. After the challah has been blessed and passed around, invite each person to set one intention around food justice for the week ahead. Examples may include cooking a healthy plant-based meal for a group of people who experience hunger, setting a goal for reducing waste in the home, supporting local farmers at a farmers market for the weekend rather than buying goods from a large-chain grocery store, or committing to advocacy for environmental legislation that would create systemic change.

BLESSING FOR CHALLAH BEFORE A MEAL:
Baruch atah, Adonai, Eloheinu Melech haolam, hamotzi lechem min haaretz.
Blessed are You, Source of blessing, our God, who brings forth bread from the earth.

NOTES
1. Psalms 95–99, Psalms 92 and 93, and Psalm 29 are traditionally included in the liturgy of *Kabbalat Shabbat*.
2. Psalm 98 as translated in the *Koren Siddur*, 315.
3. See "Shabbat Evening Blessings: *Kiddush*—Blessing over Wine," Reform Judaism.org, https://reformjudaism.org/beliefs-practices/prayers-blessings/shabbat-evening-blessings-kiddush-blessing-over-wine.
4. Torah tradition holds that two whole challot should be used on Shabbat as a remembrance of the double portion of manna that fell in the desert, so that no being should have to gather food on Shabbat (Exodus 16:22–32).

Yotzeir Or

Rabbi Evan Schultz

Yotzeir Or, *meaning "the One who fashions light," is found in the morning liturgy before the* Sh'ma. *It inspires this poem by Evan Schultz.*

we are tired.
legs.
hands.
eyes.
ears.
heart.
soul.
mind.
spirit.
of course we are.
we are re-creating a universe.
while holding on to the existing one.
close our eyes.
listen.
breathe.
pause.
mute everything. except our favorite song.
be.
nourish.
open our eyes. look around.
we are re-creating a universe.
while holding on to the existing one.
blessed are we, who daily renew creation.

Nature and Humility

A Reflection on Job

ADRIANE LEVEEN, PhD

I GREW UP in a small town nestled in rolling hills in Upstate New York, in the shadow of a glorious eucalyptus tree, a row of pines, and several maples. We lived just four houses away from a winding river. I experienced the natural world as benevolent and predictable until that same river abruptly and fiercely reminded us of nature's powers to destroy. In 1972, after days of heavy rains, the river overflowed, damaged our house, and flooded most of our town. My family briefly became climate refugees. Today hurricanes, floods, droughts, and wildfires brought on by our warming planet have created many more catastrophes. Nature is telling us we are in danger and need to wake up.

Becoming a grandmother has made this work increasingly urgent for me. On what sort of planet will my children and especially their children live? Haunted by this question, I have redoubled my efforts as a volunteer climate activist in the Jewish community in partnership with a network of climate, labor, and environmental justice organizations called NY Renews. This coalition advocated for the Climate Leadership and Community Protection Act (CLCPA) that was signed into state law on July 18, 2019. The law mandates achieving 100 percent zero-emission electricity by 2040 and an 85 percent reduction in greenhouse gas emissions by 2050. It was a historic step, but much more needs to be done. The situation remains dire. We are in the fight of our lives and must recognize our collective responsibility for the planet before it is too late. The Book of Job, a biblical source that I hold dear, has helped me recognize the paradoxical nature of that responsibility. We need to be both humble and bold. Let me explain.

In stunning poetic form, God challenges Job in chapters 38–41 to perceive the natural world differently than he had until that point and thereby acquire a deeper understanding of his place in it. God points out the appearance of the stars at daybreak, the sun's rays slowly moving across a sandy beach at dawn, the pounding of hail, and the birthing of wild goats. Such precise detail teaches Job to cherish the world on its own terms, even if just for a moment, without wanting something from it.

We are at that same moment again. Specifically, we need to question our human-centric sense of entitlement that the earth's resources are ours for the taking. We should be embarrassed at our misplaced assumption that we dominate and control the earth. We have also fatally underestimated nature's powers to fight back. God's description of the stormy forces of nature along with an array of wild creatures who repeatedly defy human attempts to subdue them offers us a lesson rather than a debate. That lesson should humble us.

In Job 39:27–30, the poet evokes the eagle, a magnificent bird that glides far above and out of our visual range. Eagles inhabit a sphere completely beyond human life, beyond our values and virtues:

> By your word does the eagle mount
> And set his nest on high?
> On the crag he dwells and beds down,
> On the crest of the crag his stronghold.
> From there he seeks out food,
> From afar his eyes look down.
> His chicks lap up blood,
> Where the slain are, there he is.[1]
>
> —*Job 39:27–30*

The poet offers us a strange world in which we are utterly insignificant to the concerns of God's other creatures. Such life is indifferent to our own.

Another fierce creature, Leviathan, perhaps a mythic god of the sea or, more likely, a large and very aggressive crocodile, strikes terror in the human heart in Job 41:1–3a:

> No one's fierce enough to engage him.
> Who could take a stand before him?
> One's hope (of doing so) is dashed—
> At the mere sight of him one's knocked down!
> Who has ever confronted him and survived?
> Of all that's under heaven—he is mine.[2]
>
> —*Job 41:1–3a*

Job, mere human that he is, does not stand a chance. Yet we continually ignore nature's powers. We willfully mine, drill and pollute, increasing global temperatures—bringing catastrophe and destroying a planet that will bring us down with it. We have ample evidence in the severe weather increasing each year in strength and destructiveness. Even when we recognize ourselves as merely a part of a threatening world and not its masters, we also need to be bold. Only we ourselves can bring the world back from the brink. Can we balance our hubris with ingenuity, our destructive powers with scientific innovation and resolve? Can we be humble and bold? Only then can we stand with God as necessary partners in preserving this one, precious planet.

NOTES

1. Robert Alter, *The Hebrew Bible*, vol. 3, *The Writings* (New York: W. W. Norton, 2019), 570–71.

2. Edward L. Greenstein, *Job: A New Translation* (New Haven, CT: Yale University Press, 2019), 180–81.

PART THREE

Encountering the Divine

A KEY MODE of engaging in Jewish ecological thought is found in existential encounters with the Divine. This section provides examples and even pathways to just such experiences.

Reflecting on his own experiences of mountains in our world, Rabbi Eric L. Abbott provides a context for understanding the imagery of mountains in Jewish text. Reflecting on the idea of God as place, Rabbi Jill Hammer, PhD, offers an innovative mystical mode of understanding God's presence in our natural world. Rabbi Eli Herb finds God in nature through *hitbod'dut*, the individual prayer practice described by Rebbe Nachman of Bratzlav. Echoing the experiences of the Torah's revelatory narrative, Rabbi Mike Comins shares having found God in the desert. Rabbi Michael Birnholz describes discovering the divine spark in the practice of composting. Detailing her approach to art, Rabbi Adina Allen charges us to find Jewish spirituality in creativity. Rabbi Efrat Rotem retranslates the traditional prayer *Ahavat Olam*. Connecting mealtime to understanding our place in the global food system, Rabbi Joel M. Mosbacher, DMin, tells a personal family story. Rabbis Daniel A. Weiner and Avi B. Fine reflect on how a walk in nature can enrich Shabbat practice. Rob Watson, the inventor of Leadership in Energy and Environmental Design (LEED), the most widely used green building rating system, recounts how his spiritual journey led him to fuse his work with personal practice. To conclude, Chaplain De Fischler Herman's poem evokes a Jewish approach to experiencing plant life.

16

Awesome Heights
Mountains in the Bible

RABBI ERIC L. ABBOTT

A CHASIDIC TALE teaches of a young child who would often skip school for hours. One day, their teacher followed, trailing behind as they traversed deep into the hilly woods, curious to discover what they did with that missing time. At one point the child paused. The teacher saw that there, amid the tranquility of nature, the child began to pray. The next day, the teacher asked what drew the child to the woods, and the child replied, "I find God there." "Why?" the teacher asked. "Can't you try to find God at school or in the synagogue? After all, God is the same everywhere." "That might be true," the child replied, "but I am not."[1]

This young child knew a profound truth: sometimes we need to change our setting, push ourselves out of our comfort zone, and escape to a different environment to experience something profound. For the ancient Israelites, mountains, with their massive heights and impressive views, often served as the setting for this experience. The mountains of the Bible evoked awe, fear, and amazement in the ancient Israelites and inspired them to encounter God in new and profound ways, and although we today may not connect to mountains in quite the same manner, perhaps we can stir ourselves to cultivate this same sense of awe and, in so doing, experience the Divine.

Rabbi Abraham Joshua Heschel, the famous professor of Jewish ethics and mysticism at the Jewish Theological Seminary, taught that awe forms the core of how we human beings begin to understand the beauty and mystery of God's Creation. When we open ourselves up to "radical amazement," as he called it, we can open ourselves up to God. "Awe . . . is the sense of wonder and humility inspired by the sublime or felt in the presence of mystery," he taught.[2] This awe can provoke a transcendent feeling and, with it, a sense of the Divine. "God begins where words end," Heschel elaborated.[3] For many people, when we leave the hustle and bustle of the city or the routine of our suburban homes and escape to nature, then words may fail us—and, in that moment, we can expose ourselves to the wonderment of Creation.

I have encountered awe on mountaintops. Though afraid of heights, I enjoy pushing myself out of my comfort zone through rock climbing. I recall a climbing trip to Rumney, New Hampshire, many years ago. After a day of scaling the cliffs, I sought one last route, pushing myself to the limits of my endurance. When I reached the top, I affixed my anchors, leaned back into my harness, and turned around. As the afternoon faded into evening, the sun splashed the scenery with warm color, painting the surrounding mountains and fields with majestic purples and deep oranges. The beauty and vastness of life took my breath away. There on the mountain, I experienced awe at God's world and felt closer to God.

Just as I felt awe on the side of that cliff, one can only imagine that for the Israelites, the mountains of ancient Israel evoked an even greater sense of wonder and humility. Due to geological features such as the Great Rift Valley, a wandering Israelite could travel the countryside seeing descents as low as thirteen hundred feet below sea level juxtaposed with heights of over three thousand feet.[4] Mountains are scattered across the terrain, from the Judean Hills surrounding Jerusalem to Mount Carmel in the north to the mountains of Moab in the south. The fact that the Bible presents a myriad of terms for massive, mountain-like topographical forms—including *har* (mountain), *tzur* ([big] rock), *marom* (elevated height), and countless others—indicates just how pervasive mountains were in the backdrop of the Bible.[5] Indeed, they were so common and compelling that Moses could not resist speaking about them, such as when he called the land "this good mountain region" (Deuteronomy 3:25) and "a land of mountains and valleys" (11:11).

With such prominence, these mountains served key geographical roles to the ancients, influencing everything from geopolitical boundaries to climate to trade routes.[6] Mountains intricately fused into the lives of the people of the Bible, guiding them as they navigated their physical space. The prophet Elisha dwelled atop a mountain (II Kings 4:25), Noah's ark rested on a mountain when the floodwaters subsided (Genesis 8:4), Solomon's workers built the Temple in Jerusalem using stones excavated from a mountain (I Kings 5:29), and armies erected fortresses on mountaintops (Joshua 15:48). Gazing upon these staggering heights, the people of the land identified many reasons to climb the ever-present mountains that framed their existence.

As the Israelites ascended these heights, they would have encountered a host of feelings. When one climbs a mountain far from a town or settlement, one experiences physical exertion coupled with intimate interactions with nature. Upon reaching the top, one discovers breathtaking views extending for miles. Add the erratic weather and intense storms that can appear on mountains, the far-reaching acoustics that can stretch over valleys, and the infinitesimal feeling that may accompany witnessing geological features that span the horizon, and there is no doubt as to why mountains conjure awe, wonder, and humility.[7]

As such, for the ancient Israelites, as for many other ancient cultures, mountains not only influenced the way they navigated their physical world but also inspired them spiritually.[8] For instance, as poets and prophets strove to convey their relationship with God, the awe they saw in the mountains became a means with which they could express the ineffable. At times, the mountains of Israel came to personify the people of Israel, such as when God commands Ezekiel to prophesy *to* the mountains (Ezekiel 36:1). In other instances, the mountains become symbols, such as when Isaiah deftly castigates Israel's enemies by comparing their arrogance to climbing a mountain (Isaiah 14:13). For other writers, mountains helped them describe God. Just as a mountain or enormous rock (think Rock of Gibraltar[9]) could shelter someone from a storm or enemy, so too could God protect God's people like a stone sanctuary (Isaiah 8:14) or a mountain stronghold (Psalm 31:3). These poets looked to the mountains and saw them quake before God, demonstrating God's supremacy over nature (Judges 5:5). The Bible takes the drop in our stomach we might feel atop a cliff or the deep dread during a thunderstorm and, through figurative language, magnifies them to express God's might.

Beyond the power of the word, the ancient Israelites used mountains to reach up toward God. In the Bible, the mountain frequently serves as an *axis mundi* (world axis), the high cosmic mountain that forms a bridge between heaven and earth.[10] The biblical scholar Theodore Hiebert has described why mountains became such important religious sites:

> With its peak reaching into the skies, it [the mountain] represents the closest connection in the environment between earth, the domain of humanity, and heaven, the realm of the gods. The splendor of the highest peaks produces a sense of awe, a sense heightened and made more mysterious when the cloud banks of the thunderstorm veil the summit from view. Once scaled, the mountain offers an unlimited vision, not only of the clouds and the heavens but also of the horizon of the earth.[11]

The mountain, with its peak extending into the sky, becomes the literal meeting point between the mortal world and the divine heavens. Through ritual, our ancestors sought to bridge the gap between the two. Hence, mountaintops serve as the setting for religious events in the Bible, such as Abraham offering a sacrifice (Genesis 22:2), Jacob and Laban forming a covenant (Genesis 31:54), Moses and Aaron dying (Deuteronomy 32:50, Numbers 20:28), and Balaam prophesying (Numbers 22:41). In fact, Solomon built the seat of the Israelite cult, the Temple in Jerusalem, atop Mount Zion (Isaiah 2:3).[12] Mountains, which offer natural amphitheaters, a platform from which one can see one's audience, and a sense of majesty mixed with the unknown, provide natural ambience for high ritual and an inspirational setting for humans to relate to God.[13]

However, in biblical theology, not only do humans reach up to God on the mountaintop; God, in return, reaches down to humans. While God occasionally chooses springs (Genesis 16:7), rivers (32:23–33), and trees (12:6–7) as sites for theophany, God predominantly elects mountains for this role.[14] Two biblical stories highlight the ways in which God reaches out to humans atop mountains and how, in response, our ancestors experienced awe on those peaks.

In the first story, one whose consequences echo throughout the Bible, God delivers Revelation at Mount Sinai. Atop this mountain—

the mountain, as the Bible sometimes refers to it (e.g., Exodus 19:2)—God reveals God's word to Moses and the people of Israel. The moment of Revelation arouses intensity and suspense. As described especially in Exodus 19 and 20, the Israelites arrive at Sinai not long after leaving Egypt. At the mountain, they experience a ferocious tumult. Lightning flashes and the storm roars; the cry of a horn pierces the air. God's voice echoes as thunder. Thick clouds cover the mountain, creating a sense of mystery.[15] The people, standing at the base of the mountain, tremble in fear. The mountain itself also trembles; perhaps it, too, stands in awe of God. This scene amplifies the intense, expansive, and transcendent feelings that one might have if one were caught in a thunderstorm atop a mountain and directed them toward awe of God's power. God, above and outside the world, controls Creation.[16]

How many of us as children or adults felt similar feelings facing the immense power of nature? Hiding under the covers during a thunderstorm? Inching back from a high cliff overlooking a deep ravine? Staring into the murky depths of the ocean with trepidation? We experience nature and respond with both wonder and fear. We respond with awe.

However, lest we confuse nature with God, the Bible presents us with a different tale set on the very same mountain, now called Horeb, in I Kings 19.[17] After destroying the prophets of Baal, Elijah flees from Jezebel and eventually arrives at "the mountain of God, Horeb" (19:8). God then calls out to him and passes by:

> God said, "Come out, and stand on the mountain before the Eternal." And behold, the Eternal passed by in a great and mighty wind, splitting mountains and smashing stones before the Eternal; but the Eternal was not in the wind. And after the wind, an earthquake; but the Eternal was not in the earthquake. And after the earthquake, a fire; but the Eternal was not in the fire. And after the fire, a still, small voice. (I Kings 19:11–12)

Like the previous story of Moses and the Israelites at Sinai, God reveals God's glory to Elijah atop a mountain, complete with a massive upheaval of the natural order. However, while the Revelation at Sinai involved powerful storm imagery to convey God's might, this narrative employs the same imagery to teach the opposite. As the biblical scholar Nahum M. Sarna wrote:

> The vivid, majestic, and terrifying depictions [of Exodus 19], which draw their ultimate inspiration from the storm and the earthquake, are meant to convey in human terms something of the awe-inspiring impact of the event upon those who experienced it. The narrative of I Kings 19:11–12 is intended to dispel any possibility of mistaking the atmospherics for the substance of theophany.[18]

Thus, while Elijah's moment on the mountain resembles Moses's, this time the awe comes not from the storm but from the quiet afterward.

Can we, like Elijah, hear the still, small voice on the mountaintop? Can we tremble in the heights, stand afraid of the power of nature, feel the awe upon looking out from a peak toward the landscape—not because of nature itself, but because we acknowledge with gratitude God as the creator of heaven and earth, the one who "affixed mountains through strength" (Psalm 65:7)? Can we feel awe not only in the big moments of fear of or amazement at impressive heights, but in the quiet moments too? Elijah teaches us that we can—if only we listen.

I recall a trip to Israel I led for college students when I guided them atop a rocky height in the desert. Far from the glow and cacophony of cities, in the pitch black of night with only stars and silence surrounding them, students came face-to-face with the still, small voice. They expressed notions of experiencing something profound, something ineffable—something radically amazing.

For many of us, however, these encounters may seem foreign. We are not all mountain climbers or hikers, and we almost certainly do not offer sacrifices or prophesy atop mountains. Nonetheless, these biblical moments on mountains have something to teach us all: how to create intentional moments in which we can open ourselves up to the possibilities of wonder. Mountains in the Bible are catalysts for awe. As Rabbi Jamie Korngold, founder and senior rabbi of Adventure Judaism, teaches:

> Perhaps God [made] Moses climb Mount Sinai to receive the Ten Commandments so that Moses would move beyond the confines of words. The physical exertion of the desert climb, coupled with the stark desert beauty, helped Moses to arrive spiritually and emotionally in a place beyond internal chatter, a place beyond

rationalization or explanation. A state often called awe, in which you open your mouth to describe what is happening and find the only thing you can say is "Wow." Only in this state was Moses able to hear the word of God, to sense God's presence, to reach out to the Divine.[19]

Only when Moses ascended the mountain could he meet God face-to-face. Only when the Israelites left Egypt, entered the wilderness, and approached the mountain could they experience God's Revelation. Only when Elijah endured the violence of nature atop the mountain could he hear the still, small voice. Mountains in the Bible, with their impressive views and terrifying heights, became impetuses to reach something greater. They forced our biblical ancestors to open themselves up to something new, feel something different, and experience awe—and, therefore, experience God.

When we cannot escape to the desert slopes of Israel, when we cannot climb the cliffs of Rumney, when we cannot skip school and enter the forested hills—the mountains of the Bible teach us that we can still find God. We can find intentional ways to see the beauty in nature. We can seek out moments that take the words right out of our mouth: the birth of a baby, the wonder in a child's eyes, the harmonies of a symphony, and the laughter of a decades-long friendship.

May we each aspire to experience the awe of the world in our own ways, just as our biblical ancestors experienced it atop mountains. As we do, may we, like them, grow closer to God.

NOTES

1. Adapted from Elie Wiesel, *Somewhere a Master: Hasidic Portraits and Legends* (New York: Schocken Books, 2005), 131.
2. Abraham Joshua Heschel, *God in Search of Man* (New York: Meridian, 1959), 77.
3. Abraham Joshua Heschel, *Man Is Not Alone* (New York: Noonday Press, 1951), 98.
4. Yohanan Aharoni and Michael Avi-Yonah, *The Macmillan Bible Atlas*, rev. ed. (New York: Macmillan, 1977), 14.
5. S. Talmon, "הר (*har*); גבעה (*gibh'āh*)," in *Theological Dictionary of the Old Testament*, vol. 3, ed. G. Johannes Botterweck and Helmer Ringgren, trans. John T. Willis, Geoffrey W. Bromiley, and David E. Green (Grand

Rapids, MI: Eerdmans, 1978), 427–47; H.-J. Fabry, "צור (ṣûr) II," in *Theological Dictionary of the Old Testament*, vol. 12, ed. G. Johannes Botter-weck, Helmer Ringgren, and Heinz-Josef Fabry, trans. Douglas W. Stott (Grand Rapids, MI: Eerdmans, 2003), 315–16; Ludwig Koehler and Walter Baumgartner, *The Hebrew and Aramaic Lexicon of the Old Testament [HALOT]*, ed. Johann Jakob Stam, trans. M. E. J. Richardson, CD-ROM ed., BibleWorks 9 (Leiden: Brill, 1994), s.v. "מרום."

6. Richard F. Townsend, "Geography," in *The Encyclopedia of Religion*, vol. 5, ed. Mircea Eliade (New York: Macmillan, 1987), 509.

7. Jeffrey H. Tigay, *The JPS Torah Commentary: Deuteronomy* (Philadelphia: Jewish Publication Society, 1996), 252.

8. Townsend, "Geography," 5:509.

9. As taught to me by Rabbi Andrea L. Weiss, PhD, in a private conversation while advising my rabbinic thesis on this subject, September 29, 2016.

10. Richard J. Clifford, *The Cosmic Mountain in Canaan and the Old Testament* (Cambridge, MA: Harvard University Press, 1972), 3; Talmon, "הר (har)," in *Theological Dictionary of the Old Testament* 3:437; Diana L. Eck, "Moun-tains," in *The Encyclopedia of Religion*, vol. 10, 130.

11. Theodore Hiebert, "Theophany in the OT," in *Anchor Bible Dictionary*, vol. 6, ed. David Noel Freedman (New York: Doubleday, 1992), 505.

12. While technically no verse ever states in clear, concise terms that the 12 sat on Mount Zion, many verses associate Jerusalem with a mountain, with Zion generally, or with Mount Zion specifically, and other verses associate the Temple with Jerusalem, Zion, and an unnamed mountain. See, for example, Ezekiel 20:40; Psalm 43:3–4, 48:10–12; Lamentations 2:6–8.

13. Tigay, *Deuteronomy*, 252. Jacob Milgrom, *The JPS Torah Commentary: Numbers* (Philadelphia: Jewish Publication Society, 1990), 169.

14. Hiebert, "Theophany in the OT," 6:505.

15. Hiebert, "Theophany in the OT," 6:506.

16. Nahum M. Sarna, *The JPS Torah Commentary: Exodus* (Philadelphia: Jew-ish Publication Society, 1991), 106.

17. G. I. Davies, "Sinai, Mount," in *The Anchor Bible Dictionary*, 6:47. While Davies argues that the mountain and region of Sinai and those of Horeb seem to be identical, some scholars disagree.

18. Sarna, *Exodus*, 106.

19. Jamie S. Korngold, *God in the Wilderness: Rediscovering the Spirituality of the Great Outdoors with the Adventure Rabbi* (New York: Three Leaves Press/Doubleday, 2007, uncorrected proof), 48.

17

The Sacred Whole of Creation
Sefer Y'tzirah and Jewish Eco-theology

RABBI JILL HAMMER, PhD

SEFER Y'TZIRAH, the Book of Creation, is an ancient work famous for inspiring many of the concepts of the Kabbalah.[1] It is less well-known as a resource for eco-theology. Yet *Sefer Y'tzirah* is one of the most ecologically sensitive sacred texts we have in our Jewish library. In its brief incantational passages, where elements are letters, time and space are books, and all of existence is one long divine name, *Sefer Y'tzirah* invites us into a cosmos that speaks. This remarkable ancient text presents the diversity of Creation as a sacred whole, offering us union (in mind and body) not only with God, but with all things.

Sefer Y'tzirah, written in cryptic, brief, polysemous passages, tells the story of God's creation of the world via the engraving of twenty-two Hebrew letters, as well as ten entities known as *s'firot*. These engraved forms carry divine intention and meaning between the One and the Many. Together they constitute a temple-like structure for the unfolding cosmos. If we read this ancient text from the perspective of eco-theology, we might say the letters and *s'firot*—which partake of the Divine at the same time that they are wholly of this world—are a divinely breathed ecology, a nurturing, organized, diversified space (*makom*) for life to grow. These elemental letter-forces proceed from the Divine "like a flame in a burning coal"[2]—ultimately, the dimensions of our physical universe are rooted in and connected to the Source of Being.

Though it is clearly in dialogue with the Bible and with later Jewish sources as well, *Sefer Y'tzirah* shows few of the hallmarks of Rabbinic literature—it may even be said to be a non-Rabbinic book.[3] It adopts Jewish magical language more than Rabbinic idiom, and its interest is primarily in the experience of the individual practitioner rather than in addressing a tribe or nation.[4] It is a mystical work, but its mysticism is entirely focused on this world, rather than on hidden worlds a seeker might try to enter. In fact, the text offers a profound solution to the problem of exile and alienation: the possibility of finding home not in a lost land of origin, but in the cosmos as it manifests in space, time, and person.

The text suggests that we begin with silence, that we turn away from the inward chatter of our ordinary consciousness and "stop our hearts from murmuring."[5] Of course, for most of us, this is impossible to do for any length of time. As we struggle with our inner voices, the text instructs that we "return to the place."[6] What does this mean? It could mean many things, but we should note that the word *makom* comes from the Hebrew root *kuf-vav-mem*, which means "to stand, to exist in place, to endure." To return to the place is to return to What Is. And, indeed, this is what we need to do, inside our noisy minds: return to the world as it exists—to our sense of emplacement, of being in a particular region of space and time. We might say that returning to the place means returning to the earth—the place par excellence for all of us.

Paths of Wisdom

The book begins by laying out the cosmos as if it were written on a page before us:

> Wisdom's thirty-two marvelous paths
> Yah engraved—
> the Becoming One who holds many—
>
> within three books:
> tome, tally, and tale.
> [*or:* book, number, and story.][7]

In this opening passage, the text invites us into the Creator's workshop, where the Creator is engraving thirty-two "paths of wisdom"—letters, numbers, and dimensions of the cosmos that will manifest the divine creative purpose. It is as if we are watching God engrave letters into the tablets of the Ten Commandments.

Yet these letters are not exactly letters on a page that form words. The three books mentioned in the opening passage are poetic terms for space (called in the text *olam*, "world"), time (*shanah*, or "year"), and

body-soul (*nefesh*, a Hebrew term that refers to both body and spirit—
we might even translate *nefesh* as "the breathing body"). A book takes up
space, numbers take time to count, and a story requires a being's experience—thus the connection between the dimensions of the cosmos
and their poetic names in this passage.

For *Sefer Y'tzirah*, word always leads to world. Indeed, the first letters God "engraves" are not words or sentences but the world itself.
The Jewish fascination with sacred word, in *Sefer Y'tzirah*, reconnects
to an embodied knowledge of a living universe. The engraved paths of
the letters are called "wondrous paths of Wisdom"—Wisdom being
a mediating entity between God and the world—a kind of proto-
Shechinah, a mediatrix between the One and the Many.[8] Wisdom, composed of elements and framing structures for the cosmos, is a kind of
placental network allowing unity to become diversity and allowing
diversity to seek back toward unity. *Sefer Y'tzirah* understands the underlying All to be revealed within the lived reality of difference. This is what
eco-theologian David Seidenberg calls "a theology of diversity."[9]

Return to the Place

Sefer Y'tzirah suggests that humans need to refine their consciousness
in order to grasp the inexpressible truth that the One and the Many are
inextricably interwoven. In 1:5, we read:

> Ten inscriptions of the void:
> Stop your mouth from speaking,
> stop your heart from murmuring,
> and if your heart runs
> return to the Place
> for Scripture says:
> "running and returning."
>
> Regarding this matter.
> a covenant was made.[10]

"Ten inscriptions of the void" is my rendering of the phrase *s'firot b'li-
mah*, which we might also render as "insubstantial dimensions." This
is based on the work of Giulio Busi, who suggests that *s'firot* could be
translated as "inscriptions"—which fits the "engraving" theme at the

heart of the book.[11] In other words, God carves out ten aspects of time, space, and being from the formless world. The reader, in contemplating these aspects, requires preparation and grounding, perhaps because it is dizzying to know ourselves as part of something infinitely larger.

It is significant that place—*makom*—is a Rabbinic term for God and is also a biblical term for the Temple.[12] The phrase in the text simultaneously invites us into relationship with the Divine and into knowledge of our world as sacred space. In 1:6, we are told that the dimensions of the cosmos "are embedded in their beginning, and their beginning in their end"[13]—that is, the physical structures of the cosmos partake of the Divine. The text adds wryly, "Before One, what are you counting?" In the face of true oneness, numbers are no longer necessary. The calculations and reasonings of our minds cannot lead us to the All—to get there, one has to let go into Being.

We might therefore understand "returning to the place" as returning to a sense of the holy within the world—not the general holy but the *specific* holiness of place, time, and being. What if, before speaking or acting or building a building or cutting down a forest, we reminded ourselves to "return to the place"? What specific holiness might we notice? What other actions might become possible and necessary?

Depths of Being

In 1:7, we learn what the *s'firot* are: a five-dimensional frame for the cosmic temple.

> Ten inscriptions of the void:
> their measure is ten yet they are infinite:
>
> A depth of beginning and a depth of end
> A depth of good and a depth of evil
> A depth of above and a depth of below
> A depth of east and a depth of west
> A depth of north and a depth of south
>
> and a singular Master—
> a faithful divine Ruler—
> rules over them all
> from God's holy dwelling
> and out to eternity.[14]

At the center of this five-dimensional structure (and really, everywhere is the center, because the lines are infinite), the Divine dwells in a *maon kodesh*, a "holy dwelling." Richard Hayman calls this "the temple at the center of the universe."[15] Indeed, the whole cosmic structure could be understood as a holy dwelling place, a sacred *makom*, for the Divine.

The God of *Sefer Y'tzirah* is an immanent God, dwelling within Creation, not in hidden worlds. God does not rule the place from outside, but rather from within: God's rule extends from the shrine at the center "out to eternity." The Hebrew phrase for "out to eternity," *ad adei ad*, has the sense of "forever forever forever" and can mean infinity in time as well as space. The threefold nature of the phrase has a kind of magical force and also hearkens back to the three books of space, time, and body-soul.

In a related vein, ecological thinker David Abram writes:

> It's likely that our solitary sense of inwardness (our experience of an interior mindset to which we alone have access) is born of the forgetting, or sublimation, of a much more ancient interiority that was once our common birthright—the ancestral sense of the enfolding earthly cosmos as the voluminous *inside* of an immense Body, or Tent, or Temple.[16]

Indeed, *Sefer Y'tzirah* seems to be sensing exactly this: the enfolding cosmos as a house or temple. This infinite temple has walls, a ceiling, and a floor. It unfolds in time, and it also contains a diversity of bodies, as we will learn throughout the book. When we return to the place, when we open the "interior mindset" to the Real, *Sefer Y'tzirah* suggests that we can again become aware of this immense temple, the *makom*, that we inhabit. There is a sense that *Sefer Y'tzirah* is inviting us into an ancient worldview in which we, God, and all Being are keeping a great house together. Space becomes less a realm of human power, and more a shrine in which we must dwell respectfully and mindfully.

Three Mothers

Chapter 3 establishes further the kinship between elements and beings, between people and the animate world. The three *imot*, or "mothers"—*alef*, *mem*, and *shin*—comprise the elements of air, water, and fire. In 3:3 we read:

Three mothers:
Fire above,
water below,
and wind in the middle.[17]

Sefer Y'tzirah names air, water, and fire as elements; the earth is framed as a kind of congealed water. These three elements, associated with the letters *alef*, *mem*, and *shin*, are called *imot*, "mothers"—implying an animate fecundity. The mothers form layers of the world: a lower layer of water (perhaps the *t'hom*, "deep," of Genesis 1:2), an upper layer of fire (comprising stars and angels), and a middle layer of air. In this middle layer, human beings, and other breathing beings, live and move. This three-layer view of the world has much in common with indigenous views of the cosmos in which humans live between an upper and a lower world.

These three layers in space, we later learn, also exist in time, forming winter, summer, and the season in between (which may refer to the "brimming" season, when rivers overflow). These layers also exist in the human body: the head, according to a passage later in the book, arises from fire, while the belly arises from water, and the chest, containing the heart and lungs, arises from the element of air; that is, the same three elements that form the world also form the body. The body has different organs that work together to support life, and so too does the world. This premise establishes a fundamental sympathy between the experience of being in a body and the experience of immersion in the world. The human is not separate from Creation, but rather a fractal of it.

Many of us have lost our sense of "embeddedness" in a larger ecosystem. Indeed, essayist Lachelle Schilling writes:

> The earth never runs out of messages. But humans as a species have lost touch with this reality. The majority of the human population lives in urban areas where we consume and live processed lives. It is no wonder too few of us make grand changes in our lives concerning excessive consumerism and waste. How can we think of what we do not encounter?[18]

Yet *Sefer Y'tzirah* reminds us that the cosmos is not just a space we live in. It is part of our very bodies—and we are part of it.

How would we treat the water, the air, the animals and plants, other human bodies (including poor, Black and Brown, disabled bodies, which our culture frequently disregards) if we truly understood these entities as part of our own bodies, interwoven with each moment of our lives? Eco-theologian Cynthia Moe-Lobeda defines "critical mystical vision" as "this three-eyed vision of seeing what is, what could be, and the presence of the sacred"—becoming aware both of the real structural obstacles to ecological sustainability and justice and of the pathways toward it.[19] *Sefer Y'tzirah* potentially offers a model for shaping our consciousness toward a critical mystical vision in which we meet the full reality of our interconnection with all life in one *makom*. Our "returning to the place" could be a return to a just and sustainable relationship with the land and all who dwell there.

Conclusion

Sefer Yetzirah frequently hints to the reader that human words and actions contain creative power, just as divine words and actions do. At the end of the book, Abraham does all the combining, forming, and engraving of letters that God does, and so becomes God's friend. In a sense, by engaging in the practices that *Sefer Y'tzirah* describes, we are following in the footsteps of the Creator. In this way too, *Sefer Y'tzirah* offers an ecologically potent observation: we are always shaping our world. In our words, and in every other way, we are creating reality for ourselves and other beings. How can we cocreate that reality while honoring the integrity and beauty of the whole? This question resonates profoundly in our contemporary age. Often we have not shaped our world with care and balance. But *Sefer Y'tzirah* suggests we could do better, if we opened our senses to the elemental forces in careful balance all around us.

Sefer Y'tzirah positions the speaking human as a creative power. Yet in the end, the book understands humans not as stewards of nature but as cocreators with the elements and dimensions of the cosmos. To the *Book of Creation*, we are beings made up of the same material as all things, part of the delicate balance of the whole. Not only we humans, but all reality is made up of a divine essence that cannot be fully named or counted. Within this sacred reality, our power can only be exercised as all powers are—as one factor in the diversity of the cosmic temple, the great *makom*. In a world where we are learning how to interweave with the rest of Creation, this ancient, cryptic book may be exactly what we need.

NOTES

1. For purposes of this chapter, I will refer to Peter Hayman's "earliest recoverable version" of the text of *Sefer Y'tzirah*: Peter Hayman, *Sefer Yesira: Edition, Translation, and Text-Critical Commentary* (Tübingen: Mohr Siebeck, 2004), 5–6. There are many variant texts of the Book of Creation—the version Hayman has derived from comparing manuscripts is briefer than most and attempts to recover the earliest possible version of the book that we have (though the original version, Hayman and most others agree, is not recoverable). Translations of the text and the numbering of passages in *Sefer Y'tzirah*, which differs from version to version, are taken from my own translation and commentary: Jill Hammer, *Return to the Place: The Magic, Meditation, and Mystery of "Sefer Yetzirah"* (Teaneck, NJ: Ben Yehuda Press, 2020).

2. Hammer, 37.

3. Tzahi Weiss, *"Sefer Yetzirah" and Its Contexts: Other Jewish Voices* (Philadelphia: University of Pennsylvania Press, 2018), 73.

4. Peter Hayman, "Was God a Magician? *Sefer Yesira* and Jewish Magic," *Journal of Jewish Studies* 41, no. 2 (Autumn 1989): 225. Yehuda Liebes notes that the text does mention circumcision and Shabbat, so it is not completely devoid of Jewish concerns; see Yehuda Liebes, *The Ars Poetica of the "Sefer Yetzirah"* (Tel Aviv: Schocken Books, 2000).

5. Hammer, 31.

6. Hammer, 31.

7. Hammer, 2.

8. For a full discussion of the mediating power of Wisdom, see Ronit Meroz, "Between *Sefer Yetzirah* and Wisdom Literature," *Journal for the Study of Religions and Ideologies* 6, no. 18 (Winter 2007): 101–42.

9. David Mevorach Seidenberg, *Kabbalah and Ecology: God's Image in the More-than-Human World* (New York: Cambridge University Press, 2015), 21.

10. Hammer, 31.

11. Giulio Busi, "Engraved, Hewed, Sealed: *Sefirot* and Divine Writing in the *Sefer Yetzirah*," *Jerusalem Studies in Jewish Thought* 20 (2005): 1*–11*.

12. Yehuda Liebes, *The Ars Poetica of the "Sefer Yetzirah,"* 96.

13. Hammer, 37.

14. Hammer, 42.

15. Peter Hayman, "Some Observations on *Sefer Yetzirah*: The Temple at the Centre of the Universe," *Journal of Jewish Studies* 37, no. 2 (Autumn 1986): 176-82.

16. David Abram, *Becoming Animal: An Earthly Cosmology* (New York: Pantheon Books, 2010), 154.

17. Hammer, 126.

18. Lachelle Schilling, "Desierto Divino: Messages from the Earth," *Feminism and Religion* (blog), February 17, 2017, https://feminismandreligion.com/2017/02/17/desierto-divino-messages-from-the-earth-by-lachelle-schilling/.

19. Cynthia Moe-Lobeda, *Resisting Structural Evil: Love as Ecological-Economic Vocation* (Minneapolis: Fortress Press, 2013), xviii.

18

Hitbod'dut

Finding the Divine through Solitude in Nature

Rabbi Eli Herb

I WOKE UP in a hopeless terror during a night in 2012, remembering that it was the year when countries were to have implemented the Kyoto Protocols. The Kyoto Protocols were believed to be "too little, too late" by many of us in the climate change movement, and here we were, in 2012, when not one country in the world was even close to making those small but important corrections. Quite the opposite—greenhouse gas (GHG) emissions had only increased. It was then that my relationship to Judaism decisively changed. I had spent years plumbing the depths of our tradition to show that Judaism possessed integral teachings that required of Jews a commitment to sustainability and stringent environmental behavior. Now I needed a way out of despair, and I turned to Judaism, desperate for a lifeline. As a result, I rediscovered the most foundational spiritual aspect of my life, which has indeed given me a deep sense of faith even in such profoundly disheartening times.

In the Ukraine, in the late eighteenth and early nineteenth century, an extremely imaginative and creative Chasidic master, Rebbe Nachman of Bratzlav, required his disciples to engage in the practice of solitary prayer in nature. Rabbi Arthur Green observes, "The most essential religious practice of [the Chasidim] Bratslav, and that which Nachman constantly taught was to be placed above all else in his disciples' hierarchy of values, was this act of *hitbod'dut*, lone daily conversation with God."[1]

Because of Rebbe Nachman's severe prescriptive criteria, *hitbod'dut*, in its most idealized format, would never become a universal practice among the rest of world Jewry. Each aspect—going out alone, nullifying the self, solitude at night in an untraveled place *outside and in nature*, and speaking to God—is an uncomfortable pursuit. However, after personally engaging in *hitbod'dut* throughout my life and having taught it primarily to unaffiliated Jews for many years, I have discovered that the practice is grounding, illuminating, and inspiring, and thus I will attempt to translate this practice from its original pietist and ascetic settings to something that can be embraced by anyone, with transformative results.

I was not introduced to this practice by Rebbe Nachman, however. Rather, I came to *hitbod'dut* through the writings of American transcendentalist John Muir. Deeply inspired by him while I was in high school, I began spending hundreds and hundreds of hours on solitary walks in the mountains around my hometown. These were particularly powerful at night, when I found the raw personality of nature and the animation of my mind markedly different from the consciousness of daytime. John Muir's solitary path was to find divinity in the natural world. Wild places are always singing with the Living God, but this is especially the case at night and amplified significantly with solitude. Though Muir certainly sought to inspire others to take to wild places through his writings, his relationship to God was very different from Rebbe Nachman's. However, because I had already been introduced to the practice by Muir, Rebbe Nachman's practice of *hitbod'dut* resonated with me.

Rebbe Nachman taught:

> To merit being subsumed into the Root of the soul, i.e., to *return* and be included in unity with *HaShem* [*sic*], may God be blessed . . . is only possible through self-nullification [*bitul*]. That is, nullifying/transforming/softening oneself completely until subsumed with God.
>
> And it is impossible to come to this place of *bitul* without *hitbod'dut* because it is *only* through solitary, deliberate conversation between you and your Creator[2] that you can nullify your cravings.[3] And only then does one merit becoming subsumed into the Source.
>
> In its most essential form, *hitbod'dut* happens at night, when the world is devoid of worldly striving. During the day, when everyone is pursuing their materialistic ventures, [all the activities of the mind and body] confound a person's ability to enter into *d'veikut*.[4] And even if you are not all caught up in this striv-

ing, nonetheless *everyone else is* chasing vanities, and this makes it difficult to achieve self-nullification.

Also, *hitbod'dut* must happen in an isolated place *outside of town*, where people do not normally go. In a place where people pursue worldly affairs, even when they are not there, *hitbod'dut* is confused by the *impression* left by all the people, and you are unable to completely become subsumed into God. Thus, you need to go at night, off the beaten path.[5] And there, you can turn your heart and consciousness away from all the business of the world and nullify everything until you are able to reach a level of true self-nullification.[6]

Talking to God

Many American Jews do not believe in God at all.[7] The majority of American Jews have an ambivalent relationship to religion, and even if they report a belief in God, they share a very impersonal, Maimon-idean theology or even an agnosticism.[8] If at the core of *hitbod'dut* is a conversation between self and Creator, we American Jews face a particular challenge to adopting this practice: *With what or whom are we talking?*

Turning to the philosopher Martin Buber has proved to be helpful in passing on *hitbod'dut* to more secularized Jews. *Hitbod'dut* can be practiced as an I-Thou contemplative meditation. In Buber's experiences of I-Thou, "the Thou 'fills the horizon.' The rest of the world has not disappeared, but we no longer see it.... I take the person in as a whole, just as he or she is." At this moment of "the Eternal Now," as Buber called it, "a window of transcendence ... opens in the very midst of the time-space universe we occupy. I-Thou breaks down subject/object dualism and creates a new unity, the relation between the I and the Thou."[9]

When you begin to speak in *hitbod'dut*, it is important to know that you can, and should, say anything that comes to your mind. However, this is done with a meditative consciousness of addressing Thou. Actually using the word "You" is helpful. Beginning with "I don't know what to say to You" or "I don't even know You, I don't know who You are" opens the door to this meditative consciousness.

In other forms of meditation, the meditator focuses on something particular, like the breath. In *hitbod'dut*, the practitioner maintains a consciousness of addressing Thou. Whenever consciousness drifts away from addressing the You, as with breathing meditations, one gently and nonjudgmentally draws attention back to addressing You. It is much like having a long conversation with someone you love when, in the midst of listening, your mind does what minds do and drifts away from focusing on the words of your friend. You notice and draw your whole attention back to your friend.

This practice is effective even if the practitioner holds no theological "belief" at all. Here we are talking about a kind of consciousness and *not* a practice of theological assertion of belief. Entering the conversation with an assumption about who you are addressing will, as it would with another person, affect the conversation. We address the ultimate You because this consciousness transforms our perceptions of ourselves and the world around us. We are addressing the Wholly (Holy) Other. What is required is that one engage the practice fully, avoiding getting pulled along by the analytical "materialistic" mind, which will, as minds are wont to do, narrate the experience for you or introduce suspicion and doubt about the practice itself.

The most important aspect of the practice is to ground ourselves in experiences of the Transcendent—a classical way of expressing that which is the *Holy* Other. These experiences calm us, make us feel deeply connected and fully alive. In our times, when despair and paralysis are so common, *hitbod'dut* offers us a way of returning to the Source, from which we can engage in what is difficult and "re-*sourced*."

Nullification of the Self

Among the elements of *hitbod'dut* that are uncomfortable to embrace as practice, *bitul*, "self-nullification," is perhaps the most frightening. Allowing the self to dissolve into the Infinite is terrifying because, in many ways, the act resembles death. Rebbe Nachman himself makes this comparison, saying that one should pray with such intensity that one stands on the edge of death. In this, he is picking up a tradition held by his great-grandfather, the Baal Shem Tov, and thus many of the Chasidic masters.[10]

Martin Buber's work *I and Thou* helps us to take in this practice in a way that is more understandable and practicable for many of us. Because *I and Thou* is experiential, like much of Rebbe Nachman's writing, it resonates with the reader. The self, as we usually understand it, disappears. What remains is a self in relationship to a You—to the Other. For Buber, no other experience is possible; there is no such thing as complete dissolution of the self. But there is "the window of transcendence" in the experience of the relationship with the Other. Buber explains this experience:

> He is no longer He or She, limited by other He's and She's, a dot in the world grid of space and time, nor a condition that can be experienced and described, a loose bundle of named qualities. Neighborless and seamless, he is You and fills the firmament. Not as if there were nothing but he; but everything else lives in his light.... When *Thou* is spoken, the speaker has no thing for his object. For where there is a thing there is another thing. Everywhere it is bounded by others; *It* exists only through being bounded by others. But when *Thou* is spoken there is no thing. *Thou* has no bounds. When *Thou* is spoken the speaker has no thing; he indeed has nothing. But he takes his stand in *relation*.[11]

Buber is speaking here of an interaction with another human being. In this experience, one also approaches the ultimate "Thou," that is, God.

> For whoever pronounces the word God and really means You, addresses . . . the true You of his life that cannot be restricted by any other and to whom he stands in a relationship that includes all others.[12]

The practice of *hitbod'dut* is a deliberate posture of I-Thou. You might begin by addressing anything in nature you see or by addressing the cosmos or the earth. Speak to a tree, an animal, the sky, or the Great Mystery, calling them "You," as you would in conversation with a dear friend. As with all meditation, if you lose yourself in thought, drifting away from that primary posture of addressing You, then pause, note your drifting away, and return to addressing You. This allows the practitioner to access a state of I-Thou without the deathlike self-nullification that Rebbe Nachman prescribes but with some of the same affect.

The Untraveled Place

While night is the optimal time for *hitbod'dut*, Rebbe Nachman describes practicing *hitbod'dut* at all times during the day. Indeed *bitul* and solitude are all aspects of *hitbod'dut* that can be achieved during the day:

> Our Rebbe, may his memory be a blessing, had a private study in his room in which he could isolate himself. Even so, most of the time, when he wanted to be alone, he would walk in the meadows and the forests; he was alone there very often. Once, he and I walked through Medvedevka, where he had previously lived; the Rebbe gestured toward the fields and mountains and said, "Upon all of these fields and mountains that you can see, and all the places all about the town, I have been in all of those places so many times, secluding myself in prayer." And he told me that there was a particular place on the top of one of the highest mountains where there was a kind of geological depression and there he loved to pray alone. Sometimes, he walked in other places while he lived in the holy community of Medvedevka after he had already become a famous tzaddik. But this practice of secluding himself in prayer outside of town, he did before he was well known, when he lived in Mezbuz and after that when he lived in Zlatipoli. So too here, in the holy community of [Bratzlav], each and every day he secluded himself. And many times, he secluded himself for the entire day.[13]

And while Rebbe Nachman also taught that *hitbod'dut* can be practiced alone in your bedroom, under your tallit, or some other solitary place, nature is the best place, by far. In nature, he taught, you can hear "the song of the grasses" and the song of your own soul. The most surprising part of this practice, for many, is the centrality of an encounter with God, especially in recent years when our relationship with the Divine has become so abstract and impersonal that many Jews have difficulty even beginning such a practice. Yet, time and again, when I see people commit themselves to this practice, they are uplifted and surprised. "I forgot," said one participant joyfully, "I can speak to God!" The practice is re-sourcing precisely because it puts us in direct contact with the vibrancy of the earth and the presence of God. Through these experiences, our faith grows, and the love of that which we are working so hard to protect, our Mother Earth and all her life forms, becomes inspired and deeply connected. The experiences lift us out of despair and give our mission a crystal-clear purpose while simultaneously cleansing us, even if only for a few hours, of the anxiety of the materialistic mind.

During a long experiment with *hitbod'dut* while living in Boston, I was alone in a city preserve, and through the practice, I suddenly became aware of the millions of trees—a living expanse stretching across New England—all deeply connected with each other, with me, and with the Creator, who is forever creative and creating. For a moment, I shared a life force with all of these gentle and stalwart beings. Coming out of the woods that night, I felt elated, rooted, committed, resilient, and re-sourced. That memory and others have fed my soul for many years. I pray that you, too, are nourished by such deep connections to the rich and spiritually exhilarating, God-given earth and natural surroundings.

NOTES

1. Arthur Green, *Tormented Master: The Life and Spiritual Quest of Rabbi Nahman of Bratslav* (Woodstock, VT: Jewish Lights, 2013), 145. See also, e.g., *Shivchei Moharan, Maalat Hitbod'dut* 3.

2. Rebbe Nachman often writes in the third person. However, because the practice is *prescriptive*, I chose to translate certain portions, like this one, in the second person.

3. *Taavah, taavot*: "craving, lust, desire, passion; delight." It may be that it is most true to Rebbe Nachman to translate this word as "lusts." Many translators, including myself, are tempted to temper the language in favor of the word "desires." There is good reason for this as well. *Taavah* is closely related to "corporeality, worldliness" in *Likutei Moharan*. However, psychologically and spiritually, it may be better understood as "materialism."

4. *D'veikut*: "cleaving, attachment, devotion." It is synonymous here with Rebbe Nachman's aspiration of being subsumed into the Source of one's soul, that is, God.

5. *Baderech y'chidi*: literally, "on the road alone." Rebbe Nachman is referring us to *Pirkei Avot* 3:4, which he quoted at the beginning of this teaching (1:52).

6. Nachman of Bratzlav, *Likutei Moharan* 1:52:3:1–4.

7. See Michael Lipka, "Americans' Faith in God May Be Eroding," Pew Research Center, November 4, 2015, http://www.pewresearch.org/

fact-tank/2015/11/04/americans-faith-in-god-may-be-eroding/.

8. See *A Portrait of Jewish Americans* (Washington, DC: Pew Research Center's Religion and Public Life Project, September 30, 2013), http://www.pewforum.org/2013/10/01/jewish-american-beliefs-attitudes-culture-survey/.

9. Mike Comins, *A Wild Faith: Jewish Ways into Wilderness, Wilderness Ways into Judaism* (Woodstock, VT: Jewish Lights, 2007), 37.

10. Green, *Tormented Master*, 33.

11. Martin Buber, *I and Thou*, trans. Ronald Gregor Smith (Edinburgh: Clark, 1942), 8.

12. Buber, *I and Thou*, 75–76.

13. Nachman of Bratzlav, *Sichot HaRan*, 162.

19

Desert Torah

Listening for God in the Wilderness

Rabbi Mike Comins

In Hebrew, the Book of Numbers is titled *B'midbar*, "in the desert."
The action occurs in the Sinai wilderness, a land so arid that water
must be miraculously wrenched from rocks and the people owe their
lives to the daily manna. I have a name for the Israelites who escaped
Egypt and traveled the Sinai for forty years: the Generation of Miracles.
No others see divine intervention on such a massive scale—Moses's
rod, the Ten Plagues, the parting of the sea, the Revelation at Mount
Sinai. As the dependence on manna is absolute, later biblical books,
midrash, and Rabbinic commentaries paint the forty-year walkabout
as a paradigmatic Torah text on faith—a model picture of the covenant
that God establishes in order to prepare the people for life in the Land
of Israel.

And yet . . . the unparalleled miracles are an educational failure.
Repeatedly, the people disobey Moses's orders and question God's
promises while pining for the onions and watermelons left behind.
God's punishments continue until the narrative arc of the book is dev-
astatingly clear. Excepting Joshua and Caleb, every single adult who
left Egypt dies in the desert. The Generation of Miracles never sees the
Promised Land.

Who *does* merit the Land of Israel? The Generation of the Desert—
those born and raised in the wilderness. Might it be that miracles are
not enough to teach faith? Might there be other gifts for those parented
by wilderness? What does the desert teach?

• • •

Come walk the Sinai, the Arava, the Negev, the Judean desert.

Some places are hot, some are cold. The desert is both at the same time. Thirty- and forty-degree temperature swings are the norm. If the day is pleasant, the night is too cold. If the night is temperate, the daytime heat will melt your candy bar, and perhaps your equilibrium. Light is too intense for comfort. The sun blinds, dehydrates, kills. Like Hagar and Elijah, you can easily lose your way, finish your water, and find yourself facing collapse in a few short hours. In the desert, you get down to essentials. Water, shade, and a bit more water. The body wants little food. A heavy pack draws moisture from your body, which evaporates before you notice that you are sweating. You'll never see a Bedouin resting in the sun.

The desert tests people physically, and thus spiritually. If you don't know which canyons still have pools from the last rain or where to find the secret water cisterns of the desert people, hope and confidence evaporate. The desert can be mentally trying even when the body is not under duress.

> Sometimes the desert horizon is as straight as the ocean.
> Indistinguishable dry riverbeds, endless plains, the hot wind.
> Nothing to cling to. Nowhere to go.
> Infinite space; infinite fear.

> The only center is the center within.
> Be patient. Fear requires effort. Be still.
> Wait for the moment when the *ruach*[1] breathes fear into awe.
> Suddenly, sight finds its anchor in the heart. Eyes see an open
> horizon; spirit sees sheer possibility.

> The soul's shadows are no match for the sun. Life is exposed.
> Beauty and grief, love and fear, hope and pain—all shimmering
> in flames that once accosted Moses.
> I want to run away, but I cannot turn away.
> Dare I close my eyes, and look?

> The desert is a place to become as straight as the horizon, as
> sharp as a thorn.
> Learn to live with little. Learn to live in light so bright that nothing can remain hidden. Learn to live at risk.
> The contract reads: courage required.
> No exceptions.

The truth is that life everywhere is just as extreme as it is in the desert. Only we do our best to believe that it isn't, and in civilization, we can delude ourselves into thinking that we're getting away with it. The desert does not indulge those who cannot tell reality from a mirage. Pretense is not an option.

The desert is one of God's most precious gifts.

• • •

A midrash: "In order to acquire Torah and wisdom, one must make oneself _____ like this desert" (*B'midbar Rabbah* 1). Of course, the midrash does not have a blank in it, but that is how it was presented to us as we hiked with Israel Hevroni, a man who moved to the Negev and spent ten years in the desert in order to understand this one sentence. Before sharing the full midrash, he asked us to look around and fill in the blank ourselves.

In my work, I have repeated this exercise with hundreds of people. Every time, at least one person says the obvious. In order to acquire Torah and wisdom, one must make oneself *thirsty* like this desert. Thirst is the greatest fear in the desert. It is said to be the most painful way to die. And yet, we can't live without thirst. One who doesn't want to drink is one who *wants* to die.

Plants and animals everywhere are thirsty, but water's scarcity in the desert demands ingenuity. Lizards, rodents, and even larger mammals get their water directly from the food they eat. Unlike their forest relatives, many plants evolved to survive by spreading roots wide along the surface *and* deep into the earth. The desert rhubarb's broad, corrugated leaves, a rarity in the desert, enable it to collect dew and irrigate itself. The list of adaptations goes on and on.

My favorite is the Jericho rose. Unlike North American deserts, the lower Judean desert can go years without rainfall. When that happens, the Jericho rose shrivels into a small ball of tangled fibers. It can detach from its roots and travel like a tumbleweed. When the drought is prolonged, a part of its seeds will feed on the rest to stay alive. And when the rain comes, the Jericho rose fully expands in four hours, turning green and reproducing before the moisture in the soil evaporates. Christian pilgrims named it the "resurrection plant."

Thirst spawns creativity, patience, extreme receptivity, growth, and so much more that a student of Torah does well to emulate. Like the desert, we might feel the preciousness of every drop.

The original midrash fills in the blank with *hefker*. "Open" is a good translation for our context. One should be receptive to new insight when studying Torah. But *hefker* is often translated as "abandoned." Must I feel forsaken to acquire wisdom and Torah?

One path forward is to understand *hefker* in its legal meaning, the term for a thing not owned. To acquire wisdom, you cannot be owned by a false god, whether a pagan deity or the subtle gods of fame or wealth, or selfishness or . . . fill in your own blank. One must be available if one is to succeed in Torah study.

Well and good. But the common meaning of *hefker* is "abandoned." The desert is indeed indifferent to my survival. Must I feel like a motherless child to receive its gifts? Must I be deserted in the desert to feel God's love? Must I know the despair of separation to acquire wisdom? In reality, these are false questions; they imply a choice I do not actually have. At some point, every human feels separated and unloved, threatened by a hostile world and humbled by the unfairness of life. We all know abandonment.

Because there are moments when I am battered and defeated, the Torah's command to choose life (Deuteronomy 30:19) is significant and powerful.

Naaseh v'nishma (Exodus 24:7), said the Israelites in response to the Revelation at Mount Sinai: "We will do and we will understand," seemingly the opposite order of the way we moderns practice education. But when my will surrenders and follows the command, my heart begins to understand that I am not alone and that fear and despair need not be permanent.

Like a desert plant, I choose life. I seek connection.

On a good day, I walk the desert as if I were walking in God's womb. At my best, I study Torah like a Jericho rose.

• • •

The most noticeable sound in the desert is silence, an irony encapsulated in biblical Hebrew long before Simon and Garfunkel. *Dalet-bet-*

reish, the three root letters of *midbar*, "desert," are best known as the root letters for *dibur*, "speech." Those who walk the desert cannot escape the koan: *hamidbar m'dabeir*, "the desert speaks." What does desert silence say?

This is the challenge for Elijah. Near the end of his career, he is brought by God to Mount Sinai,[2] where he hears the *kol d'mamah dakah*, the "still small voice" (I Kings 19:12). An iconic phrase from the King James translation, it was often understood by Reform Judaism's founders as the voice of one's conscience. Modern scholarship, however, begs to differ. Contemporary, mainstream translations of the Hebrew include "a soft murmuring sound," "a tiny, whispering sound," "a gentle little breeze," and "a sound of sheer silence."[3]

Some context is in order. Elijah lives an astonishing life of divine service—chastising King Ahab on God's behalf, being fed by ravens while hiding afterward, miraculously multiplying flour and oil, reviving a dead boy, and finally, defeating the prophets of Baal in the famous contest on Mount Carmel (I Kings 17–18). God's supernatural intervention is normal for Elijah. But I Kings 19 finds Elijah seemingly abandoned by God. When Ahab's wife, Queen Jezebel, threatens to kill him, he flees to the Negev desert. After a day of wandering, he lays down in the sand. Once the right-hand man of God, the mighty prophet resigns himself to die in a nameless, dry riverbed. One can only imagine Elijah's despair.

But the miracles are not over. An angel wakens Elijah and feeds him. Without further food or water, he travels forty days (the period of Revelation) to Mount Sinai (the place of Revelation). Wind, earthquake, and fire ensue, reminiscent of the sounds and sights Moses experienced as the Torah was given. God has not abandoned Elijah! The reward for his service awaits: nothing less than the second Revelation from God on Mount Sinai! One can only imagine Elijah's elation.

And then, shock. The narrator repeats it three times. Elijah and the reader share the surprise. God is "passing by" the mountaintop, but God is not in the wind, not in the earthquake, and not in the fire (I Kings 19:11–12). Instead, Elijah hears a shattering question through the *kol d'mamah dakah*: *Mah l'cha fo, Eliyahu?* (I Kings 19:13). "Why are you here, Elijah?" the Jewish Publication Society translates. Many Christian translations concur,[4] while others offer, "What are you doing here?"[5]

Both play loose with the Hebrew to offer a colloquial interpretation that, to my mind, makes little sense. Did God miraculously bring Elijah to Mount Sinai in order to ask him why he came or what he thinks he's doing? Clearly, it was God's idea, not Elijah's!

I propose a literal translation: "What is for you here, Elijah?" What is for you here, *in the desert?* Elijah found what any of us find when we walk deep into wilderness. Bank accounts and stock portfolios are worthless. Past accomplishments do not lead to water.

After fleeing from Jezebel into the desert, Elijah surrendered to the heat and asked to die. "It is enough! Take my life now, O God; I am no better than my forebears" (I Kings 19:4). Better than his forebears? Rather than ask for water, he thinks about his life and those who came before him. After years of being God's chosen, after so much personal sacrifice, he is unable to accept abandonment. Elijah would rather die.

Elijah faces a challenge that many of us experience in our lives. What do I do when the qualities I have intentionally cultivated, when the past achievements I stand upon, when the story I tell myself about my place in the world—when everything that has worked for me in the past—no longer serves? When my old ways lead directly to suffering and, possibly, to death?

God responds to Elijah's depression by bringing him to Mount Sinai. The divine therapy takes the form of a question: *Mah l'cha fo,* "What is for you here?" Not where you were, but where you are. If I were to offer a translation according to the context, it would be "What *are* you here, Elijah?"

Who is anyone when stripped of all that seemed important, when all we have achieved means nothing? How will I survive when friends and loved ones have left or been taken, when it seems only a miracle can save me—when life is suddenly reduced to the minimal and the essential?

Who am I?

Equally important: Who will I be?

Elijah listens for God in the expected places: the wind, the earthquake, the fire. But he only hears God in the silence. While most modern translations of *kol d'mamah dakah* posit that Elijah hears an audible sound, I side with Abraham Joshua Heschel ("a voice of silence")[6] and King

James ("a still small voice"). The Torah recognizes soundless voices (Genesis 4:10), and that, I believe, is described here. An inaudible voice that can only be "heard" from within, but clearly does not come from within. A holy voice, emerging from an open sky, a limitless horizon, and a thirsty landscape where life thrives despite the odds; a voice that shatters expectations and points to possibility; a voice that confronts and consoles; a voice with a question.

When it comes to Revelation, perhaps silence is for questions as thunder is for commandments. Moses receives Torah to the sounds and sights of major pyrotechnics, while Elijah is forced to listen in the silence, to the silence, from the silence. He hears a question that thunder would overwhelm and conceal.

When the Torah we inherit through study and deed guides us to undeniable truth—in those luminous, prescient moments when we glimpse what God wants of us—do we not tremble in awe as if before lightning and thunder? And when we are quiet enough to hear what the clutter and noise have blocked from our vision and imagination, do we not hear questions only we can answer? Do we not find wisdom no book can give: intuitions, understandings, and perceptions only we can discern?

The Revelation of Moses and the Revelation of Elijah—do we not need both?

•••

God provided the Generation of the Desert with the daily manna to keep them alive, but it was the bare minimum. The Israelites still needed to find water and build shelter. They needed to track wild goats and search for edible plants; they had to learn to protect themselves from enemies, whether human or natural. Even in the desert—especially in the desert—it takes more than food to survive. The Israelites no doubt gazed in awe at the mountains, the stars, and the moon, and took comfort in the early morning sun of winter and the midnight breeze of summer. I imagine as wilderness dwellers they might learn to appreciate that God's world is a good world, an expression of God's love.

In the desert (b'midbar), the Israelites received a different kind of education. No more reliance on onetime, spectacular miracles. Instead, they developed an appreciation for daily miracles and a hard-earned belief that even the harshest place in the world is a good place: where living beings rely on their ability to listen to the terrain and creatively adapt, and where the people's fate depends mostly on their own initiative, even as they realize their dependence on God's grace with every bite of manna and splash of rain.

Near the ancient, spiritual center—the Temple in Jerusalem—if one stands in the right place, rain falling on one foot drains to the Mediterranean while raindrops on the other head toward the Judean desert. Jerusalem rises between the fertile plains to the west and the wilderness to the east. From the hilltops, one gazes on the Dead Sea. The view is the message: No matter how prosperous your farmlands make you, never forget the wilderness from which you came. Never let the desert out of your sight. Never forget the desert's gifts.

NOTES

1. The Hebrew word for wind and for spirit.
2. The text refers to the mountain as Horeb, the northern tradition's name for Mount Sinai.
3. In order, translations are from the new Jewish Publication Society translation of the *Tanach*, the New American Bible, *The Harper Collins Study Bible*, and the New Revised Standard Version of the Bible.
4. New American Bible (Revised Edition), Common English Bible, and more.
5. New International Version, New Revised Standard Edition, and more.
6. Abraham Joshua Heschel, *God in Search of Man* (New York: Harper Torchbooks, 1955), 186. Heschel writes, "Literally: *a voice of silence.*" And in the next paragraph, "The voice he perceived was almost stillness."

20

Composting and Sacred Time
Lessons from a Pumpkin

Rabbi Michael Birnholz

By nature and training, I am a curious learner. I frequently try new activities, learn new skills, or taste new foods. In doing so, my rabbinic training is activated, and I weave that experience into an act of study to be shared with other people. On this occasion, I began with a desire to harvest the seeds from a pumpkin and to roast them and the flesh for a tasty snack. I could certainly have done this for my own pleasure, but I also needed an activity for an outdoor Shabbat program—a perfect outdoor fall experience to share. In Judaism, we don't use an artifact, share a text, or do a ritual in isolation; we connect these to other people or to elements of our culture or tradition. I was challenged to find a way that the act of carving a pumpkin could illustrate Torah (study), *avodah* (ritual action), or *g'milut chasadim* (acts of loving-kindness).

As I considered the round pumpkin—the rind, flesh, and seeds—an image came to mind. We humans tend to perceive time linearly, moving from past to present and into the future. Jewish tradition describes the flow of time as a cycle or bubble of time. The outer circumference is shalom—the ideal of wholeness, harmony, and peace. Connected to descriptions of the Garden of Eden, the world-to-come (*olam haba*), and the messianic age, these "ends" or "edges" are times and places of perfection where all is working in balance and in concert. Within this bubble of shalom is this world we inhabit, this world (*olam hazeh*). From the moment that Adam and Eve ate from the Tree of the Knowledge of Good and Evil until the future arrival of the Messiah (or the messianic age), we have and will continue to exist in this time and place of separate parts and broken systems. We have free will, but we are obligated to seek and build order in the chaos and shards of Creation. Jewish tradition is full of rituals, artifacts, and stories that we use to try to get back in sync with the ideals that we "remember" from Eden or we imagine from the messianic era. The past and future are bound to and guide our present. We work toward the best in "this world" as we are inspired by the ideal "shalom" of the world-to-come.

Bringing in that pumpkin to carve and to harvest the seeds and flesh to roast for our Shabbat program offered a powerful model of Jewish time and awareness. Consider what we do to consume that pumpkin. First, we slice open the inedible, protective rind to reveal the flesh and the seeds; next, we separate all three layers: seeds, flesh, and rind—the outer, middle, and center layers. While we use most of the seeds and flesh, we need to discard the stem, rind, and the gooey bits still containing leftover seeds. Should we throw them in the trash or into compost? If we discard the waste into trash and send it on the way to the landfill, it is easy to see a pumpkin linearly. It is merely trash to get rid of. However, once we start composting the "waste" of the pumpkin, a very different image emerges. The rind and seeds placed into the compost tie the past and the future together in unexpected ways.

One might say that the rind and innards are the past and the seeds are the future. The rind is the part of the pumpkin one cannot consume and is left behind. The seeds can be planted to create a new generation of plants to bear more fruit. On the other hand, the equation can be flipped completely. With the act of composting, one can see the rind decomposing with other vegetable waste, becoming the soil, ready and full of nutrients for the next generation. The seeds, in contrast, are the link to the past, holding the genetic memory of the plant at its core, ready to bring that past through the present into the future.

In addition to roasting just the seeds and some of the flesh and discarding the rest, gaining a sense of the pumpkin as a bubble with many layers, having experienced cutting into the pumpkin, having eaten and discarded what remains, we found an illustration of the flow of time around us. The physical appearance of the pumpkin is a concrete model of the dynamics of Jewish time. The pumpkin has outer, middle, and inner layers, allowing us to ponder past, present, and future. This act of eating touched the transcendent and expanded an everyday experience. We could see ourselves connected across time and space to something eternal and infinite. This act of finding Torah in the consumption of a pumpkin led to a wonderful lesson and discussion. I, and I think the participants as well, left with an incredible visual experience of Jewish time.

The words of *Pirkei Avot* 3:21, *Im ein kemach, ein Torah; im ein Torah, ein kemach* ("If there is no sustenance, there is no [values of] Torah; if there is no [values of] Torah, the food you consume won't sustain you"), echoed in my consciousness. Food and Torah are bound together. Just a few weeks later, in the midst of a group Torah study, I found myself witnessing the same illustration. How often (pre-Covid) did we sit for a nosh during Torah study? On this morning, in addition to the bagels and cream cheese, I ate pieces of melon. It was a bit of sweetness and refreshment to offset the salty starch of my bagel bites. The pumpkin had offered an act of eating and discarding, leading me to the Jewish understanding of time; here was an act of Torah (study) reminding me of a valuable and vital act of *avodah* (ritual action) that applies to our consumption of food. Instead of eating food as a supplementary activity to our study of Torah, this connection added the action of eating and disposing of the melon as a window into Jewish time to the spiritual experience.

What was true for the pumpkin was true for the melon. I experienced the same dynamic, but a different, additional layer of connection and action presented itself as well. Clearing the table and remembering the pumpkin, I considered how to discard the waste left over after our nosh. I could work linearly, sending the trash to the landfill, where it would contaminate the land and generate destructive greenhouse gases to fill our atmosphere. Yet, I wanted to embrace the *avodah* of the pumpkin and Jewish time, moving in a way that preserves that matter in the flow of energy and time and protects the earth. By recycling and composting what we were able to, we did not just illustrate Jewish time; we applied that spiritual connection to the work of our hands and the way we care for our resources. There is a whole movement dedicated to "farm to table," focused on being aware and appreciative of where our food comes from. This window into the cycle and motion of Jewish time challenges us to see the experience of food in its largest circle and to take responsibility after we eat for getting the back to the "farm."

Many Jewish values and stories remind us that we should be limiting our waste and dedicating our efforts to recycling and composting what we can. If we cannot do this in all of our acts of eating, then we must apply it to at least some of them.

I typically think of Rabbi Ben Bag Bag's quote "Turn it, turn it for everything is within it" (*Pirkei Avot* 5:26) as a search for meaning in the study of Torah. The experience of pumpkins and melons in Jewish time offered insight into a different dimension of motion in our world. Time and resources are moving around us. As we consume food, we work not just to appreciate the source of our food, but to invest awareness and action into the full cycle of food—what we eat and what we can return to the earth to honor our past and enrich our future.

Time is a hard value to illustrate concretely. Composting is an action that is still not the norm in much of the United States. That said, seeking to embrace the values and practice of composting from a Jewish perspective will assuredly connect the act of eating to the powerful cycle of time and resources.

FOR MORE INFORMATION ON JUDAISM AND COMPOSTING:

Koenig, Leah. "Composting: A Jewish Practice?" My Jewish Learning. https://www.myjewishlearning.com/article/composting-a-jewish-practice/.

Weinbach, Eliezer. "Judaism and Food Waste." https://drive.google.com/file/d/1l405wDokq9z6X38NgRexkr2Ei-mG2sd0/view?ts=5efb8791.

21

The Weight of the World
Spiritual Grounding through Making Art

RABBI ADINA ALLEN

As we navigate this time of increasing climate chaos, most of us are aware on an intellectual level of the profound effect human activity is having on the earth and the life systems that support us. We read every day in the news, and experience in our own lives, the challenges brought on by increased drought, more frequent and severe wildfires, more intense flooding, rising temperatures, hurricanes and storms, the rapid spread of disease, crop failure, species extinction, and the list goes on. These changes affect our lives in real and tangible ways in terms of our physical health, housing, financial stability, and strains placed upon community programs and resources, to name a few. Even when we are not directly in harm's way, we can emotionally, psychologically, and spiritually shut down such that we cannot process or respond to what is happening in generative ways.

Less seen and often unacknowledged is the psychological toll climate change can take, including fatigue, depression, overwhelm, and anxiety. Underlying and encompassing all of these is the toll that living through the intensity of this time can take on our spiritual lives, which is rarely, if ever, named. Whether we have a sense of ourselves as "spiritual" or not, this can manifest as a profound sense of grief and disconnection. It "impoverishes our emotional and our sensory life," impeding "our capacity to process and respond to information" in generative ways, writes environmental activist Joanna Macy in her seminal work *World as Lover, World as Self*.[1] Yet, as she teaches, these feelings are precisely what we need to adapt and survive.

This chapter explores the ways in which the Jewish Studio Process, a methodology that incorporates traditional Jewish text study and hands-on engagement with art materials using tools from the field of art therapy, can help us to experience, honor, and creatively channel our despair, grief, and anger. Through personal narrative, exploration of Jewish texts, and creative exercises, we can shift our orientation so that rather than being crushed by these emotions, new energy, creativity, and empowerment can come forth and new visions for our future can emerge.

Whenever we reach the limits of our own ability to process, make sense of, and respond to the world around us, we need ways to move out of our intellect and into our other ways of knowing—intuition, imagination, memory, emotions. When we are overwhelmed by an experience, we need tools that help us calm our nervous system, regulate our emotions, and bring ourselves back into an open and receptive state. When we feel cut off from God, we need practices that help reweave us into the fabric of Creation. Creativity is this power, this practice, this wellspring—the tool that helps to make challenges bearable and brings possibility to that which seemed impossible.

Creativity in our society is often seen as something frivolous or extra, something we can indulge in in our free time, if we are privileged, or, alternatively, focus on in our careers, if we are talented. In fact, creativity is the life force energy that exists within every human being. We learn this foundational truth from Torah. The opening line of our most sacred text begins: B'reishit bara Elohim, "In the beginning, God created" (Genesis 1:1). God, first and foremost, is the creative force of the universe. A few verses later, we read that human beings are made b'tzelem Elohim, "in the image of this Divine Creative Force" (1:27). Each and every one of us is created as inherently creative simply by dint of being human. It is the source of our deepest power and is our access point to connection with God. Our creativity is where we and the Divine meet to partner in the ongoing work of shaping and reshaping our world.

In Torah, God creates out of an innate impulse and the mess of what existed prior. The world was not, as we are so often taught, created from nothing. Instead, as Torah teaches, before Creation there were raw materials on hand: water, wind, darkness, the depths, chaos, and void. So too we all contain these elements within us, and increasingly in our world, so too can we use our creativity to work with what is on hand

and transform it to what comes next. Rather than turn away from these materials, God turns toward them, changing chaos and void into the sparkle of stars, the swell of sea, the colors of sunset. From the beginning of the Torah, God shines a light on the power and purpose of creativity as a means for being with challenge, transforming what is into what comes next and bringing forth the world we desire.

In my role as rabbi and creative director of Jewish Studio Project (JSP), I have helped to bring forth a process for accessing and activating creativity in service of personal healing and collective change. The method we have created, the Jewish Studio Process, comes from the foundational work my mother, Pat B. Allen, PhD, ATR, has brought forth in the field of art therapy. Pat created the Open Studio Process, a methodology now used in diverse communities across the globe. The core components of this process are (1) intention setting, (2) art making, and (3) witness writing. To this method we have added spiritual grounding and *beit midrash* (textual inquiry), creating a new iteration: the Jewish Studio Process. Each element of the Jewish Studio Process offers useful practices for helping us to process the emotional, psychological, and spiritual effects of climate change.

Spiritual grounding is a way to come into resonance with ourselves and with each other, if we are practicing in a group setting. Spiritual grounding can consist of song, silence, movement, check-in, art warm-up, or any other ways we have of settling into the space, connecting with one another, and inviting something bigger and beyond ourselves into our process. Spiritual grounding is especially important when using this process to interface with challenging personal or societal issues, such as climate change, as a way to begin to decrease our level of activation and regulate our nervous system. And it is a way to begin to reweave strands of connection—to ourselves, to community, and to the Divine when the fabric of our being has become torn and frayed.

Spiritual grounding prepares us for *beit midrash*, the ancient place and practice of Jewish text study. The word *midrash* comes from the Hebrew word *lidrosh*, meaning "to seek or inquire." In the Jewish Studio Process *beit midrash* we explore a text—be it Jewish, secular, poetry, news article, or something else—with the goal of seeing what that text brings up for us. When we are experiencing something acute in our environment, *beit midrash* can be a practice of coming into contact with what we are feeling. We may turn to the weekly Torah portion or a beloved collection of poetry, open to a page, and allow ourselves to rest on one sentence or phrase and to see what it evokes for us in light of what we are dealing with. In this way, text study can be approached almost as an experience of serendipity in which we imagine that whatever we need to read or hear is close at hand. On other occasions, we may look at texts on a particular topic, such as a recent news article predicting sea level rise over the next decade, a report detailing the effects of particulate matter in our air long after the smoke has cleared, or even something more hopeful such as the role fungi can play in bioremediation. We may use any text as a mirror to see what it reflects back to us about ourselves and our situation.

Intention setting follows *beit midrash* as a way of grounding in the present moment and asking oneself: What do I need now? In this process, an intention is written down in one to two sentences as a simple statement of what one seeks to receive from the art-making practice. An intention is written without any striving words such as "try" or "want," but rather in the present tense as though it is already happening. For example, sentences may begin "I open to . . . ," "I release . . . ," or "I explore. . . ." With regard to working with the emotional and spiritual effects of climate change, intentions I have written include "I receive guidance on how to be of highest service at this moment in the world," "I feel the grief of this moment and create space for it to open into something else," and "I reconnect with God in this moment of feeling abandoned and forlorn." Intention is a way we set the parameters of our experience and decide what we want to invite into our process. On a spiritual level, intention is a way we align ourselves with a force greater than ourselves. Intention comes from the Latin *intendere*, meaning "to reach toward." As my mother teaches, we decide what we are reaching out toward and imagine that what we call to is reaching back toward us.

From here, we move into art making, that is, exploration with materials. Materials can be anything from paints, pens, sculpture, or collage to writing, music, vocal improvisation, arranging found natural materials on the forest floor, or movement. The goal of this part of the process is to work with materials in a way that is pleasurable, with the understanding that when we are in an open and relaxed state, things that have been stuck can move to us and through us. This is vital when attending to the emotional, spiritual, and psychological strain of living through this time of increasing climate chaos. So often when it comes to climate change, we suffer not only from what is happening directly to us, but also from what we witness others going through, and from our predictions for the future. A 2019 *Mother Jones* article quotes Sarah Myhre, a former senior research associate at the University of Washington's School of Oceanography, as saying that she experiences "a profound level of grief on a daily basis because of the scale of the crisis that is coming, and I feel I'm doing all I can but it's not enough."[2] So much of the psychological and spiritual impact of climate change comes from what we are sure will happen in the future—the story has been written, and there is no way to change how it ends.

In contrast to the feelings climate change elicits in us, the primary guideline in this process of art making is to follow pleasure. In the face of the realities and catastrophic predictions of climate change, the truth is we are here now, alive on this planet. I believe we have an obligation to advocate, educate, and organize to mitigate the effects of climate change in order to create a more just and livable future, *and* we also have an obligation to bask in, enjoy, celebrate, and give gratitude for our lives, for this planet, and for the incredible web of interconnectedness that supports us in every moment. The principle of following pleasure instructs us to surrender the idea of "working on" whatever issue we have been holding, of trying to "understand" or "solve" an issue, and instead allow it to work on us. Another way to say this is to follow the energy, to follow what calls to us, to create, but, in our creating, to let ourselves be led. Here, the focus is on the somatic experience of materials. For instance, if we are working with two-dimensional art materials, we allow ourselves to follow the way a brush moves on the page, the depth of a particular color, and the way it feels to make certain shapes or patterns. Art making invites us back into our own vitality and life force as we, through the use of materials, access the flow of our creativity and come back home to ourselves.

We harvest from our art making through witness writing, that is, we sit back and receive from our creative output. What do we see on the page? What do we sense in our body? Witness writing is a practice of writing in response to both our piece and our process. We let all thoughts, feelings, associations, stories, and even the extraneous thoughts we think do not matter, onto the page. All of it goes into our witness. In a world where we so often live in our heads, art making takes us into our other ways of being and of knowing—intuition, imagination, emotion, and memory. Witness, then, is a practice for beginning to translate what occurred in art making back to our mind. At the end of witness writing, we check back in with our intention and ask: In what, if in any way, does my piece and/or my process speak to what I originally wrote down? Witness writing is a way to harvest ideas or insights from our process, to check in with ourselves to see where we are now, and to listen for what we are being called to next. When using the process in connection to climate change, we may have come in with a particular idea of what we "must" do to take action on a particular issue. The process is a way, ultimately, of inviting God to partner with us, to guide us, and to help us sense where we are truly being called rather than what we "think" we must do.

Of course, we do not always end in a place of clarity. It is often the case that we end with a new question or become aware of another issue or struggle we need to work with. The process is meant to be cyclical. Engaging this way is a practice. What comes to us in our witness writing serves as fodder for our next session.

Anyone who is awake to the reality of climate change has at some point spent sleepless nights or anxious days asking: Is it too late? Do we deserve to die? Who will save us now? Is this how humanity ends? These were the thoughts running through my head as I sat at my desk in the eerie light of a sunless, smoke-filled day, trying to write about *t'shuvah* and the power of change while feeling that the worst predictions for the future had already become inevitable.

In the throes of despair, unable to evoke anything of hope to say, I turned to the Jewish Studio Process. I closed my computer, set an intention, opened my paints, and let myself be soothed by the way water and color flowed onto the paper, one hue of blue mixing into another, clouds, heavens, sea, sky swirled together as one. The movement of brush on paper absorbed my attention, and my thoughts *about* the world began to dissipate as my sense of connection *to* the world began to grow. At some point as I was painting, I looked up at the bush dotted with purple flowers outside my window. All morning as I had been trying to write against my grief and certainty, it had seemed as though the world was deserted—no pedestrians passing by on the sidewalk, no insects buzzing around, not a chirp of birdsong or flutter of a wing. As I painted, something changed; the world began to open to me again. I paused midway through my painting and looked up to see a hummingbird, iridescent wings catching whatever light there was, shimmering in her blue-green and red-throated colors, diving expectantly into the open blossoms, gathering the sweet nectar and pollinating as she went from flower to flower, nourishing and being nourished, giving and receiving all in the same breath.

This is creativity. It is a practice of coming back, again and again, to pleasure, to vitality, to the open, awaiting flower and all that gives us life in the face of everything that is dying. In the ever-changing nature of our creation—it looks like sky at first and then it is the sea—we can feel certainty's grip on us loosen as we are reminded of the truth that nothing is ever one thing and everything is always changing. In the messy, untamable-ness of our art, we are reminded that we have agency and power to act, but we are not in control. In the serendipity and surprise of what comes through us onto the page, we soften into the knowing that we and the Divine create together, and that we can ask for and open to what it is we need no matter what it is we are facing.

NOTES

1. Joanna Macy, *World as Lover, World as Self* (Berkeley, CA: Parallax Press, 2007), 93.
2. David Corn, "It's the End of the World as They Know It: The Distinct Burden of Being a Climate Scientist," *Mother Jones*, July 8, 2019, https://www.motherjones.com/environment/2019/07/weight-of-the-world-climate-change-scientist-grief/.

Infinite Love

Rabbi Efrat Rotem

אַהֲבַת הָעוֹלָם אֲהַבְתָּ,

With infinite love You have loved the planet.

אוֹתָנוּ לִמַּדְתָּ, עַל כֵּן, יָהּ אֱלֹהֵינוּ,

Therefore, You taught us, Yah our God,

בְּשָׁכְבֵנוּ עַל אַדְמָתֶךָ, וּבְקוּמֵנוּ

that when we lie down on Your earth and when we rise up

לֶאֱכֹל מִפְּרִי אַדְמָתֶךָ,

to eat of the produce of Your land,

נָשִׂיחַ בִּגְבוּל יְכָלְתֵּנוּ

we should meditate on the limits of our capacity

לְהָבִין אֶת עוֹלָמְךָ שֶׁבָּרָאתָ,

to understand the world that You created,

הַמֻּרְכָּב מִנִּי־עַד,

in its incalculable complexity.

וְנִשְׂמַח בְּעָצְמָתוֹ וּבְיוֹפִיו הַנִּמְצָא בַּכֹּל.

We will rejoice in its potency and beauty found in everything.

מִצְוֹתֶיךָ לִשְׁמֹר וְלַעֲבֹד, לְהִזָּהֵר,

You have commanded us to cultivate and preserve, be mindful,

לְהָגֵן וּלְלַמֵּד הֵן בָּנוּ לְעֹלָם וָעֶד.

protect and inculcate these responsibilities deep in our hearts forever.

כִּי הָאֲדָמָה וְהַמַּיִם, הַשָּׁמַיִם וְהָאֲוִיר

For the soil and the water, the sky and the air—

הֵם חַיֵּינוּ וְאֹרֶךְ יָמֵינוּ,

they are our life and they lengthen our days,

וְקִיּוּמֵנוּ כָּרוּךְ בְּזֶה שֶׁלָּהֶם, יוֹמָם וָלַיְלָה.

and our very existence is intertwined with theirs, day and night.

וְאַהֲבָתְךָ אַל תָּסִירִי מֵהֶם וּמִמֶּנּוּ לְעוֹלָמִים.

May Your love never leave them and us.

בָּרוּךְ אַתָּה יְיָ, אוֹהֵב הָעוֹלָם וְכָל אֲשֶׁר בּוֹ.

Blessed are You, Adonai, who loves the planet teeming with life.

Text co-translated to English with the help of Rabbi Levi Weiman-Kelman.

The Story of the Pizza

Rabbi Joel M. Mosbacher, DMin

WHEN MY WIFE and I would take our first child out to dinner at a restaurant, they would get impatient, as kids do, in what seemed like the interminable time between when the server took our order and when the food actually arrived. At some point, when our oldest was six or so, they whined at me, "Why is the food taking so long?" And in a moment of inspiration, I began to explain in exquisite detail.

"Well, Ari, you know, the pizza doesn't grow here in the restaurant. In order to make the pizza dough, the chef first has to travel to Iowa to get the grain to make the flour that is in the dough we love so much. Then, she has to fly to Rome to get the Roma tomatoes to make the yummy pizza sauce and then on to Wisconsin to get milk from the Holstein cows to make the cheese. And that's not all. Then, because she doesn't want to serve the pizza on napkins, she has to fly off to China to buy the china that we will eat the pizza on." And on and on. And, if I timed it just right or if my creative juices were really flowing on an extra-slow night at the pizza joint, Ari would be transfixed by my story until the moment that delicious pizza showed up.

Thus was invented "The Story of the Pizza." There were other volumes, of course. There was "The Story of the Grilled Cheese," "The Story of the Pasta with Pesto," and "The Story of the Matzah Ball Soup." To my surprise, it worked almost every time.

It was only sometime later that what began as a stalling tactic to keep the restless natives a little less restless became a spiritual practice for me around saying *HaMotzi* before I eat.

Of course, traditionally, we are blessing "the Holy One who brings forth bread from the earth" when we say that prayer. And that's important to note.

But it turns out that for me, and my family, and even for my congregation as I sometimes frame a communal *HaMotzi*, the moment before we eat can be transformed into a moment that we take to reflect on the immensely complex and intricate series of things that took place to make that food appear on our plates, to appreciate the innumerable people who were involved and the miraculous earth on which we live.

Challah doesn't grow at the store, you know. Someone tilled the land, and then someone planted the wheat seed, and someone watered the earth, and someone weeded the soil around the growing plant. And then, someone harvested the grain, separated the wheat from the chaff, and ground the wheat into flour. And someone put that flour in a bag and put the bag on a truck, and someone drove that truck to the grocery store, and someone unloaded the truck, and someone put the bag of flour on the shelf. And then, the baker came to buy flour. A cashier sold it to the baker and put the purchase into another bag.

And that's just the flour! How about the sugar, and the yeast, and the eggs, and the salt, and the sesame seeds!

The Rabbis of our tradition encourage us to say one hundred blessings a day. That can sound overwhelming, but if, in saying *Motzi*, we could silently bless and thank the earth for its abundance and also bless and thank every person who made it possible for that yummy challah to appear on that plate on the bimah, we'd be at one hundred blessings before we ever put that first olive's worth of bread in our mouths.

"The Story of the Pizza" is the way we thank the planet, and everyone on it, and the Holy One of Blessing for conspiring to make it possible for us to sustain our bodies and our souls. Six-year-old Ari taught me how to truly say *HaMotzi* and really, really mean it.

The Sacred Power
of the Shabbat Stroll

RABBI DANIEL A. WEINER and RABBI AVI B. FINE

THE PACIFIC NORTHWEST has the dubious distinction of the designation of the "none zone," where the responses of a significant cohort to questions of religious affiliation elicit the terse answer "None." What is now more commonplace across the country began more than a decade ago here in Seattle, with the pride its populace places in nonconformity and a rugged spiritual individualism. At its worst, it is a kind of solipsistic narcissism that marks the broader contemporary culture. At its best, it inspires a creative and entrepreneurial approach to faith formation and community.

A potent driver of this trend is the inherent and overwhelming natural beauty of the region. For many, nature is their "cathedral" or "sanctuary," and a personal immersion in and connection to the natural world provides a sufficient, if not complete, experience of the transcendent. For these and other "seekers," their rejection of established religious communities is often more a result of a lack of knowledge and experience, many having rejected their faith at a young age, never to double back for a more adult reassessment. Those who have returned to a more mature engagement with their faiths of origins are often surprised to find meaning and purpose that awaited them all along.

And so, providing opportunities to bask in the power of nature within a Jewish context offers the chance to engage skeptics and cynics with a vehicle for holiness with which they are comfortable while introducing them to spiritual insights that can greatly augment the experience. The Shabbat stroll, a staple of traditional Sabbath observance, framed within this larger context, offers a mutually reinforcing embrace of both the rest and retreat of the day with the rejuvenating energy of Creation. Rabbi Avi B. Fine blends these affirming forces in the following ritual:

Jewish liturgy may spiritually move us in any space, but in the outdoors the words of our prayers give me the language to express my innermost feelings. After a lifetime of learning the words of our prayer book, I now call on them when I am outside. The fixed practice of praying in a synagogue equips me with the structure that shapes my more spontaneous worship in the expanse of the outdoors.

I recall one particular morning during a stay at a cabin by a river with a few friends. While everyone was still sleeping, I slipped my way down to the river. I found a perch on a smooth boulder, surrounded by rushing water and warmed by the rays of the sun. Inspired by the nature around me, I prayed the highlights of our morning liturgy. I began by offering the words of Modeh Ani, *expressing my profound gratitude to God and the universe for the present moment. I sang* Elohai N'shamah, *breathing in the fresh air with a renewed connection to my own soul.*

You need not have memorized the entire service to deeply connect with yourself, Judaism, and God while outdoors. Nor do you need to find yourself a pristine flowing body of water. Taking a walk on a trail, in a park, or in a green space offers the opportunity for deeper spiritual connection. Instead of working through the entire service, turn your focus to a single prayer or even a line from a prayer, such as "Mah rabu maasecha, Adonai—*How numerous are Your works, Adonai!" We recite this line every morning in the* Yotzeir Or *prayer, though it originates in Psalm 104. As I am struck by the beauty of the natural world, I say to myself and to God,* "Mah rabu maasecha, Adonai!" *Try saying it next time you are on a walk and encounter the majesty of Creation. After you say it, pay attention to how it makes you feel. How is your awareness and appreciation enhanced when you say,* "Mah rabu"? *Do you notice anything different in the way you see the world? How does inviting God into that multisensory moment transform you?*

As you feel comfortable (or even a little uncomfortable), try this practice more often and for longer. Go for a hike and see how long you can sustain your sense of Mah rabu. *Cultivate what Rabbi Abraham Joshua Heschel called "radical amazement." Open yourself to wonder, and let the world inspire you.*

The second half of the verse containing "Mah rabu" continues: "Kulam b'chochmah asita, malah haaretz kinyanecha—Everyone You created in wisdom, filling the world with Your creatures/possessions." Ask yourself how would you relate to the world if you saw each and everything—from a speck of sand to a person to an elephant to a glacier—as a purposeful and essential creation?

Spending time outdoors transforms our awareness. Looking up at Mount Rainier on a clear day shocks me into realizing how minuscule I am relative to the world, as the scope of my problems diminish in comparison to this enormous mountain. I imagine the Psalmist shared this very thought when writing the words of Psalm 121, "I lift my eyes to the mountains, from where will my help come?"

In addition to this transformative perspective, the act of moving our bodies through space shifts our focus from mind to body. By ensuring the ground beneath my feet is stable, in feeling my muscles strain as my legs climb, and by focusing on pushing myself along the trail, I stop experiencing the world through my intellect and instead become present in my body. This binds me to the physical realm and my place in it more fully than when praying statically indoors.

As you can see, the merging of fixed with free-form prayer, moved hearts with moved limbs, the words of tradition with the rapture of the natural world, synthesizes to elicit an experience far greater than the sum of its parts. Moreover, in helping those who feel disconnected from religion to discover a wisdom and wonder that they might not have pursued otherwise, the binding of Shabbat worship with immersion in nature could reclaim many who have dismissed more established forms of Judaism, while providing new possibilities for those same institutions to more successfully engage future generations.

Radical Confidence

Rob Watson

When my former Natural Resources Defense Council (NRDC) colleague asked the Dalai Lama what would be required to solve the world's environmental challenges, the Dalai Lama responded, "Radical confidence." He explained that the small act of planting a date tree, which could take decades to mature, is an act of radical confidence, as the planter will never benefit from the fruit of their labor. This echoes the lesson from the Talmud (Babylonian Talmud, *Taanit* 23a) that Choni the Circle Maker learned from the old man who was planting a carob tree: he had enjoyed the fruit from trees planted by his ancestors and wanted to pass on the blessing to his progeny. These are both beautiful lessons about the power of *tikkun olam*, or "healing the world": acts of radical confidence that are about doing the right thing—what's needed when needed, regardless of the risks or delays in the reward. It is the essence of faith, and it lies at the heart of Judaism; it is environmentalism, and my own life choices, even before I consciously knew it.

As a child, some of my most enduring memories involved the natural world: a slash of sunlight across still water in a glade; the perfume of gardenia blossoms in a pool; coastal fog weaving through the spires of a craggy shoreline; the miracle of a grove of towering redwoods. I was destined to work on big issues to protect all life on earth and have enjoyed a successful career in environmental advocacy, working on international energy and sustainability challenges on four continents.

However, my life fundamentally changed when I met my wife, Peg, along with the early arrival of our son, Max. Although Peg and I were taught to be good, moral people, neither of us was raised in a religious household. The miracle of Max's birth and the wonder we experienced as new parents made us realize that we wanted Max to have a deeper relationship to Judaism and the Divine, which in turn activated and cemented our own recommitment to *HaShem*.

During college, in a course on comparative religion, I learned about the Hindu concept of three paths to the Divine: the path of knowledge, the path of love, and the path of service. It was always service that resonated with me as the truest manifestation of my faith. Thus, it is the practice of *tikkun olam* that has crystallized the meaning of my life purpose and path.

To put this in perspective, years ago as part of our son's community service, my family accompanied our temple's *tikkun olam* group to assist in the cleanup and restoration of the Elizabeth Hubbard Memorial Garden, located on the Lower East Side of Manhattan in the Sara D. Roosevelt Park, named for the first African American dancer with the Radio City Hall Corps de Ballet. The site was formerly occupied by tenements that housed many of the earliest Jewish immigrants to the United States. The garden's neighborhood is one in transition, full of hope and dreams, and dozens of cultures and spoken languages, as well as the specter of poverty, homelessness, drug abuse, and a host of other urban ills.

My commitment to Judaism's sacred community has grown over the years through my work in the garden, and the fruits of this commitment are beginning to show delicate shoots beyond its gates. Neighborhood residents stop by to appreciate the flowers of the garden and the beauty of nature in the many stages of its life, while helping to collect trash and correct others who litter. The garden has become an oasis in a sea of concrete and occasionally a safe haven for those unhoused New Yorkers living rough under the stars.

What began as one day of service has evolved into seven years of weekly cutting back weeds, relocating bushes, planting seeds, and practicing radical confidence. I have come to know many of the locals by name, including the homeless, and I have learned that healing comes in many forms, such as small acts of kindness without judgment. As I have learned and thought more about *tikkun olam*, it confirms that "healing the world" is what I am meant to do in this life. As a lifelong environmentalist, "saving the world" has been a continual refrain. There is a lot of ego in the concept of being a "savior" and on some level a fundamental separation of actor and action. With *tikkun olam*, there is commitment, a cocreation, a partnership, and through this, the healer also becomes the healed.

Gardening in a small plot in a disadvantaged neighborhood of New York City may seem trivial compared with some of the market transforming systems I have put in place throughout my professional environmental career. However, I think my work in the garden each week is the purest manifestation of *tikkun olam* in my life and the highest expression of radical confidence in our shared future.

Ferns/Passage

CHAPLAIN DE FISCHLER HERMAN

Chlorophyllic cells
Harnessing sun, rain, and soil
Gather, in community, every spring,
Form willowy fronds, unfurl—
Reveal the fresh spirited green of youth
And the wonder of Nature's bounty

Soft and delicate in the warm breeze,
Feathery ferns
Congregate beside the dirt road,
Cozy up to moss and lichen,
Wave at chipmunks, squirrels, deer,
Catch dew drops on a summer morn
And prepare for the cool nights to come

As summer yields to autumn,
Ferns shed their emerald frocks
And, as a last hurrah, take on new hues,
Harvest gold, amber, rust
Before surrendering to first frost, then decay—
Resting under the blanket of winter

Year after year
Century upon century
Spiraling through eternity
These ancient plants, bound to Earth time,
Mark their perpetual passage of the seasons
With vitality, simple beauty, and grace

PART FOUR
Sacred Time

Jewish time is integrally related to our natural world, charted on the lunar-solar calendar, with each holiday correlating to different aspects of the cycles of the seasons. This section highlights time as a deep connector between humanity and the earth. Each chapter guides us to find the ways our tradition links us and our environment together through time.

Rabbi Dvora E. Weisberg, PhD, writes about the explicit connection between the Jewish calendar and the environment in the Talmud. Inventing new modes of practice, Kohenet Shamirah Bechirah shares her reimagination of the ancient rituals of the Jerusalem Temple. Thinking about how biblical ideas can help us today, Nigel S. Savage writes about revolutionizing the *Sh'mitah* (Sabbatical) year in our contemporary world. Rabbi Shoshana Meira Friedman provides a guide for connecting to our local plant life during Sukkot by reinvestigating the *lulav*. Through a close read of an ancient prayer, Rabbi Dennis C. Sasso, DMin, discerns a thread of environmental awareness winding through the *Birkat HaMazon*. Reconsidering atonement for today, Rabbah Gila Caine writes on Yom Kippur as a day to reflect on our responsibilities to the earth. Rabbi Warren G. Stone shares an original prayer designed for Tu BiSh'vat. Finally, we are blessed with reflections by the next generation of thinkers in our community. Michael Pincus, Anna Dubey, Raphaela Gold, Penelope Kopp, and Tali Deaner, youth leaders in the Jewish climate movement, share their stories of bringing climate activism to the center in their lives, both as young people and as Jews.

22

The Climate and the Calendar
A Talmudic Perspective

RABBI DVORA E. WEISBERG, PhD

In the aftermath of a flood that destroyed every living thing on the earth, God vows never again to bring doom upon the earth in response to the sins of human beings. God proclaims:

> As long as the world exists,
> planting and harvesting,
> cold and heat,
> summer and winter,
> day and night
> will never end.
> —*Genesis 8:22*

God's pronouncement seems to promise that the rhythms of nature are protected from the impact of human activity. With the possible exception of the land of Canaan, which the Torah tells us will show the evidence of God's anger when the people of Israel stray, the cycle of the seasons and the weather patterns that accompany them are constants. Never again will there be radical disruption to the entire world.

Today, we know that this pronouncement is far from true. Human activity is having a massive impact on the world around us. Temperatures are rising, ice is melting, areas impacted by drought are expanding, and habitats are being destroyed. We are facing radical disruption. It may not include destruction of all life on the earth, as described in Genesis, but it threatens entire species and human populations across the world. Although we would not describe these changes as God's punishment for the sins of humanity, much of the damage is the consequence of human beings' actions.

What does Judaism have to teach us about the interplay of human activity and the natural world? Is it possible to craft a religious approach to the environment that acknowledges our capacity to shape the world around us while affirming the need to respect nature? One element of the Jewish calendar discussed in Rabbinic literature suggests that Jewish tradition is aware of the tension between human manipulation of the environment and respect for the ecosystem that sustains life. This element, the need to adjust the largely lunar calendar of Judaism to the solar year through *ibur hashanah*, the periodic addition of a thirteenth month to the twelve-month year, underscores the intersection between human calculations and natural phenomena. This process, known as intercalation, dates back approximately four thousand years and was a feature of the Sumerian and Babylonian calendars.

The Jewish calendar is primarily lunar; months are 29 or 30 days, reflecting the 29½-day cycle of the moon's orbit around Earth. A lunar calendar year is 11 or 12 days shorter than the solar year of 365 days. In order to keep the holy days in the season associated with them in the Torah, an additional month is added to the year seven times in a nineteen-year cycle. Since the Jewish calendar was fixed in the fifth century CE, the additional month has occurred regularly in the third, sixth, eighth, eleventh, fourteenth, seventeenth, and nineteenth years of a nineteen-year cycle. Before the standardization of the calendar, the Rabbis asserted that the extra month, a second month of Adar, was added when it was determined that without that additional month, Passover, which was to take place in "the month of spring" (*bachodesh haaviv*; e.g., Exodus 23:15, 34:18), would occur out of season.

How was the determination to add a thirteenth month to the year made, and who had the authority to make that decision? The Babylonian Talmud, *Sanhedrin* 18b, offers this information in its discussion of the limits on the power of the High Priest and a Davidic monarch:

> We seat neither the king nor the High Priest on [the court that decides] when to intercalate the year. The king [is excluded] on account of the soldiers' pay; the High Priest [is excluded] on account of the cold.
>
> Rav Pappa said: We learn from this that [weather of] the year follows the month. Is that so?

Mishnah Sanhedrin 2:1 states that a High Priest may serve as a judge, but a king may not. Our passage indicates that there is a particular type of court on which neither the king nor the High Priest could sit, namely a court that is convened to decide whether the year should be lengthened by the insertion of a second month of Adar before the month of Nisan. The reasons given relate to the personal concerns of the men who hold these two offices. In the case of the king, the concern relates to the salaries of a standing army. According to Rashi, soldiers were paid an annual salary, rather than a monthly salary. It would be in the king's interest to intercalate the year, because by doing so he would obtain thirteen months of service for the same cost as twelve. Other commentaries suggest that while taxes were paid annually, soldiers were paid monthly; in this scenario, the king would have reason to avoid intercalating the year. The High Priest has incentive not to intercalate the year, because the additional month will delay the observance of Yom Kippur, forcing the High Priest to wash in colder water and then walk barefoot on a colder floor.

At this point in the passage, it is unclear if there are fixed criteria that shape a court's decision to add a thirteenth month to a year. There is no question that astronomical observations played a role in determining the beginning of the new month and deciding when to intercalate the year. We learn in *Mishnah Rosh HaShanah* 2:6 that witnesses who claimed to have seen the new moon were asked about its position in the sky relative to the sun and its appearance. Rabban Gamliel, a first-century rabbi, is said to have had pictures of the moon in various phases that he used to examine witnesses (*Mishnah Rosh HaShanah* 2:8). In the early centuries of the Common Era, scholars were familiar with the course of the sun and some of the planets; Rabbinic literature indicates that the Rabbis knew the timing of the equinoxes and solstices. When the Talmud, later in our *Sanhedrin* passage, asserts that "the Rabbis relied on their calculations" in deciding to intercalate the year, it is presumably speaking of astronomical data.

At the same time, we know that the interpretation of information, particularly when relying on eyewitness testimony, can be a matter of dispute. The exclusion of the king and the High Priest could suggest that the decision to intercalate a year, even when based on evidence, is somewhat subjective, and therefore we need to bar individuals with a clear stake in the decision from sitting on the court. It is also possible that the Talmud believes that there are set criteria for adding a month to the year, in which case it is concerned that the king or High Priest, individuals with significant power, could ignore those criteria and pressure others on the court to do the same.

Rav Pappa addresses the explanation given for excluding the High Priest from the court seated to consider intercalating the year. He asserts that the idea that adding a month to the calendar before Passover would make the month of Tishrei later that year colder indicates that "[weather of] the year follows the month." That is, in the standard twelve-month year, we can expect each month to feature a particular weather pattern. Cheshvan is typically colder than Tishrei; ergo, if the year is intercalated, the weather in Tishrei will be the weather that is "normal" in Cheshvan. *Sanhedrin* 18b goes on to question this assertion, relating an incident in which the Sages overheard a conversation among three herders regarding the weather:

> But what about the three cattle herders who were hanging around and were heard by the Rabbis speaking [about the criteria for intercalating the year]? One said: When the early and late grains sprout at the same time, it is Adar, but if not, it should not be Adar [that is, we need to add a second month of Adar, lest we arrive at Nisan too soon]. The second said: If the ox comes close to dying from cold in the morning and at midday lies down in the shade of the fig tree rubbing his hide, it is Adar, but if not, it is not Adar. The third said: If there is a strong east wind, but the air you expel goes out toward it, it is Adar, but if not, it is not Adar. And the Sages intercalated that year!
>
> Does it make sense to say that the Sages relied on cowherds? Rather, the Sages relied on their calculations, and the words of the cowherds served merely as confirmation.

Each of the three individuals offered wisdom about the anticipated weather for Adar, the month in which one would have to decide whether to intercalate the current year. According to the herders, Adar is a transitional month. In the morning, it is cold enough to support snow or to feature a strong east wind, but as the day progresses, it can become quite warm. When that is not the case, they said, it is not Adar; that is, it is too cold to be Adar. That year, the Sages did intercalate the year, which suggests that the Rabbis accepted the "evidence" contained in the herders' conversation. If so, then the notion that the solar year guarantees a reliable weather pattern is incorrect.

The Talmud now pushes back against the idea that the Rabbis would base a legal decision on the word of three, presumably uneducated, herders. Rather, states the Talmud, the Sages used calculations that happened to lead them to the same conclusion as the herders. However, these calculations were not based on the weather or the growing cycle, but on astronomical indicators. A year based on twelve lunar months is simply not in sync with the solar year. Unless one adds days to the calendar periodically, there will be significant disruption to the festivals and other markers of time, the fall and spring equinox and the summer and winter solstice. The Rabbis, according to the Talmud, did not need to check the weather to know that it was necessary to make an adjustment to the calendar every few years.

Sanhedrin 18b presents two ways of thinking about the relationship between human activity and desires and the natural world. The Talmud imagines the Rabbis working to harmonize the various natural cycles that impact a human construct through the Jewish calendar. They achieve their desired outcome—ensuring that festivals associated with certain seasons occur in those seasons—through the study of the natural world.

The Talmud's explanation of why the king and the High Priest would not be allowed to make decisions about the calendar shows an awareness that human beings may opt to shape a reality that advantages their interests rather than take into account the workings of nature. Decisions might be made for financial gain or for personal comfort. These biases are understandable, but they must not be allowed to influence decisions based on what can be properly described as the science of late antiquity.

The commentators view the Talmud's rejection of the evidence of the three herders through the lens of elitism. Surely the Sages would not base their decisions on folk wisdom! We can see the issue differently. The words of the herders underscore a sense of displacement or disconnect between the evidence of our senses and our expectations. If the calendar tells me it is Adar, but the weather doesn't *feel* to me like the weather I associate with Adar, I have two choices. I can accept the fact that Adar is not inextricably tied to a particular weather pattern, or I can deny that it is Adar. The latter option may be satisfying insofar as it confirms that my expectations are reasonable, but it is problematic, unless I am living alone in a cave.

Today, we confront the reality of climate change. The disruption to our lives goes far beyond the annual complaints of rabbis and Jewish educators about the fall holidays being "so early" or "so late" in a given year. Our summers are hotter, tropical storms are more frequent and more deadly, and our coastlines are eroding. In some places, droughts threaten the water supply, and in others a normal level of rainfall causes flooding in our neighborhoods. While there are people who still deny that we are experiencing serious climate change, as well as those who argue that climate change is unrelated to human activity, we cannot escape the fact that large numbers of people live in places that are becoming increasingly inhospitable and dangerous.

The Talmud cannot supply answers to our current situation. The Rabbis of late antiquity were not climate scientists. However, the Talmud offers us several models for responding to the disparity between what we want and what we see. We can be like the three herders, attempting to force the world to adjust to our desires, insisting that the weather we are experiencing cannot be the weather that is normal—or the new normal—for a certain time of year or a certain location, or we can acknowledge that what we see around us is the reality that we must confront and to which we must respond. We can be like the king and the High Priest, prioritizing the financial or personal well-being of the powerful over the needs of the many. Or we can be like the Sages, recognizing that whatever our preferences, we must work in harmony with the natural world. Just as the Rabbis of late antiquity used the science of their time to establish the calendar, we can use climate science to determine what is required to protect the planet.

Mishnah Rosh HaShanah 2:8–9 describes a dispute between two first-century CE rabbis about the accuracy of testimony in the sighting of the new moon. The disagreement resulted in confusion about the proper date of Yom Kippur. One of the sages, Rabbi Y'hoshua, was forced to submit and to present himself before Rabban Gamliel carrying his wallet and his walking stick on the day he held to be Yom Kippur, thus desecrating what he believed to be the holiest day of the year. For us, the stakes are higher. We are in a moment that can legitimately be compared to the period leading up to the Flood, a moment when all living things are under threat. We cannot build an ark, nor can we anticipate divine intervention. We must act.

23

Yizal Mayim
Water Rituals and Meditations

⋅ KOHENET SHAMIRAH BECHIRAH (Sarah Chandler)

Their boughs drip with moisture, their roots have abundant water.
—*Numbers 24:7*

UNLIKE DIASPORA JEWS today, our ancestors were an agricultural people who depended on the cycle of the seasons and rain, in particular, to meet their most basic needs. It is not surprising that our holidays and prayers reflect this history. Even our calendar is based on the growing seasons in ancient Israel.[1] In contrast, our modern-day Jewish study and practice are often disconnected from the earth. We pray indoors, read words from a book, and are often more in our heads than in our bodies. Yet, throughout the year, our calendar calls us to align our liturgy and rituals with the cycles of rainfall. We call for rain on Sukkot and for dew on Passover, but how many of us actually feel the rain or touch the dew as a component of our rituals? *Yizal mayim*, the flow of water, was essential to our ancestors' spirituality, and yet most modern Jews do not interact with this element in a ritualistic manner.

By reengaging in water rituals, we can through our liturgy bridge the gap between those from an ancient Middle Eastern climate for whom the liturgy was created and those living in any climate today. Moreover, we can honor the earth and her elements in a direct, embodied manner, through Jewishly rooted rituals.

Fall: *Simchat Beit HaSho-eivah*

Sukkot, which begins on the full moon of the month of Tishrei, is a time when we celebrate water and pray for the rainy season to begin.[2] *Nisuch HaMayim* (Pouring of the Waters) is a Sukkot ritual that came about during the time when the Temple stood in Jerusalem.[3] Every morning during Sukkot, priests descended to a pool of water collected from a spring called Shiloach; they then carried the water back up through the hills to the Temple. Water was especially sacred at this time of year, because water stores were low at the end of the dry season. The priests made a careful yet joyous journey back up to the Temple, doing their best not to lose a single drop of water as they went. The water drawing was accompanied by a huge celebration called *Simchat Beit HaSho-eivah* (Rejoicing of the House of Water Drawing). This celebration was full of joy, dancing, singing, and music played on lutes, harps, cymbals, and trumpets. Large torches were lit at the Temple, lighting up all of Jerusalem.

Ritual Preparation and Instruction

1. Choose a place to pour out the water (a specific place outdoors or indoors into a plant or beautiful vessel). Provide song sheets for all.

2. Gather the water in a bowl, one per participant: The water can come from any source (rainwater, pond, river, lake, spring, or sink), though natural sources are preferred.

3. Make present an intention: Take a deep breath, look at the water in your hands. Imagine that this vessel of water is literally the last few drops of last year's rain. Prepare yourself to release it on the altar with faith that more rain will soon fall. Feel its value in your hands, and feel what it is like to prepare to pour it out.

4. Proceed with the water: Just like the priests' procession from the spring to the Temple, the journey from your gathering space to where you pour the water is a part of the ritual itself. Process in silence, or join in with a song or poem. Bring along a shofar to sound as you process; sing or read.

5. Pour it out in the chosen place: Say thank you to the water for sustaining you.

6. Recite the closing words of *t'filat hageshem* (prayer for rain):

Shaatah hu Adonai Eloheinu

שָׁאַתָּה הוּא יְיָ אֱלֹהֵינוּ

mashiv haruach umorid hagashem.

מַשִּׁיב הָרוּחַ וּמוֹרִיד הַגֶּשֶׁם:

Livrachah v'lo liklalah. Amen.

לִבְרָכָה וְלֹא לִקְלָלָה. אָמֵן:

L'chayim v'lo lamavet. Amen.

לְחַיִּים וְלֹא לַמָּוֶת. אָמֵן:

L'sova v'lo l'razon. Amen.

לְשׂוֹבַע וְלֹא לְרָזוֹן. אָמֵן:

> You are Adonai our God,
> Who causes the wind to blow and the rain to fall.
> For blessing and not for curse. Amen.
> For life and not for death. Amen.
> For plenty and not for lack. Amen.

Winter: Sap Rising

If you live in the northeastern United States or eastern Canada, you may have a sugar maple or two in your backyard—trees that produce sap that can be turned into maple syrup. Around the full moon of Sh'vat or a few weeks after, the daytime temperatures finally rise just above freezing. At night when the temperature goes back below freezing, it creates pressure in the tree as the tree awakens and draws water from the earth. By drilling a hole into the tree, you can collect the sap as it flows during the warmer daytime hours. The *P'ri Eitz Hadar* (the kabbalistic guidebook for Tu BiSh'vat) describes this time of year with the phrase *alah hasaraf*, "the sap is rising."

RITUAL GROUNDING AS THE SAP FLOWS. This outdoor or indoor ritual is meant to bring you into a balanced relationship with the earth and to connect with the season of the rising sap. Visualize, standing or sitting with your feet planted on the floor/ground, that you are a tree whose sap just began to flow again, as you listen to the following guided meditation:

> Feel your feet in connection with the ground
> Widen your feet, spreading out your toes
>
> Feeling supported by the earth
> Notice the warmth of the sun shining above you

Draw up *shefa*/flow tapping into feeling consider:
What is my connection
To the earth?

From that place
Feel the soles of your feet drawing in
Drinking up water
From the earth, from the soil

What sensations are you feeling?
Draw that water up through your feet
Through your ankles
Up toward your knees, your thighs, your belly, your heart

Feel into sensation, texture
Is there any spot it might get caught on or need to move around?

As you allow that water to continue to move up your body
To your fingers, arms, elbows
Let it reach the top of your head

What does it feel like for this moment to be filled with
This earthly water body
This cold
In an environment that has created just the conditions
For this exact experience?

Spend a moment there in this water space
What are your impulses?
What do you want to do with this water?
Does it want to move?
See if there are any ways you want to move or shift your body in
     this place
With these sensations
Coolness, flow

This new water allows for more reaching in the body
Cracking open of the cold hard places
Allow your being to sway
Allow your rooted tree to find a bit of motion

How might you express or share what you are experiencing?
Reaching out to meet the air

Allow your arms to also reach into the air, opening
Expressing expansion that has come through you
In the receiving of new flow—of new water—of new life force

Sharing the abundance and aliveness with your neighbors
If your eyes are closed, allow them to now open
Allow your eyes to gaze at the others
Honoring and noticing the orchard you belong to
This community of trees
          Dance with this flow state
This water state

NOW

Something shifts
There's a warmth
The light of the sun from above
Feel that energy radiating upon you
Allow that warm energy to move from the top of your head
To the tops of your fingers
Through your trunk
It starts from the top and allows that water to shift
To begin to move back down the body

With this feeling of connection
You now feel a quality of warmth
          What do you sense?
Can you let in a little bit more warmth?
Allow the motion that has moved upward
Begin to flow back downward
Toward the earth
Toward that rootedness
Toward the relationship

As you feel the warmth
Allow yourself to root even more deeply
Bring that warmth into your center
Flow the warmth down to your roots, rooting you more deeply, as
you allow the flow to continue to move through you

Do you want to move?
Is there a gesture or an impulse?

As you feel the warmth of the sun
Is there any relief?
Is there an emotion that comes up?
Notice how it moves and moves until it comes to rest.[4]

Spring: Welcoming Dew

Jewish liturgy slices the year into two seasons. The poetry we recite when the seasons change indicates what is coming. On Sukkot, the end of the dry season, we pray for the coming rainy season. On Passover, with the dry season beginning, we pray for the blessing of dew.[5]

Praying for rain is more instinctual than praying for dew. Rain can be seen and quantified. Metaphorically, rain represents abundance and the flow of life. It is more difficult to pray for dew. We are literally calling in something small, difficult to see, and often fleeting. Praying for the tiny droplets of morning dew invites us to shift our outlook to enough-ness. So much of our society defines thriving as acquisition: more money, more possessions, more titles, and more education. Dew reminds us that huge life achievements are not the best measurement of happiness.

DEW MEDITATION. Sit comfortably with your eyes open. Find some dew on grass or rocks, or dip a hand or a few fingers in some water. Watch and feel the texture and sensation of the water. How long does it take for the water to evaporate or be absorbed into your skin? Notice how the textures and sensations change. Which thoughts and feelings arise? Is the water enough—enough for what? Do you want more? Less? Breathe through it all.

Dew is our teacher, reminding us about the sacredness of sufficiency. May our prayers for dew be an opportunity to express joy, even when it is fleeting. May the ephemeral dew of spring reinvigorate our capacity for small drops of loving-kindness, toward ourselves and toward others.

Summer: *Bikurim*/First Fruits

By the time the month of Sivan (the month when Shavuot falls) arrives, our agrarian ancestors hoped that the wheat in the field had dried on the stalk. Our first harvest is an opportunity for celebration, but not yet for feasting. The biblical and Mishnaic origins of Shavuot (Exodus 23:15–16, 34:22; Leviticus 23:9–21; Numbers 28:26; Deuteronomy 16:9–10; *Mishnah Bikurim*) discuss the first wheat harvest of the year, as well as the ritual of bringing your *bikurim*, "first fruits," to the Temple.

REENACTING A FIRST FRUITS PROCESSION: "The choice first fruits of your soil you shall bring to the house of the Eternal your God" (Exodus 23:19).

The original rite of offering first fruits was the bringing of the fruit of trees during their fourth year of fruit bearing (Leviticus 19:23–25). One should also make a grain offering with freshly harvested wheat in the form of two loaves of baked leavened bread (23:17). Observing Shavuot at the start of the harvest season included a pilgrimage to the Temple in Jerusalem but also included weeks of preparation. The Mishnah gives clear instructions for designating your first fruits. In addition to watching your wheat dry on the stalk while you harvested your barley:

> How does one set aside *bikurim*? One goes down into one's field, one sees a fig that ripened, or a cluster of grapes that ripened, or a pomegranate that ripened; one ties a reed-rope around it and says: "Let these be *bikurim*." (*Mishnah Bikurim* 3:1)

1. Choose a date for your first fruits reenactment, on or near the holiday.
2. Ask volunteers to bake challot (use locally sourced wheat flour if you can) and bring produce from their garden or farmers market.
3. Recite: "Historically, how were the *bikurim* taken up [to Jerusalem]? All [the inhabitants of] the cities . . . would spend the night in the open street and they would not enter any of the houses. Early in the morning the officer would say: 'Let us arise and go up to Zion, into the house of the Eternal our God' (Jeremiah 31:5)" (*Mishnah Bikurim* 3:2).
4. Gather your offerings in a *bikurim* basket and decorate it with ribbons or colorful fabric. Rather than gather around the table for a banquet, you will act as pilgrims making an *aliyah l'regel*, walking up to Jerusalem by foot. If you have goats, dogs, or

other pets who can join you in the procession, include them as you dress up for the occasion. At Adamah Farm, where we partake in this ritual annually, we process with a chuppah covering the person who holds the offerings. Designate one site to be "home" and another location to represent "Jerusalem."

5. By giving up the first of this bounty, one demonstrates that one has faith that more is coming. Whether holding a real object or an imaginary one, prompt each person to turn to someone next to them and share: What is something in my life I have a small amount of and feel I could release, if only it meant that I would receive more later on? After each person shares, process collectively to the "Jerusalem" site.

Gathering the Waters

These rituals will support you and your community to flow in an authentic relationship with the elements, grounded in ancient Jewish texts and aligned with the seasons of where you live. Whether you gather before a holiday to use these as spiritual preparation or infuse your observances with these ceremonies, honoring the flow of water will bring you in sync with the Jewish calendar and all of Creation.

NOTES

1. Sarah Chandler, "Why Shemini Atzeret Is the Pinnacle of the High Holidays Season," Jewish Telegraphic Agency, October 1, 2015, https://www.jta.org/2015/10/01/lifestyle/why-shemini-atzeret-is-the-pinnacle-of-the-high-holidays-season-2.

2. Becca Heisler cowrote a longer version of this Sukkot section in her role as curriculum research assistant for the "Yizal Mayim" workshop series I created. This Sukkot ritual also draws upon the ritual cocreated with Rabbi Jill Hammer, which can be found here: https://zeramim.org/past-issues/volume-ii-issue-3-spring-2018-5778/offering-to-the-foundation-stone-jill-hammer/.

3. See Babylonian Talmud, *Sukkah* 51a, for a description of the entire *Simchat Beit HaSho-eivah* ritual.

4. Original composition by Kohenet Shamirah Chandler. Janna Diamond, CCEP (jannadiamond.com) and Elana Brody (elanabrody.com) advised imagining and writing the sap grounding exercise.

5. Sarah Chandler, "Tefillat Tal: Cultivating a Mindset of Sufficiency," My Jewish Learning, https://www.myjewishlearning.com/article/the-prayer-for-dew-cultivating-a-mindset-of-sufficiency/.

24

Resetting the Planet through *Sh'mitah*

Nigel S. Savage

WHAT DOES IT MEAN to be Jewish? How can, could, or should Jewish tradition inflect how we live today? Are there Jewish ways to relate more deeply to the wider world, to friends and family, and to oneself? How can Jewish tradition guide how we as Jews respond to and cope with the multiple ways that we are overconsuming the planet? *Sh'mitah* offers a frame to address all of these questions.

What Is *Sh'mitah*?

Sh'mitah is cited in many places in the Torah, often using different terms, and with slightly different foci:

- In Exodus 23:11: *sh'vi-it*—simply "seventh year"
- In Leviticus 25: *Shabbat l'Adonai*—"a Sabbath for the Eternal" (verse 2); *Shabbat Shabbaton*—the quintessence of the Sabbath (verse 4); and *Shabbat haaretz*—"the Sabbath of [*or:* for] the land" (verse 6)
- In Exodus 23:11: *tishm'tenah untashtah*—"letting go and letting be" (the first word is from the same root as *Sh'mitah*)
- In Deuteronomy 15:1: *Sh'mitah*—"letting go" or "releasing"

In all but the last instance, the injunctions apply to the land. They guide us not to plant or reap; to leave food for the poor of our community (and then for the wild beasts); to allow the land to rest, either for its own sake or for God. The last text instructs us to release monetary debts.

Here are parts of three of the key texts, and they give a sense of the range of *Sh'mitah*—the different ways that the Torah describes what *Sh'mitah* is:

Six years you shall sow your land and gather in its yield; but in the seventh you should let it rest and lie fallow. Let the needy among your people eat of it, and what they leave let the wild beasts eat. You should do the same with your vineyards and your olive groves. (Exodus 23:10–11)

When you enter the land that I assign you, the land should observe a Sabbath of the Eternal. Six years you may sow your field and six years you may prune your vineyard and gather in the yield. But in the seventh year the land should have a Sabbath of complete rest [*Shabbat Shabbaton*], a Sabbath of the Eternal: you shall not sow your field or prune your vineyard. You shall not reap the after-growth of your harvest or gather the grapes of your untrimmed vines; it shall be a year of complete rest for the land. But you may eat whatever the land during its Sabbath will produce—you, your male and female slaves, the hired and bound laborers who live with you, and your cattle and the beasts in your land may eat all its yield. (Leviticus 25:2–7)

Every seventh year you shall practice remission of debts [*Sh'mitah*]. This shall be the nature of the remission: all creditors shall remit the due that they claim from their fellow [Israelites]; they shall not dun their fellow [Israelites], or kin, for the remission proclaimed is of the Eternal. (Deuteronomy 15:1–2)

Why Has *Sh'mitah*, in General, Been Overlooked?

Most Jews growing up (and even rabbis and rabbinical students) become Jewishly literate without paying much attention to *Sh'mitah*. Given *Sh'mitah*'s references to land and to farming, we assume that *Sh'mitah* is only for farmers. And since most of us are not farmers (and even if we are, the provisions of *Sh'mitah* don't apply, in a formal halachic sense, outside of the Land of Israel), we assume it's not for us.

Yet we forget that the world of the Torah, twenty-five centuries ago, was an agrarian world. Everyone was a farmer or, if not, certainly in direct relationship to the process of growing food and producing wine, bread, and olives. And, so, we should understand that the provisions of *Sh'mitah* are not about "farming," in our terms; they are about *life*. *Sh'mitah* is about what we could call economics, politics, culture—in fact, all aspects of human society.

What, Then, Could or Should *Sh'mitah* Mean for Us Today?

Sh'mitah, in fact, addresses specifically some of the most intractable questions of society today. How do we, as a society, ameliorate inequality? How—and when—do we construct transfers of resources from those who have more to those who have less? What is our relationship to ownership? What does it mean that something is "mine"? When should I share what is mine with you? How hard should we work and for how long, and how and why should we rest? What is or should be our relationship to the physical land? What is or should be our relationship to the other living creatures with whom we share this planet? How do we both ensure that credit is available to those who need it and find ways to ameliorate debt burdens for those who are overly indebted?

As we begin to understand the questions that *Sh'mitah* is addressing, their salience for us becomes clearer. I first started thinking seriously about *Sh'mitah* in 2000, and I have been learning and teaching about it quite consistently since 2007. I have discovered that when one starts to learn the primary texts of *Sh'mitah* with any group of people—Jewish or non-Jewish, learned or not learned—and simply asks questions about what those texts mean, what their underlying values seem to be, and how they might apply to the world we live in today, we see that conversation comes alive in remarkable ways.

The COVID-19 pandemic has been, in a sense, the partial equivalent of a global involuntary *Sh'mitah* year. It was a time in which economic life was constricted, travel was reduced, and all sorts of social interactions were curtailed. People lost their jobs and could not see loved ones; normal life was disrupted. And yet, in its aftermath, many have also talked about what was good: it was *good* to travel less; it was good to focus on one's closest loved ones; it was good to spend more time (for those who could) with parents or children.

Governments also rose to the challenge in some ways. In both the United States and Israel, governments provided significant additional support for those who had lost jobs, had less money, or needed help in general. At least some of that additional support was of a kind, and on a scale, that people would have said was "impossible" only a few months prior.

Our reflections on the coronavirus enable us to see *Sh'mitah*, through fresh eyes, as a significant frame for contemporary life. We're in this strange world of postindustrial capitalism, in which so many things feel askew and out of balance; and the driving forces for those imbalances seem to come from the constant encouragement to buy more, to acquire more.

It is against this that *Sh'mitah* comes as a radical and profound critique. It is an *injunction* to rest, periodically—not just on the Sabbath, but once every seven years, for a whole year—and in resting, to acquire much less. What would it be like if, one year in seven (with prior planning, and without a life-threatening virus to prompt it), the pace of an entire community or society or country slowed? What if every person, every institution, every government chose to reduce air travel, one year in seven? What if, every seven years, we reduced our sense of what is *mine* and shared it with *you*?

Making This Real

Ahead of the *Sh'mitah* year of 5775 (2014–15) I decided, somewhat randomly, not to buy any books (and I love buying books) and not to buy any liquor. There is no halachah, no Jewish law, no Jewish tradition that forbids either of these two actions. I chose to (try to) do this because I wanted to explore the spirit of *Sh'mitah*. To my surprise, I kept to both for the whole year—and loved and was fascinated by the experience. Every time I wanted to buy a book or a bottle of Scotch, I was reminded that it was the *Sh'mitah* year. And going the whole year without buying either was a reminder *that I already had* enough, that many of us already have too much.

For the following *Sh'mitah* year, in 2021–2022, I decided again not to buy books or liquor, and added to this the decision not to buy clothes either. (A year of COVID made clear that I have more than enough clothes. Also, when will I ever again *need to buy a tie*?!) I was struck that the Sabbatical year in the biblical narrative is not simply about having less, acquiring less, and living more simply. It is also very much focused on *aniyei amecha*—the poor of your community. Not buying books or liquor may have caused me to consume a little less, but it did not help anyone else. My intention was to put aside what I otherwise would have spent on books, liquor, and clothes in the course of a year and to find ways to give an equivalent amount of money directly to those in need, over and above whatever I normally give. This is how Jewish tradition should influence us on a daily basis, inspiring and encouraging us to acquire less and to give more. This is also how the tradition understands that we change the world—moving out from ourselves, in concentric circles.

What if you followed this *Sh'mitah* practice? And your parents, and your kids? And your friends? And your rabbi? And the people in your temple? And those in your school, in your college, and in your camp? And those in your law firm, in your restaurant, in the company you work for or own, and in the nonprofit you work for or support? What if every Jewish institution saved money over the first six years of a seven-year cycle and then made sure that at least one year in seven funds were saved for those who had less?

What if our governments and our institutions set aside money, six years out of seven, to offer paid sabbaticals to at least some people and more each successive sabbatical year? What if all museums and swimming pools were free one year in seven? What if one year in seven our governments reinvested in parks and gardens, small and large, and committed to cleaning them up? What if one year in seven we decided to drive less, fly less—and walk and bike more?

Student loan debt in the United States has grown immensely since 2000. What if the US government decided to find some mechanism to release those who are most indebted or to forgive all debts for those who go into public service? What if, one year in seven, we created additional resources for public services and funded, for example, everyone, ages sixteen to twenty-five, to spend one year serving people in need, animals, or the land itself?

What if we devoted one year in seven to simply *discussing* these topics—learning together, brainstorming, ideating, and envisioning?

Looping back to my opening frame, it becomes clear that *Sh'mitah* is central to the Torah's understanding of living, as it were, a good life. It is a challenge, and it prompts us to change. It reminds us that the Torah does not just see the earth as *sacred*, but more significantly, it sees the earth as *not ours*. Ownership in the Jewish understanding is relative, not absolute. We are tenants in a world that the Torah understands to be God-given. Regardless of our personal theology, this understanding is central to *Sh'mitah*—if the land is not *mine* in the first place, then I can be enjoined to share what I have with others. Indeed, the Babylonian Talmud, *B'rachot* 35a, teaches that any property we acquire must be through the voicing of a blessing; otherwise, we are stealing from what belongs to God.

Broadening the Frame: *Sh'mitah* in a Wider Context

This notion that the world is not *mine* is critical to enabling us to begin to address the multiple environmental crises we face. The world today is bound up with *rights*: I have the right to do what I like with my land, my trash, my money; and I have the right to drive a carbon-emitting SUV, to own three homes, and to take thirty flights a year. To be clear—I am not arguing for prohibiting these actions. But I *am* arguing that Jewish tradition is focused not on *rights*, but rather on *responsibilities*—not on what I have or what I'm entitled to, but rather on what I must give to others and whom I'm obligated to help.

In the Torah, *Sh'mitah* is not just an individual or even familial or communal obligation; it is societal. You cannot observe *Sh'mitah* by yourself, according to the Torah's understanding, nor should you. *Sh'mitah* is a societal slowdown and a societal reset.

Whatever you choose to do or not do in the remaining *Sh'mitah* years of your life is merely a starting point for a wider conversation in your community, and that is, in turn, a prompt for a societal conversation. Shouldn't rabbis be speaking up, to offer these frames for public conversation? Shouldn't our elected officials be thinking about how to use these values to enact new laws that will reduce inequality and renew the land? If we engage in this way, Jewish law and practice will lead us toward a deeper commitment to environmental sustainability and, indeed, environmental justice—that is, helping those who have been most hurt by the actions of wealthy countries or individuals. We may come to understand halachah not solely as Jewish law but as a form of self-restraint that is inculcated within the family and that spreads out, in concentric circles, into the wider culture and society. We may acknowledge our blessings and our responsibilities, especially in a post-pandemic world. I hope and pray that this path will lead us to be better Jews—and ultimately to engender a healthier, more sustainable, and more equitable world for all.

25

Creating a Local *Lulav*

RABBI SHOSHANA MEIRA FRIEDMAN

I WAS BLESSED to study Torah in the company of trees. At Hebrew College rabbinical school, poring over *mishnayot* and midrashim, my study partners and I would regularly lift our eyes from the text to look out the giant wall of windows at the small woodland outside the *beit midrash*. We marked each passing semester by green summer foliage in Elul, maples' crimson on Sukkot, the birch leaves blanketing the ground in yellow by Chanukah. At Tu BiSh'vat, the branches were still bare, but little tufts of baby leaves would begin to bud after Purim, opening into a new riot of green as we prepared for our season of liberation and the giving of the Torah.

Every year as a rabbinical student, I looked forward to Hoshana Rabbah, the seventh day of Sukkot, when Jews march seven *hakafot* around the Torah, crying out *Hoshana! Save us!* I loved the stunning aesthetic of a community wearing white (a Hoshana Rabbah custom), holding green palm fronds and yellow citrons. I loved the long, loud shofar blast that signaled the final, lingering end of the High Holy Day season. I loved kneeling after the service to whack my willow branches on the ground in total abandon alongside my teachers and friends, a custom that certainly proves to any cynics that Judaism is an earth-based religion, with its own healing plants, its own rain dances, its own sun and moon festivals. Sukkot marks the beginning of the rainy season in the Land of Israel, and before modern irrigation, the right rain in the right season meant the difference between abundance and famine. The refrain of the day gives voice to what was a time of intense communal vulnerability for the ancient Israelites.

Yet, as the years ticked by toward my ordination, droughts and storms increased around the world, and I learned the haunting truth that most of us are feeling the first effects of climate change as too much or too little water. As much as I loved the ancient rain dance of Hoshana

Rabbah and how it connected me to the biblical Land of Israel and my ancestors, I needed a rain dance that would speak to the peril of climate disruption.

The mitzvah to wave what we now call the *lulav* and *etrog* comes from the Torah. In describing the festival of Sukkot, Leviticus 23:40 stipulates, "On the first day you shall take the product of *hadar* trees, branches (*kapot*) of *t'marim*, boughs of *avot* trees, and *arvei nachal*, and you shall rejoice before the Eternal your God seven days."

While the biblical Hebrew is somewhat vague, about two thousand years ago, Jews settled on which plants the Torah meant, and we have been sacredly waving them ever since: a palm frond, two willow branches, three myrtle branches, and one *etrog* (citron) fruit. Put together, they are known as the *lulav* and *etrog* (literally "palm frond and citron fruit"), or the *arbaah minim* (literally "the four species"). The tangy smells of *etrog* and myrtle leaves have always told me it is Sukkot.

Most *lulav* and *etrog* sets are grown in pesticide-laden monoculture and shipped to the United States across the ocean. As much as we may intend them to symbolize tradition and joy, they also inherently signal business as usual in the overseas travel and agricultural industries that are directly causing climate disruption in Israel and around the world. *Mishnah Sukkah* 3:5 famously teaches that we may not perform a mitzvah with a stolen *etrog*. Large-scale monoculture steals from the land. The carbon emissions of overseas shipping steals from the future. How could I walk around the Torah in Boston with a sacred intention for rain in the right season in Israel—or anywhere else—waving four perishable, fragile parts of plants shipped to me from across the Atlantic?

Traditions bind communities together. They signal stability and group cohesion. They ground us in social connection. But as the climate changes around us, Judaism—along with human civilization—faces another major paradigm shift. Like everything, our rituals will have to adapt. For a few years I simply did not buy a *lulav* and *etrog* set. Then my husband and I moved to a new home with a shaded garden in the back, and as we unpacked our boxes, I couldn't take my eyes off the trees. Basic tree identification had been on my bucket list for years, and here was a perfect challenge. There were a dozen species of trees and large shrubs on our property alone. I decided to learn not just their names, but *how* to learn their names. In learning how to identify them, I would learn their natural history. And in studying their bodies and stories, I would be able create a meaningful local alternative to a traditional *lulav* and *etrog*.

I dove into studying trees with the zeal of a *baalat t'shuvah* (someone practicing Orthodoxy for the first time). I learned how to use a dichotomous key, using a series of yes/no questions to identify a tree based on leaves or bark. I invested in a variety of guidebooks and spent the evenings learning my way around them, reading up on tree natural histories on the side. Going on walks with me became rather frustrating for my husband, as I stopped to identify every tree I did not yet know. But the practice worked. That first fall, as my toddler gained confidence in walking, I learned the common and scientific names and habits of the trees in my neighborhood.

And I fell in love with them. I loved the shockingly straight-limbed arrowwood viburnum (so called because Indigenous tribes used the branches for arrows), whose branch became the middle spine of my four species, standing in for the palm. I loved the American elm in front of our house (blessedly untouched by the blight of Dutch elm disease, which killed the beloved elms of American streets), whose eye-shaped leaves stood in for my first myrtle. I loved the weeping willow hybrid who towered in a field just a ten-minute walk from my home, whose branches were indistinguishable from those in a traditional *lulav*. And I loved the golden apple I'd picked up at our farm stand. Just as the *etrog* is not native to Israel, the edible apple is not native to New England, but like the *etrog* it has become a symbol of abundance and delight.

Since we cannot do a mitzvah with stolen property, I touched the trees' trunks lightly and asked quietly before I cut their branches.

As I twined my four species together, I missed the sound of waving palm branches and the smell of *etrog*. And I felt halachically uncomfortable. Jewish law and practice are clear that we should not change the four species.[1] Who was I to mess with centuries of practice? But I realized that this, too, is the power of the local *lulav*. It may cause discomfort and, for those familiar with traditional sets, a sense of loss. Yet climate change is only going to disrupt our way of life more as the years go by. As we wave our local four species, we are signaling the need to end what Joanna Macy calls a business-as-usual economy.[2] And as we bless and dance with these new creations, we are also practicing the emotional skill of moving through grief and loss into the joy that is at the heart of Sukkot.

When I carried my four species to synagogue with me that first year, I felt shy and a little proud, like I was introducing new friends to my community. As I recited the blessing and waved my unusual bundle in the six directions, I sent out prayers of gratitude to all the trees I'd come to know and love, to the soil they grew in, and to the air we both breathe. I prayed with a strong, clear intention for rain in the right amount, at the right time—where I lived, in Israel, and around the world.

During the morning blessing before the *Sh'ma*, we ask God to "gather us in peace from the four corners of the earth and lead us upright to our land." The composers of the liturgy yearned for Jews to come out of exile, back to the Land of Israel. Many communities today even sing this paragraph to "HaTikvah," the Israeli national anthem. Yet in true rabbinic fashion I like to play with the meaning of the words. The blessing does not say lead us upright to the Promised Land or to the Land of Israel. It says simply, "Lead us upright to *our land*."

When I chant, "Lead us upright to our land," I have a practice of stomping my feet on the ground, reminding myself that I am asking God to bring me home *here*, *now*, to *this* soil underneath the foundation of *this* building, to the proud foliage of New England, to our edible and medicinal plants, to the Charles River watershed, to the changing seasons, changing ever more as the earth warms. To be led upright to our land means to rise before her as we rise before an elder or a revered teacher. It means to learn about her—her wildlife, plants, topography, water, stones, growing seasons. It means to see the neighborhoods built around us as one snapshot on a geologic journey, designed by blips of human choice on a planet who will most definitely have the final word.

As Jews, we have lived with a narrative of exile for two thousand years. When we wave a traditional *lulav* and *etrog*, we are enacting an ancient communal connection to and longing for the Land of Israel. But the Jewish Diaspora is not the only form of exile. Most of us alive now, in the age of the industrialized global economy, are twice exiled, once from the lands of our ancestors and once again from the lands where we live. We spend our days in the physical exile of indoors and in the spiritual exile of an extractive economy that views the earth, animals, and other human beings as resources to colonize and extract, instead of as teachers, elders, and beloveds and kin.

When I wave a local four species, I am enacting my connection to and longing for the land on which I live. In this age of climate change and ecological collapse, I am called to root myself passionately and proactively on the actual land upon which I live, day after day. For me that is the land now known as Massachusetts, and specifically the land of the Wampanoag people, on whose soil I breathed my first breath and took my first steps. I will never be descended from people native to this land. But I am striving to, as Robin Wall Kimmerer puts it, become indigenous, to have a relationship of mutual love and belonging here, to know the ecosystem as intimately as I possibly can, and to treat the land and her animals, plants, and fungi as my elders and teachers.[3]

The homecoming that I long for is not informational. It is not platonic or casual. It is at the core of my devotional life. It is a passionate lunge toward aliveness, toward the specific aliveness that could be mine in this specific place. It is a longing for God's love as manifest through the earth, a stance that the ancient Israelites with their agrarian, place-based covenant would certainly have understood.

Years ago, I ran into a rabbi and teacher of mine on a public bus. As I was trying to avoid motion sickness, he was bent reverently over a book of Rebbe Nachman's teachings. I said something about being impressed, and he responded in his characteristically gentle way: "I carry a *sefer* [holy book] with me wherever I go. I don't want to waste a moment when I could be studying Torah."

On my journey to become indigenous to the land where I live, I keep thinking of that moment on the bus. When our sacred places and practices were destroyed, Rabbinic Judaism arose as an answer. We grieved and survived by studying what was lost. And in studying, we came to honor, to intimately know, to love with the passion of black fire on white fire.[4] The sacred places are being lost again, but we need not retreat into written text alone this time. When we study the more-than-human natural world, as when we engage in the study of Torah, we unfold into that which we learn, and it unfolds into us. As our Rabbinic ancestors discovered, by studying we can retain intimacy with that which is threatened or lost.

The spiritual work of returning from ecological exile is not the same as activism. To have a chance at a livable future, we must put strategic money, time, effort, and political capital behind what I like to call the Movement to Sustain Life—the decentralized movement for ecological health and social justice. As we organize, march, sit in, lobby, and put our bodies in the way of the business as usual that is destroying our world, we can sustain our souls by growing an intimacy with the land where we live.

NOTES

1. See Babylonian Talmud, *Sukkah* 31a. For those who want to follow the halachah and also signal an end to business as usual, encourage individuals in your community to forgo purchasing their own *lulav* and *etrog* and instead invest in a small number of sets that all community members can use. This allows people to complete the mitzvah of waving the traditional *lulav*, but it also requires communal coordination of resources, a great skill set in the age of climate change.

2. See much of the writing of Joanna Macy, including *Active Hope: How to Face the Mess We're In without Going Crazy* (Novato, CA: New World Library, 2022).

3. See Robin Wall Kimmerer, *Braiding Sweetgrass* (Minneapolis: Milkweed, 2020), 9.

4. The verse Deuteronomy 33:2 is creatively interpreted to include reference to God's "fiery law." The Jerusalem Talmud, *Sh'kalim* 6:1, 49d, speaks of the letters of Torah as "black fire upon white fire, sealed with fire."

26

Birkat HaMazon

A Call to Environmental Awareness

RABBI DENNIS C. SASSO, DMin

BEYOND A RITUAL of thanksgiving for food, recitation of *Birkat HaMazon* (the Blessing after Meals) is a manifestation of ecological concern and environmental awareness, acknowledging our dependence on the gifts of nature and our duty to reciprocate graciousness with gratitude.

The prayer is enthusiastically chanted in Jewish youth group and camp settings. Among traditionally observant Jews, its recitation is a daily practice, but even among the less observant, many will join in its words and strains during weddings, *b'nei* and *b'not mitzvah* celebrations, and synagogue meal gatherings. It is a piece of liturgy that we honor more by rote repetition than by thoughtful reflection. This chapter is an invitation to taste *Birkat HaMazon* as a savory morsel of Jewish spirituality.

The practice of reciting the Blessing after Meals was derived by the Rabbis from the Torah: "When you have eaten your fill, give thanks to the Eternal your God for the good land given to you" (Deuteronomy 8:10). The biblical context of this verse is suffused with ecological language: "For the Eternal your God is bringing you into a good land, a land with streams and springs and fountains issuing from plain and hill; a land of wheat and barley, of vine, figs, and pomegranates, a land of olive trees and honey; a land where you may eat food without stint, where you will lack nothing; a land whose rocks are iron and from whose hills you can mine copper" (8:7–9). Then, the next verse (8:10) elicits the human response of gratitude for that bounty. Giving thanks implies protecting nature's gifts and recognizing that these gifts are not of our own creation, but are graciously bestowed. They are not guaranteed, but require our vigilance, nurturance, and gratitude.

The Bible honors our relationship with the natural environment. Genesis 1:28, which entrusts the gift of Creation to the human, has been misinterpreted as a license for the despoliation of nature. In fact, the thrust of the Bible, even in the verses that immediately follow (1:29–31), is to tame the human instinct to abuse the natural world and to position the human being, the image of the Divine, not as owner, but as steward and cocreator of nature's bounty. The prophetic hope for a perfected world envisions that "the wolf shall dwell with the lamb . . . and a child shall herd them. . . . In all My sacred mountain [the world] nothing evil or vile shall be done" (Isaiah 11:6, 9). The Sabbath,[1] the Sabbatical,[2] and the Jubilee[3] give socioeconomic reinforcement to the idea of codependence between nature and humans. Rabbinic tradition underscores those biblical values with legislation against wanton abuse or the destruction of nature or human creations. According to a Rabbinic homily, God introduces the first human to the earthly habitat and says, "See how beautiful and perfect . . . ! Be ever mindful not to abuse or desolate My world. For if you abuse it or desolate it, there is none to repair it after you."[4] The human being is not only a worker and fabricator, but a trustee, agent, and curator appointed "to work and keep" (Genesis 2:15), to protect and enhance the earth. *Birkat HaMazon* is a grateful reminder of that obligation and privilege.

Like much of our synagogue liturgy, *Birkat HaMazon* combines universal and particular themes. It opens with wonder and gratitude at the divine order of nature and moves on to concerns of the household of Israel. As in the *Sh'ma* and Its Blessings, God is first discerned in nature's creative processes and then in Israel's experiences of revelation and redemption. Like the *Amidah*, *Birkat HaMazon* concludes with *Oseh Shalom* and the hope that blends the cosmic welfare (*bimromav*) with the particular (*aleinu v'al kol Yisrael*).

The recitation of *Birkat HaMazon* is preceded on weekdays by Psalm 137, which resonates with nostalgic remembrance of the Land of Israel. On Shabbat and holidays, the more celebratory Psalm 126 is recited. Appropriate invitationals, whose wording is determined by the number of the assembled, turn the private prayer into a public liturgy of thanksgiving. Tradition allows for expanded and briefer versions of the prayer, depending on circumstances and occasion.[5]

Birkat HaMazon is the oldest biblically established prayer; it precedes the destruction of the Second Temple.[6] The prayer consists of four distinct blessings. According to Rabbinic tradition (Babylonian Talmud, *B'rachot* 48b), the first benediction, *Birkat HaZan* (the Blessing for Sustenance), was composed by Moses; the second, *Birkat HaAretz* (the Blessing for the Land), by Joshua; the third, *Boneh Y'rushalayim* (the Rebuilding of Jerusalem), by David and Solomon; and the fourth, *HaTov V'HaMeitiv* (the Good and Beneficent), was added by the Sages at Yavneh after the failed Bar Kochba rebellion.

Birkat HaZan: The Blessing for Sustenance

Birkat HaZan is the most ancient section of the prayer. Some of its core ideas are reiterated in the three subsequent blessings.

The first striking element of this beautifully crafted paragraph is its unabashed universalism. In typical benediction formula, it opens and closes with divine address. But the prayer reads as a panegyric to nature as it continues to address the Divine in the third person. It is nature's abundance that is celebrated here. God is manifest through the earth. The richness of the natural world sustains not only humans: "Goodness, grace, loving-kindness, and compassion" nourish *kol basar*, "all flesh."

Nature's plenitude is expressed in the affirmation that *tamid lo chasar lanu, v'al yechsar lanu mazon l'olam va-ed*, "we have never lacked, and we shall never lack sustenance." The prayer is trusting and hopeful. It speaks of abundance rather than scarcity. God is *El zan um'farneis*, "the Power that nourishes and sustains," terms that serve not just as a description, but as a name.

This blessing calls for a moral charge. Sustainability is God's intention for a world that contains all that makes life possible. It doesn't ignore the reality of those who lack resources, but recognizes that the earth provides abundance if we respect and do not hoard or abuse its gifts. Shefa Gold gives poetic expression to these sentiments in theological terms:

> You are the source of everything . . .
> You nourish the world with goodness and sustain it with grace,
> We find You in the dust and in the vastness of space.[7]

This ecological awareness is further captured in the English rendition of the invitational to the *Birkat HaMazon* in the Reconstructionist liturgy: "Godly is the energy pent up in the seed and in the soil's wondrous chemistry."[8]

Birkat HaAretz: The Blessing for the Land

While the first paragraph of *Birkat HaMazon* is unabashedly universalistic, the prayer turns to the particular experience of the people of Israel in its subsequent blessings. The second blessing, *Birkat HaAretz*, gives thanks for the "desirable, good, and ample land" entrusted to our ancestors, for deliverance from bondage, for the ancestral covenant, and for the gift of Torah. These are common elements in the traditional liturgy. Yet, the core theme of *Birkat HaMazon* remains: gratitude for the constancy ("life, grace, and loving-kindness") that sustains the world. It is in this second blessing that the biblical verse that informs the recitation of *Birkat HaMazon* is referenced: "When you have eaten your fill, give thanks to the Eternal your God for the good land given to you" (Deuteronomy 8:10).

The particular focus of this blessing does not compromise its universality. It underscores the trust that even in times of adversity, gratitude is concretized in relationship to the land, a relationship of appreciation, reciprocity, and stewardship, rather than entitlement.

Boneh Y'rushalayim: The Rebuilding of Jerusalem

The third blessing expands on the particularity of Israel's experience. The good land now becomes concretized in "Jerusalem, Your city, and Zion, the dwelling place of divine glory." The yearning for messianic redemption resonates with the urgent needs of the people for a land ravaged by foreign domination. Yet, travail does not dull the hopeful assurance that God, who is now referenced nurturingly as "Parent," will "feed, nourish, sustain, support, and relieve us . . . from all our troubles." The theme of abundance is reiterated in the affirmation that "Your helping hand, which is full, open, holy, and ample," will be a source not only of material sustenance, but of personal and national honor.

This third blessing is petitionary, not just celebratory. God is now a providential agent, acting through history, not just nature. Yet, attachment to nature and a yearning for the land continue to inform the proto-environmentalism of the prayer. This blessing ends with a fervent plea, *uv'neih Y'rushalayim*, "for the restoration and rebuilding of the holy city of Jerusalem," a theme that resonates throughout synagogue liturgy and life-cycle celebrations. For, in Jewish piety, Jerusalem is more than a holy city; it is the *axis mundi*, the "center" or "navel" of the world (Ezekiel 38:12). Psalm 24 regards the site of the Temple at the heart of Jerusalem as the microcosm of the world. The restoration of Jerusalem is symbolic of the restoration of the earth's wholeness.

HaTov V'HaMeitiv: The Good and Beneficent

The fourth and last blessing is called *HaTov V'HaMeitiv*, "The Good and Beneficent." Acknowledgment of God's goodness and graciousness toward the people and the land are at the heart of this paragraph. The second and third blessings had addressed God in the second person. The fourth blessing, like the first, uses third-person address. As the people mourn the destruction of the Temple, God's proximity is now more a yearning than a felt reality.

And yet, the paragraph includes a litany of names for God, who "day after day has bestowed goodness, bestows goodness, and will bestow goodness" and brings "relief, deliverance, prosperity, blessing, and salvation . . . life, peace, and all that is good." Even in times of distress, the many-named Source of abundance can be counted upon to keep faith with Creation and the household of Israel. This nurturing relationship is reinforced in a series of implorations, each beginning with the term *HaRachaman*, "the Motherly Merciful." Perhaps the most popular line among these is the allusion to Eliyahu HaNavi, Elijah the Prophet, who will announce *b'sorot tovot, y'shuot, v'nechamot*, "good news, salvation, and consolations."[9]

Birkat HaMazon builds to a climax of praise, gratitude, and confidence in *mishmeret shalom*, an "enduring decree of peace": fullness, wholeness, and completeness, both ecological and theological. Following special implorations for the Sabbath and Festivals, the benediction ends, once again, with the oft-repeated hope for peace: *Oseh shalom bim-romav hu yaaseh shalom*, "May the Source of peace [fullness] grant peace [fullness] for us, the household of Israel (and all who make of earth their home)."

Birkat HaMazon begins and ends with awe and gratitude. It celebrates a universe that is capable of providing for the needs of humans and all living creatures. It acknowledges times of crisis and yet invites us to participate in restoring wholeness to a broken world, to create a new climate of coexistence, an environment of peace between the people Israel and the earth and between the earth and its inhabitants.

The recitation of *Birkat HaMazon* gives us hope, awakens gratitude, and affirms the Divine-human partnership in addressing the urgent existential need of restoring balance, realigning our priorities, and keeping faith with Creation.

NOTES

1. Genesis 2:1–3; Exodus 35:1–3: The seventh day is a day of armistice between humans and the earth. Even as God rested/paused from work/creation on the seventh day, so must humans not impose themselves on the earth on the Sabbath.

2. Leviticus 25:3–7: Every seventh year the land enjoys a "Sabbath of complete rest" (25:4). It is a time of noninterference and "coexistence" between the land its inhabitants.

3. Leviticus 25:8–17: The fiftieth-year Jubilee, at the end of forty-nine years (seven times seven), is a supreme expression of the Sabbath—a time of care, release, and renewal in the relationship of humans to the land and to one another.

4. Adapted from *Kohelet Rabbah* 7:13, as found in Sidney Greenberg, *Likrat Shabbat: Worship, Study, and Song: for Sabbath and Festival Services and for the Home*, ed. Jonathan Levine (Bridgeport, CT: Prayer Book Press Media Judaica, 1997), 40.

5. For variations in ritual and customs, see A. Z. Idelsohn, *Jewish Liturgy and Its Development* (New York: Schocken Books, 1960), 124–25. See also Saul Kaiserman, "Teaching Birkat Ha-Mazon: The Grace after Meals" (master's thesis, Jewish Theological Seminary of America, New York, 1999), 52–53, https://www.lookstein.org/resource/birkat_hamazon.pdf.

6. For historical and textual studies of *Birkat HaMazon*, the reader may consult any number of liturgical works, including A. Z. Idelsohn, *Jewish Liturgy and Its Development*, 122–27; Reuven Hammer, *Entering Jewish*

Prayer (New York: Schocken Books, 1994), 263–74; Elie Munk, *The World of Prayer*, vol. 1 (New York: Philipp Feldman, 1961), 210–22. Arthur Waskow, *Down to Earth Judaism* (New York: William Morrow, 1985), 65–67, provides relevant spiritual insights.

7. Shefa Gold, in *Kol Haneshamah: Shirim Uv'rakhot; Songs, Blessings and Rituals for the Home* (Wyncote, PA: Reconstructionist Press, 1991), 46.

8. *Kol Haneshamah*, 20.

9. *B'sorot tovot*, "good tidings" or "good news," is a term that will also be associated with the Christian notion of Gospel (Mark 1:14; Luke 1:19, 2:10). Restoration prophecies use the term *m'vaseret/m'vaseir* (Isaiah 40:9, 52:7; Nahum 2:1). In traditional Jewish circles, the expression *b'sorah tovah* (pl. *b'sorot tovot*) is a congratulatory term in anticipation of the birth of a child, hence the association with Elijah, who will announce the birth of the redeemer.

27

Yom Kippur
A Jewish Earth Day

RABBAH GILA CAINE

THE FIRST TIME I felt a rush of the Sacred while in shul was on Rosh HaShanah about a decade ago, prostrating myself on the floor during the Great *Aleinu*. In all the noise and emotion of the day, I found an island of silence and rest lying on the floor in front of the open ark. It would have been better to pray the Great *Aleinu* outdoors, where we could feel the dirt in our hands as we bow down to Creation, but the shul's clean floor was second best.

Then came Yom Kippur of that year, and of every year since, when I bring myself to the highest moment of *Avodah*, the sacred priestly ritual of Yom Kippur. At that moment when we all submit ourselves to the name of *Adonai*, like generations of *Am Yisrael*, I'm back there with the earth.

Yom Kippur can then be seen as a Jewish Earth Day. It is about our striving for an attitude of humility in the face of Creation. It is about the possibility of forgiving wrongs and cleansing sins, cleansing contamination, pollution, and sorrow. It is about the reality of forgiveness and hope.

Yom Kippur's origins lie in the tragic story of Nadab and Abihu, the sons of Aaron and nephews of Moses and Miriam. Here is the story:

> Now Aaron's sons Nadab and Abihu each took his fire pan, put fire in it, and laid incense on it; and they offered before the Eternal alien fire, which had not been enjoined upon them. And fire came forth from the Eternal and consumed them; thus they died at the instance of the Eternal. Then Moses said to Aaron, "This is what the Eternal meant by saying:
>> Through those near to Me, I show Myself holy,
>> And gain glory through all the people."
> And Aaron was silent. (Leviticus 10:1–3)

In her book *Leviticus as Literature*, Mary Douglas reads this as "[a] parable about trespass on forbidden ground"[1] and situates it within the wider context of the Levitical text as embodying, in written form, the structure of the *Mishkan* (Tabernacle). In a nutshell, Douglas suggests that by reading Leviticus, we are invited to walk through the (memory of the) *Mishkan*, thus acquainting ourselves with its inner workings and perhaps even its secrets. She also reminds us that we find only two narrative pauses in this book, mostly about priestly ritual, and both deal with trespass and death.[2] It would be helpful to remember at this point that Douglas understands "dirt" or contamination as that which is out of its place in the ordered structure of society.[3] Within the sacred structure of the *Mishkan* or *Gan Eden* (Garden of Eden), the out-of-place presence of fire or humans becomes a defiling contamination of holiness. We'll get back to this a bit later on, but at this point let us notice that beyond being a story of religious trespass, this is also a story of hubris and retelling of Eve's misadventures around the Tree of Knowledge.[4] To understand and begin tying this story with our relationship to the earth, we should remember that Rabbinic tradition parallels the construction story of the *Mishkan* with the creation of the world. In that sense, the *Mishkan* is parallel to the earth, and the priests (and perhaps all of Israel) to the guardians of the earth, that is, humanity.

In *Midrash Tanchuma* (*P'kudei* 2) we find, "Why does it say, 'I love the habitation of Your house, and the place where Your glory dwells'? Because the Tabernacle is equal to the creation of the world itself." In the Talmud we read, "Bezalel knew how to join the letters with which heaven and earth were created" (Babylonian Talmud, *B'rachot* 55a), meaning that the artist and designer Bezalel had access to the blueprint of Creation, on which he modeled the *Mishkan*, the meeting place with God.

However, if we have all of Creation around and within us, why would God command us to build a *Mishkan*? Why do we need a Tent of Meeting when meeting can and does happen all around us? In another midrash, Moses asks the exact same question, "The glory of the Holy One fills the upper worlds and the lower, and God said to make for God a Tabernacle?" to which the Eternal answers, "I do not see things the same way as you do. . . . Furthermore, I will come down and contract My Presence within a space of one cubit by one cubit" (*Sh'mot Rabbah* 34:1).

Contrary to my natural inclination to believe God/dess has no measure and cannot be contained within buildings no matter how wonderful they are, there is something very compelling in this answer. In the *Mishkan*, we were given the opportunity to create a virtual structure in which to practice stewardship, a space where we could potentially learn care and caution. This space echoed the "real" world outside, but inside it we found a "condensed" presence of God/dess, very close to our touch. Any divergence from the blueprint of Creation brings with it a reaction. If in the wide space of Creation we can heat up the atmosphere and wait decades until Arctic ice begins to melt, here the fire hits us instantly.

Torah ends the story of Creation and consecration of the earth with a human action and God's reaction (Eve and the Tree of Knowledge), and the telling of the creation and consecration of the *Mishkan* similarly ends with the story of priestly action and God's reaction (Nadab, Abihu, and the fire). Earth and *Mishkan* were both contaminated by a human act that could be read either as a mistake or as hubris. The consequence is painful in both instances because if regular/secular space allows itself to become defiled and then must wait until it is cleansed, surely sacred space *cannot* allow itself to hold dirt, contamination, or defilement and must eject that which is out of place.

Some chapters later, we return to the silently grieving father Aaron when Moses instructs him on the correct way of entering the sacred zone (הַקֹּדֶשׁ, *hakodesh*). And there, in chapter 16 of Leviticus, we learn the laws of cleansing the sacred space and of the ritual that will evolve to become Yom Kippur:

> And this shall be to you a law for all time: in the seventh month, on the tenth day of the month, you shall practice self-denial; and you shall do no manner of work. . . . He shall purge the innermost Shrine; he shall purge the Tent of Meeting and the altar; and he shall make expiation for the priests and for all the people of the congregation. This shall be to you a law for all time: to make atonement for the Israelites for all their sins once a year. (Leviticus 16:29, 33–34)

If ritual cleansing of the *Mishkan* was done correctly and *if* atonement was achieved, a year of plenty in all aspects of life was ensured. Why? Because this sacred structure represented the world, and the world must be purified for life to continue. In acknowledgment of our great power in the world, it is our job as humans to perform the ritual of cleansing, on both a spiritual and a very practical level. Whereas the story of *Gan Eden* ends with banishment and suffering, here we are offered a way to cleanse our sins and mishaps and begin again—not from an Edenic start, but by continuing within our often broken, but fixable world.

Torah and mythology create an origin story from which to draw energy to do our sacred work of cleansing the earth. Rabbi Glenn Jacob offers an in-depth exploration of *Avodah*, the sacred service of the Temple, as a model for the urgent climate work that needs to be done in our times, and he reminds us that a theology of *purification* could be a more robust tool at this point than that of *Creation*.[5] His distinction is important not only in that he offers us a new theology, but also in that we can use this idea to develop an active, ritual and halachic (Jewish legal) response to our current climate crisis. Below are a few suggestions from within the Yom Kippur ritual as to how we may do this.

Vidui—Confession

"Aaron shall lay both his hands upon the head of the live goat and confess over it all the iniquities and transgressions of the Israelites" (Leviticus 16:21). First, we offer a communal acknowledgment of guilt, because as we remember, Yom Kippur's *Vidui* involves the whole community speaking our sins together, in the same way that in Jewish theology redemption is communal and not individual. In our days of climate crisis, mass extinction, and social upheaval, we must reconnect the "I" and the "we." To bring a deep confession to our lips on Yom Kippur, we must first be able to imagine the terrible outcome of not recognizing our sins and offer a *Vidui* for our collective guilt.[6]

To know where the world is broken and what we are atoning for, we must first remember what a "working planet" looks like. We need to make sure that part of our ritual is in learning and relearning the science of our planet—the physics, biology, zoology, geology, chemistry—the whole of the ecosystem. That is, we must study the Torah of observing life and the universe:

> [We] should know the importance of ritual in building human community, but also understand the function of mycorrhizal fungi and soil microorganisms in the natural community in which the human community is embedded. . . . Our culture is afflicted with a vast disconnection, an abyss of ignorance that becomes apparent whenever an issue involving the natural world arises.[7]

As part of our preparation for the High Holy Days, and perhaps even as part of our spiritual work during *Aseret Y'mei T'shuvah* (the Ten Days of Atonement prior to Yom Kippur), we should make space in our communities and congregations to learn some hard science and educate ourselves on the current knowledge of our planet's rhythms and workings. It will be easier to know what we have done wrong when we know how life on earth is sustained.

Sa-ir LaAzazeil—The Scapegoat

The goat designated by lot for Azazel shall be left standing alive before the Eternal, to make expiation with it and to send it off to the wilderness for Azazel. . . . Aaron shall lay both his hands upon the head of the live goat and confess over it all the iniquities and transgressions of the Israelites, whatever their sins, putting them on the head of the goat; and it shall be sent off to the wilderness through a designated agent. Thus the goat shall carry on it all their iniquities to an inaccessible region and the goat shall be set free in the wilderness. (Leviticus 16:10, 21–22)

In the Book of Leviticus, we find a description of two rituals for cleansing the "house": the first deals with the case of a house being contaminated by *tzaraat* (skin disease), and the second tells of the Yom Kippur ritual. In both rituals we have "twin" animals—bird and bird (Leviticus 14:49–53), he-goat and he-goat (16:7–10, 20–22)—one of which will be sacrificed to God, and the other released away from human habitation. The "twinning" of animals might not indicate two parts of a ritual happening to two animals, but rather two aspects of the ritual happening to the "same" animal (but since we cannot both kill an animal and set it free, we need to use two identical animals). The two birds in the first ritual represent a single bird (and one house) going through a ritualized process of healing. One bird is sacrificed over "living waters," and then the live bird is dipped in her blood (talk about traumatizing someone!) and set free into the field (*sadeh*). The two goats stand next to each other as the lot is cast and together symbolize a single goat, who is enacting both the house of God (the *Mikdash*, which is being cleansed) and no-man's land—a covenant both with the house of God and of freedom in the wilderness. By sending out a portion of ourselves (represented by the bird and the goat) into the wild, we are acknowledging the presence of chaos, pain, and fright in Creation. Through this aspect of the ritual, we remind ourselves that "the world is not inherently safe; it is inherently unsafe"[8] and that the power of God/dess to confine chaos rather than to eliminate it is the essence of Creation. By sending a part of ourselves out to the borders of our habitation, we are redefining the edges of our "home," our place as humans, and making space for the unpredictable, nonhuman others who are as much a part of Creation as we are. This moment of the Yom Kippur ritual reminds us of the forces that lie outside our human home but are as much part of the wider cosmic home as we are. These forces strike fear in our hearts and are worthy opponents to our God of order and borders, though some of our theology knows how to make *them* a part of God: "I form light and create darkness, I make peace and create woe—I the Eternal do all these things" (Isaiah 45:7). Like the two birds and the two he-goats, the verse from Isaiah expresses that the two are one—both part of the covenant, both part of the wilderness and part of God. I am not suggesting we reintroduce animal sacrifice into our ritual, but it is critical that we find new liturgy and ritual to help us remember the awesome power of Creation around us and appreciate the delicacy of the islands of civilization we live within.

Kodesh HaKodashim—Holy of Holies

And he shall take a panful of glowing coals scooped from the altar before the Eternal, and two handfuls of finely ground aromatic incense, and bring this behind the curtain. He shall put the incense on the fire before the Eternal, so that the cloud from the incense screens the cover that is over [the Ark of] the Covenant, lest he die. (Leviticus 16:12–13)

Behind the curtain and within the Holy of Holies lies the Ark of the Covenant. The Day of Atonement aims at cleansing the contamination we have brought into our sacred spaces—the *Mishkan*, *Mikdash*, synagogues, and the earth—and so into our covenant with God. The *Mishkan* mirrors the earth, and Eve and Adam mirror Nadab and Abihu. So what is the sacred covenant or assignment that we are breaking again and again?

"So God Eternal took the man, placing him in the Garden of Eden to work it and keep it" (Genesis 2:15). Our original covenant, or assignment on earth, was to "work it and keep it" (*l'ovdah ul'shomrah*). The Hebrew here is interesting, especially relating to the word *l'ovdah*, "to work." The assignment *l'shomrah*, "to keep," is quite understandable; we are to be wardens of this place. *L'ovdah*, on the other hand, is usually understood as working the earth, being good gardeners. But the root for *ovdah* (*alef-vet-dalet*) has another meaning in biblical Hebrew, which is "to worship." In this reading, our role is to guard the earth and pay homage to it, that is, to realize once again the sacredness that dwells within its soil and ecosystems, just as the *Shechinah* (God's presence in the world) came and rested within the *Mishkan*. The earth is the *Mishkan* and should now be the focal point of our spiritual and religious work as Jews.

I find Leviticus in general, and especially the scapegoat ritual, to be fascinating in the way it deals with contamination (both physical and spiritual) and purification. Similarly, much of the spiritual language around the climate crisis is apocalyptic and draws its theology and imagery from traditions where the world must be destroyed for it to be renewed (e.g., the "second coming of Christ," the Ragnarok, Gog and Magog in our own mythology). These are theologies that call for the ruin of our world and society before new life emerges. Leviticus suggests a different way, one in which we recognize that part of our human existence is sin, mistakes, and contamination. By recognizing this fact, we are not divesting ourselves from responsibility, but rather we are taking on a much greater commitment to our original assignment here on earth—*l'ovdah ul'shomrah*, to work and pay homage to it. On Yom Kippur during *Seder HaAvodah*, bring your body down to the floor, to the ground. Touch the earth. Feel yourself breathing, and feel the earth breathing with you as you commit to guarding and seeing the sacredness of it all once again.

NOTES

1. Mary Douglas, *Leviticus as Literature* (Oxford: Oxford University Press, 1999), 200. For an expansion on her idea of Leviticus as a written projection of the Tabernacle and as a form of "Memory Palace" holding the structure and meaning of that sacred space, see 195–200.
2. The other story, found in Leviticus 24, tells of the stoning of a blasphemer.
3. Mary Douglas, *Purity and Danger: An Analysis of Concept of Pollution and Taboo* (London: Routledge, 2004 [1966]), 44.
4. Another, more midrashic, reading could connect Nadab and Abihu with the Titan Prometheus, who, in Greek mythology, stole fire from the gods and introduced it to humans. He thus enabled us to become fully "human," which is where it parallels with Eve and her consumption of wisdom. But, like Eve, he too was punished by the gods with unending physical suffering. Nadab and Abihu did not steal fire from God, but rather brought "alien fire" into the *Mishkan*. Having been entrusted with the sacred role of taking care of the communal fire, they misappropriated their position and brought in another fire. In this reading, their sin was the sin of pride, of thinking they understood the inner workings of something that was perhaps beyond their grasp.
5. Glenn Jacob, "A Jewish Theology of Climate Change," *CCAR Journal: The Reform Jewish Quarterly*, Winter 2020, 108–29.
6. You can find one such *Vidui* in Andrew Ramer, *Fragments of the Brooklyn Talmud* (Eugene, OR: Resource Publications, 2019), 57–58.
7. Starhawk (Miriam Simos), *The Earth Path: Grounding Your Spirit in the Rhythms of Nature* (New York: HarperOne, 2004), 7.
8. Jon D. Levenson, *Creation and the Persistence of Evil: The Jewish Drama of Divine Omnipotence* (Princton, NJ: Princeton University Press, 1994), 17.

A Tu BiSh'vat Prayer for Creation

RABBI WARREN G. STONE

SOURCE OF CREATION and Life of the Universe, we gather on Tu BiSh'vat as Jews of conscience, with a deep spiritual bond to Your natural wonders, to affirm and preserve Creation.

We are grateful for Creation in all its majesty: the ever-flowing waters, the azure blue skies, the complex life of the earth's forests, the myriad of life forms—amoebae and falcon, black-footed ferret and wild turkey, human being and soaring eagle.

The life of all creatures and our own lives are One, profoundly dependent upon each other.

We call our ancient scroll of wisdom, the Torah, an *eitz chayim*, a "tree of life," for it, like the earth's great forests, sustains us. Torah teaches us that Creation, in its great diversity, is harmoniously interconnected. Like the trees, we too need strong and deep roots for nourishment. The uplifted branches of trees point to our future. God, let us be strong, as strong as ancient trees. The Psalmist was right in saying, "Like a tree planted by the waters, we shall not be moved."[1]

We are grateful for the life we are lent. We pledge to lift up our voices both in praise of You and in defense of Your Creation.

NOTE
1. Adapted from Psalm 1:3.

First published by the Religious Action Center of Reform Judaism
as an environmental worship resource.

Voices of the Future
Stories from the Jewish Youth Climate Movement

MICHAEL PINCUS, ANNA DUBEY, RAPHAELA GOLD,
PENELOPE KOPP, AND TALI DEANER

THE JEWISH YOUTH CLIMATE MOVEMENt (JYCM) was founded by Hazon in 2019. We are dedicated to mitigating climate change by empowering teens, mobilizing our communities, and taking action. We are in a global climate crisis, and Jewish tradition compels us to respond. We aim to live as the midrash *Kohelet Rabbah* instructs us: "For if you corrupt it, there is no one to repair it for you" (7:13:1). JYCM believes that our greater purpose is to be a resource for people of all ages and religions, spreading a multigenerational message to stand in the name of climate justice. Composed of a National Leadership Board and over forty chapters within synagogues, schools, and other Jewish institutions across the country, JYCM understands that young voices should not only be heard but be recognized as having the power to make change. As a movement, we exist to make taking collective action toward climate justice a central, defining feature of Jewish identity and existence over the next decade and *Sh'mitah* cycle (the biblical Jewish period of land restoration), empowering the next generations of Jewish youth to be leaders in our fight for a sustainable and equitable world for all.

Written by five members of JYCM's National Leadership Board, the following essays share what it means to be a young Jewish climate activist in our world today.

Michael Pincus

Standing outside a random door in suburban Florida with a "Lauren Baer for Congress" sticker on and a clipboard in hand is pretty much a death wish. And yet, starting in July 2018, a month full of humidity and Drake's new hit single "In My Feelings," I did it door-to-door four hours a day, four days a week. I got used to classic Florida greetings like

"I'm gonna shoot you," "They oughta send kids like you to Bible camp," and "I'm calling 9-1-1." Throughout it all, I kept knocking, right up until election day.

I joined Lauren Baer's campaign for Florida's Eighteenth Congressional District seat after hearing her speak at a community event. Lauren was my first exposure to someone like me—a queer Jewish person—running for political office. She inspired me to join her campaign as an organizing fellow, recruiting volunteers, phone banking, and most importantly, canvassing.

This experience took me out of my comfort zone. I had preconceived notions about certain areas where I was knocking on doors, whether about a community's class or its general political alignment. Yet, surprisingly, I forged strong connections with many of the people behind the doors on which I knocked.

While campaigning for Lauren, I learned a lot about her views on both local and global climate issues, and my learning was enhanced because she spoke as a Jewish woman. In a guest column for *TC Palm*, Lauren wrote, "We need a representative who is clear-eyed about the challenges we face and appreciates the potential we have—someone who won't just pay lip service to the environment, but will back up rhetoric with action." It was Lauren who taught me how urgent the climate crisis is, and it was through knocking on doors for her campaign that I learned what local residents thought about it.

There is something truly thrilling about standing in front of a closed door, waiting to see who opens it. While canvassing, I was constantly on my toes. For every negative experience and door slammed in my face, there was a person eager to speak with me and share their story.

There was a time when I spoke with a woman on her porch for over an hour. She wanted to know which mental health services my candidate would include in health-care proposals. For her, it was personal. She told me about her son—politically active, like me—who committed suicide after not having access to mental health resources. Her son was a vocal proponent for climate justice and would have agreed with Lauren's campaign. She said that door-to-door canvassers like me gave her the same hope for the future that her son had. I had not expected to end up crying on a porch with a woman I had just met.

I think of that woman on the porch in suburban Florida every time I march in a protest, attend a Jewish Youth Climate Movement meeting, or write about my experiences. My experiences taught me the importance of individual climate stories, like the one I am telling now. Everyone joined this fight for a different reason, but together we form a unified front putting in the work for climate justice. Our interpersonal connections can go a long way in moving other people to take action.

> MICHAEL PINCUS *is the Jewish Ritual and Culture Fellow for the Jewish Youth Climate Movement (JYCM). They are originally from West Palm Beach, Florida, and are now a second-year student at the University of Southern California in Los Angeles. At USC, Michael studies journalism with two minors in philosophy and screenwriting. They are a USC Admission Center student ambassador (campus tour guide) and a USC Hillel service engagement intern. In high school, Michael served on JYCM's executive board and public relations team. Outside of school and JYCM, Michael loves playing with their two cats (Latke and Gelt) and their two dogs (Teddy and Dreidel). Michael is trying to rekindle hobbies in cooking, rollerblading, and hiking.*

Anna Dubey

A peasant man accused of romantic entanglement with a princess faces an unusual punishment: he must open one of two identical doors. Behind one, a noble lady awaits his hand in marriage. Behind the other lies a tiger salivating at the thought of human flesh. The princess, knowing which door is which, gestures for her lover to choose the one on the right. But the narrative ends at the moment the man opens the door. Did the princess save her lover from death, or did jealousy of the other woman overwhelm her?[1] I pored over the text of Frank Stockton's well-known short story, "The Lady or the Tiger," scrutinizing for telltale language, and between the lines I found the crux of the tale. Are humans fundamentally vindictive and selfish, or do we have each other's best interests at heart? Is there reason for hope, or are we doomed to irredeemable cruelty? I had my answer, then: the tiger.

As my junior year English class contemplated the story, I persuaded most of the students that the princess must have sacrificed her lover to the tiger's claws. But the topic still rattled around my mind, prying at my cemented theories of the world.

I had long ago emerged from my childhood daze of blurry smiles and soft colors into a blunt and uncaring world. Marine life poisoned by oil spills, chickens crushed into cages with their beaks slashed off, refugees fleeing the devastating climate of their home countries—this was the world I knew. So I stored each new fragment of information in my brain, confident that it would fuel me to deliver more impassioned speeches, write more letters to legislators, do more, more, more. But instead of strengthening me to make a change, the constant influx of devastating news made me wonder: Why bother working so hard to fight the inevitable? How could I, one teenager, possibly prevent the end of the world as we know it?

Yet in the weeks after reading the story, a peculiar feeling overcame me. The first wisp of this feeling drifted by when my sister read about poor animal treatment in factory farms and pledged to become a vegetarian like me. It came again, stronger, when thirty people from my school accompanied me to a climate strike in Lower Manhattan. And as I began working with other teens in JYCM to plan panels, campaigns, and "Get Out the Vote" events, it came stronger still: A feeling that I shouldn't have been so certain the princess sent her lover to his death. A feeling that I, one teenager, could make a difference—because I was not alone.

Let me tell you another story. Humanity squanders its resources faster than the planet can replenish them. The humans—alas!—do not know how to react to their impending doom. They must make a choice.

I stand before two doors, but I know which is which. Behind one door is the future of hopelessness. It is the future of the ravenous ocean swallowing my home city. It is the future in which I don't think we can change for the better. It is the tiger.

Behind the other door is the future of hope. It is the future of living in harmony with the earth and repairing what we've broken because we have each other's best interests at heart. It is a future fueled by aspiration and not by fear; it is the future in which I bring my vision for the planet to life. It is the lady, eyes wide and unbelieving, astonished by our ability to improve.

And so, as does the princess's lover, I open a door. But this story has an ending, and I bet you can figure it out.

ANNA DUBEY is a student at Brown University, where she currently studies ecology and works in a biogeochemistry lab. She served as a member of the National Leadership Board of the Jewish Youth Climate Movement, where she is now part of the inaugural JYCM Amitim College Cohort. Her writing has previously appeared in Encyclopedia Britannica *and* The Peoplehood Papers.

Raphaela Gold

There once was a man with two pockets, each containing a note on which was written a quotation from Jewish tradition. When the man felt disconsolate, he reached into one pocket and read the words: *Bishvili nivra haolam*, "The world was created for me." When he felt prideful, he reached into his other pocket and read: *V'anochi afar v'efer*, "I am but dust and ashes." Thus he lived a balanced life.

I grew up hearing this Chasidic teaching often. The crux of the tale: how can we aim to change the world while maintaining humility?

Thus far, fighting the climate crisis has mostly filled me with moments of discouragement in which I am compelled to look to the words "the world was created for me" for comfort. When I learn that deforestation is responsible for at least 15 percent of global greenhouse gases per year, hear about fires ravaging California, and recall the myriad natural disasters that have rendered millions of people climate migrants over the past few years, I feel like I am but dust and ashes. I can't possibly make a difference. Nothing I do is enough. When I was ten years old and became a vegetarian, it felt like that was enough, like I was finally taking concrete actions that would result in concrete change. But then I discovered that humans eat sixty-five billion chickens per year. I understood that my individual decision wasn't nearly enough. When my neighborhood's farmers market opened a composting service and my mom and I began composting, I felt righteous each time we placed our batch of compost into the bin. But somehow we are still headed toward a positive feedback loop of climate change, and scientists have been telling us that we have 12, then 11, 10, 9, 8 years left until the effects of climate change would become irreversible. My righteous acts were clearly having no impact. Even when helping to found my school environmental club, hosting guest speakers, and working to make our school more sustainable, I knew that the microcosm of my school was only one small battle in the larger war of climate change—and that whether we won or lost our little battle would not significantly change the outcome of the war. Now, working with the Jewish Youth Climate Movement, I finally feel as though I'm part of something big, something important. However, discouragingly, I still don't see that we've made any appreciable difference.

Growing up in New York City, where we're definitely beginning to feel the effects of climate change—even if not as significantly as they are felt in other places—I learned that being an environmentalist meant stopping people from littering and always recycling. I learned very little besides that. When we had hurricanes, few people linked them to climate change. But now there will be a seawall around Staten Island by 2025. Now people are waking up. Still, there's that nagging voice that nothing is enough. That we are but dust of the earth, and that a seawall is putting a Band-Aid on a problem that requires far more than that. I love snow and cold weather, I love looking at the sky, I love the changing seasons, and I love the feeling of possibility that rises within me at the beginning of each of them. I don't want to lose winter or parks or beautiful weather or my future, but until recently, I was convinced that a dim future was inevitable.

Over the summer, however, along with many other JYCM members, I read Jonathan Safran Foer's book *We Are the Weather*, and it changed my thinking immensely. In the chapter "Dispute with the Soul," Foer narrates a conversation between himself and his own soul.

His soul asks, "Have you noticed how often conversations about climate change end with the question of hopefulness?"

Foer challenges, "Have you noticed how often conversations about climate change end?"

This is why collaboration in the climate movement is so crucial: Multiple people are required in order to hold a conversation. It is our job to ensure that conversations about climate change don't end. Perhaps *I* am but dust of the earth. But upon converging our molecules of dust by coming together and mobilizing our communities, *we as a group* are significant. *We* are for whom the world was made. I know this when I listen to the stories of my friends who are on the frontlines of the climate war or when my school environmental club works with the administration to reduce waste. The world was created for *us*, and our collective power is reason for hope.

> RAPHAELA (RAPHI) GOLD *is a first-year student at Princeton University where she is currently studying English and environmental studies. Due to her belief that climate change is the most urgent issue of our time, Raphi joined the Jewish Youth Climate Movement in 2019 and has gained so much from the opportunity to work with other Jewish teens similarly committed to environmentalism. She worked on the public relations team and served as the creative arts and writing director on the JYCM executive board from 2020 to 2021. She is now a service engagement intern through Repair the World, working to connect Jewish college students with environmental activism.*

Penelope Kopp

"*Olam chesed yibaneh!* We will build this world from love!" We belted our song, dancing arm-in-arm under the stars in our Shabbat dresses after a full day of picking cucumbers, soothing bug bites with dandelion leaves, and giggling through a lightning storm. We were lucky to be at Eden Village Camp (EVC), the place I lovingly refer to as my hippie-Jewish-farm camp.

During the forty-eight weeks of the year I wasn't at camp, I held onto its *Environmentalism, Social Justice, and Spirituality!* motto. When I was in eighth grade, I designed and sold *Heal the World* tote bags to raise money for Hurricane Maria victims, which connected me to Eden Village's "Attitude of Gratitude"—being grateful for what we have and channeling that energy into helping others.

The summer before high school, EVC led us on a three-week camping trip through the Deep South. After our days working in community gardens, we cooked yummy dinners on portable stoves and ate together around campfires, then dropped off our compost scraps each morning at the next farm. Every day, we engaged with each other and connected to the Earth in a harmonious partnership.

I came home ravenous to learn more about food systems and climate change. I studied Earth science and deepened my understanding of the size and complexity of the crisis. I phone-banked, lobbied, and walked out. Yet as natural disasters became more frequent, I grew overwhelmed with existential dread, because I feared our leaders would never take action. I teared up as my cousins were evacuated from wildfires, when my friend sheltered in his basement during a tornado, and as I saw the photos of refugees fleeing barren farms. The impacts of climate change were only getting worse. This systemic crisis was so much bigger than me, and I didn't believe my efforts could make *the* difference. Would I even make *any* difference? Change takes time. Could we win before it was too late? The task ahead seemed impossible. Time was running out.

Then, in the spring of 2020, I became a co-founder of the Jewish Youth Climate Movement, an initiative of Hazon. I had never built a movement from scratch, much less during a global pandemic! In Zoom after Zoom, the other leaders and I hashed out action plans and defined our principles: to agitate for change within Jewish institutions and enlist our communities in the broader fight. JYCM reminded me of what I absorbed as a kid at EVC—that Jewish tradition instructs us to pursue justice and heal the Earth. I was grateful to learn that the Torah guides farmers to set aside the corners of the field (*pei-ah*) to feed the hungry. I started to appreciate that my religious and cultural values support my progressive ones. It's beautiful that people have gathered for thousands of years to recommit to these ideals, to connect to those who came before, and to dedicate ourselves to those who will come after. I cannot just focus on tearing down destructive and oppressive systems. I am committed to creating a more sustainable and equitable world, and JYCM has helped me find connection, gratitude, and joy along the way.

At our first JYCM retreat, as the first three stars appeared in the sky, marking havdalah, we sang our way into the woods, arm-in-arm. Our voices grew louder; my voice grew louder. We danced around the fire as it crackled a flurry of red into the sky. We shared strategies for making perfect s'mores: I always push my stick right into the heart of the flames. I looked around at the kids I had grown close to that past year, and the new recruits I had just met, then up again to the stars. These were my people. I've been able to cultivate a strong sense of belonging that has kept me positive and full of love in this sometimes devastating fight. I squeezed them closer, inspired to return next summer, with countless more in our movement. "*Olam chesed yibaneh!* We will build this world from love!"

> PENELOPE KOPP *is a member of the class of 2026 at Tufts University. Penelope joined the Jewish Youth Climate Movement as a founding board member in 2020 and served as the actions director on the executive board from 2021–2022, where she led programming, facilitated lobbying, and spoke at rallies. She has also engaged with climate efforts on national and local political campaigns, as an organizing intern in her city council-man's office, through volunteering or working at community gardens and farmers' markets, and at her high school. For fun, Penelope loves drawing, sewing, and trying new food. Penelope grew up in Brooklyn, New York.*

Tali Deaner

In February of 2020, my friend and I were asked to lead a session and have a booth at a conference called "The Intersection of Climate and Politics" as representatives of the Sunrise Movement in our town. We had to arrive early in the morning, and as my mom drove us down the dirt road to reach this nature center, she asked me, "Are you sure we're going the right way?"

Once we arrived, we quickly felt out of place. On our table, we displayed a sign-up clipboard to attend our climate strike and posters with passionate phrases like "Green New Deal" and "Organizing for Our Future." Meanwhile, we were surrounded by wildlife conservation groups, a testament to the environmentalism of another era, one our generation had left far behind. My friend, who is also in high school, and I stuck out because of our ages: we were some of the few people there under thirty. She gave me a look that said, "I don't think we fit in here very well—how can we possibly have something to say that these people think is worth listening to?"

At midday, I was standing at our table, and an older woman approached me. I started telling her about Sunrise, and she told me how cool she thought it was. The time for people to visit the booths ended, and we were supposed to split off into the conference presentations, but the woman stayed talking at my booth. She told me how she worked tirelessly on the 1972 presidential campaign between McGovern and Nixon and that McGovern lost every single state except one. She had a sad look in her eyes, and well, I did too. Being hopeful about the future of our world, especially during the pandemic, is something I struggle with too—how can we know that any of this will work? Especially with the fear of the 2020 election over our heads back then and the pandemic now that has ravaged the world, uncertainty abounded. After listening to her talk and sharing her sense of sadness, I felt a little stuck. How could I possibly help someone who had felt down so many times feel optimistic about the future of our world? How could I make her believe we can actually stop climate change? It's hard talking to strangers about our capacity to realize our visions and enact change, especially to a stranger who had been let down by politics so many times.

At this moment, I had a choice: I thought about saying, "I'm sorry to hear that," and continuing on with my day, but I dug deep inside and thought, "I probably have a perspective that she doesn't yet." I told her about my excitement for the Green New Deal, the presidential primary in Michigan, and our major upcoming Earth Day climate strike. She smiled at me while I talked and started to tear up. She told me, "I'm so hopeful because of your generation." She said she was going to try to come to our climate strike a few months later because she was so impressed.

In that woman I was talking to, I saw who I could be in fifty years: sadly telling a young person that despite trying my hardest to create a better world, my efforts had not been enough. Yet, I have a lot of optimism that something different will happen this time; I know we can do it. To me, this is what activism is all about—helping our neighbors and communities feel hopeful again. The climate crisis is scary and devastating, but if we only feel sadness, we're not going to get anywhere. If we take the time to talk to people from all walks of life and make them feel heard, they'll listen to us, too.

Ultimately, I don't know where my conversation with this person took her in life. Sadly, I don't even remember her name. Even so, I like to think that maybe our conversation encouraged her to go home from that conference and strike up a similar conversation with a friend or family member. Maybe our conversation had a ripple effect. And I know the effect this conversation had on me: it caused me to want to work so much harder at getting out the vote and organizing for an equitable and sustainable world. Even though I was younger than most people at the conference, my voice made an impact. Just as my mom was unsure whether we drove the right way to the nature center, we may not know exactly what our path is—but not knowing doesn't mean that it is not worth doing.

> TALI DEANER *is a second-year student at Kalamazoo College in Kalamazoo, Michigan, majoring in sociology and minoring in Spanish and environmental studies. She joined the Jewish Youth Climate Movement (JYCM) in 2020, was on the JYCM board in high school, and was a college organizing fellow in the spring of 2022. Tali became interested in this work after growing up at a social justice oriented Jewish summer camp in Michigan, which she now has the joy of working at each summer. She works at her college's Center for Civic Engagement as the student coordinator and is part of an after-school program, Club Grub, which teaches cooking skills to third graders.*

PART FIVE

Contemporary Responses

We end with a section focused most specifically on today and on the future. Each chapter presents a clear contemporary issue, situating it in our world while using ideas and tools from our Jewish tradition to connect us with the ongoing unfolding of Torah.

Rabbi Mark Washofsky, PhD, provides a framework for building a new category of Jewish law: environmental halachah. Alon Tal, PhD, a former member of the Knesset, explores the history of Zionist environmentalism and suggests how Zionism can inform our current environmental activism. Reflecting on the concept of *galut* (exile), Daniel Delgado uses postcolonial theory to understand Jewish environmental responsibility. Rabbi Dr. Shmuly Yanklowitz describes his work on global interfaith activism. Looking toward a sustainable future, Rabbi Dean Shapiro creates a new mission for synagogues as community organizations. Rabbi Jonathan E. Blake, Ron Schulhof, and Michelle Sterling share their process for moving their synagogue toward a zero-waste building. Centering eco-justice and sustainable eating, Rosa Fink, Tanya Fink, MS, RD, and Rabbi Daniel B. Fink consider the ways in which Jewish tradition can guide our response to the environment today. Considering those who tended the land before us, Rabbi Jessica Rosenberg outlines her Jewish grounding for the practice of acknowledging Indigenous peoples whose lands have been colonized. Rabbi Sandy Eisenberg Sasso, DMin, reflects on the image of stones in Torah. To end the volume, Rabbi Jennie Rosenn shares her story of founding Dayenu, an organization mobilizing the American Jewish community to confront the climate crisis with spiritual audacity and bold political action.

28

Beyond *Bal Tashchit*

Developing an Environmental Halachah

RABBI MARK WASHOFSKY, PhD

AS COMMITTED JEWS who are also committed environmentalists, we like to think that our concern for the fate of our planet reflects authentic Jewish values. We'd like to think that our activism is what our Jewish tradition, as expressed in its sacred literary sources, requires of us. And by "sources," I mean the halachic sources. That's because halachah, the Jewish legal tradition, is the language of Jewish sacred action, the discourse that puts those "authentic Jewish values" into practice. When our tradition discusses and argues questions of how we should *act* in relationship with God or other people, we usually find those discussions and arguments recorded in the halachic literature. Given the vital importance of environmental protection to humanity's future, we'd expect the halachah to recognize it as a mitzvah, as a set of actions we Jews ought to take in response to the covenant that makes us a people.

Such, however, is not the case. Jewish law does not speak of environmental protection as a mitzvah. The concept does not appear in lists of the 613 commandments like Rambam's *Sefer HaMitzvot*. Nor do the great halachic codes contain a section bearing a name like *Hilchot Eichut Has'vivah*, "Laws of Environmental Quality." That silence contains multitudes. The codes, which organize the vast corpus of Talmudic discussion and post-Talmudic commentary under subject headings, function as maps of the halachic universe,[1] identifying those aspects of life in covenant that ought to be of concern to the traditionally religious Jew. Rambam's *Mishneh Torah*, for example, is divided into fourteen "books" (*s'farim*) and subdivided into eighty-four sections of halachot, each of which codifies the rules governing a department of Jewish practice either weighty (*Hilchot Shabbat*, Laws of Sabbath Observance; *Hilchot*

Eidut, Laws of Evidence) or abstruse (*Hilchot N'zirut*, Laws of the Nazir-ite; *Hilchot M'chusarei Kaparah*, Laws concerning One Whose Ritual Atonement Is Incomplete). The absence of a *Hilchot Eichut Has'vivah* testifies that the tradition has never defined environmental protection as a self-standing mitzvah.

Yet none of this means that Jewish law is indifferent toward the environment. It means rather that while various halachot and principles relating to environmental issues are scattered throughout the Rabbinic legal literature, the idea of environmental protection does not exist as a recognized concept of halachic thought, readily available in an off-the-shelf form in the Talmud and codes. It follows that such a category could be constructed by gathering those scattered materials, putting them into systematic form, and updating them so that they address contemporary realities. I am suggesting that we, the Jewish environmentalists who are the intended audience of this book, take on this project.

This sort of work is nothing new; it has been done before, in law and in halachah. A famous example in the history of jurisprudence is the 1890 article in which Samuel Warren and Louis Brandeis argue for the existence of a right to privacy in the Anglo-American common law, even though the literary sources of that law do not mention that term. They locate this right by assembling a number of existing common law protections and identifying a moral principle that unites them, namely the protection of "the inviolate personality."[2] The discovery of this new right, controversial for some years, was ultimately accepted by jurists working in common law and in American constitutional law.[3] In Jewish law, as well, some scholars infer from various provisions in halachah the existence of a substantive Jewish legal value they call "privacy," even though the sources do not expressly mention such a value. Their findings are aimed at providing material to Israeli lawmakers who are interested in drawing upon Jewish sources in crafting their legislation.[4] The same thing happens in classical halachah. While the Talmud contains numerous texts that relate to the subject nowadays called "medical ethics," and while Rambam codifies a number of these in the *Mishneh Torah*, neither of those works speaks explicitly of a legal category called *Hilchot R'fuah* (Laws of Medicine) or *Hilchot Rofim* (Laws Pertaining to Medical Practitioners). We do find those categories, however, in later works

(*Tur* and *Shulchan Aruch, Yoreh Dei-ah* 336), which organize the diffuse halachic material under its own distinct department of the law. Some contemporary rabbis, mostly in Israel, have gathered Talmudic and traditional halachic material to create a new field of halachah that speaks to issues of government and politics, sometimes referred to as *Hilchot M'dinah*, "Laws regarding the State."[5] In all these cases, the legal writers do not claim to be inventing anything new. They insist, rather, that they are simply making explicit, through the act of collection and systematization, aspects of their legal traditions that until now have existed only implicitly. The impetus to engage in this process is the recognition that history often demands that the implicit be made clear, that "political, social, and economic changes entail the recognition of new rights" and the "law, in its eternal youth, grows to meet the new demands of society."[6]

What existing halachic rules and principles might we draw together to construct "Laws of Environmental Quality"? The most obvious starting point is the mitzvah known as *bal tashchit*, "do not destroy," based upon Deuteronomy 20:19, "When in your war against a city you have to besiege it a long time in order to capture it, you must not destroy [*lo tashchit*] its fruit-bearing trees." The tradition reads this mitzvah expansively as forbidding destructive behavior in general: "[This mitzvah applies] not only to trees. On the contrary, anyone who in a wanton and destructive manner [*derech hashchatah*] breaks implements, tears clothing, demolishes a building, stops up a well or spring, or spoils foodstuffs transgresses the rule *bal tashchit*."[7]

The scope of the prohibition leads some to cite this rule as *the* basis for the Jewish conception of environmentalism.[8] The classical halachah also contains rules dealing with the pollution of the air and water. *Mishnah Bava Batra* 2:9 instructs, "Animal carcasses, graves, and tanneries must be distanced at least fifty cubits from a town," because of the foul odor they emit (Bartenura *ad loc.*). A passage in the *Tosefta* (*Bava M'tzia* 11:31, ed. Lieberman) prohibits one from utilizing a public bathing facility if one's hands and feet are filthy, and it forbids any bathing in water sources reserved for drinking.[9] Environmental concerns are present in rules concerning land use: an ancient *takanah* (ordinance) forbids the raising of sheep and goats in *Eretz Yisrael* (Land of Israel) "in order to preserve the land for human habitation [*mishum yishuv Eretz Yisrael*]," that is, to protect farmers' crops.[10] We also find zoning regulations in early Rabbinic sources: residents may prevent the operation of certain businesses in their neighborhood due to concerns over traffic (*Mishnah Bava Batra* 2:3) or noise (Babylonian Talmud, *Bava Batra* 21b, *baraita*).

As with the issue of privacy, we can stitch these individual provisions together with a common conceptual thread, and on the basis of that commonality we can organize them into a general category, *Hilchot Eichut Has'vivah*. This is no mere matter of semantics. To assert the existence of this category is to claim that "Jewish environmentalism" is more than simply a high-minded sentiment backed by a few choice quotes from the Bible and the aggadic literature. It is a substantive matter of Jewish *law*, which means that the tradition sees the protection of the environment as an obligation, a demand that Torah places upon our behavior as individuals and as communities.

To be successful, however, this assertion will have to overcome at least two obvious difficulties. The first is that the scope of these rules is seriously limited. For example, the rule *bal tashchit*, as we have seen, prohibits only those acts of "destruction" that are performed *derech hashchatah*, in a wanton manner, for no socially useful purpose but simply to destroy. Indeed, the rule permits one to chop down fruit-bearing trees and to destroy other objects "if one may derive some benefit from the action, for example, if one can sell the wood of that tree for a profit."[11] That's a significant loophole, given that individuals, corporations, and governments that undertake activities harmful to the environment routinely justify those activities as economically beneficial to the community. If their argument is reasonable, then *bal tashchit* and the other environmental halachic rules would not necessarily stand in their way. The second difficulty is that the environmental halachah we find in the sources is woefully outdated. The rules reflect the legal and economic conditions that prevailed in ancient agricultural societies and medieval urban neighborhoods. They do not address the questions we face today, challenges of worldwide dimensions posed by industrialization, the consumer economy, and climate change. If "the Laws of Environmental Quality" offer no substantive guidance as to how we should confront those challenges, it is questionable whether they deserve to be called "laws" at all.

These difficulties, though serious, are not insurmountable. Every healthy legal tradition encounters and overcomes such problems in the course of its development. The halachah's environmental rules are "limited" only in the sense that any legal value, because it must coexist with other, potentially conflicting legal values, is limited. A legal system that wishes to protect the environment will also wish to facilitate economic activity. In cases of conflict between these values, the environment does not always and automatically prevail over economics. Environmental law will therefore consist largely of efforts by jurists to balance the competing claims, to determine in particular cases just where the line between environmental protection and economic activity should be drawn. This might be done through sweeping legislation, but it is more often accomplished through case law, in which existing rules and principles are interpreted so that they can be applied to resolve new and specific questions. This brings us to our second difficulty: environmental halachah is "outdated" only because we don't yet have that case law. Rabbis and Jewish communities have not as a rule been called upon to apply existing halachic rules to those new and specific questions. The remedy, of course, is to do the work, to ask the questions, to interpret the sources, and to arrive at the appropriate answers. For example, we have seen that the rule *bal tashchit*, which prohibits wanton and pointless destruction (*derech hashcharah*), traditionally gives way before claims of profit and economic benefit. But the rabbinic authors who made this determination did not work within the context of today's climate crisis. Had they done so, it is at least arguable that they would have arrived at a different understanding of what counts as "wanton destruction." Our times require a new definition of *derech hashchatah*, in which the short-term profitability of individual economic activities is balanced against the substantial and permanent risks they present to the environment and the human future. This, obviously, is a complex task. Whether framing general rules or responding to individual cases, those constructing this new department of halachah cannot do the work all by themselves. They will have to draw upon the findings of environmental scientists, economists, and policy makers. But that's nothing new; after all, halachists who write in the field of Jewish medical ethics seek guidance from physicians and public health specialists. To repeat: this sort of thing has been done before.

I suggest here that we do it again. If there is such a thing as a Jewish response to the environmental crisis—that is, a response rooted in the Jewish texts that speak to our duty to the world around us—it ought to speak the halachic language in which those texts are composed. It should come into being in the traditional Jewish way: as halachic literature, essays and responsa that address the entire range of issues of concern to Jewish environmentalists. That literature, and the effort involved in its creation, is what I mean by *Hilchot Eichut Has'vivah*.

NOTES

1. Rambam's *Mishneh Torah* codifies all matters of observance, including practices that disappeared with exile and the destruction of the Temple. Most other halachic compilations, like the *Tur* and the *Shulchan Aruch*, content themselves with codifying present-day halachah (*halachah hanoheget baz'man hazeh*).

2. Samuel D. Warren and Louis D. Brandeis, "The Right to Privacy," *Harvard Law Review* 4 (1890): 193–220.

3. See Mark Washofsky, "Internet, Privacy, and Progressive *Halakhah*," in *The Internet Revolution and Jewish Law*, ed. Walter Jacob (Pittsburgh: Rodef Shalom Press, 2014), http://www.freehofinstitute.org/uploads/1/2/0/6/120631295/the_internet_privacy_and_progressive_halakhah.pdf, at 88ff.

4. Among them Nachum Rakover, *Hahaganah al tzin'at hap'rat* (Jerusalem: Ministry of Justice, 2006).

5. The title of a multivolume work by R. Eliezer Y. Waldenberg (d. 2006).

6. Warren and Brandeis, "The Right to Privacy," 193.

7. *Mishneh Torah, Hilchot M'lachim* 6:10, based upon Babylonian Talmud, *Shabbat* 105b and Babylonian Talmud, *Bava Kama* 91b.

8. See Eilon Schwartz, "*Bal Tashchit*: A Jewish Environmental Precept," in *Jewish Environmental Ethics: A Reader*, ed. Martin Yaffe (Lanham, MD: Lexington Books, 2001), 230–49.

9. The early twentieth-century *Aruch HaShulchan* includes this detail in a chapter dealing with "public harm," suggesting that environmental damage is a tort.

10. *Mishnah Bava Kama* 7:7 and Bartenura *ad loc.*, following Rashi to the mishnah on Babylonian Talmud, *Bava Kama* 79b.

11. *Sefer HaChinuch*, mitzvah no. 529. See Babylonian Talmud, *Bava Kama* 91b and *Mishneh Torah, Hilchot M'lachim* 6:8.

29

The Land's Still Small Voice Beckons Us All
Preserving a Collective, Zionist Environmental Ethic

ALON TAL, PhD

ZIONISM has always been focused on meeting needs of the Jewish people as a collective entity.[1] The Land of Israel and its environmental health were part of the common cause to which private interests were expected to yield. The needs of individual Jews were secondary. Indeed, for most of the past century, Zionism was synonymous with sacrificing for this greater good.

Sacrifice was surely required. During the first half of the twentieth century, Palestine was a hard sell, even to an oppressed and restless Eastern European Jewry that suddenly found it had options.[2] The universal vision of Trotsky and a new classless, Soviet society surely had appeal for young idealists. The American "Golden Medina," or even the Canadian, Australian, and Argentinian versions, offered unprecedented economic opportunities for the more pragmatic or materialistic.

And then there was Palestine, with an "attractive" package that included malaria, violent Arab attacks, abject poverty, Tel Aviv summers without air-conditioning, and absolutely no guarantee that anything would come of the Jewish people's nascent national aspirations. It is little wonder, therefore, that only about 3 percent of the Jews who emigrated from Europe during this period purchased tickets to the Jaffa port. And sooner than later, most of this intrepid cohort found the challenge to be too much. David Ben-Gurion may have been exaggerating when he noted that 90 percent of his peers in the second *aliyah* eventually left.[3] Nonetheless, disillusionment among immigrants has always been a prevalent phenomenon.

What the Zionist idea could offer, however, was an inspirational ideology of the collective. For the first seventy-five years of the twentieth century, the kibbutz movement wielded a disproportionately powerful influence, expecting its members—and its country—to "take according to their needs and to give according to their abilities." Regardless of the ideological camp, Zionist thinkers—from the pragmatic politics of Herzl to the selfless socialism of Borochov to the religious mysticism of Rabbi Kook—all called for casting one's lot "all in" with the national revival of the Jewish people. Even Revisionist-Zionist leader Ze'ev Jabotinksy, who is often presented as an advocate of radical individualism and capitalism,[4] in fact also appealed to a sense of collective Jewish responsibility. He argued that at the very least, a Jewish state was duty bound to ensure the "elementary" needs of all citizens: "food, housing, clothing, education, and health."[5]

Environmental stewardship was a common denominator among these disparate, principled, Zionist visions of collective responsibility. The Land of Israel, neglected and exploited for almost two millennia, awaited an ecological makeover. Zionism expected its agents to be partners in this transformation, contributing to both the renewal of the Land's ecological identity and the Jewish people's renewed identity as an indigenous people in a Promised Land.[6]

IN 1904, at age forty-eight, Aaron David Gordon left his comfortable life as an estate manager in Russia and moved to Palestine, where he began to espouse Romantic philosophy about the meaning of a Zionist identity. His was a secular spiritualism with a strong ecological passion that called for an organic harmony between Jews and their rediscovered homeland. It was a green spiritualism that captured the hearts and minds of the young pioneers. In an entire monograph dedicated to "The Human and Nature" he wrote:

> Moreover, the more man develops and the more his emotions and awareness become deeper and broader, and his knowledge becomes richer, he is in greater need of direct attachment inside of nature. To suckle directly from this vast global experience. . . . And you shall learn Torah from the mouth of nature, the Torah of building and creating. And you shall learn to do as nature does in all you build and in all you create. And so in your ways and in your life, you will learn to become a partner in creation.[7]

Such views were not merely philosophical musings. They also were quickly translated into operational public policy in the *Yishuv*. The Jewish National Fund / Keren Kayemet L'Yisrael (JNF/KKL) first articulated Zionism's land ethic, later adopted by the State of Israel, in 1901. Its refusal to ever sell the lands it acquired in Zion became axiomatic, informed by the prohibition appearing in Leviticus 25:23: "The land must not be sold permanently." This was not so much a religious ethos that assumed that environmental responsibility was a divine obligation, but rather that ultimate ownership of all land belongs to God. The traditional Jewish view that "the earth is the Eternal's" is not unlike the assumptions of Native American tribes. But the Zionist ethic was steeped in a devotion to the Jewish peoplehood. These were "national lands" that belonged to the nation. They were only to be utilized for the benefit of the Jewish people and the creatures with which it shared the land.[8] Much as the first Zionists gave little thought to the national aspirations of the Arabs living in Palestine during the early twentieth century, neither did local land practices and land ethics warrant meaningful attention. Theirs was a decidedly European, Romantic ideology that prioritized national and ecological restoration.

As the Zionist movement came to assume a significant presence in Palestine, additional environmental manifestations of this commitment to the collective emerged. Exceptional programs in afforestation, land reclamation, malaria eradication, and agriculture were part of a higher collective purpose and love of homeland. The craving of the young Zionist settlers for intimacy with Israel's natural world and vistas was extraordinary.[9] A high value was placed on "knowing the land"— with all the biblical double entendre intended. This was not an individual aspiration but part of a renewed, national culture that provided a meaningful—and for many, a transformative—outdoor experience in return for the tribulations that the Land of Israel imposed on immigrants.

Even the ecological follies of the nascent Jewish state were performed in pursuit of collective visions rather than individual enrichment. The Huleh Lake and its magical ecosystem were drained in the 1950s with the high-minded (albeit misguided) goal of creating fertile, arable land for new immigrant farmers. Israeli novelist Meir Shalev shares a story—which may well be apocryphal—that reflects Zionism's deep faith in the insuperable capacity of Jewish communal effort: Dutch consultants had come to advise the JNF/KKL engineers as they began to plan the massive drainage project. After evaluating the soils, the visiting engineers concluded that once deprived of dampness from the wetlands, the underlying peat soils in the valley would combust and collapse, undermining any anticipated agricultural production. But the JNF professionals were indignant, insisting that such a scenario was unthinkable: "Our peat is Zionist peat. Our peat will not cause damage," they railed. "As is known, the Dutch have much experience in the reclamation of land. But even they had not yet met land with a political conscience."[10]

Other environmental crimes and misdemeanors were committed without thought of personal gain by the polluters. For instance, in the 1960s, Israel's government insisted on expanding Tel Aviv's Redding polluting power plant. The motivation behind a project that was already recognized to be a public health insult involved energy supply for the local economy that had to grow rapidly in order to meet the needs of a burgeoning population.[11] Indeed, cities and factories were allowed to dump their wastes into the public sphere because their economic resources were so limited, domestic and international environmental standards were still low, and the needs for jobs and a reasonably viable economy in a new nation were so great. Indeed, the major polluters in Israel for the country's first forty years were government corporations: Israel Chemicals, the Israel Oil Refineries, the Israel Electric Company, and the Eilat-Ashkelon Pipeline.[12] For Israel's early governments, worrying about environmental damage was a luxury that simply needed to wait.

The collateral damage that the zeal for national development left behind did not go entirely unrecognized by the general public. By the 1960s, the Society for Protection of Nature in Israel (SPNI), a conservation and educational NGO, emerged as the country's largest nonprofit organization of any kind. The SPNI began to draw attention to the loss of ecosystems and landscapes, conducting innumerable successful campaigns during its first decades of work.[13]

When they were successful, it was because their arguments appealed to the shared, societal love of the Land of Israel and its commons.

The year 1977 brought with it the first Israeli government that was not driven by a socialist economic orientation. The free-market reforms instituted by the Begin administrations unleashed the power of the profit motive as an engine of economic growth. After decades of austerity and a tax system that produced the world's lowest Gini coefficient (or highest level of society equality), it was now possible to become rich in Israel. It would not take long before the entrepreneurial genius of Israelis became an international sensation and the "start-up nation" phenomenon was born.

Slowly but surely, within mainstream Israeli society, the focus on individuality became pervasive. In the past, it was something of an ideal to study for careers in agriculture or engineering, professions so important to nation building. In the new economy, MBAs, law programs, and accounting programs produced a glut of managers, attorneys, and accountants who opted for the lucrative incomes offered by less productive professions. The kibbutzim, once a beacon to idealistic Israeli youth as well as to young volunteers from around the world, became increasingly privatized. Members preferred personal freedom and pursuing individual affluence to embracing national challenges. Even Israeli museums, which had traditionally been a forum for presenting communal treasures or customs, began to reflect the narratives of individual heroes,[14] with Yitzhak Rabin and Menachem Begin lionized in museums that blurred the lines between history and hagiography.

Israel's new culture of prosperity and individual self-actualization began to redefine the financial aspirations of citizens, along with the societal perceptions of material comfort and economic opportunity. It should not be surprising that the country's environmental dynamics dramatically reflected these changes. Air pollution was now an externality, which a reasonable company might try to impose on society as its CEO sought to maximize the corporation's profits. Developers identified previously unimaginable bonanzas associated with construction projects that primarily benefited the wealthy on scenic, open spaces. Proposals to build marinas and coastal resorts flooded the country's planning commissions. Top local (and in certain cases, international) environmental experts were brought in as consultants to help rationalize projects with environmentally destructive outcomes.

Frequently outgunned and always underfunded, Israel's Ministry of Environment sought to assume a new identity as a regulator of private enterprises and their environmentally destructive activities —rather than a partner, working in sync with government corporations. As the range of environmental insults expanded, Israel's local environmental community became more aggressive, sophisticated, and diverse: over a hundred environmental active organizations, local and national, along with local and national green parties, fought for an alternative, sustainable paradigm. The power wielded by Israel's environmental movement was due to the tremendous public backing it enjoyed.

This support suggests that the new era of Israeli individualism and entrepreneurial creativity has not entirely eliminated Israel's Zionist communal ethos. A deeply engrained concern for the commons remains a central theme in the remarkable culture and education of the country's many youth movements and an increasingly green public school curriculum. The high percentage of Israeli high school graduates who volunteer for a gap year of national service and then seek to complete their mandatory service in combat military units reflects a selfless ethos. The best and the brightest continue to dedicate "the best years of the life" to their country's defense and well-being.

When there are terrorist attacks, Israelis continue to line up to donate blood. Rocket fire from the Gaza Strip only strengthens citizens' resolve. And this idealism goes beyond solidarity in time of existential threats. The social-protest movement of summer 2011 was a reminder that a majority of Israelis still expect their country to be a paragon of social justice. The country's general solidarity with environmental campaigns suggests that environmental justice is part of this modern vision for a healthier State of Israel. Whether you call it that or not, it is a very Zionist vision.

So it seems that Zionism's long-held collective orientation is hardly irrelevant in Israeli society today, even as the country venerates its eighteen billionaires and ninety thousand millionaires.[15] The Zionist ideal, that all Jews pitch in for the greater good of the Jewish people, is still quite valid and not only in hours of crisis. It resonates in small acts of patriotism—from paying enormously high taxes (along with growing donations to Israel's charities and civil society) to a culture of volunteering—a culture that is celebrated by tens of thousands of citizens involved in environmental activism.

The truth is that Israel does not need to go back to a time when its citizens were asked to forgo personal ambitions and endlessly sacrifice for the country's greater good. Those days are probably better left in the past.

To be sure, the discipline imposed on the *Yishuv* and then Israeli society during the early years of Zionism may have been necessary, given the extraordinary exigencies facing the incipient nation. Without a selfless national ethos, the young country would not have been able to meet such a formidable array of challenges; it would not have built an incredible water infrastructure, absorbed over three million immigrants, and established world-class universities, while withstanding constant attacks from its neighbors. Today, however, those expectations are unnecessary. Zionism's success means that the country need not live according to a Spartan code of ethics that suffocates individual creativity and initiative.

The challenge for Zionism is finding the balance between an ideology that expects totally self-abnegation and the nihilistic self-indulgence that can be found in some of the greedier pockets of Israel today. There is nothing new about such a balance. Indeed, it is simply a societal application of Hillel's famous adage from the Mishnah's "Ethics of the Fathers": *"If I am not for myself*, who will be for me? But if I am only for myself, who am I?" (*Pirkei Avot* 1:14).

As an extreme example of a multicultural society, it is no small challenge to maintain a shared sense of purpose within Israel. The environment is probably the most natural area for galvanizing all sectors in Israel to work together, providing the kind of higher, common purpose that was a unifying force in the country's earlier years. There is ample empirical experience that supports this notion. One invariably finds meaningful cooperation and friendships when Arab and Jewish, secular and Orthodox, urban and rural environmental organizations join together to protect a common natural resource.

Israel's environmental laws are not perfect, but they are sufficient to give the environment a fighting chance when facing competing interests. The courts have shown time and again that Israel's legal system creates an even playing field in which public interests can successfully compete with private revenues. The environment can come out a winner if there is a righteous cause and an unwavering effort.

Just like the early Zionists found spiritual sustenance in the local natural world, when Israel's secular Jews today seek a consequential, modern, Jewish identity, their environmental heritage offers one salient area of meaning. From its laws about Sabbatical years to the prohibition on wasteful consumption, for the most part Judaism and environmentalism are synonymous. The Bible offers a rich treasure chest of environmentally inspirational legends—from the biodiversity conserved in Noah's ark, to when Abraham's sensitivity to overgrazing and carrying capacity with his herds competed with those of his nephew Lot. But Judaism also gave rise to a tradition of laws that reflect environmental ethics. For instance, as Israel finally begins to face the ecological implications of its consumer culture, the ancient Jewish proscription on wasting contained in the precepts of *bal tashchit* offers a wonderful starting place. It is an inspirational place where their Israeli and Jewish roots overlap.

If Zionism is to claim a modern environmental identity, however, it will have to show the kind of open-mindedness and nimble thinking that allowed it to evolve over the years to meet the ever-changing reality and challenges facing the Jewish people. That means that it might not make sense any longer to focus on maximum agricultural production, but rather preferring to leave more public lands as habitats and natural parks. It means that the government no longer needs to obsessively subsidize large families or immigration programs when the country's population is already exceeding its carrying capacity; rather, demographic stability needs to be a paramount Zionist goal in order to ensure that population density in the Land of Israel does not destroy quality of life and ecological services.

At the same time Zionism needs to double down on its historical commitment to public land ownership and prioritization of the commons. Zionism always sought to heal the land. But for too long this impulse was overshadowed by the country's zeal to build a robust economy. This neglect created toxic brownfields, anaerobic streams, and decimated inventories of mammals, birds, reptiles, and amphibians. Israel still faces the enormous task of becoming a true ecological restoration movement that can transform the Jewish people's tiny corner of the planet into a Garden of Eden. It will need to redefine its priorities and return to its historical commitment to collective solidarity with the Land of Israel and its natural resources.

For Jews living around the world, the call for ecological harmony with the homeland offers a challenge and a vision for the future. To truly understand our past and the heritage of the Bible, we should all look more intently to the Land of Israel, which for millennia has provided inspiration to prophets and pilgrims. People seeking meaning in the ancient narratives that inform Jewish life will most easily find it when they bring their hearts and heritage to the very land that produced the Jewish people. If you listen closely, a still small voice whispers that the dream of returning to the homeland is still germane. The Land of Israel beckons, reminding us that making the Zionist dream a sustainable one still requires a collective effort.

Notes

This chapter previously appeared in *The Fragile Dialogue: New Voices of Liberal Zionism*, edited by Rabbi Stanley M. Davids and Rabbi Lawrence A. Englander, DHL (New York: CCAR Press, 2018).

1. Anita Shapira and Derek Jonathan Penslar, *Israeli Historical Revisionism: From Left to Right* (London: Routledge, Abington, 2002), 37.

2. Judith Shuval and Elazar Leshem, "The Sociology of Migration in Israel: A Critical View," in *Immigration to Israel, Sociological Perspectives*, ed. Elazar Leshem and Judith Shuval (New Brunswick, NJ: Transaction Publishers, 1998).

3. David Ben-Gurion, "At the Half-Jubilee Celebration" [in Hebrew], in Bracha Habas, ed., Sefer Ha-Aliyah HaShniyah (Tel Aviv: Am Oved, 17–18, as quoted in Gur Alroey, "The Jewish Emigration from Palestine in the Early Twentieth Century," *Journal of Modern Jewish Studies* 2, no. 2 (2003): footnote 44.

4. Ezra Mendelsohn, *Studies in Contemporary Jewry*, vol. 12 (New York: Oxford University Press, 2003), 47.

5. Ze'ev Jabotinsky, *The Social Redemption* (Warsaw: D'ar Mament, 1934), 297–98.

6. Alon Tal, *Pollution in a Promised Land: An Environmental History of Israel* (Berkeley: University of California Press, 2002).

7. Aaron David Gordon (tr. Frances Burnce), *Selected Essays* (New York: Arno Press, 1973).

8. Tal, *Pollution in a Promised Land*, 25.

9. Oz Almog, *The Sabra: A Profile* [in Hebrew] (Tel Aviv: Am Oved, 1997), 255–59.

10. Meir Shalev, *Primarily about Love* [in Hebrew] (Tel Aviv: Am Oved, 1991), 34.

11. Richard Laster, "Reading D: Planning and Building or Building and then Planning," *Israel Law Review* 8 (1973): 480.

12. Tal, *Pollution in a Promised Land*, 253.

13. Ofer Regev, *Forty Years of Blossoming* (Tel Aviv: Society for the Protection of Nature in Israel, 1993).

14. Michael Hollander, personal communication, October 31, 2016.

15. Roee Bergman, "Israel in 2015: 17 Billionaires, over 88,000 Millionaires," *Ynet*, October 14, 2015, http://www.ynetnews.com/articles/0,7340, L-4711244,00.html. In 2022, there were approximately 131,000 millionaires and 70 billionaires in Israel.

30

"You Are but Tenants and Settlers"

Ecology, Anti-colonialism, and the Theology of *Galut*

Daniel Delgado

For the land is Mine; for you are but tenants and settlers with Me.
—*Leviticus 25:23*

WHAT DOES IT MEAN to have a specifically *Jewish* relationship with the land?

By all appearances, the question is a pressing one for many Jews today. According to the Jewish Outdoor, Food, Farming & Environmental Education (JOFEE) Network, "Tens of thousands of people engage in JOFEE activities every year, from learning about Jewish harvest rituals, to composting, to . . . standing up for our environment, to praying outside."[1] These activities bespeak a desire to connect, *as Jews*, with the earth—whether through direct spiritual practice or through seemingly secular activities stemming from Jewish values. This phenomenon goes by many names, including "JOFEE" and "earth-based Judaism"; for the sake of brevity and clarity, I prefer "eco-Judaism."

For all its transformative potential, eco-Judaism has a deep and largely unexamined problem: as an outgrowth of trends within the Euro[2] world, it relies heavily on colonialist ideas of what it means to inhabit, possess, and interact with land. These presumptions—discussed below—are so deeply rooted that they remain invisible to many Jews. Yet even accidental colonialism still propagates harm toward Black and Indigenous[3] people, produces unsafe spaces for Jews of Color, and undermines efforts toward radical healing of the dominant culture's relationship with the earth.

Here I present a potential correction for the distortion that colonialist thought has inserted into Jewish perspectives on land: the theology of *galut* (exile), which interprets the destruction of the Temple and sub-sequent exile as an expression of the divine plan for the Jewish people. For obvious reasons, the idea of *galut* as God's will has fallen out of favor among many Jews, particularly since the advent of Zionism. Yet many kabbalistic and Chasidic traditions actually interpret *galut* as a positive state that establishes a framework for the particularly Jewish mission in the world. This chapter presents an overview of a theology of *galut* with potential to inject a much-needed anti-colonialist ethos into eco-Judaism.

The Problem of Colonialism

The question of colonialism is neither academic nor merely historical. Rather, the term describes modern structures of power with real conse-quences for human and nonhuman lives. The most well-known form of colonialism is *exploitation* (or *external*) *colonialism*, in which a relatively small number of colonizers forcibly extract material resources for the benefit of a colonizing power. A classic example is the British occupa-tion of India; a contemporary example is the activity of extractive cor-porations in the so-called Global South.[4]

In contrast, *settler colonialism* is based on *replacing* the Indigenous pop-ulation with settlers from the colonizing culture. Settlers take control of land via a combination of overt tactics—such as the killing or forced removal of Indigenous people—and more indirect techniques, such as criminalizing Indigenous practices in order to force assimilation into settler culture. A classic example of settler colonialism is the British colonization of North America; contemporary examples include the United States and Canada as successor states to those initial colonies. The continued existence of both states is predicated upon the ongoing negation of Indigenous sovereignty and control of land.[5]

The enduring colonial structures of settler states—enshrined in property law, in criminal law, and indeed in every legal and social insti-tution—exact horrific and quantifiable tolls on the bodies of Black and Indigenous people in particular, as well as upon the earth itself.[6] The state-backed violence in response to the Oceti Sakowin's anti-pipeline resistance at Standing Rock in 2016 represents but a single example of how systems of law and violence intertwine to deny Indigenous people the ability to access, protect, or manage their sacred lands.

Note that as defined here, colonialism is a *material* condition, characterized by who controls land and social institutions and how. As such, it is correct to identify the State of Israel as also settler colonial in nature—notwithstanding the ancient and unbroken Jewish religious connection with *Eretz Yisrael*. It is the *structures* of colonialism that turn Israeli Jews into settlers, rather than any abstract philosophical questions about Jewish versus Palestinian claims on belonging.[7]

Thus, the critiques of eco-Judaism made below apply as much within Israel as within Diasporic settler colonies. Indeed, one strength of the theology articulated here is that it guides us toward a Jewish land ethic that is equally applicable whether we reside in *Eretz Yisrael* or not.

Whose Land?

Eco-Judaism's search for a connection with land thus raises the question: Whose land is it anyway, and what sorts of relationships are appropriate for settlers to have with it?[8]

As writers including Eve Tuck and K. Wayne Yang,[9] Dina Gilio Whitaker,[10] Philip J. Deloria,[11] and Leanne Betasamosake Simpson[12] have discussed, Euro environmentalism and eco-spirituality developed out of cultures founded upon colonialism. Thus, these movements have often been more concerned with preserving colonizer privilege than with disrupting it—such as by focusing on pollution's effects on the health and living spaces of white people or by lauding a "wilderness" violently emptied of Native people but still available for white hunters, backpackers, and spiritual seekers.

As a descendant of these movements,[13] eco-Judaism likewise tends to take certain colonialist premises for granted, including not just the idea of wilderness but also of land ownership (whether by individuals, farming collectives, or the settler state via so-called public lands) and the assumption that Indigenous land rights have been annulled or otherwise rendered irrelevant to settlers. This often leads eco-Judaism to ignore preexisting, mutualistic, and communal Indigenous relationships with the land in favor of personal connections by individual Jewish settlers.

The problem can be stated another way: The Jewish ethical paradigm centers on injunctions to protect the most vulnerable and oppressed. Fulfilling these mitzvot is literally impossible if we refuse to acknowledge the requisite Black and Indigenous underclass upon which the societies we inhabit are built.

A Holy Exile

In fact, our religion explicitly teaches us to *never* feel entitled to a connection with the land—not even in *Eretz Yisrael*. The Torah is clear: no human can own land, "for the land is Mine" (Leviticus 25:23).[14] Although God has "given" *Eretz Yisrael* to the Israelites, they should more properly consider themselves tenants or temporary interlopers— that is, settlers. Although the chapter refers specifically to *Eretz Yisrael*, the wider *Tanach* makes it clear that God owns the entire earth. For humans to presume that they can own land is blasphemous, even disastrous. On this point, many Indigenous peoples would wholeheartedly agree.

What relationship, then, do humans have with land? Whereas Genesis 1–2 positions humans as caretakers of the earth on behalf of God,[15] Leviticus 25 clarifies that each parcel of land is cared for by a *mishpachah*, an extended patrilineal kin group (distinct from the word's more generic meaning of "family" in Modern Hebrew). In the mitzvah of *Yoveil* (Jubilee), God commands that all land sold since the prior *Yoveil* be returned to its *mishpachah* and that all Israelite slaves be freed: "Each person shall return to their *achuz*, and each person shall return to their *mishpachah*" (Leviticus 25:10).

Achuz literally means "holding" or "possession" and is often used for inherited property. Used here to refer to land, the word reinforces the connection between the individual, their family, and their land— together forming a single unit. So essential is this unit to preserving the health of the land and the people that the entire system of *Yoveil* is designed to prevent its disruption.

In a modern context, this passage reads as positively anti-colonial, insisting that the ancestral connections between peoples and their lands never be permanently severed. It also poses a stark challenge to

Jews living as settlers on lands forcibly stolen from other nations: When will the land be given back?

Could this reading imply a permanent Jewish claim to *Eretz Yisrael*? It might, if the very same chapter did not so strongly emphasize that God reserves the right to sever Israelite title: "For the land is Mine; for you are but tenants and settlers with Me" (Leviticus 25:23). Indeed, in traditional Jewish theology, the destruction of the Temple and subsequent exile were in fact willed by God (e.g., Babylonian Talmud, *Yoma* 9b). To this day, the traditional siddur reads, "Because of our sins, we have been exiled from our land."[16]

Yet the idea of exile as punishment is an oversimplification. Rabbi Shimon bar Yochai taught, "Every place they were exiled, the *Shechinah* [Divine Indwelling Presence] went with them" (Babylonian Talmud, *M'gillah* 29a). The kabbalist Isaac Luria, also known as the Ari, explained that the *Shechinah*'s descent and exile reflects the brokenness of the world: how profoundly God is hidden! At the same time, the *Shechinah*'s descent makes it possible for us to redeem holy sparks that would have otherwise remained too deeply hidden for us to find. Since God's Indwelling Presence is always accessible, we can follow that Presence to even the most concealed of places.[17]

According to the Ari, the purpose of human existence is to elevate concealed sparks of holiness, thereby transforming the world. While in one sense *galut* distances us from holiness, it also, paradoxically, makes holiness easier to uncover. Thus, the Ari taught that the Jews were exiled precisely in order to find and elevate holy sparks throughout the world.[18] Put another way, Jews are *supposed* to be in exile. *Galut* is the only place we can do the work of healing brokenness.

If *galut* is our purpose, then we are not supposed to settle permanently in *any* land. This is more a question of orientation (*kavanah*) than location: the Ari specified that because *galut* is a spiritual state, the term applies even to those living in *Eretz Yisrael*.[19] Thus, we might dwell in a given land indefinitely, so long as we maintain the perspective of Leviticus 25: *we are not supposed to try to own the land.*

Moreover, in Kabbalah, *Shechinah* is another name for the earth itself.[20] If the *Shechinah* dwells more closely with us when we are in *galut*, then we dwell more closely with the *Shechinah* as well. Might we take this to mean that our home should be no single land, but rather the entirety of the earth?

People of the Earth

The Haskalah, Zionism, Bundism with its *doykeit* (hereness)—Jewish movements of the last few centuries sought belonging and power in colonial states. They sought to force an end to *galut*. Our ancestors warned against this path in the folk tale of Joseph Della Reina, who tried to force the coming of the Messiah, with disastrous consequences.[21] Indeed, to the extent that Jews (and other peoples) have embraced private land ownership and colonial nation-states, we have become collaborators in the destruction of our entire biosphere. What greater disaster could there be?

The theology of *galut* suggests a different path: that of belonging with the earth, a path of humility rather than power. In this worldview, we see *galut* as a gift, a chance to generate holiness wherever we live. We see Judaism as both a land-based religion and a Diasporic one. We see any land we live in as a place with holy secrets to teach—but only if approached in the right way, with the right action and intention.

This does not require us to deny or abandon our ancient connection with *Eretz Yisrael*. For two thousand years, Jews prayed toward Jerusalem without thinking to own it.

What would a *galut*-informed land ethic look like? It would direct us away from identifying with any colonial state, regardless of what citizenships we might hold. Instead, it would direct us to see ourselves as Jews living on Indigenous land.[22] It would direct us away from projects that reaffirm settler ownership and toward following Indigenous laws and defending and returning Indigenous land. It would direct us away from casting ourselves as Indigenous to *Eretz Yisrael* and toward seeing ourselves as tenants and settlers, a people of Diaspora, a people of the earth.

It would make every place we live holy, imbue our every act with meaning, make justice and repair the focus of our every thought—precisely, that is, what Judaism is meant to do.

NOTES

1. JOFEE, "About," https://jofee.org/about/.

2. I use the term "Euro" instead of the more common "Western" both to undercut the Eurocentrism of the latter term and to highlight the cultural continuity between Europe and its colonial successor states. From an Indigenous perspective, Western thought and institutions are in fact painfully European, regardless of which modern country they manifest in.

3. Throughout this chapter, I use the term "Indigenous" in its modern, political sense of distinct peoples who persist in opposition to colonization and in relation to ancestral lands, rather than the (lowercase "i") sense of "originally from a given place."

4. I prefer the terms "Decolonizing World" and "Colonizing World" to replace the Cold War terms "Third/Fourth World" and "First World," respectively.

5. US chief justice John Marshall explicitly admitted as much in *Johnson v. M'Intosh* (1823): "However extravagant the pretension of converting the discovery of inhabited country into conquest may appear . . . if the property of the great mass of the community originates in it, it becomes the law of the land, and cannot be questioned."

6. See, for instance, Roxanne Dunbar-Ortiz, *An Indigenous People's History of the United States* (Boston: Beacon Press, 2015); David Treuer, *The Heartbeat of Wounded Knee: Native America from 1890 to the Present* (New York: Riverhead Books, 2019); and Chelsea Vowel, *Indigenous Writes: A Guide to First Nations, Métis, and Inuit Issues in Canada* (Winnipeg: HighWater Press, 2016).

7. To take just one example, Peter Beinart has recently written on the question (without using the term "colonialism") in regard to the Palestinian refugees of 1948: "Teshuvah: A Jewish Case for Palestinian Refugee Return," *Jewish Currents*, May 11, 2021, https://jewishcurrents.org/teshuvah-a-jewish-case-for-palestinian-refugee-return.

8. Black and Indigenous Jews inhabit a different position relative to settler colonialism than other Jews. Yet because the majority of Jews are still settlers, the issue remains a pressing one for Judaism as a whole.

9. Eve Tuck and K. Wayne Yang, "Decolonization Is Not a Metaphor," *Decolonization: Indigeneity, Education & Society* 1, no. 1 (2012): 1–40.

10. Dina Gilio Whitaker, *As Long as the Grass Grows: The Indigenous Fight for Environmental Justice, from Colonization to Standing Rock* (Boston: Beacon Press, 2020).

11. Philip J. Deloria, *Playing Indian* (New Haven, CT: Yale University Press, 1999).

12. Leanne Betasamosake Simpson, *As We Have Always Done: Indigenous Freedom through Radical Resistance* (Minneapolis: University of Minnesota Press, 2020).

13. It is worth clarifying that ancestral Jewish communities persisting in non-colonialist contexts in North Africa, Southwest Asia, Europe, and elsewhere may have traditions of Jewish relationship with land that are beyond the scope of this discussion.

14. *Tanach* translations are mine.

15. "The image of God" is the same language used in Mesopotamian writings to refer to the king who rules on behalf of the gods; its use in Genesis 1 implies that humans care for the earth on behalf of God, the true owner.

16. Rabbi Nosson Scherman, ed., "Mussaf for the Festivals: Kiddush Hayom," *The Rabbinical Council of America Edition of the ArtScroll Siddur, Weekday/Sabbath/Festival* (Brooklyn: Mesorah Publications, 1990), 679.

17. E.g., *Shaar HaGilgulim* 15.

18. E.g., *Shaar HaGilgulim* 15.

19. E.g., *Shaar HaGilgulim* 15.

20. See, e.g., *Tikkunei Zohar*, 70, 131a, quoted in David Seidenberg, *Kabbalah and Ecology* (New York: Cambridge University Press, 2015), 274.

21. See, e.g., Howard Schwartz, "The Chains of the Messiah," *Gabriel's Palace* (New York: Oxford University Press, 1993).

22. Within most of Europe, we might instead see ourselves as Jews living in societies built upon stolen Indigenous wealth and filled with displaced Indigenous peoples.

Thanks to rabbinic student Sasha Perry for their collaboration in researching and developing many ideas in this chapter.

31

Healing the Environment through Global Interfaith Activism

Rabbi Dr. Shmuly Yanklowitz

Today, when someone mentions "religion in a global context," one's first association may be "conflict." Religious groups throughout history have struggled, disagreed, and killed each other over all aspects of life, including questions on how to pray, whom to pray to, what theological and moral ideals to aspire to, and how to interact with other religions. Religious pluralism was rarely a philosophical or political ideal in centuries past. Today, however, in the modern/postmodern era, another way to think about "global religion" is evolving: competition and an assumption of scarcity are no longer the default approaches to interfaith encounters. Instead, collaboration has become established as the primary means to move the world toward repair and healing.

One of the most pressing needs for our contemporary moment is controlling climate change and mitigating looming environmental disaster. If there is no habitable environment to live within, it will be the end of humanity and therefore the end of the rich faith traditions we have inherited. The time has come to develop an interreligious and collaborative approach to the protection of the environment. Only together can we stave off the ill effects of economic and climate politics that cause devastation for communities all over the world.

Sir David Attenborough, the noted naturalist, commented, "Right now we are facing a man-made disaster of global scale, our greatest threat in thousands of years: climate change. If we don't take action, the collapse of our civilizations and the extinction of much of the natural world is on the horizon."[1] If we do nothing, if we stay in our corners, then we do so at *our own peril*.

I've seen this devastation firsthand. As I traveled the world pursuing social action relief work, I saw with my own eyes the detrimental effects of climate change on communities in developing nations. Without any access to natural resources or political power, many people in rural villages have to endure living in proximity to unprocessed sewage and waste, contaminated water sources, and polluted skies. They are sick. They are malnourished. They are alone. There is no one to advocate for these vulnerable communities, no one within the community with the influence to ask for protection.

Such problems cannot be solved unilaterally. And this reality saddens me. But, counterintuitively, this reality has also emboldened and inspired me. It made me realize that to create a thriving future for the most at-risk communities all over the world, it is my sacred obligation to carve out space in my religious activism work for the care of the environment. As I reflected on the issue at hand, I thought about the need for people of faith to speak out and foment a new spiritual revolution, one that rejects the need for dominance and power and instead calls for unity and equity. Only together can we repair a world brought to the brink by exploitation and plundering of its beauty. Modern societies as a whole have, in many ways, often belittled and outright rejected the call of religion to heal the global problems, yet there is much wisdom to be found within religious traditions—wisdom that can help us to assess, acknowledge, and heal.

It is for this reason, among many, that I was moved by how Pope Francis talked about the work of combating climate change. In 2015, the pope addressed the ecological crisis in *Laudato Si: On Care for Our Common Home*.[2] In his address, Pope Francis connected the inner, spiritual lives of human beings with the planet's health. He noted that to address the environmental crisis, we need a new mode of spirituality where the virtues of humility, gratitude, and sobriety overcome the vices of greed and overconsumption—in short, our fear of scarcity. A statement from the United States Conference of Catholic Bishops in 2014 presages the pope's encyclical: "At its core, global climate change is not about economic theory or political platforms, nor about partisan advantage or interest group pressures. It is about the future of God's creation and the one human family."[3]

According to the Buddhist thinker Thich Nhat Hanh:

Our way of walking on the Earth has a great influence on animals and plants. We have killed so many animals and plants and destroyed their environments. Many are now extinct. In turn, our environment is now harming us. We are like sleepwalkers, not knowing what we are doing or where we are heading. Whether we can wake up or not depends on whether we can walk mindfully on our Mother Earth. The future of all life, including our own, depends on our mindful steps.[4]

Once I fully understood my sacred obligation to activism work on behalf of the environment, I cofounded, together with Mayim Bialik and Matisyahu, SHAMAYIM: Jewish Animal Advocacy. Our organization encourages those in the Jewish community and beyond to follow an animal-friendly, plant-based diet. The reason for this is personal: I saw how the factory farming industry, more than any other industry on the planet, destroys our land, our water, our animals, and our bodies. I saw the practices that treated living creatures, divine creatures, as nothing more than a product subject to abuse. By being a voice against brutal and inhumane practices, I join the interfaith and international struggle against needless cruelty—while, at the same time, also promoting the health of the human body and soul.

Let us consider some theological proposals that all of us, regardless of our faith, might come to agree on, to different degrees:

1. God created the earth, water, air, fire, and sky; these elements possess inherent purity and sanctity (Genesis 1).
2. God owns the land. We merely borrow that land from God while living here on the earth (Leviticus 25:23).
3. Because of the sacred task of stewardship, we are responsible for the state in which we hand over the earth to the next generation (Genesis 1:28).
4. To preserve the environment, we have to cultivate character traits such as modesty, gratitude, and equanimity (*halachta bidrachav* [*imitatio Dei*], as learned from Deuteronomy 28:9).
5. We will not be punished by the courts of our time for destroying the land, air, or water as long as our actions comply with secular law—but we are, indeed, religiously culpable for the damage we cause (Deuteronomy 20:19–20).

There are many different approaches that could be taken to increase meaningful interfaith dialogue for the sake of the environment. We could offer different articulations of the points listed. However, this must be done in order to mobilize us all to action, not just for the sake of virtue signaling and sermonizing. We must ask ourselves, as faith leaders, how we will model the following:

1. Maintain sustainable communal practices
2. Cultivate modesty in our personal practices
3. Reduce the consumption of animal products (moving toward veganism)
4. Advocate for environmental policy changes
5. Develop theological language for universal collaboration

Interreligious dialogue is one of the most dynamic paths toward reconciliation and hope. If we are able to seek teachers from across the faith spectrum and look beyond leaders within our own faiths, we will be able to learn from each other and to live in peace both with humanity as a whole and with our planet. In his 1989 address after being awarded the Nobel Peace Prize, the Holiness, the Dalai Lama noted, "Because we all share this small planet earth, we have to learn to live in harmony and peace with each other and with nature. That is not just a dream, but a necessity."[5] Opportunities for collaboration allow us to plant seeds of change among all the great religious traditions. Our world needs this change urgently. Spiritual leaders, myself included, must do more to facilitate this interreligious dialogue focused on our shared planet. The cross-cultural, intra-communal, and broadly human project is urgent given how rapidly we have polluted the air and sea, destroyed and exploited the earth's natural resources, and accelerated natural disasters and pandemics. The ability to have spaces for true interreligious dialogue will, hopefully, one day save humanity from its worst impulses. Nothing less than the future of the world is at stake.

For me personally, my clean break with the comfort of the status quo is ever challenging, but always invigorating. My religious activism has been motivated by personal experiences and by leaders of various faiths—but also, indeed primarily, by Jewish texts. I personally draw on a passage in the Talmud when I think about the necessary, essential work to protect and care for our fragile environment. In the Talmud, there is a man named Choni. One day, as Choni walked along a road, he saw a man planting a carob tree. Choni asked the man, "How long will it take for this tree to bear fruit?" "Seventy years," the man replied. Choni then asked, "Are you so healthy that you expect to live that length of time and eat its fruit?" The man answered, "I found a fruitful world because my ancestors planted it for me. Likewise, I am planting for my children" (Babylonian Talmud, *Taanit* 23a).

There are countless other Jewish legal and theological models for the value that Choni expresses, our limitless responsibility for our world and the generations to come:

- *L'ovdah ul'shomrah*—our divinely mandated work to protect Creation (Genesis 2:15)
- *Pikuach nefesh*—the Torah command to save life (Babylonian Talmud, *Shabbat* 150a)
- *Bal tashchit*—the Torah prohibition against waste (Deuteronomy 20:19–20)
- *Avodah b'gashmiyut*—making our interactions with the material world into something that is spiritually deep[6]
- *Anavah* (humility)—not being *baalei gaavah* (filled with arrogance and self-absorption)[7]
- *Hakarat hatov* (gratitude)—channeling "gratitude" for our blessings[8]
- *Halachta bidrachav* (*imitatio Dei*)—God is merciful; we cultivate our mercy in "emulation of the Divine"[9]

It is obvious that Jewish practices teach us to be more mindful, modest, and open to transformational experiences. What is less obvious is how we create sustainable behavioral change. Leadership scholars teach that we should not operate from fear when attempting to "weather the storm."

The danger in the current economic situation is that people in positions of authority will hunker down. They will try to solve the problem with short-term fixes: tightened controls, across-the-board cuts, restructuring plans. They'll default to what they know how to do in order to reduce frustration and quell their own and others' fears. Their

primary mode will be drawing on familiar expertise to help their organization weather the storm.[10]

In all we do, we need to cultivate *tamidiyut* (consistency), and ritual
commitment can help us do that. If we live with religious discipline, this
concept can carry over into the discipline of environmental discipline.
Indeed, history is filled with stories of religious leaders who were able
to adapt to change—and those who refused:

1. Joseph interpreted Pharaoh's dreams to mean that seven years
   of abundance would be followed by seven years of famine.
   Because of his interpretation, the grain surplus was stored
   during the years of abundance and helped save Egypt during
   the succeeding famine. Joseph could have become acquies-
   cent, as Egyptians were used to regular flooding from the Nile
   that annually replenished the soil, seemingly guaranteeing
   a perpetual plentiful food supply. However, he understood
   that—eventually—there would come a time of scarcity, and
   he acted accordingly (and proactively) (Genesis 41:25–36).
2. On the other hand, the last king of Babylon, Belshazzar,
   ignored the literal "writing on the wall" at his peril and decided
   to celebrate what he thought would be a long, secure reign. In
   reality, a large force of Persians and Medes were about to over-
   throw him and bring about the downfall of Babylon (Daniel
   5:25–28).

To my religious colleagues and friends who don't know where to
begin with this vast charge, I want to say: We must come together to
have more meaningful interreligious dialogue about climate change.
We need to bring about change. Our world needs this change urgently.
The ability to create this change will heal humanity. I have found that
the most helpful way to carve out time for environmental activism,
while there are so many other demands in life, is to make very small but
consistent changes in one's daily habits. Though it is difficult, I try to
remind myself every day of how much I love my children and how badly
I want the world to be inhabitable for them.

We cannot wait for change. *We must be the change.*

In my work as a spiritual leader, I often teach that we must change the world from the inside out, that we have to change our behavior to allow for self-transformation. Such a method will then, hopefully, lead to outer change. This pedagogical technique should not be misunderstood to mean that we must perfect ourselves before we can begin to work for social change, since then, of course, we would never even begin. The beginning date for our work is today, and it has no set end date except for our deaths. It is never complete; this fact makes life challenging yet so exciting.

To everyone, whether you're a believer or nonbeliever, a neophyte or an expert, or someone simply invested in the notion that a single person can make an enormous difference: We are responsible for the state in which we hand over the earth to the next generation. Let us transform our world, not only for ourselves but for our descendants for years to come.

NOTES

1. "Sir David Attenborough: Time Is Running Out," *BBC News*, December 3, 2018, https://www.bbc.com/news/av/world-46428260.

2. Pope Francis, *Laudato Si: On Care for Our Common Home* (Huntington, IN: Our Sunday Visitor, 2015).

3. Most Rev. Thomas G. Wenski and Most Rev. Nicholas DiMarzio, "Climate Change Justice and Health Initiative," United States Conference of Bishops, 2014, https://www.usccb.org/resources/climate-change-justice-and-health-initiative.

4. Thich Nhat Hanh, "The Sun My Heart," in *Engaged Buddhist Reader*, ed. Arnold Kotler (Berkeley: Parallax Press, 1966), 162–70.

5. "The 14th Dalai Lama's Nobel Lecture," December 11, 1989, https://www.dalailama.com/messages/acceptance-speeches/nobel-peace-prize/nobel-peace-prize-nobel-lecture.

6. See Joseph Dan, *The Teachings of the Hasidim* (Millburn, NJ: Behrman House, 1983), 24.

7. See Norman Lamm, *Seventy Faces: Articles of Faith*, vol. 2 (Hoboken, NJ: Ktav, 2002), 110.

8. See Harold M. Schulweis, *In God's Mirror: Reflections and Essays* (Hoboken, NJ: Ktav, 2003), 64.

9. See Dov Schwartz, *From Phenomenology to Existentialism: The Philosophy of Rabbi Joseph B. Soloveitchik*, vol. 2 (Boston: Brill, 2013), 116.

10. Ronald Heifetz et al., "Leadership in a (Permanent) Crisis," *Harvard Business Review*, April 4, 2020, hbr.org/2009/07/leadership-in-a-permanent-crisis.

32

Beit Atid
Synagogues as Laboratories for the Future

Rabbi Dean Shapiro

Humanity—and, indeed, all life on earth—is now entering a new era. Some call it the Sixth Great Extinction, the die-off of countless and uncounted species. Some say we are living through the end of the Anthropocene, a geological epoch marked by substantial human impact on the earth. Weather will grow more intense, food and fresh water scarcer. It will be harder to breathe. Migration and sea level rise will upend societies. The window has most likely already closed on avoiding substantial degradation to human life and culture within the lifetimes of today's adults. Today's children's futures are even more untenable.[1] In order to effectively prepare for these future hardships, synagogues need to become *batei atid*, "places for the future."

In the Book of Genesis, Joseph interprets Pharaoh's dreams of cows and grain. First, he proclaims that there will be seven years of plenty during which the land will produce. Afterward, there will be seven harsh years of famine. Joseph crafts a plan to feed the people:

> Have them gather up all the [surplus] food of these good years that are coming, and let them store up grain in the cities under Pharaoh's control, and put it under guard. The food will then be a reserve for the land during the seven years of famine that will prevail in the land of Egypt; thus the land will not perish through famine. (Genesis 41:35–36)

Joseph uses the time of plenty and stability to prepare for the years of future want. With plan in hand, he speaks with those in power and enacts his vision.

Synagogues often understand themselves through a tripartite division—*beit k'neset, beit midrash, beit t'filah*—places of gathering, study, and prayer. As human society enters a substantial, all-systems transformation, congregations should add a fourth leg to that tripod: *beit atid*—a place for the future. Congregations can follow in the footsteps of Joseph and become incubators, visioning, training, and transforming into the centers Jews (and, indeed, human beings in general) will need in changing environments burdened with storm, fire, and drought, scarcity of food and fresh water, unhealthy air, worsening medical outcomes, the substantial movement of people, and the struggles over diminishing resources. Although large-scale policy is set in government capitols and in corporate boardrooms, it is local communities who will weather the storms together, according to their own realities, protecting human life and Jewish culture as best they can, alleviating as much suffering as possible.

Many Jewish communities are involved in climate advocacy, seeking to impact governmental and corporate policy for the good. This approach, called *mitigation* because it seeks to mitigate the worst impacts of climate change, is important. In addition, we need to start *adapting* to the changes that are, in fact, inevitable. How will we cope when we realize our children will not lead the flourishing lives we've dreamt of for them? How will we live as the systems that distribute our food, water, and clothing disintegrate? As our buildings cease to protect us? We'll need to shift our expectations and learn to take care of ourselves. This is a different kind of conversation, painful but necessary. It's a conversation that's overdue.

Some might ask how it is possible to anticipate the distant future. In Western culture, the present often eclipses any other concern. We are trained to consider only the "now" of quarterly reports, "sale ending soon" (or "Buy now!"), and instant gratification in all its guises. Judaism, by contrast, encourages us to think across longer periods of time. Through festivals, rituals, and readings, we regularly commemorate events that took place even thousands of years ago. These events stay active in our consciousness despite the passage of time. Like the Passover seder reminding us to cherish freedom and the Chanukah candles that bring us hope in the darkness, they influence our behavior. Through the holy days, we understand time to move in a spiral, not a line. Our ancestors yearned for our return to Zion twenty-five hundred years ago, embedding the vision deep in our collective psyche and laying the groundwork through the charged languages of prayer, metaphor, and symbol. Further, the Jewish people is experienced in pivoting. We transitioned from the agrarian lives of Genesis to the urban lives of the prophets. We lived as slaves in Egypt, and then as a liberated people. After the Second Temple was destroyed, Yochanan ben Zakkai reimagined Judaism, and it has transformed repeatedly ever since. As liberal Jews, we proudly proclaim the right—indeed, the obligation—to reimagine Judaism as our circumstances and our culture evolve.

Batei atid are congregational laboratories for long-range thinking and action, incubators for evolution, experimenting, and preparing now for what we know the future will bring. Teams of laypeople, staff, and especially young adults could plan for the coming decades and beyond, engaging in the physical plant, learning, ritual, experimentation, and new clergy roles, to name a few areas of primary focus. We are looking for betterments, not fixes.

Physical Plant

Many synagogue buildings were designed for the twentieth century. In order to stave the inevitable and disastrous effects of the environmental crisis on their viability for the future, we need to redirect our focus: What heating and cooling will our buildings need three decades from now? How will energy be sourced and stored? Can synagogues in hot and dry places install outdoor drinking and washing fountains for the public, and synagogues in wet climates install outside coverings to protect people from the elements?

Further, storms are growing more powerful and destructive. Crisis response is part of climate response. When disaster strikes, how can the synagogue building provide succor for the neighborhood? Consider meeting with disaster relief specialists in your area to talk through how your synagogue can serve the community during and after a crisis—and prepare for one ahead of time. How can the sanctuary be converted to a dormitory? Can you build the infrastructure to provide showers to displaced people? Can you provide storage for relief supplies?

Most synagogues are buildings with land that requires tending. Is your landscaping adapted to changing environmental realities? Can it be upgraded to provide food and shade, to improve the way the earth absorbs groundwater (recharging aquifers), and to provide habitat for insects? Can you use less water and collect rainwater? Who cares for the synagogue's landscaping, and how are they paid and treated? Beyond the needs of the synagogue, mutual aid societies within congregations can organize to use their collective buying power and shared labor to reduce costs, enabling any household in the community to improve its trees and landscaping.

Learning

Our religious schools teach Hebrew and holidays, prayer and values. Educators and religious school committees should ask themselves what other skills and abilities our young people will need toward the end of the twenty-first century, well within the span of their lifetimes. These might include group decision-making and listening. If systems collapse, they might benefit from practical skills like first aid, gardening, cooking, sewing, and knitting. How can we teach our young people flexibility, resilience, and teamwork? While these are important for all people, our children and grandchildren may well depend on them.

We also need Jewish communities to provide the opportunity to engage in robust study of moral reasoning and environmental/regional awareness from a Jewish perspective. As resources diminish, we will be forced into complex decision-making, as individuals, families, communities, and nations. Now is the time to hone our understanding of ethics by discussing our lived experiences (which helps us develop empathy) and by studying the many Jewish texts exploring food, water, responsibility, and sharing.[2]

Synagogue groups can research what is happening in their region—not only environmentally, but politically as well. Deeper dives should include hearing the lived experience of neighbors (including Indigenous, marginalized, and impoverished communities) and other experts. Who makes key decisions (about watershed, for example), and how are they elected or appointed? How can they be influenced? Study groups can then present their findings to the wider community and invite the congregation into informed advocacy.

Many synagogues already have walking or hiking groups. Ask participants in these groups to include environmental and systems learning, even just an article each month, to their exploration. In these ways, we prepare ourselves for a turbulent future.

Ritual

An uncertain future is distressing and overwhelming. Our minds can't process the possibilities, but our souls are already grieving the loss of ease, freedom, opportunity, and privilege that's expected this century. Rituals, shared basic behaviors that resonate deeply, can help.

Impactful ritual brings us out of "standard" time, allowing us to experience a sense of timelessness. Rituals often demarcate "before" and "after" their performance. Because ritual actions are symbolic, participants generate their own meanings from their experience. Indeed, effective rituals are sufficiently abstract to allow a range of meanings—some shared, some personal. How could our clergy and ritual/worship committees create rituals that allow us to integrate both the hope we hold and the grief that comes from anticipated loss?

Take, for example, these two Jewish rituals (among others) that could benefit from updating for changed environmental realities: bet mitzvah and Tishah B'Av.[3] Today's celebrations are valuable and, for most, transformative for young people and families. They are largely twentieth-century rituals that inculcate text study, analytical thought, public speaking, Hebrew, memorization, advocacy, and independence. How could bet mitzvah change to promote teamwork, resilience, *chesed*, and *tzedakah* more holistically? As a starting place, I envision mitzvah projects involving four or five students working together, rather than individually. Students could edit one another's *divrei Torah*, offering and accepting feedback. The entire class could contribute a percentage of their gifts to a shared *tzedakah* fund, decide together how to donate the money, and then see how it is put to use. These small changes would shift the individualistic focus of this life-cycle event.

Contrasting with the joy of becoming bet mitzvah, the fast day of Tishah B'Av commemorates the great losses our people has suffered: the destructions of the Temples, the expulsion from Spain, and the

Holocaust. Reform Judaism celebrates the Rabbinic Judaism that emerged from the Second Temple's ashes, making mourning on Tishah B'Av less meaningful, and therefore less frequently observed, in our communities.

Without Tishah B'Av, however, we have lost the practice of collective grief and lament. As the climate deteriorates, our lives will grow harder. So, too, our expectations of what's possible for ourselves and our families will shrink. We will need a space to name our losses, mourn together, and ask God, "How could this happen?" Imagine if our Jewish communities gathered on Tishah B'Av to confront our climate grief.[4] We could recite *Eichah*, Lamentations, and allow ourselves to cry together: to cry for the real pain that we and our children will inevitably experience in times of collapse, and to feel the shame of our complicity in the environment's degradation. We could study Ezekiel's "valley of dry bones," understanding that we exist in an enduring cycle of collapse and growth. We could journal and share pictures of loss and promise. Since Tishah B'Av generally occurs around the time of the anniversary of the first moon walk, the service might conclude with a contemplation of planet earth as seen from space and Carl Sagan's famous vision of our "Pale Blue Dot." In these ways and others, we can inculcate a culture of the collective, even as we celebrate the individual.

Experimentation

Few synagogues have a deep culture of experimentation or even an organized program that encourages it. We do what we have always done, whether or not it works. Amy Asin, the URJ's vice president and director of Strengthening Congregations, has encouraged us to pursue "transformational and disruptive change."[5]

What if boards of directors appointed a particular board member to speak for the descendants?[6] The position might rotate, but at each meeting, and especially at board retreats, someone would be tasked to consider the implications of all decisions and budgets on the grandchildren of current bet mitzvah kids and to speak for them. This is *midor l'dor vador* (from generation to generation to generation).

What do our children's grandchildren need us to do today? Where would they want us to place our communal funds? What would they want their parents and grandparents to learn through the curricula we teach? Which cleaning products would they want us to use in the synagogue? Would they want us to serve meat at our events? Do our policies and practices promote the Jewish engagement of our children's children's children? In this way, we can be a light not only to the nations, but to the generations.

Clergy

The work of anticipating and preparing for uncertain futures falls to the entire community, but it requires leadership. In my own work as director of the Joseph Project for the Global Future at Arizona State University, the focus is on clergy as leader. Clergy have a unique ability to engage in long-term thinking. Like time travelers, clergy move between past, present, and future so often that the lines blur into meaninglessness. When we explore texts that are thousands of years old, we see beyond the present moment. Ancient wisdom, characters, and images come alive in us, as real as the things of everyday life. Moreover, we interact daily with people at all stages of the life cycle, enabling us to see the child that seniors once were and the elders that little ones may one day become. Thinking generationally, the future does not seem so far away.

Too often today's clergy serve as functionaries, spending hour after hour on the secondary Jewish tasks of administration, organization, preparation, and development. Clergy have the gifts of deep listening, assimilation of complex inputs, and creative symbolic communication, including storytelling, song, and teaching. People listen when clergy speak.

How can we put these gifts to use? We need rabbis and cantors to contemplate the future, to express the severity of the present moment, and to rally the community and prepare it for hardships to come as the climate continues to change. In order to nurture the gifts clergy bring, what would it take to provide them with some amount of time—an hour a week, perhaps—to read and think deeply about the future; to develop new liturgy, rituals, and lessons to engage their community with the changing environmental reality; to reenvision life-cycle rituals for lives lived in different times; and to learn to hold people in their climate grief?

At the Joseph Project for the Global Future, we are building digital learning environments so that clergy of all faith traditions can take time to focus on these questions and craft experiments and solutions. Clergy skills are needed to envision, inspire, plan, teach, organize, and engage with healthier local outcomes. In the Jewish community, congregational rabbis and cantors must be granted the time to undertake the task of pondering the future and the resources to do so meaningfully. Synagogue leadership must create a structure that allows them to lead not only this generation, but also the generations to come.

Synagogues are seeders, in that their choices radiate into the wider community through member families and businesses, into neighborhoods, and, through the URJ, from congregation to congregation. Let us produce and exchange knowledge for the good of humanity. Let us store up grain now for the hardships we know will happen.

Just before Moses dies, God leads him up to the summit of Mount Nebo, there to peer into the land he will not enter. "Moses went up from the steppes of Moab to Mount Nebo, to the summit of Pisgah, opposite Jericho, and the Eternal showed him the whole Land . . . as far as the Western [Mediterranean] Sea" (Deuteronomy 34:1–3). Although we are tempted to read the verse geographically, Rashi offers a different meaning: "Do not understand the verse as stating *hayam haacharon* (the last *sea*—that is, the Mediterranean), but read it as *hayom haacharon* "until the very last *day*." Moses looks forward, into extreme time. He is concerned not only for his living tribe, but also for the descendants of his descendants. In this way, he adopts a perspective that is godly and eternal.

Let us be like Moses, looking toward the furthest future. Let us be like Joseph, preparing for hardship. Let us create a better future. Let us be good ancestors.

Notes

1. "Code Red for Humanity," UN Secretary-General António Guterres on the UN's Intergovernmental Panel on Climate Change's Sixth Assessment Report, August 2021, https://www.ipcc.ch/2021/08/09/ar6-wg1-20210809-pr/. "The transitions required to avoid the worst climate impacts are not happening fast enough"; "State of Climate Action 2021," World Resources Institute, October 2021, https://www.wri.org/research/state-climate-action-2021. "It looks pretty bleak"; Shane Harris, "Intelligence Forecast Sees a Post-coronavirus World Upended by Climate Change and Splintering Societies," *Washington Post*, April 8, 2021 (on the National Intelligence Council Global Trends report of March 2021), https://www.washingtonpost.com/national-security/.

2. Consider, for example, Genesis 21 (Hagar in the wilderness); Genesis 25 (Jacob, Esau, and the stew); Genesis 47 (Joseph and the starving Egyptians); Babylonian Talmud, *Bava M'tzia* 62a; Babylonian Talmud, *Bava Batra* 1:15; and *Vayikra Rabbah* 4:6.

3. Bet mitzvah is used here as a gender-inclusive or collective term for all Jewish coming-of-age ceremonies.

4. See Panu Pihkala, "Climate Grief: How We Mourn a Changing Planet," BBC Future (BBC, April 2, 2020), https://www.bbc.com/future/article/20200402-climate-grief-mourning-loss-due-to-climate-change. Panu Pihkala, PhD, a professor at the University of Helsinki, defines "climate grief" as "a wider loss and anxiety related to the overall effects of climate change."

5. Amy Asin, "What We've Learned about Congregations and Movements during the Pandemic," Union for Reform Judaism, July 20, 2020, https://urj.org/blog/what-weve-learned-about-congregations-and-movements-during-pandemic.

6. Alexander Rose on "Continuity: Discovering the Lessons behind the World's Longest-Lived Organization," Long Now Seminars, September 24, 2021. The Long Now Foundation (longnow.org) promotes thinking in longer periods of time—even in centuries and millennia.

33

Achieving Zero Waste

A Synagogue Case Study

RABBI JONATHAN E. BLAKE, RON SCHULHOF,
AND MICHELLE STERLING

Introduction: Going "Zero Waste"

NEAR THE LOADING DOCK behind the temple kitchen sits a solitary trash bin. Westchester Reform Temple (WRT) is the largest Jewish congregation in Westchester County, serving over one thousand households in and around our suburban village of Scarsdale, New York—twenty miles from Times Square. We have only one trash bin because we need only one trash bin, and even that one rarely gets filled before collection time. It is flanked by seven—count them!—*seven* bins for compostable waste and a few for recyclables.

We are three people who call WRT our spiritual home: one of us, Jonathan, is senior rabbi of the congregation. Ron and Michelle are active congregants who also serve as volunteer leaders of our local village's Sustainability Board. It was they who, back in 2013, approached their rabbi with an intriguing proposal: Let's make WRT the first local house of worship to begin a comprehensive composting and recycling program. Let's get WRT to go "zero waste."

They understood that "green" was already an important byword of our congregation, WRT having distinguished itself as only the second—and by a significant measure, largest—LEED-certified[1] synagogue upon completion of a comprehensive campus construction and renovation project in 2009. Our synagogue's physical plant was designed to be built and used with a minimal negative impact on the environment and with the intention to inspire other houses of worship to "live their values" through their architecture and operations. Over the last ten years, the number of LEED-certified synagogues has proliferated all over the country.

For the last eight years, we have embarked on our zero waste initiative together, transforming how WRT handles all food service and associated materials, as well as all programming that would ordinarily have drawn upon single-use (i.e., disposable) resources. In the process, our congregation has influenced several other institutions (including, but not limited to, other faith-based institutions) both in our community and in the wider geographical context of the North American Reform Movement.

In this chapter, we will outline the values, process, and outcomes of our effort to achieve zero waste in our synagogue operations and programming, through combined efforts to *reuse, compost,* and *recycle* what otherwise would have become waste (i.e., trash that winds up in a landfill). We will outline both successes and setbacks, opportunities seized and those yet to be. We will examine the Jewish values that have informed our efforts toward zero waste and map the impact of this effort both on our congregational community and on others whom we have catalyzed to adopt same or similar practices.

From Theory to Action

In translating our values into action, we adhered to one Jewish precept, the phrase known as *naaseh v'nishma*, which is translated to mean "we will do, and only then will we hear" (Exodus 24:7). These words spoken by the Israelites at Sinai in acceptance of God's Law have been taken, through the interpretive genius of the Rabbinic tradition, to mean that often the best way to understand a precept deeply and authentically is to begin with the doing; to start with action before analysis, to "heed" before we "hear." *Naaseh v'nishma* provided us with the "push" we needed to begin the work of zero waste at WRT, convinced, as we were (and remain), that our congregation and community would best learn *about* zero waste—the reasons for these practices, the benefits of adopting them—by *doing* them. The learning would come *through* the doing.

Zero Waste: What and How

What is zero waste? A zero-waste setup or event is one where little or no trash is generated. Everything is reusable, recyclable, or compostable, so nothing ends up in the trash! All food scraps and compostable serveware are sent to a commercial compost facility to be composted and turned into soil. Imagine having an event with hundreds of people where virtually nothing goes into a trash bag. WRT has been successfully holding such events for years and has created a model that makes it easy for other houses of worship to start their own zero-waste programs.

There are three main components to setting up a successful zero-waste house of worship:

- Setup: setting up the facility with the proper bins and signage at appropriate locations
- Items used: using reusable or compostable serveware
- Awareness and education: building awareness and providing education to clergy and lay leaders, facility staff, congregants, and guests

Each of these aspects, implemented together, is needed to launch a zero-waste program successfully.

Setting Up the Facility with the Proper Bins and Signage at Appropriate Locations

How many times have we been somewhere where it's hard to find a recycling bin or a bin isn't clearly labeled, so that we don't actually know what goes in it? A successful zero-waste setup makes it *easy* to dispose of items in the proper bin. There are a few key aspects to this success:

- Bins are always together as sets, with the appropriate types of bins for each location. For example, in a space or event with food, you will find bins for compost in addition to bins for recycling and trash.
- Bins are color-coded (e.g., green for compost, blue for recycling, gray for trash).
- Bins have lids with corresponding slots (e.g., a lid with a slit for a paper recycling bin; a lid with a round hole for plastic and metal recyclables).
- Bins have signage that is picture-based and at eye level.
- Bins are sized appropriately for the location.

- Bins are placed in easily seen and accessible locations.

An important note: There should be no solo trash cans anywhere in your facility. A solo trash can is like a magnet for whatever is in a person's hands—even if it's recyclable. A trash bin always needs a recycling bin right next to it, so that it's easy for people to do the right thing: stop, sort, and recycle. Having an easy-to-use setup will make it simple for people to properly place items in the correct bins.

The food scraps and compostable items will not be composted on site; rather they will be picked up by a hauler and brought to a commercial composting facility. Most areas have a composting facility nearby and a hauler that handles food scrap recycling for venues such as restaurants. It may take some calling around to different haulers, but we have found it is always possible to find one who picks up food scraps and has a facility to compost the food scraps into soil.

Building Awareness and Providing Education to Clergy and Lay Leaders, Facility Staff, Congregants, and Guests

Education and awareness are just as important as having the appropriate facility setup. Those who use the facility need to know how to appropriately dispose of items and be reminded throughout the first months and sometimes years of a program in order to effectuate a smooth transition to zero waste. Many people have a "muscle memory" of throwing out all their items into the trash bin, a habit that can take time and frequent reminding in order to change.

There are several ways that we have accomplished this at WRT and other zero-waste houses of worship.

KICKOFF ZERO-WASTE EVENT. Holding an initial zero-waste event, ideally a celebratory function with a lot of people and food, is a great way to introduce this program to your congregants. The clergy and lay leaders make a brief announcement at the beginning of the event explaining what will be different at the event to make it zero waste, how it will work, and why zero waste is important.

VOLUNTEERS HELPING AT EVENTS. It is important to have volunteers staffing the event by standing next to the bins to help congregants sort their items and answer any questions. This staffing is probably the most important aspect of education and awareness, as it provides a personal connection and an opportunity right there at the bin to explain the program. While it does require a number of volunteers to devote time to these events, staffing the bins will make the transition to zero waste much easier and smoother in the long run. When launching a zero-waste program, you should expect to have volunteers staff the events for at least the first few months.

At the end of an event, we ask people to "please peek quickly into the bins as you are leaving." What they will see—whether it's a twenty-person or two-hundred-person event—is that there is no trash, and instead there is a green bin full of compostables that are going to be turned into soil. We let them know this—and often ask how it feels to leave an event knowing that they have now contributed to the benefit of the earth. The universal responses range from surprise to happiness to pure joy.

REMINDERS. At WRT, at the end of services, or right before heading into an event with food, we ask the clergy to remind congregants politely and consistently (1) that we are a zero-waste facility; (2) that everything at the event is reusable, recyclable, or compostable; and (3) to take a few extra moments to sort your items correctly and make sure that everything you have used goes into the correct bins. This is also a reminder to congregants that zero waste is how we, in our everyday lives, can contribute to healing the earth—*tikkun haolam*.

EDUCATING THE FACILITIES/MAINTENANCE/CUSTODIAL STAFF. Just as a zero-waste program may be new to congregants, it will likely be new to your institution's facilities staff. While there likely won't be more work, the work for the facilities staff will be different. For example, collection bins will still need to be lined with bags, but some bins will have a compostable liner bag rather than a plastic bag. It is important to set up training meetings with the facilities staff and also to ensure there are volunteers available to answer any questions or concerns that might arise. Educating facilities staff and supporting them during the rollout will both make their jobs easier and contribute to the success of the program.

Success Comes in Phases

PHASE ONE: BASIC RECYCLING AND FOOD SCRAP RECYCLING. Shifting your facility to zero-waste is a journey best accomplished through multiple phases. It is important to make sure that basic recycling of plastic, metal, glass, and paper is in place in a facility before undertaking further recycling such as adding food scrap recycling. Once basic recycling is in place, a facility can add food scrap recycling. Sometimes this is done just at a few events first. At WRT we started out by having food scrap recycling only at the food events that were run by our synagogue. Next we expanded the program to the preschool program run by the synagogue. Lastly, we expanded it to bet mitzvah[2] and other synagogue events where outside caterers were brought in and therefore the synagogue wasn't in control of the food service at the event.

PHASE TWO: TRANSITION TO REUSABLES. At events such as weddings and bet mitzvah at WRT, mostly reusables are provided, which makes having a zero-waste event easy. The zero-waste volunteers at WRT met with the caterers in regular use at the synagogue and got them on board with placing all of the food scraps in the green food scrap recycling bins in the kitchen and taking the bags of food scraps to the special outdoor compost receptacles at the end of the event. At smaller or more casual events, the shift to reusables can take more time. Most institutions and people have a long-standing habit of using disposable items at casual events. Even though WRT uses all compostable products, the best shift is to reusable, durable goods. This is still our challenge.

Part of the shift to reusables can be subtle. At WRT we have begun shifting from disposable tablecloths to reusable ones. When we began looking into making the shift, we discovered that we were disposing of two thousand tablecloths each year! That's a lot of trash year over a single year, and we are proud to be making this switch.

Where Challenges May Lie

One key to success is having a head of facilities who reinforces the need to change to their staff. Change is hard for some. If the head of facilities is present and enforcing best practices, it can make the difficulty of change much easier. It's important to explain to the facilities staff that as times change, jobs change. In the past the facility staff's job description may have indicated to get rid of everything and that filling a dumpster was not consequential. The new mantra needs to be that a full trash dumpster *is* consequential and that part of the job of the facilities staff now needs to be to make 100 percent sure that everything that ends up in the trash dumpster could not have been reused or recycled. Once this new mantra is embraced by facilities staff, the zero-waste program will thrive.

Paying It Forward

We have had the pleasure of passing on our program to other houses of worship and have seen those facilities pay it forward as well. We are indebted to those who run composting facilities that we are able to contract with to take our food scraps and turn them into compost. We have figured out how to set up programs with them and will always help anyone who asks. What we ask in return is that the facility we teach put the time and energy into making their program a success—and, when the time comes and someone asks, that they then help another facility start their zero-waste program.

Note
1. Leadership in Energy and Environmental Design, the preeminent US benchmark in sustainable construction and operational practices: https://www.usgbc.org/leed.
2. Bet mitzvah is used here as a gender-inclusive or collective term for all Jewish coming-of-age ceremonies.

34

Sustainable Eating and Eco-justice
Lessons from Jewish Tradition

Rosa Fink, Tanya Fink, MS, RD,
and Rabbi Daniel B. Fink

We Are What We Eat: Diet and Climate Change

W HAT WE EAT—and how it is produced—matters a great deal. As Paul Hawken noted in his book *Drawdown,* "If you add to livestock all other food-related emissions—from farming to deforestation to food waste—what we eat turns out to be the number one cause of global warming.[1] While evidence-based knowledge about the critical relationship between climate and diet is relatively new, our Jewish tradition has long recognized that food cultures raise profound ethical questions. In this chapter, we will discuss how Jewish texts, traditions, and values can guide us toward more sustainable food production, with the larger goal of mitigating global warming. Tanya Fink is a registered dietitian with a master's degree in nutrition and works at the intersections of diet and public health. Rosa Fink is an environmental engineer with a special interest in green food production. Daniel Fink is a rabbi who publishes and teaches about Judaism and environmental ethics and is the father of Tanya and Rosa. Together, we will draw upon our experiences to address diet and food production from both a scientific and Jewish textual framework.

Patching Up and Tearing Down—At the Same Time

We begin by acknowledging the tension between individual/communal choices and wider systemic challenges. While affirming that our personal practices matter and each of us should do what we can to green our own dietary habits, we also recognize that such lifestyle changes often depend upon levels of wealth and privilege that relatively few enjoy. Furthermore, such a narrow focus can distract us from holding

government and corporations accountable for their actions—and inac-
tions—which play a disproportionate role in climate change. Personal
responsibility is necessary but not sufficient; we must also address the
deep systemic failings and inequities that demand major shifts in public
policy.

By way of analogy, the Book of Leviticus describes how a mysterious
plague known as *tzaraat* can afflict houses (14:34). When a home-
owner suspects that their house is affected—as evidenced by colored
streaks on the walls—they call a priest to inspect the building. In some
instances, it suffices to scrape away the plaster and remove the contaminated stones; in other cases, the entire house must be torn down and its
materials disposed outside the city. Applying this metaphor, our food
production system is our "house." We have numerous opportunities
to make surface repairs through greener personal choices. At the same
time, we must recognize that there is a level of deep-seated rot demand-
ing we unearth the foundation and build anew. The challenge is that we
now must be working in both of these modes at the same time.

A Failed System

As we consider our decision-making around diet, we want to acknowledge the fundamental inequities in our system. "Food apartheid," a
term coined by activist Karen Washington, makes clear that the lack
of access to nutritious products in marginalized communities is not a
naturally occurring phenomenon, as implied by the popularized phrase
"food deserts." Neighborhoods that lack access are "the result of systematic racism and oppression in the form of zoning codes, lending
practices, and other discriminatory policies rooted in white supremacy."[2] Sound ecological ethics are inextricably bound with economic
and racial justice.

Land plays a crucial role in the pursuit of both equity and
sustainability. As Malcolm X taught, "Land is the basis of all independence. Land is the basis of freedom, justice, and equality."[3] Alas,
most contemporary farming fails badly by both of these measures. Of
the nearly 40 percent of the world's land that is used for agriculture,
most is not managed sustainably or equitably. The model of American
agribusiness, which has spread across the globe, is built upon highly

mechanized, large industrial farming of monocultures using vast quantities of pesticides, herbicides, and chemical fertilizers. In the American Midwest, two crops—corn and soybeans—account for over 75 percent of production.[4] After decades of intensive tilling and lack of crop diversification, the region has lost almost one-third of its topsoil, the upper layer of nutrient-rich organic matter that naturally feeds healthy plants, filters water, reduces erosion, prevents flooding, and sequesters carbon.[5] Almost all of our food production now depends on this failed approach, which prioritizes profit and yield over sustainability and diversity. Industrial agriculture crowds out small farmers, concentrating land and wealth among an elite few, who benefit at the expense of the rest of humankind and all the other creatures whose survival is tied to robust ecosystems. With each passing year, agribusiness wrings more empty calories out of our land, offering nothing in return.

Unfortunately, our government is highly complicit in this unsustainable and unjust system; as a result, the true cost of our food is not reflected in what we pay at the grocery store. Massive governmental subsidies promote the sale of highly processed foods filled with corn and soybean by-products (including corn-fed beef and poultry); as a result, these products, which hold little nutritional value and exact a steep toll on the environment, tend to be significantly cheaper and more accessible than foods that are far healthier for us and our planet.

Looking Backward, Looking Ahead: Toward a Better Way, Rooted in Torah

While corporate agriculture is deeply entrenched, there are time-tested alternatives. The path forward may well begin by looking back—and outside the industrial mainstream. Small-scale local farmers and Indigenous communities around the globe continue to practice what we now call regenerative agriculture. Some of its more common techniques include no tillage, crop rotation and fallowing, and zero (or minimal) pesticides and synthetic fertilizers. Particular practices vary according to ecosystem, culture, and geography, but the general goal is consistent: to steward our resources sustainably in a manner that provides for the welfare of the entire community of living and nonliving things.

Classical Jewish teachings around land use and food production dovetail with that aim. While Torah clearly dates back to prescientific times, many of its lessons around what we now call regenerative agriculture are stunningly prescient, grounded in both ecological sustainability and economic justice.

Core tenets of Jewish agronomic practice appear in Exodus 23, Leviticus 25, and Deuteronomy 15, which introduce the laws around the Sabbatical (Sh'mitah) and Jubilee (Yoveil). Every seventh year, debts are forgiven and we are commanded to give the land—and the people and animals who work it—a complete rest: "In the seventh [year] you shall let it rest and lie fallow. Let the needy among your people eat of it, and what they leave let the wild beasts eat" (Exodus 23:11). After seven cycles of these Sabbaticals—every fiftieth year—we celebrate a Jubilee, when all land is returned to its original family holdings. At the heart of this endeavor is the still-radical notion that land ownership is a legal fiction: "When you sell property to your neighbor, or buy any from your neighbor . . . what is being sold to you is a number of harvests. . . . But the land must not be sold beyond reclaim, for the land is Mine; you are but strangers resident with me" (Leviticus 25:14, 16, 23).

These principles are far-reaching and transformational. While sowing and harvesting annual grains is forbidden during Sabbatical years, consuming perennial grasses, fruits, and vegetables is permissible. Sh'mitah practices, therefore, model alternatives to annual monocultures that can save soil from being lost, depleted, and chemically poisoned. The Sabbatical also teaches the virtues of a local, seasonal diet with a significantly lower carbon footprint than our current system of food transportation and storage. Since the Sh'mitah effectively renders private agricultural land into temporary public commons, all of its produce is declared "ownerless" and shared equally. Taken together with biblical and Rabbinic laws that require farmers to leave the corners and gleanings of their fields for the poor during non-Sabbatical years and preserve public green spaces, these policies offer a blueprint for environmental and economic justice.[6] Above all, Sh'mitah provides a potent countercultural critique of corporate capitalism: land is not to be treated as a mere commodity, and the ultimate purpose of harvesting is not the profit of agribusiness but the nourishment of the community and the sustainable health of God's Creation.[7]

Choosing Life: Eco-justice through Public Policy and Personal Practices

Our window of opportunity to mitigate global warming will close if we do not start making serious changes soon. The stark choice that the Holy One presents in Deuteronomy 30:19–20 now feels existential: "I have put before you life and death, blessing and curse. Choose life—if you and your offspring would live . . . and shall long endure upon the soil that the Eternal swore to your ancestors." At the systemic level, the necessary work will take decades—but we must begin now, guided by the best contemporary science and the wisdom of our tradition.

Urban farmer and author Will Allen urges us to "reverse course from subsidizing wealth to subsidizing health."[8] If we wish to create a more just food system, this shift is crucial. Instead of supporting corporate food monopolies, we must invest in local and regional food systems, incentivizing biodiversity and regenerative agricultural practices. Government occupies a central place in this endeavor. Every five years, the Departments of Agriculture and Health and Human Services publish the Dietary Guidelines for Americans. These recommendations inform federal nutrition programs and policies and impact health-care providers, the food industry, and agricultural subsidies. Unfortunately, current guidelines ignore the suggestion of the Advisory Committee to "support efforts to consider sustainability of the food system."[9] Next time, we need to do better. The American public is invited to submit comments throughout the five-year process of the USDA, Health and Human Services, and the Advisory Committee's development of new guidelines. We can all use our voices to shift their attention to both personal and planetary health.

As voting consumers, we should call for farm subsidies that prioritize human and ecological wellness. We can buy from local farmers and vote for politicians who endorse a climate-conscious agenda. We can also support organizations that promote greener food production.[10] Together, we might reimagine our cityscapes with urban farms and hydroponics, which require zero soil and can be built vertically on any scale, from kitchen herb gardens to commercial farms producing millions of cherry tomatoes. By way of example, Rosa volunteers at a rooftop garden atop central Tel Aviv's Dizengoff Mall; there, a greenhouse supports hydroponically grown lettuce, broccoli, tomatoes, and all types of herbs. This system requires less water, space, fertilizer, and maintenance than modern conventional farming and thrives within the urban landscape.

For those of us privileged with access and bandwidth, there are numerous things we can do at home, even as we lobby for a more sustainable, equitable food system. Between 30 and 40 percent of the American food supply is currently wasted—with a carbon footprint greater than the airline industry. With the largest proportion of food waste happening at home, it's a great place to start making small changes with big impact. Preplan meals and cook based on what's available in your fridge. Buy only what you'll actually use. Learn how to store and freeze fruits and vegetables to maximize shelf life. And in a world filled with fad diets, ultra-processed foods, and powerful corporate lobbies, heed Michael Pollan's sage advice, "Eat food. Not too much. Mostly plants."[11]

Here Jewish tradition offers time-tested wisdom. Today we know that plant-focused diets significantly reduce our carbon footprint and lower incidents of obesity, cardiovascular disease, and hypertension. The Torah, too, implicitly recognizes the value of limiting meat consumption. In the Genesis Creation narrative, humans do not receive permission to eat meat until after the Noahide Flood. Based on this chronology, Richard Schwartz argues that vegetarianism represents God's original vision of the biblical ideal.[12] He draws on the wisdom of Rabbi Abraham Isaac Kook, who interpreted the permission to eat meat as a temporary concession, since a God filled with mercy for all Creation would not institute an everlasting law permitting the killing of animals for food. In that spirit, while not everyone will choose to stop eating meat, we can all consume less, to the benefit of both ourselves and our planet.

Conclusion: Thinking Big, One Small Step at a Time

Wes Jackson, the visionary founder of the Land Institute, has spent over four decades developing perennial crops that would radically shift the dominant agronomic paradigm, based on the natural model of prairie ecology. He has no expectation that he will live to see this project to its conclusion, yet he continues to labor, daily, toward an agriculture that is both highly productive and truly ecologically sustainable. When asked why he persists, he responded, "If your life's work can be completed in your lifetime, you're not thinking big enough."[13] In the second chapter of the Mishnah's tractate *Avot*, Rabbi Tarfon offers the ancient Jewish precursor of Jackson's wisdom: "It is not incumbent upon you to finish the work, but neither are you free to desist from it" (*Pirkei Avot* 2:21). The task of transforming our unhealthy, unjust, and unsustainable food system is more than a lifetime's labor for any and all of us, but over the course of our work on this chapter, we have found that when we draw upon our distinct areas of knowledge and the wisdom of our tradition, together we can begin to forge a path forward.

NOTES

1. Paul Hawken, ed., *Drawdown: The Most Comprehensive Plan Ever Proposed to Reverse Global Warming* (New York: Penguin Books, 2017), 36.

2. Nina Sevilla, "Food Apartheid: Racialized Access to Healthy Affordable Food," NRDC, April 2, 2021, https://www.nrdc.org/experts/nina-sevilla/food-apartheid-racialized-access-healthy-affordable-food.

3. Malcom X, "Message to the Grass Roots" (speech), in *Malcolm X Speaks: Selected Speeches and Statements*, ed. George Breitman (New York: Grove Press, 1994), 9.

4. "Agriculture in the Midwest," USDA Climate Hub, https://www.climatehubs.usda.gov/hubs/midwest/topic/agriculture-midwest.

5. Susan Cosier, "The World Needs Topsoil to Grow 95% of Its Food—but It's Rapidly Disappearing," *The Guardian*, May 30, 2019, https://www.theguardian.com/us-news/2019/may/30/topsoil-farming-agriculture-food-toxic-america.

6. See Leviticus 19:9–10, Numbers 35:2–3, and Babylonian Talmud, *Arachin* 33b, which mandate greenbelts of open spaces around cities to be maintained as agricultural and park lands, which provide environmental benefits to help sustain urban life.

7. See Hazon's *Shmita Sourcebook*, edited by Yigal Deutscher, Anna Hanau, and Nigel Savage, https://hazon.org/shmita-project/overview/.

8. Will Allen, "A Good Food Manifesto for America," Community Alliance for Global Justice, May 10, 2009, https://cagj.org/2009/05/a-good-food-manifesto-for-america-by-will-allen/.

9. Marion Nestle, "Dietary Guidelines Advisory Committee Releases

Report," Food Politics, July 16, 2020, https://www.foodpolitics.com/2020/07/dietary-guidelines-advisory-committee-releases report/.

10. A very partial list might include World Food Programme, EAT Forum, Food and Agriculture Organization, Food and Water Watch, National Sustainable Agriculture Coalition, National Resource and Defense Council, Land Institute, International Food Policy Research Institute, and Rodale Institute.

11. Michael Pollan, *In Defense of Food* (London: Penguin Press, 2008), 1.

12. See Richard Schwartz, "A Vegetarian View of the Torah," Jewish Vegetarians of North America, https://www.jewishveg.org/schwartz/view-torah.html.

13. "About the Land Institute," *Land Institute*, 2022, https://landinstitute.org/about-us/.

35

Indigenous Land Acknowledgments
A Jewish Perspective

Rabbi Jessica Rosenberg

I write these words from Dakota homeland, Mni Sota Makoce, the land where the water reflects the sky. I sit a few miles from Bdote, where two waters come together, the sacred land and creation place of the Dakota people. This land has also long been home to and stewarded by Anishinaabe people. It was in this place that I began to learn what it means to be a settler on stolen land. I dedicate this writing to the Indigenous teachers through whose writing, teaching, and organizing I began to shift my relationship to land, place, earth, and life. I pray that this offering brings more of my beloved Jewish community into the holy work of interweaving ourselves into deeper, more responsible and accountable relationships to the First Nations of this land, honoring tribal sovereignty, working for land return, and collectively caring for the earth for the sake of all life.

Dr. Robin Wall Kimmerer teaches:

It's not just the land that is broken, it's our relationship to the land that's been broken, that allows us to make these footprints all across the landscape. And so that *we must invest as much effort in healing our relationship to place as we do in healing places* . . . How do we once again restore those bonds of affection and respect for a place? How do we remember and help regenerate those bonds of reciprocity? That land takes care of us, so that the plants that we are helping grow back on land should include those plants that are part of a cultural landscape, that are part of feeding people. Because when the land takes care of you, you take care of the land.[1]

There are infinite creative ways to remember and restore our bonds of reciprocity with the places where we live. As Jews committed to environmental justice, Indigenous land acknowledgments are one way to regenerate our relationship to place. The process of researching, writing, creating, offering, and concretely and intentionally recognizing through ritual practice lands long stewarded by First Peoples can transform our consciousness and actions to be more aligned with healing, caring for, and sustaining life on earth.

Why Land Acknowledgments:
As Ecological Stewards, as Settlers, as Jews

Ecological destruction and colonization are deeply intertwined; those who are passionate about stopping and reversing climate change must also work for decolonization. One of the driving forces of the colonial project on this land has been and continues to be capturing the earth and her resources for the sake of commodification, extraction, exploitation, and profit. The cities and states in which we live, govern, and pay taxes were all created through the forced removal and genocide of Indigenous people. Prior to colonization, the original inhabitants of this land enjoyed relationships of sacred and reciprocal care, conscious and ecological balance, to the places in which they lived. Part of the myth of "tabula rasa," that the places we live were wild and uncared for before the arrival of European settlers, is an erasure of the intentional and sustainable land management practiced by Indigenous communities. At times, Indigenous communities and their connection to land is romanticized by settlers, who speak about Native American cultures and relationships to place as pre-historical, mystical, existing in a pure time that is now gone. In fact, Indigenous people are still here and leading fights for their land, water, hunting, and fishing rights. Those of us concerned with transforming our ways of living to be in balance with the earth have an obligation to repair relationships with and respect the rights of Indigenous communities.

Land acknowledgments do not, through the power of their recitation, account for centuries of violence. They do not restore broken treaties or return land, nor do they magically restore Indigenous land practices and ecological balance. The process of researching and creating an Indigenous land acknowledgment, however, can deepen our relationships to Indigenous histories and contemporary life. Indigenous land acknowledgments, to be meaningful and effective, must be integrated into our Jewish ritual life. In this way, land acknowledgments, like ritual and prayer, can transform our consciousness and our actions, individually and collectively.

Part of the work of decolonization is rooting deep into our own traditions, naming who our people are and where we come from. We can make our traditions visible to safeguard against the stance of appropriation that so often dominates settler interactions with Indigenous people. And we, as Jews, have so much rich tradition to draw on when we shift our relationships to Indigenous people and land. Rabbi Dev Noily of Jews on Ohlone Land[2] teaches that we can apply the laws of *gerim* to how we live on Turtle Island.[3] Leviticus 25:23 teaches:

וְהָאָרֶץ לֹא תִמָּכֵר לִצְמִתֻת כִּי־לִי הָאָרֶץ כִּי־גֵרִים וְתוֹשָׁבִים
אַתֶּם עִמָּדִי:

But the land must not be sold beyond reclaim, for the land is Mine; you are but *gerim toshavim* with Me.

Gerim toshavim is often translated as "resident strangers," sojourners or temporary inhabitants. Seeing ourselves as *gerim toshavim* provides a halachic and spiritual framework through which to understand our sacred duty to live respectfully in a place, caring for it on behalf of our neighbors and future generations. All the laws of *Sh'mitah* and *Yoveil* that follow flow from this principle: the land does not belong to us.

As Jews working to restore those bonds of affection and respect for the places where we live, we can acknowledge and work with our cultures' conflicted histories with Diasporism. On one hand, there is much in our tradition that celebrates Jewish thriving on every continent. At the same time, the Zionist project invests in expanding and highlighting the strands of our tradition that decry living outside *Eretz Yisrael*. For those who want to restore ecological balance and transform settler relationships with Indigenous people, we must orient politically and spiritually toward lands, water, and food-sheds in which we reside. When, for example, we say the *Amidah*, even as we turn our hearts and faces to the east, we plant our feet and our roots firmly in the spots where we are. We can use these moments, three times a day, to pause, notice, and name these places (e.g., "I live on Lenni Lenape Land") and recommit to living in right relationship with the original inhabitants of these lands.

Creating Land Acknowledgments

In order for land acknowledgments to be more than rote formalities, we must create them and continually engage them in ways that bring us into deeper knowledge, relationships, and accountability. Jews on Ohlone Land offers "four aspects of a land acknowledgment":

- Gratitude for the land
- Acknowledging Indigenous histories/names, and the waves of colonization and genocide
- Acknowledging Indigenous survival, creativity, resilience and generosity
- Acknowledging our relationship to this land[4]

In this framework, each aspect requires research and internal spiritual processes, both with the land and with the people on whose land we reside. Native Land Digital is an Indigenous-run interactive map, educational tool, and community-organizing project (at Native-Land. ca). They invite groups creating land acknowledgments to reflect on the following questions:

- Why is this acknowledgment happening?
- How does this acknowledgment relate to the event or work you are doing?
- What is the history of this territory? What are the impacts of colonialism here?
- What is your relationship to this territory? How did you come to be here?
- What intentions do you have to disrupt and dismantle colonialism beyond this territory acknowledgment?[5]

Kate Beane, director of Native American Initiatives for the Minnesota Historical Society, digs into the question of why this acknowledgment is happening and invites us to be honest about the answer: "Are you doing it to make yourself feel better and/or ease your guilt? Are you doing it because you agree that education is really important? Is there something that can come out of it?"[6] If your community is not aligned about why and how the acknowledgment process will happen or not clear about seeking pathways for greater engagement, it is important to slow down and take the time to wrestle with these questions. There is a risk that the weight of guilt and grief can freeze us into complete inaction. By working through these questions in community, we can create those pathways to move forward and, in this process, deepen with integrity.

We begin with researching the original inhabitants of the land and other Indigenous peoples who have lived there over the years. Given the long history of forced removal, displacement, and relocation of people by the US government, this may number multiple peoples. The opening of the Native Governance Center's land acknowledgment reads:

> Mni Sota Makoce (Minnesota) is the homeland of the Dakota people. The Dakota have lived here for many thousands of years. Anishinaabe people reside here, too, and reached their current homelands after following the megis shell to the food that grows on water (manoomin, or wild rice). Indigenous people from other Native nations also reside in Minnesota and have made innumerable contributions to our region.[7]

While it is powerful for settlers on Indigenous land to name ourselves as settlers, we must acknowledge that some Jews have Indigenous heritages and identities, that some members of Jewish communities are part of Indigenous communities. Those of us who are settlers can humbly invite Indigenous community members to contribute to or give feedback on the process of creating a land acknowledgment as much or little as they choose.

Offering gratitude for the land and naming specific relationships to the land and the people are important moments to ground in Jewish tradition and ritual. Some questions to consider:

- When did Jews first arrive in the place where you live? What were their relationships to tribal governments? To settler infrastructures? How were they part of colonization?
- How does your Jewish community continue to benefit from the ongoing colonization of the land?
- What from Jewish tradition, history, spirituality, theology, and practice inspires you to engage in Indigenous sovereignty, solidarity struggles, and environmental justice?

Mitsui Collective's "Land Acknowledgement through a Jewish Lens" resource invites Jews to weave the *Sh'ma* into acknowledgments, writing:

> In this time of isolation we must simultaneously hold the needs of ourselves as individuals, the needs of our individual communities, and the needs of all other communities who make up the larger ecosystems in which we live. So as a closing ritual to our land acknowledgment, we turn to the Shema, a beautiful Haiku that holds both the particular and the universal in Jewish tradition.[8]

An "Indigenous Land Acknowledgement" for Toronto by Dr. Aurora Mendelsohn opens with the prayer *minhag* of intention setting and Torah study before moving into *hakarat ribonut haaretz*, literally, "the recognition of the sovereignty of the land."

INTENTION	כַּוָּנָה
Here we are, ready and prepared	הִנְנִי מוּכָן וּמְזוּמָן/מוּכָנָה וּמְזֻמֶּנֶת
to acknowledge the sovereignty	לְקַיֵּם מִצְוַת
of the land as we are commanded	הַכָּרַת רִבּוֹנוּת הָאָרֶץ
for the sake of unification.	לְשֵׁם יִחוּד.
As it is written:	כַּכָּתוּב:
God said	וּנְטַעְתִּים עַל־אַדְמָתָם
I will plant them on their land	וְלֹא יִנָּתְשׁוּ עוֹד מֵעַל אַדְמָתָם
and they will no longer be	אֲשֶׁר נָתַתִּי לָהֶם
removed from their land	אָמַר יְיָ אֱלֹהֶיךָ: (עמוס ט:טו)
which I gave them. (Amos 9:15)	
	וְהָאָרֶץ לֹא תִמָּכֵר לִצְמִתֻת
The land shall not be sold permanently	כִּי־לִי הָאָרֶץ
because the land is Mine,	כִּי־גֵרִים וְתוֹשָׁבִים
since you are all immigrants and	אַתֶּם עִמָּדִי: (ויקרא כה:כג)
resident-settlers	
according to Me. (Leviticus 25:23)[9]	

Land acknowledgments should not only name the original inhabitants, but also acknowledge the specific relationships of place over time. Corinna Gould, tribal spokesperson for the Confederated Villages of

Lisjan/Ohlone and cofounder of Sogorea Te' Land Trust,[10] teaches:

> If you live in the San Francisco Bay Area, you have to know that
> this place is full of magic. There's movements that have come
> out of the Bay Area, like the takeover of Alcatraz, the American
> Indian movement, Indians of All Tribes, the Brown Berets, the
> Black Panthers, all kinds of technology and ideas have come out
> of here. But why would this bubble place be that place? Because
> our ancestors for thousands of years put down prayers on this
> land. This land is magic. It's our responsibility to take care of this
> place in such a way. But, taking care of this place is not just for us
> to do. There are thousands of people that live in our lands now,
> and so now that you live in our lands, it is also your responsibility.
> Because this land also takes care of you. Those prayers that our
> ancestors put down for thousands of years also take care of you
> and your family.[11]

Over the years, as land acknowledgments have become more commonplace, the questions—what action does this call us into, and what
actions are we committing to take?—have become more central. Offering public land acknowledgments without being engaged in active
support for Indigenous sovereignty, environmental justice, and land
rematriation, following the specific calls of Indigenous leadership, is
hypocritical and empty. The work of creating opportunities for ongoing learning about Indigenous histories and relationship building with
Indigenous peoples is more important than quickly inserting a land
acknowledgment into our rituals.

Offering the Acknowledgment

For Jewish communities taking on the practice of land acknowledgments, we can turn to the Jewish practice of *chevruta*, of learning and
deepening our understanding of this issue, through study and with partners, in order to dig into these questions in a genuine and engaged way.
In synagogue life, creating land acknowledgments could involve part-
nerships between members of a social action or *tikkun olam* committee
and a ritual or spiritual life committee. In this way, what is created can
be rooted in both the justice work and prayer life of a community, as
land acknowledgments are truly both.

Ritual and prayer leaders can bring intention to when and how land acknowledgments are offered. Options include the following:

- At the beginning of a service, before anything else
- Between *Kabbalat Shabbat* and *Maariv* or between *P'sukei D'zimrah* and *Shacharit*, to incorporate Indigenous sovereignty into the ritual act of making a minyan
- During a Torah service, bringing the *kavod* and increased sanctity of having the Torah out and open

The community and ritual leadership can experiment with different timings for the land acknowledgment, exploring for what creates impact and engagement in the service. We can create specific land acknowledgments for different holidays and rituals, each time asking ourselves: What deeper action does this ritual call us into?

Social justice leaders in our communities can build the ongoing work of decolonization and Indigenous solidarity into the work of *tikkun olam*. Everywhere we live has or is near to Indigenous communities working for cultural revival, rights, reparations, and justice. We can support fights for treaty rights and land to be returned, fund language and cultural projects, and pay land taxes. We can engage our building and financial leaders in integrating action for Indigenous-led environmental efforts into all aspects of our communities: Land acknowledgments and commitments to action can live on synagogue and organization websites, be included in printed materials, and be visible in the spaces where we gather. Paying land tax to the original inhabitants of the land can be built into organization budgets. And every time we offer an Indigenous land acknowledgment can be a moment to publicly commit, recommit, and update the wider community on what work is happening for *t'shuvah* with Indigenous peoples.

Acknowledgment Is the Beginning, Not the End

Creating and regularly offering Indigenous land acknowledgments and *acting* in ways that acknowledge the sacred relationships between people and place are a central, holy part of moving toward embodying a transformed relationship to earth. Colonization is a process that has taken centuries and is ongoing. Decolonization must also be an ongoing process. We must make moves toward decolonization in ways that repair the immense harm caused by settlers, restore human and ecological balance, and move us toward a livable future for all who are on and in relationship with this living earth.

NOTES

1. Dr. Robin Wall Kimmerer, speaking on *The Native Seed Pod* podcast "Trusting in Abundance: Finding Your Regeneration Niche," August 10, 2018, 58:17–59:23, https://www.nativeseedpod.org/podcast/2018/episode-4-robin-kimmerer; emphasis mine.
2. See https://www.jewsonohloneland.org/.
3. In some Indigenous Creation stories, the land is supported on the back of a turtle; Turtle Island is a name for the North American continent used by many Indigenous people and allies. See Robin Wall Kimmerer, *Braiding Sweetgrass: Indigenous Wisdom, Scientific Knowledge, and the Teachings of Plants* (Vancouver, BC: Milkweed Editions, 2013), 3–5.
4. "Guidelines for Doing a Land Acknowledgement," Jews on Ohlone Land, https://docs.google.com/document/d/1H6FJ_DihbOJWyDohbX7ToHxH7Wd_68vyMWTdoAlEsnA.
5. "Territory Acknowledgement," Native Land Digital, https://native-land.ca/resources/territory-acknowledgement/.
6. "What To Consider When Acknowledging You Are On Stolen Indigenous Lands," Healing Minnesota Stories, (October 20, 2019), https://healingmnstories.wordpress.com/2019/10/20/what-to-consider-when-acknowledging-you-are-on-stolen-indigenous-lands/.
7. "Land Acknowledgment: The Land We're On," Native Governance Center, https://nativegov.org/about/our-land-acknowledgement-statement/. This acknowledgment goes on to teach the specific histories of state and federal governments' "genocide, ethnic cleansing, and forced removal against the Dakota" and concludes with affirming, "Indigenous people are not relics of the past. We are still here, and we continue to demonstrate our talents and gifts amidst a backdrop of ongoing colonialism and oppression. We are worth celebrating."
8. "Land Acknowledgement through a Jewish Lens," Mitsui Collective, https://mitsuicollective.org/resources/.
9. Aurora Mendelsohn, "Indigenous Land Acknowledgment," Ritualwell, 2020, https://www.ritualwell.org/ritual/indigenous-land-acknowledgment.
10. See https://sogoreate-landtrust.org/.

11. Julian Brave NoiseCat, Ruth Orta, Jonathan Cordero, and Corrina Gould, "Landless in the Bay Area," SFMOMA's Open Space, November 11, 2019, https://openspace.sfmoma.org/2019/11/landless-in-the-bay-area/.

36

Learning from Rocks
Sacred Stones in the Torah

Rabbi Sandy Eisenberg Sasso, DMin

I HAD NEVER really considered looking at the world from the perspective of a stone or a rock. A rock was something on which I stubbed my toe or skipped on the water. I knew if I resided in a glass house, I should not throw stones nor cast the first one. But then I read a book by Jeffrey Cohen entitled *Stone*.[1] The idea that hard rock holds stories billions of years old, stories of our planet's history and its changing climate, offered new ways to talk about who we are as human beings and what our place is in the history of our planet.

We are living in a time of rapid, devastating climate change that is producing rising sea levels and temperatures, melting our glaciers, and threatening our animal and plant life. Jewish tradition is replete with biblical and rabbinic teachings, psalms, and blessings marking the wonders of nature, reminding us that the earth is but lent to us and not ours in perpetuity. On Tu BiSh'vat, the New Year of the Trees, and Sukkot, one of our harvest festivals, we celebrate the earth and its gifts. Yet, the downward spiral of our threatened planet continues.

I propose that we look at this time from the perspective of stone—that we stand between a rock and a hard place in order to reimagine our relationship to the larger environment. Because we see our history in the face of a mountain, sacred moments in stone, we join the rabbinic imagination where rocks are the bearers of story. We usually celebrate texts of nature alive with animals, plants, and trees in order to recognize our obligation to care for the earth. Rock appears permanent and lifeless, but rocks contain fossils of ancient life and markings of how our climate has changed over the millennia. The inanimate is alive with narrative that calls us to treat the earth as sacred, to understand the places on which we stand as holy. We may come to recognize our need to rethink our relationship to the earth—that it is not ours to use as we wish, but God's, and that the earth is to be sanctified.

How do our Jewish texts relate to stone? Rather than an encumbrance to be cast aside or a stumbling block to be avoided, it is surprisingly alive with revelation and sanctified.

1. Our itinerary begins with the stone altar on which Abraham bound Isaac in order to fulfill what he believed was God's command to sacrifice his son. Only at the last minute is the tragedy averted. The place is Mount Moriah, which, as we will see, is linked to other stories of revelation (Genesis 22:2).

2. The stone shows up again at the place which Jacob names Beth El. Escaping the wrath of his brother, Esau, Jacob stops for the night on his way to Haran. The midrash imagines that this was not a chance resting spot. Rather, God made the sun set prematurely, so that Jacob could not pass by (*B'reishit Rabbah* 68:10). There he sleeps using a rock as his pillow and dreams of a ladder with angels of God going up and down. When he awakens, Jacob realizes that God was in that place, although he had not known it. In the morning, as he is about to leave this spot, Jacob takes the stone that he had put under his head and sets it up as a pillar and pours oil on the top of it. He names that site Beth El (Genesis 28:18–19). Midrash identifies this stone pillar with the keystone of the earth and calls it "the foundation stone" (*Pirkei D'Rabbi Eliezer* 35:8–9).

   Commentary suggests that Jacob's stone pillow is the same stone that formed the altar upon which Isaac was bound.[2] The place that Jacob stopped for the night is identified as Moriah. It is not hard to imagine that Jacob wanted nothing to do with the spot where Isaac had been bound, wishing to avoid the God who would ask such a frightening deed of a father. But God made certain that night fell, so that Jacob was forced to sleep and to confront the God who was called *Pachad Yitzchak*, "the Fear of Isaac." Only then could his God become *Tzur Yisrael*, "Rock of Israel," and Moriah could be called Beth El, "the House of God."

3. Time passes, but the rock remains. There Moses encounters the burning bush that is not consumed and recognizes a divine presence he had not realized abided there. God calls out to Moses from the burning bush, as God once called out to Abraham: "Moses! Moses!" He answers, "Here I am!" (Exodus 3:4). The rock of Isaac's binding, the pillow stone on which Jacob dreamed, is now the place of the burning bush at which God appears to Moses.

Tradition connects this stone to the rock, the ancient aquifer, from which Moses must draw water to quench the thirst of his people crossing the Sea of Reeds. It, too, is called Horeb, which is Sinai, which is the place where Moses carves in stone the Ten Commandments. It is the foundation stone, the beginning of the world's creation and the site of the Temple.

From Moriah to Beth El, from the burning bush on Horeb to Moses on Sinai, revelations abound. Acts leave imprints, the consequences of which last for generations. Every stone unturned contains multitudes of stories, millennia old. To see the world through the Rock of Ages and the ages of rocks reveals our urgent obligation to care for our earth.

The Jewish people have always placed stones on graves to remember those we have loved. Now let us gather stones to remember the earth that is our home.

> God calls each of us
> by name
> and we listen.
> Rocks tell stories
> weather beaten, metamorphosized:
> hills into mountains,
> mountains into plains
> sacrificial altars, places of dreams
> and gushing water.
> Remember—
> we stand
> between the rock
> pulsing with life
> and the hard place

of our warming planet
Stop—
Turn aside to see
Remove your shoes
Pay attention
The ground on which we stand is holy.

"Truly, the Eternal is in this place, and I did not know it! . . . How awe-inspiring is this place! This is none other than the house of God, and this is the gate of heaven" (Genesis 28:16–17).

NOTES
1. Jeffrey Cohen, *Stone: An Ecology of the Inhuman* (Minneapolis: University of Minnesota Press, 2015).
2. Rashi on Genesis 28:11.

Dayenu!
A Jewish Response to the Climate Crisis

RABBI JENNIE ROSENN

FOR THE PAST TWO DECADES I have worked as a rabbi mobilizing the American Jewish community to address issues of social and economic injustice. For me that had always meant people-oriented issues, such as poverty, immigrants and refugees, and hunger. Like many, I thought of the environment as something "out there" and was less viscerally moved by the issue. In a few short years, this changed dramatically, and once I saw, I could not "unsee."

I remember reading one of the critical reports of the Intergovernmental Panel on Climate Change and realizing that climate devastation was coming much faster and more furiously than even predicted, which terrified me. Without major change, climate collapse would happen in my lifetime, and the future for my children, let alone my grandchildren, was in peril. Would there be enough food to eat? Water to drink? Clean air to breath? I felt like where the hell had I been?! People had been talking about this for years. How did I not get it?!

At the time I was working at HIAS and listening to the stories of refugees and witnessing their pain. Imagining that we could have a billion climate refugees (the number many experts estimate) if we don't make massive change was unfathomable. In this same period, while visiting my father in San Francisco, a heat wave hit. It was a minor event in the scheme of climate events, but it was unbearable, and the city, unaccustomed to heat and unprepared, completely shut down. Empty streets, closed businesses, insufferable homes. It felt apocalyptic.

I was also coming to realize that the climate crisis at its core *is* an issue of social, economic, and racial justice. It is about who is bearing the brunt of climate change already and who will be most severely impacted. Like the coronavirus, climate change is a force multiplier, exacerbating historical inequities even as it impacts everyone.

While integrating the reality of living in this moment of climate emergency, I was having conversations with friends and colleagues about how the Jewish community was not showing up in all our people and power to confront this crisis. To be honest, I was not looking to start a new organization in my early fifties. I knew that launching a start-up is risky and takes thick skin (which I do not have). I asked myself, *Am I up for this?* My answer was *No, but I still need to do it.* We are living at a time when we all need to do uncomfortable things.

For me, that meant founding Dayenu: A Jewish Call to Climate Action (Dayenu.org) and building a Jewish movement working to confront the climate crisis with spiritual audacity and bold political action. In partnership with a nationwide network of Jewish and interfaith grassroots environmental groups, we are building a robust Jewish climate movement. American Jews of all generations are forming Dayenu Circles and engaging in powerful national campaigns, calling on leaders to take bold climate action that centers justice and equity, and joining together with other communities to work for a more just and sustainable world.

We are living in a devastating time. As Jews, we have faced existential crises, disruption, and destruction many times throughout our history. Each time we have not only survived, but we have envisioned and rebuilt a different future. The destruction of the Temple, for example, meant a complete paradigmatic and societal transformation—a shift from sacrificial offerings on the Temple's altar to a practice of deeds and prayer. What comes after the Temple is a story of rebuilding, not the same structures but ones that transformed Jewish civilization and brought about a new era. We can think of many other times throughout history when there have been profound reinventions. Right now we are in such a time—one that calls for bold, not incremental, action. This moment in history demands responses and solutions at the scale that science and justice demand. None of us can sit this out.

Some may ask: Why should we do this as Jews? Beyond the many Jewish values that call us to rise to the challenge of the climate crisis, we need all hands on deck. Every community must fully show up, including the Jewish community. While we are only 2 percent of the population, we have a strong voice in American society and politics. Furthermore, religious voices play an important role in shaping our national narratives and solutions. We must ensure the centrality of human dignity, social justice, and the public good. There is power in spiritually rooted activism. We bring Jewish history and experience, teachings and tradition, and faith and song to the movement. Finally, our people are grappling with this existential crisis, feeling unsafe and unsure of humanity's future. We must support them Jewishly to live with greater integrity and wholeness, attending to the spiritual issues raised by the crisis and moving into courageous action.

Dayenu: We've had enough! Enough destruction. Enough valuing of fossil fuel companies over human life. Enough letting the impacts of climate destruction fall disproportionately on Black, Brown, Indigenous, poor, and marginalized communities. *Dayenu!* But *dayenu* also means that we have enough. We have what we need to confront the climate crisis. We have the science. We have the resources. We have the people, and we have the power. We have what we need so that everyone can have enough. Now is the time to join together in this urgent and sacred work. Nothing less than the future of humanity is at stake.

Contributors

Rabbi Andrue (Andy) J. Kahn (he/they) grew up in Tacoma, Washington, and has lived in New York since 2009. Prior to starting rabbinical school at Hebrew Union College–Jewish Institute of Religion, he received a BA from Kenyon College in Ohio, an MA from Queen's University in Kingston, Ontario, and an MA from the Jewish Theological Seminary in Manhattan. He has served as associate rabbi at Congregation Emanu-El of the City of New York since 2018, where he has invigorated community members in their twenties and thirties, organized interfaith programming, and led people of all ages in deep Jewish learning geared towards spiritual development and *tikkun olam*. Rabbi Andy currently resides in Brooklyn with his spouse Mia and their dog Babka.

Rabbi Eric L. Abbott serves as the spiritual leader of Bethesda Jewish Congregation in Maryland, where he lives with his inspirational wife Rabbi Eliana Fischel and two children, Ezra and Rebecca. Having grown up in Warwick, Rhode Island, he earned his BA in Judaic studies from the University of Massachusetts Amherst, and later master's degrees in religious education and Hebrew literature, plus rabbinic ordination, from Hebrew Union College–Jewish Institute of Religion in New York. He believes that Judaism can change lives and better the world and strives to lead his community toward that shared vision.

Rabbi Adina Allen, cofounder and creative director of the Jewish Studio Project (JSP), is a spiritual leader, artist, writer, and educator whose work is dedicated to helping people reclaim their creativity as a powerful tool for spiritual connection and social transformation. A recipient of the Covenant Foundation's 2018 Pomegranate Prize for emerging educators, Adina has pioneered a methodology for integrating Jewish learning, spiritual reflection, and creative expression that she has brought to thousands of Jewish educators, clergy, professionals, and lay leaders across the country.

Rabbi Elizabeth Bahar joined the Temple Beth Israel family in Macon, GA, on June 1, 2020. She previously served as a spiritual leader in Jacksonville, FL, and Huntsville, AL. She was ordained in 2009 by Hebrew Union College–Jewish Institute of Religion in Cincinnati, and recognized by *The Forward* as one of "America's 33 Most Inspirational Rabbis" in 2015. Rabbi Bahar is the proud parent of her daughter Aiden and two sons, David and Daniel.

Jeremy Benstein, PhD, is a senior staffer at the Heschel Center for Sustainability in Tel Aviv and editor at 929-English (www.929.org.il). He holds a BA from Harvard, a master's in Jewish studies, and a doctorate in cultural anthropology. He is the author of *The Way into Judaism and the Environment* (Jewish Lights), and *Hebrew Roots, Jewish Routes: A Tribal Language in a Global World* (Behrman House). He lives with his wife Professor Annabel Herzog in Zichron Yaakov, Israel.

Rabbi Michael Birnholz arrived at Temple Beth Shalom in Vero Beach, Florida, in 2002 following his ordination from Hebrew Union College–Jewish Institute of Religion. Over the twenty years that Rabbi Birnholz has been in Indian River County, he and his family have had a chance to grow in body, mind, and spirit right along with his congregation and community. One vital aspect of his work has been the creation of a garden project—engaging in the garden to teach Jewish values, illustrate Jewish stories, and generate Jewish ritual artifacts and food, all while demonstrating the Jewish value of caring for the earth.

Rabbi Jonathan E. Blake is the senior rabbi of Westchester Reform Temple. In that position, he shares his love of God, Torah, and Israel through education, preaching, writing, public advocacy, and sacred relationship with the congregational community. Rabbi Blake is a prominent commentator on Judaism and spiritual life and has been featured in print, film and TV, and podcast media. A graduate of Amherst College (1995), he was ordained by Hebrew Union College–Jewish Institute of Religion in 2000.

Rabbah Gila Caine was born and raised in Jerusalem. She graduated from Hebrew University with an MA in contemporary Judaism and received her rabbinic ordination from Hebrew Union College–Jewish Institute of Religion's Israel program in 2011. She now serves as rabbi at Temple Beth Ora congregation in Edmonton, Alberta, Canada, where she lives with her husband Ariel and children, Shaqed and Alon.

Rabbi Nina Beth Cardin has been a leader in environmental advocacy for over fifteen years. She co-wrote with her husband the Conservative Movement's *t'shuvah* on sustainability, which was adopted unanimously by the Committee on Jewish Law and Standards. She is currently working to ensure environmental human rights in her home state of Maryland.

Sarah Chandler, also known as Kohenet Shamirah Bechirah, is a Brooklyn-based Jewish educator, artist, activist, healer, and poet. She teaches, writes, and consults on a national level on a variety of topics, including earth-based spiritual practices, mindfulness, and Jewish dreamwork. Sarah is the founder and lead teacher for Shamir Collective and Soft as a Rock: Public Speaking for Sensitive Souls.

Rabbi Mike Comins is an Israeli desert guide and founder of the TorahTrek Center for Jewish Wilderness Spirituality (RabbiMikeComins.com). He is the author of *Making Prayer Real: Leading Jewish Spiritual Voices on Why Prayer is Difficult and What to Do about It* and *A Wild Faith: Jewish Ways into Wilderness, Wilderness Ways into Judaism*. He created the video-based Making Prayer Real Course, available for free at the Hebrew Union College–Jewish Institute of Religion College Commons (collegecommons.huc.edu/course/making-prayer-real).

Rabbi Nate DeGroot currently serves as the associate director for The Shalom Center, helping to renew the Jewish holiday cycle to inspire public prophetic action. Ordained at Hebrew College in 2016, he previously served as the associate director and spiritual and program director at Hazon in Detroit and was the inaugural Jewish Emergent

Network Rabbinic Fellow at IKAR in Los Angeles. Based in Michigan, Rabbi DeGroot also serves as a congregational rabbi, educator, writer, and speaker.

Daniel Delgado (he/him, Quechua and Ashkenazi) lives on O'odham and Pascua Yaqui land in the so-called Arizona borderlands. He is an ALEPH rabbinic student, a graduate of ALEPH's Earth-Based Judaism program, and a former editor of *Earth First! Journal*. His short fiction has appeared in publications including *Lamplight Magazine* and *Cossmass Infinities*.

Rabbi Avi B. Fine serves as the associate rabbi at Temple De Hirsch Sinai in Seattle and Bellevue, Washington. He was ordained in 2019 from the Los Angeles campus of Hebrew Union College–Jewish Institute of Religion, where he also earned a master's in Jewish nonprofit management from the Zelikow School. As a student rabbi, Avi served congregations in Juneau, AK, Lake Tahoe, CA, and Los Angeles, CA. In his life and work, Avi is inspired and called to action by the beauty of nature.

Rabbi Daniel B. Fink has been the rabbi of Congregation Ahavath Beth Israel in Boise, Idaho, since 1994. He has written several books and articles on Judaism and environmental ethics. He is a certified forest therapy guide and an avid backpacker and kayaker. He is the very proud father of Tanya and Rosa Fink.

Rosa Fink is a food studies MA candidate at New York University with a focus in sustainable food production and distribution. She received her BS in environmental engineering from the SUNY College of Environmental Science and Forestry.

Tanya Fink, MS, RD, is an integrative registered dietitian at Tilth Alliance in Seattle, Washington. She graduated from Bastyr University with a master's of science in nutrition and received a BA in anthropology and peace and conflict studies from the University of Colorado, Boulder.

Rabbi Shoshana Meira Friedman is a queer and Autistic rabbi, writer, mother, and climate activist in Boston. Her writing has been published in various venues including *The New York Times*, *YES! Magazine*, WBUR's *Cognoscenti*, *Tablet Magazine*, and *Rooted & Rising: Voices of Courage in a Time of Climate Crisis* (Rowman & Littlefield, 2019). She has adapted her popular climate anthem "The Tide is Rising" into a picture book (Beaming Books, 2025). More at rabbishoshana.com and @rabbishoshana on Instagram.

Rabbi Shefa Gold graduated from the Reconstructionist Rabbinical College and also received *s'michah* from Reb Zalman Schacter-Shalomi, *z"l*. She is the author of four books, has ten compilations of music, and is a spiritual director and a popular teacher of retreats and Zoom classes. Shefa travels the world, teaching Torah and promoting a Judaism that centers love (www.RabbiShefaGold.com).

Mirele B. Goldsmith, PhD, is an environmental psychologist, educator, and activist. She is an expert on how to change human behavior to solve environmental problems and build a sustainable future. Dr. Goldsmith cofounded Jewish Earth Alliance (www.jewishearthalliance.org), a grassroots network calling on Congress to act on climate. She has shared Jewish environmental teachings from Kathmandu to the Salisbury Cathedral, and written for the *Jerusalem Report*, *Jewish Week*, *Times of Israel*, the *Forward*, *Shma*, and *The Huffington Post*.

Karenna Gore is a teacher, lawyer, and climate activist. She is the founder and executive director of the Center for Earth Ethics at Union Theological Seminary in New York City. Karenna has also worked as a writer and is also the author of *Lighting the Way: Nine Women Who Changed Modern America*.

Rabbi Jill Hammer, PhD, author, scholar, ritualist, poet, dreamworker, and midrashist, is the director of spiritual education at the Academy for Jewish Religion (www.ajrsem.org), and cofounder of the Kohenet Hebrew Priestess Institute (www.kohenet.org). She is the author of a number of books, including *Undertorah: An Earth-Based*

Kabbalah of Dreaming, Return to the Place: The Magic, Meditation, and Mystery of Sefer Yetzirah, The Hebrew Priestess: Ancient and New Visions of Jewish Women's Spiritual Leadership (with Taya Shere), *The Jewish Book of Days: A Companion for All Seasons, Sisters at Sinai: New Tales of Biblical Women,* and *The Book of Earth and Other Mysteries.*

Rabbi Eli Herb (he/they) was ordained by Hebrew College Rabbinical School in 2016. Eli is a certified river guide in Utah and leads Jewish wilderness expeditions every year in Canyonlands National Park. A congregational rabbi, Eli lives with his wife Kim and son Saadyah in Salem, Oregon, on the ancestral lands of the Kalapuya, who are today represented by the Confederated Tribes of the Grande Ronde.

Chaplain De Fischler Herman, ordained as a rabbinic pastor by the ALEPH Ordination Program, is a poet, writer, calligraphic artist, retired hospice chaplain, and climate activist. She cofounded Shomrei Adamah of the Washington area and the Green Shalom committee of Temple Emanuel of Kensington, Maryland, in 1990. She edited *The Green Shalom Guide: A How-To Guide for Greening Jewish Synagogues, Schools, and Offices,* published by Shomrei Adamah in 1995. Chaplain Herman writes for and serves on the editorial board for the online, peer-reviewed *Journal of Health and Human Experience.*

Adriane Leveen, PhD, is senior lecturer in Hebrew Bible at Hebrew Union College–Jewish Institute of Religion, having previously taught at Stanford University. Her books include *Biblical Narratives of Israelites and their Neighbors: Strangers at the Gate* (2017) and *Memory and Tradition in the Book of Numbers* (2008). She is also a grandmother, and therefore a ferocious community organizer on behalf of our one precious planet.

Rabbi Mordechai Liebling is the senior advisor at POWER Interfaith, the largest faith-based community organizing group in Pennsylvania. Before that, he founded and directed for ten years the Social Justice Organizing Program at the Reconstructionist Rabbinical College, from which he graduated. Previously, Rabbi Liebling served as the executive vice president of Jewish Funds for Justice (now Bend the Arc) and was the executive director of the Jewish Reconstructionist Federation for twelve years. He leads workshops on race, antisemitism, and Christian hegemony; and on the Work That Reconnects practice developed by Joanna Macy.

Rabbi Devorah Diana Lynn graduated from the University of Maryland with an undergraduate degree in anthropology and zoology, received a Master of Fine Arts from the Art Institute of Boston, and was ordained by Hebrew Union College–Jewish Institute of Religion. She previously was the director of Elderhostel (now known as Road Scholar) at the Bermuda Biological Station for Research (now known as the Bermuda Institute of Ocean Sciences). She was formerly the spiritual leader of the Jewish Community of Bermuda and Temple Beth Sholom of Fredericksburg, VA. She is now the cofounder of Jewish Earth Alliance, a grassroots network of communities calling on Congress to act on climate.

Shaul Magid, PhD, is a professor of Jewish studies at Dartmouth College, senior fellow at the Center for World Religions at Harvard University, and Kogod Senior Fellow at the Shalom Hartman Institute of North America. His most recent book is *Meir Kahane: The Public Life and Political Thought of an American Jewish Radical* (2021). His forthcoming book is *The Necessity of Exile: Essays from a Distance* (2023).

Rabbi Joel M. Mosbacher, DMin, has been the senior rabbi of Temple Shaaray Tefila in New York City since 2016, after serving congregations in Mahwah, NJ, and Atlanta, GA. He was a contributing author to three publications from the Central Conference of American Rabbis: *The Sacred Table: Creating a Jewish Food Ethic*, *Moral Resistance and Spiritual Authority*, and *The Sacred Exchange: Creating a Jewish Money Ethic*. He is a national cochair of the Do Not Stand Idly By campaign to reduce gun violence.

Rabbi Iah Pillsbury (she/they) is a graduate of the University of Chicago and an ordinee of Hebrew Union College–Jewish Institute of Religion in Cincinnati. She is honored to serve as the rabbi of Temple Beit Torah in Colorado Springs, CO.

Rabbi Avram Israel Reisner, PhD, is rabbi emeritus of Congregation Chevrei Tzedek in Baltimore, MD. He is a longstanding member of the Conservative Movement's Committee on Jewish Law and Standards. He co-wrote with his wife the Conservative Movement's *t'shuvah* on sustainability which was adopted unanimously by the Committee on Jewish Law and Standards.

Rabbi Jessica Rosenberg currently resides on Dakota land, long home to the Anishinaabe, known as South Minneapolis. Ordained at the Reconstructionist Rabbinical College, she is a collective member of the Radical Jewish Calendar and Matir Asurim: Jewish Care Network for Incarcerated People. She has worked as a national organizer at Bend the Arc: Jewish Action, at Keshet's LGBTQIA Teen Shabbatonim, with the Jewish Congregation at SCI-Phoenix Prison, and as part of the Jewish Voice for Peace Rabbinical Council. She authored *Introduction to Trauma, Healing and Resilience: For Rabbis, Jewish Educators and Organizers*, published by Reconstructing Judaism.

Rabbi Jennie Rosenn is the founder and CEO of Dayenu, an organization mobilizing the American Jewish community to confront the climate crisis with spiritual audacity and bold political action. She has spent over two decades advocating for social change and creating dynamic new initiatives at the heart of the Jewish social justice movement through her leadership at HIAS, the Nathan Cummings Foundation, and Columbia University Hillel. Ordained by Hebrew Union College–Jewish Institute of Religion, where she was a Wexner Graduate Fellow, Rabbi Rosenn has twice been named one of the *Forward* 50.

Rabbi Efrat Rotem was ordained by Hebrew Union College–Jewish Institute of Religion in Jerusalem in 2015. She served as the rabbi of Kehilat HaLev in central Tel Aviv and now serves as an independent rabbi in Israel. She is a queer environmental activist who integrates pluralist Judaism, critical feminism, and queer identity and worldview into her work as a rabbi. In addition, she holds an MA in literature from Tel Aviv University and is a translator and editor.

Rabbi Laura Rumpf serves as the director of Project Kavod/Dignity for Jewish Family Service of Seattle, where she crafts service learning, workshops, and diverse engagement opportunities for the greater Seattle Jewish community. She was previously the associate rabbi at Peninsula Temple Beth El in San Mateo, CA, where she led their congregation to take important climate action through community organizing. She is currently in an immersive fellowship exploring the intersection of Judaism, creativity, and social transformation with the Jewish Studio Project.

Rabbi Dennis C. Sasso, DMin, has served as the senior rabbi of Congregation Beth-El Zedeck since 1977. He obtained his BA in Near Eastern and Judaic studies at Brandeis University, an MA in religion from Temple University, and was ordained at the Reconstructionist Rabbinical College in Philadelphia in 1974. He holds a Doctor of Ministry from Christian Theological Seminary, where he is an affiliate professor of Jewish studies. He and Rabbi Sandy Eisenberg Sasso are the first rabbinical couple in world Jewish history.

Rabbi Sandy Eisenberg Sasso, DMin, is rabbi emerita of Congregation Beth-El Zedeck in Indianapolis, Indiana, where she served for thirty-six years. She is presently the director of the Religion, Spirituality, and the Arts Initiative at Indiana University–Purdue University in Indianapolis. Rabbi Sasso was the first woman ordained at the Reconstructionist Rabbinical College in 1974. Author of award-winning children's books, she is a cofounder of Women4Change Indiana, a statewide organization focused on creating positive change for women.

Nigel S. Savage founded Hazon and led it from 2000 to 2021. Under his leadership, Hazon (now renamed Adamah) grew to be the largest environmental organization in the American Jewish community. He studied at Georgetown and Pardes, received an honorary doctorate from the Jewish Theological Seminary in 2015, and has twice been recognized as a member of the *Forward* 50. He is thought to be the first English Jew to have cycled across South Dakota on a recumbent bike.

Ron Schulhof and Michelle Sterling develop and implement sustainability solutions as volunteers. As members of Westchester Reform Temple, Ron and Michelle developed a zero-waste program for the temple and have helped many other houses of worship around the region implement similar programs. Ron and Michelle also work on various other sustainability programs with municipalities and schools.

Rabbi Evan Schultz currently serves as the senior rabbi of Congregation B'nai Israel in Bridgeport, CT. His writings have been included in *When We Turned Within*, edited by Rabbi Menachem Creditor and Sarah Tuttle-Singer, and *The Way of the Empath* by Elaine Clayton. His writings can be found on Instagram @barefoot_rabbi.

Rabbi David Mevorach Seidenberg is the creator of neohasid.org and the author of *Kabbalah and Ecology: God's Image in the More-Than-Human World* (Cambridge University Press, 2015). He is well-known for his liturgy and translations, and his writing and teaching focus most often on ecology and the environment, human rights, and/or animal rights. He served as the Shmita scholar-in-residence at Abundance Farm in Northampton, MA, and holds ordination from both the Jewish Theological Seminary and Reb Zalman Schacter-Shalomi, *z"l*. David is also an avid dancer and a composer of Jewish and secular music.

Rabbi Dean Shapiro serves as the rabbi of Beth Shalom: The Progressive Jewish Synagogue in Auckland, New Zealand. He also runs The Joseph Project, a platform to train clergy of all faith traditions to lead communities through climate change and crisis. Rabbi Shapiro received rabbinic ordination from Hebrew Union College–Jewish Institute of Religion and a BA from Harvard College.

Rabbi Warren G. Stone, a longtime Jewish environmental activist, represented the Union for Reform Judaism and the Central Conference of American Rabbis at the Kyoto (1997) and Copenhagen (2009) United Nations environmental conferences. At these summits, he blew the shofar and called for greater environmental activism. He currently serves as rabbi emeritus at Temple Emanuel in the greater Washington, DC, area.

Alon Tal, PhD, was a member of the Knesset, Israel's parliament, from 2021 to 2022, during which he served as chair of the subcommittee for environmental and climate impact on health. Presently he has an appointment as professor in the Department of Public Policy at Tel Aviv University. Tal has held faculty posts at Stanford University, Ben-Gurion University, Hebrew University, Michigan State University, the University of Otago, and Harvard University. He has founded several Israeli environmental organizations including Adam Teva V'Din, the Israel Union for Environmental Defense, and the Arava Institute. He plays fiddle and mandolin in the Arava Riders, a leading Israeli bluegrass band.

Hava Tirosh-Samuelson, PhD (Hebrew University, 1978) is a Regents Professor of History, Irving and Miriam Lowe Professor of Modern Judaism, and the director of the Center for Jewish Studies at Arizona State University in Tempe, AZ. As an intellectual historian, she writes about Jewish philosophy and Kabbalah; religion, science and technology; and religion and ecology. She is the author of *Religion and Environment: The Case of Judaism* (2020), as well as the editor of *Judaism and Ecology: Created World and Revealed Word* (2002) and numerous essays on Judaism and ecology.

Rabbi Mark Washofsky, PhD, is an emeritus professor of Jewish law and practice at Hebrew Union College–Jewish Institute of Religion in Cincinnati. He served as chair of the Responsa Committee of the Central Conference of American Rabbis from 1996–2017 and is currently chair of the Solomon B. Freehof Institute of Progressive Halakhah. He is the author of *Jewish Living: A Guide to Contemporary Reform Practice*, which is drawn from the halachic literature of the Reform movement.

Rabbi Arthur Ocean Waskow, PhD, founded (1983) and directs The Shalom Center (www.theshalomcenter.org). Since 1969, he has been a leader of the movement for Jewish renewal. He is the author of many books—some that have reexamined American society—including *The Limits of Defense* and *From Race Riot to Sit-in*. Others have renewed Jewish and multireligious spiritual and political life, including the original *Freedom Seder, Godwrestling—Round 2, Seasons of Our Joy,* and *Dancing in God's Earthquake,* which he calls the harvest of his life-work. He taught at the Reconstructionist Rabbinical College from 1982 to 1989. With Reb Zalman Schacter-Shalomi, *z"l,* he cofounded ALEPH: Alliance for Jewish Renewal. He was also among the cofounders of the National Havurah Committee and Rabbis for Human Rights/North America (now T'ruah).

Rob Watson is an international leader in market transformation in solid waste, green buildings, and sustainable tourism. He is best known as the "Founding Father of LEED." Under Mr. Watson's direction, LEED became the largest and fastest-growing international standard by which green buildings are measured. In 2016, as part of transforming the solid waste sector, Mr. Watson launched the SWEEP (Solid Waste Environmental Excellence Performance) Standard, a comprehensive framework for triple bottom line performance of municipal solid waste programs. Author Thomas Friedman called Rob "one of the best environmental minds in America."

Rabbi Daniel A. Weiner has served as a rabbi for more than thirty years. His current tenure is as the senior rabbi of Temple De Hirsch Sinai in Seattle, WA, for more than twenty years. He writes and teaches widely, authoring *Good God: Faith for the Rest of Us* in 2009. He enjoys the fusion of the rabbinate with his love of classic rock guitar, and enjoys walks through the Pacific Northwest with his wife, Cindy, and black lab, Sadie.

Rabbi Dvora E. Weisberg, PhD, is the Rabbi Aaron Panken Professor of Rabbinics and rabbinical school director at Hebrew Union College–Jewish Institute of Religion. She received an MA and PhD in Talmud and Rabbinics at the Jewish Theological Seminary of America and rabbinic ordination at HUC-JIR. She is the author of *Levirate Marriage and the Family in Ancient Judaism* and *A Feminist Commentary on the Babylonian Talmud: Massechet Menahot.*

Rabbi Dr. Shmuly Yanklowitz is the president and dean of the Valley Beit Midrash (a national Jewish pluralistic adult learning and leadership center), the founder and president of Uri L'Tzedek (a Jewish Social Justice organization), the founder and president of Shamayim (a Jewish animal advocacy movement), the founder and president of YATOM, (the Jewish foster and adoption network), and the author of twenty-three books on Jewish ethics. *Newsweek* named Rav Shmuly one of the top fifty rabbis in America and *The Forward* named him one of the fifty most influential Jews.